So you can see it will take time to transform society. In recent years, Chairman Mao himself has paid attention to the fact that it can be said that the United States is now on the eve of a great storm. But the question of how this storm will be developed exactly is your task, not ours. We can only tell you about something of our hopes. And this can promote the solution of the normalization and improvement of the relations between the two countries. But what are the obstructions to the improvement of the relations between China and the United States? What would you say?

—from an exclusive interview Chou En-lai gave to the Committee of Concerned Asian Scholars

Bantam Books by the Committee of Concerned Asian
Scholars

CHINA! INSIDE THE PEOPLE'S REPUBLIC
THE INDOCHINA STORY

CHINA! INSIDE THE PEOPLE'S REPUBLIC

by the Committee of Concerned Asian Scholars

A NATIONAL GENERAL COMPANY

CHINA! INSIDE THE PEOPLE'S REPUBLIC
A Bantam Book / published March 1972

The interview with Chou En-lai has appeared in the
BULLETIN OF THE COMMITTEE OF CONCERNED ASIAN SCHOLARS,
Summer-Fall, 1971, Vol. 3, Nos. 3 & 4. Copyright © 1971
by The Committee of Concerned Asian Scholars.

Published simultaneously in the United States and Canada

Bantam Books are published by Bantam Books, Inc., a National
General company. Its trade-mark, consisting of the words "Bantam
Books" and the portrayal of a bantam, is registered in the United
States Patent Office and in other countries. Marca Registrada.
Bantam Books, Inc., 666 Fifth Avenue, New York, N.Y. 10019.

PRINTED IN THE UNITED STATES OF AMERICA

To the peoples of China and America

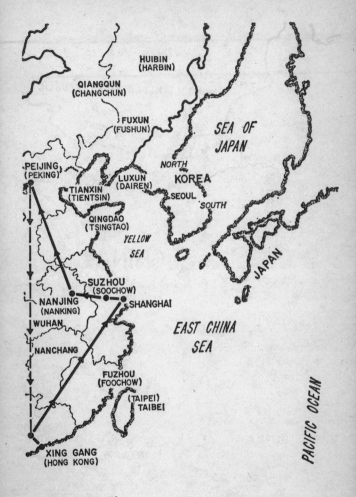

Arrows indicate the itinerary of the CCAS group.

Contributors

Andrew Andreasen
Lorraine Broderick
Halsey Beemer
Cynthia Chennault
Helen Chauncey
Maryruth Coleman
Joel Coye
Robert Delfs
Richard Doner
Thomas Englehardt
Robert Entenmann
Gardell Feurtado
*Anthony Garavente
*Jean Garavente
June Gordon
Harry Harding
Kathleen Hartford
Theodore Huters
*Kay Ann Johnson
*Dorothy Kehl
*Frank Kehl
David Kelly

*Ann Kruze
*Uldis Kruze
Michael David Lampton
*Kenneth Levin
*Paul Levine
Daniel Lindheim
Jonathan Lipman
Jonathan Livingston
Earl Martin
Vera Morrissey
Felicia Oldfather
*Paul Pickowicz
Sue Ann Ritchie
*Susan Shirk
Stephen Thomas
Christena Turner
Jonathan Unger
Carter Weiss
Judith Welch
*Raymond Whitehead
*Rhea Whitehead
*Judith Woodard

*Kim Woodard

*Members of the Committee of Concerned Asian Scholars who visited the People's Republic of China

Contents

INTRODUCTION

We are Americans. We too have been shut off from China for most of our lives . . . until this summer, 1971, when we walked across a bridge from Hong Kong over the Shumchun river, and entered the People's Republic of China.

For four weeks we traveled through the People's Republic, visiting industrial cities and rural communes, schools, factories, hospitals, and homes. We were free to wander the streets and we talked with Chinese from all walks of life: workers, students, farmers, children, factory managers, officials, and army men and women. Although translators from the China Administration for Travel and Tourism were provided, many of us speak fluent Chinese—some in two dialects—and nearly all of us speak passably, so we were encouraged to wander off on our own.

We are almost all young, in our twenties, and all of us are students or teachers. We had applied for our visas as members of the Committee of Concerned Asian Scholars (CCAS), and called ourselves the "CCAS Friendship Delegation." We represented a new generation of China scholars.

Thirty-one days later we walked back across the bridge. What had we seen? Even now, we are not quite sure. And not all of us agree with each other. Like most visitors, we were taken to certain cities, certain factories, certain communes, and there was a great deal we did not see. But we speak Chinese, we read Chinese, and we have studied China for many years.

So we think that our observations, honestly presented and with all our questions and hesitations intact, will begin to break through the wall of ignorance which has separated Americans from China. We hope you will remember that we did not see all of China. In a country slightly larger than the United States, with three and a half times the population, any generalizations are dangerous. Instead, we have tried to give just the minimum background necessary for the reader to understand what we saw.

The questions we carried with us into China reflected our American concerns. Drugs—in 1949, the newborn People's Republic faced the worst drug problem in the world; today, that problem has been totally eliminated. How? Cities—would they too have slums, ghettos, rich suburbs? Or would everyone be equal—in equally squalid poverty? Schools—if there were any dissident group in China, surely it would be the students, we reasoned. But were the students too regimented to express their criticisms? Disease—for the young people of the United States, the most serious problem after drugs is venereal disease, now officially an epidemic. Again, China has totally brought this disease—which in 1949 affected tens of millions of her people—under control. And again, how?

In the course of a month, we discovered that—despite all our study of China—we still had, deeply ingrained, many of the American stereotypes. We had not really expected rigid conformity, but we were surprised that schoolchildren did not wear uniforms. Instead, their playgrounds were a riot of nonconformist color! And although we did not accept the idea that "in China, the army runs everything," we were surprised to find young men and women soldiers in clean but very baggy outfits working cheerfully at the most menial jobs. Most surprising, perhaps, was the contrast between physical China, which to an American is still a very poor and struggling country, and the people of China.

For the overwhelming impression of China is vitality —the enthusiasm, the humor, and the tremendous commitment of her people to this new China.

Studying Asia, we came to realize that the American public has been grossly misinformed by the press and politicians of the last two decades. We had not endured the anti-Communist witch-hunts of the fifties, and we were uncowed by academic pressures to remain silent; instead, angered by America's war against the Vietnamese people, we were determined to be heard. In 1968, CCAS was formed with an antiwar program, opposed to Japanese expansion and in support of the normalization of relations with China. Soon after, similar organizations were formed in Britain, Australia, and New Zealand.

In the struggle to change America's mind about Asia, we've used every weapon we have. We have written four books: *The Indochina Story,* a handbook on the history of the Indochina War; *Cambodia, the Widening War,* one part of our response to the invasion of Cambodia; then *Laos: War and Revolution,* to reveal that almost unknown war, now in its ninth year; and most recently, *America's Asia,* an investigation of American images, attitudes, and policies about Asia. We have chapters or members almost everywhere that students study Asia, and we give speeches, write articles, publish a quarterly *Bulletin* and a (sometimes) monthly newsletter. If all of this sounds like an invasion of young Asia experts, remember that we are still, like the Asian studies field itself, fairly small. But we are also, as we told Premier Chou En-lai in our meeting this summer, very determined!

The greatest problem encountered in this undertaking —to change the mind of America—has been the mythology which grew up around China during the McCarthy period. Compounded by twenty-two years of ignorance and reinforced by sensationalist "China watchers" in Hong Kong, these images were tenacious. Disputing their validity was sometimes like fighting a jellyfish; each minor myth that was overcome was simply replaced by another. The worst of it was working from books alone, even from pictures and books and movies. "Book learning" was never quite convincing enough. Now, finally, we could see for ourselves. But what would we find? Where would the line be drawn between the myths we had fought and the "reality" we had studied?

One advantage our group had was the tremendous range of differences among us. Bound loosely by our commitment to CCAS, we were still fifteen highly individualistic Americans, with fifteen particular ways of looking at what we saw together. We must have seemed a disparate lot to our Chinese hosts . . .

Rhea and Ray Whitehead have lived in Hong Kong for the last ten years, and their Cantonese is excellent; Cantonese is the dialect of Chinese spoken in Hong Kong, in the southernmost coastal province of China, and in the first city we visited, Canton. Ray is the Hong Kong representative of the World Council of Churches. One of the ten children of a truck driver, he grew up around Buffalo, New York, and graduated from Union Theological Seminary; he is now finishing a thesis on the philosophy of the Cultural Revolution. Ray and Rhea, both in their mid-thirties, have three children. Rhea, who has taught elementary school, paid close attention to the schools we saw. Kay Ann Johnson grew up in the Midwest outside Chicago, and is now working toward a doctorate in Chinese foreign policy at the University of Wisconsin. When the China Travel Service asked us to appoint one member of the group to serve as "liaison" man for them, we decided to choose a woman, Kay. The youngest member of our group was Paul Levine, a twenty-four-year-old graduate student in history from Berkeley. He was also interested in the Cultural Revolution and constantly asked questions about political leadership, asking "who runs things here" in each place we visited.

Dorothy Kehl was one of the few women to join in the pickup basketball game we played with the hotel workers in Yenan; she had been raised in Hong Kong, where girls play basketball just as much as they do in China. Dorothy is Chinese—she was born in Hong Kong but fled with her grandmother to a village in Guangdong Province when the Japanese invaded Hong Kong on Christmas Day, 1941. She had not been back to China since the end of the war in 1945. Educated in the U.S. as well as Hong Kong, Dorothy was teaching English to university students there for two years preceding the visit to China. Her husband, Frank, has himself spent almost five years in Hong Kong, and his Cantonese is as good as Ray Whitehead's (both he and Ray speak the common language, Mandarin, as well). Frank is in urban anthropology at Columbia, doing a thesis on the squatter settlements of Hong Kong. Tony Garavente, a graduate student at UCLA and the oldest member of the group at forty, was also the only one willing to try acupuncture when we were offered the opportunity at the Canton Deaf-Mute School. There we watched as they pressed a small needle firmly into his hand; no response and no pain. Later, perhaps because of this demonstration, Rhea actually underwent a treatment of acupuncture to cure an illness—in this case, faintness brought on by the heat of summertime Yenan. We had been walking through the cave houses used by Mao and the revolutionary government during the war against Japan when she suddenly sat down, then fainted completely. By the time a doctor arrived, she was awake again, but still faint; the doctor advised acupuncture. With some hesitation, Rhea agreed, and the doctor bent over her to slip a tiny silver needle into the skin above her lips under her nose . . . her nose wrinkled, but she says she felt almost nothing. In any event, she was soon up again, and back with us.

Ken Levin also took a great interest in medicine in China—his father is a doctor in a small town in Ohio. Ken's work at the University of Wisconsin, however, is in Chinese literature. In addition to Rhea, there were two other schoolteachers in the group. Ann Kruze grew up in Mississippi, and has lived all over America. She taught elementary school for several years, and at the time we left for China she had just finished a year of teaching English in Hong Kong. Jean Garavente taught Spanish and English-as-a-second-language in the United States, at Belmont High School in Los Angeles. Since Belmont serves the Chinatown area, many of her students in the English-as-a-second-language class were Chinese-Americans. This, plus her desire to see a revolutionary society in action, gave her a strong interest in China. She also shared a steady concern for the condition of women in China with Judy Woodard, who had already spent time in Taiwan and Hong Kong. Judy's Mandarin was quite good, and she made friends easily with the young women we met. Our hosts grew used to her "women's lib" questions! Kim Woodard, a political science student at Stanford, is doing his dissertation on the last two decades of China's foreign policy; at six foot three and bearded, he stood out everywhere.

Paul Pickowicz was the pride of our basketball team at Yenan; four years of playing in college had served him well. In more serious moments, he is working on a thesis on Chinese culture, specifically on a literary critic of the 1930s. When we were in Peking, he took some of us with him to visit the home of a famous writer from that period, Lu Hsun, who had been a good friend of the literary critic Paul was writing about and had often hidden him from the police. Uldis Kruze was interested in the Cultural Revolution and also in Chinese cities. He and Ann, with the Woodards, shot three hours of Super-8 color film while they were in China. Although they had had no experience before, parts of it were very good and this "home movie" has now been edited down into an hour-long film which is being used on their speaking tour. Susan Shirk, from Long Island, New York, was one of the few members of our group who smoked—and in a country where almost everyone smokes, she had a far easier time than the rest of us. Every time we sat down to talk with some Chinese friends, the table was laid with tea and cigarettes, and cigarettes were offered everywhere. Susan's work has been concerned with education, and she is writing a dissertation on Chinese middle schools.

This was our group. We had begun to prepare our application many months earlier, before the American ping-pong team walked atop the Great Wall and applications for visas began to flood in from the United States. For years, we had studied China, watched films, seen slides and pictures, interviewed visitors, read its newspapers and monitored its radios, even stood at the border with binoculars, trying to peer into the People's Republic. And we had said to each other, "Maybe in ten or twenty years . . ." or "When the war in Vietnam is over . . ." speculating about the far-off magic moment when China would "open" to us.

To all of us, and all our friends in the "China field," the news of the ping-pong team's visit was electrifying. Maybe, just possibly, the moment was at hand. Overnight, our basic assumption—that we would never see firsthand what we might spend our lives studying—seemed to be overturned. Our application was almost ready, after months of discussion, and now we rushed to complete it.

Finally, we were ready, and Ray, Susan, Kim, and Kay took the application down to the Kowloon office of the China Travel Service which represents the People's Republic in visa and travel matters. The clerk, a young woman with a serious face, looked at it with interest and turned away. We watched it disappear into her files. Then we went home and waited.

It was close to the end of the academic year, and for many of us our stay in Hong Kong was finished. Our funds had run out, our leases were up, and the Garaventes had even bought charter tickets back to the United States for June 1. Still, we hung on, those without housing doubling up, moving in with friends and living out of a suitcase because everything else had been shipped home. How long could we stay without encouragement? It was easy to believe that our own hopes had led us astray.

On Memorial Day, word came through friends in Hong Kong that something was happening . . . not definite yet, no dates, but enough so that Jean and Tony rushed out to sell their charter tickets back, only to find that the charter flight had never existed. In the midst of our own excitement, Hong Kong papers were full of this news, for dozens of Canadians had been left stranded by the failure of the charter. Jean shrugged wryly and began the task of finding a baby-sitter for the potential trip, still unsure how long it might be for.

The next week, at a meeting with the "patriotic" (pro-People's Republic) press of Hong Kong called ostensibly to discuss the Hong Kong press, we were told—pick up your visas at China Travel Service in two days, prepare to leave in two weeks! That Monday, the seventh, we received our official invitation from the China Administration for Travel and Tourism. We would be the guests of the Chinese government, beginning June 23, "to tour various places in China for one month." We had exactly sixteen days to prepare.

Preparation for us was largely a matter of equipping

ourselves with the requisite number of cameras, tape recorders, and notebooks. For in some ways the most recent years of our lives had all been a preparation for this day. We had been trained to study China's history, anthropology, political science, literature, and economics at some of the best universities in America. But our greatest task would be to untrain ourselves, to try to abandon all the preconceptions we had of China; to enter China observant but open.

The weeks before we left were also spent trying to ensure that Frank and Dorothy Kehl would be able to come with us. Their applications had gone in separately, and they were now living in Macao. But we had worked closely together on CCAS projects and on the drafting of the applications and wanted very much for them to be a part of our delegation. By the night before our departure there was still no final word, and we would have to go on, hoping they could join us en route.

By the time we boarded the train for Canton that Monday morning, we were liberally draped with cameras, tape recorders, notebooks, and handbags full of film. "Tourists in China," Kay jibed; our excitement overflowed, and we laughed helplessly. New shorts for comfortable traveling in the hot weather ahead, with all our equipment, made us look like thirteen overgrown campers. Then, sobered by a sudden deluge of reporters, we felt the train begin to move. Slowly it pulled out of Tsim Sha Tsui Station, tunneled through the hills above Kowloon and headed for the British New Territories that lie between the city of Hong Kong and the People's Republic. It was the same train we rode for Sunday sightseeing, or to visit friends doing research in the villages of the New Territories.

But this time we did not get off at Sheung Shui. Instead we posed once more for the friends riding with us, and saw them off the train. By this time there were only a few passengers aboard the train. We stared out the windows and waited impatiently for the five minutes it took us to reach the border. The fields were bright green, and the day was getting hotter with each hour. Camera straps pulled and we practiced greeting phrases for the border formalities. Our impatience mounted until we could all feel the tremendous excitement in the car.

Then suddenly we were there. The train slowed to a halt, we jumped down the steps, and turned to look at the bridge. But we still had the British guards to pass. There was a delay of twenty minutes, and we wondered if there might be some problem. But the guard returned with our passports, and nodded us on with a smile for our excitement. Now, first foot on the bridge, walk across slowly, halfway there—we were in China! There could have been brass bands to welcome us and we never would have noticed; the thrill of simply thinking "I'm in China" absorbed us all.

At the Chinese border station, a soldier of the People's Liberation Army (PLA) greeted us and took our passports. He opened the first one and noticed the official injunction "not valid for travel in China." We looked at him anxiously, but he simply looked up and said to us, "This was issued by your government, not by you. We welcome the American people."

As we walked toward the reception building, three men and a woman came forward to greet us. They introduced themselves: Lao Xi (the leader of the group), Lao Shi, Lao Li, and Xiao Li; they would serve as our interpreters and guides, accompanying us throughout our stay. After a short lunch together, we boarded the train for Canton. The train had a steam engine; it was modern and gleamed from constant washing. The cars were not air-conditioned, and the windows were wide open to let the wind in through a fine screen. We passed through rice paddies shimmering in a hundred shades of green, from the faint pale of newly planted paddy to the rich green of full young plants. Occasionally we would stop at a small town; one was Bao An, and at another, Shi Long, we got out and walked around the platform. There were only a few people around, and they seemed to be used to the sight of foreigners. We felt a little deflated, and climbed back on again. Finally, two hours later, we passed through the outskirts of Canton and pulled into the main station.

Standing on the open platform as we arrived were a small group of men and women, part of the Canton staff of the China Administration for Travel and Tourism (CATT). They took us to a special bus and we rode back toward the edge of the city. Our hotel, an old cavernous tall brick building, was in an old suburb of Canton. The manager of the hotel met us at the door and led us into the lobby, a large plush room decorated with pictures of Mao and quotations from his works. Here again there was tea, but the meeting was brief, and we soon were taken to our rooms, given a few minutes to unpack and wash up, and then asked to meet again in the lobby.

Since no itinerary had been set before we left Hong Kong, we spent the rest of the afternoon discussing with the staff of CATT what we wanted to see in China. Although our list was long, almost all of our requests were filled. The places we visited are listed in the itinerary (pp. 13–22). It is difficult to remember the things we didn't see, but among them was Sichuan (a mountainous province in the southwest, famous for its hot food and tumultuous politics) and one of the autonomous regions where the minority nationalities live. Since both of these requests would demand transporting us almost the length of the country, and far from the other areas we wanted to see, we were not surprised to find these items struck. Our greatest surprise, however, came as the result of another request—to meet with one of China's leaders. Almost a month later, in Peking, we had a long discussion with Premier Chou En-lai.

There had been no customs inspection at the border, and now we asked under what conditions we would be allowed to take pictures or tape conversations while we were in China. There were virtually no conditions—we were asked only to refrain from photographing small-town airports, but since we were never in any this did not become an issue. Tape recorders could be used everywhere and we were free to take all of our undeveloped exposed film with us when we left.

We also asked if the Kehls would be joining us and were told that they would arrive soon. We found out later that night that Frank and Dorothy had made a mad dash from Macao in a small van provided by CATT, after only a half day's notice.

The four friends who had met us at the border—Xi,

Shi, and "big" Li and "little" Li—would travel with us and serve as translators. Because most of us spoke Chinese, in many cases this turned out to be only a formality, often ignored when we felt confident. There were, however, a number of times when we had to ask their assistance, partly because (especially in the south of China) there are so many local dialects, and partly because of the highly technical language we ran into at some of the places we visited—the Nanking Observatory, for example. Whenever we wanted to, we were free to go off without one of the interpreters, and all of us frequently went for strolls. The only obstacle to our obtaining an "objective" picture was the huge instant crowd that so often formed whenever we stopped.

In reading the following chapters, the reader might like to know how we obtained the figures we quote, and how we evaluate them. In each visit to a commune, hospital, factory, housing area, or other unit, there was a basic pattern. We would arrive, chat for a few minutes, and then be shown into a room for a short briefing. Inevitably there were glasses of hot tea, cool, damp small towels for freshening our faces, and packs of cigarettes. These sessions were usually conducted by a "responsible person," that is, some sort of leader of the area we had come to see. After his or her talk, we asked questions for a while, and then were given a tour of the area. While this was going on, we often stopped to talk with workers or children, or wandered away from the group for a few minutes. We never saw anything to indicate that our briefings had not given a very good representation of the situation. After these tours, we would come back to relax and talk some more; this was our chance to ask questions about what we had seen. Sometimes we asked for a chance to see another part of the area, or to meet with someone later who could explain a matter of national policy relating to the unit we were visiting. The only hesitation we met with was rather understandable: we wanted to try working on a commune! Finally, at Hongqiao Commune, the peasants broke down against their better judgment and allowed us to pick a few rows of tomatoes. Predictably, we snapped the vines, tore the tomatoes, and managed to eat far more than we picked.

Finally, a short note about the pronunciation of Chinese names. For one hundred years, since the time of the Western missionaries' first intrusion into China, Europeans and Americans have used a variety of conflicting and confusing methods to represent Chinese sounds. By now one set, the Wade-Giles system, has come to be used fairly regularly by American and British scholars, but it gives misleading and undependable indications of the true Chinese sounds, and it ignores the fact that the Chinese themselves have devised and use a perfectly adequate system called pin yin, which we are mostly using in this book. If in the future Americans are to come to know and appreciate China, they ought to learn to use the romanization system used by the Chinese themselves. In the meantime we'll have to "walk on two legs," using both old and new systems. The old for names most Americans are familiar with, like "Peking" and "Chou En-lai"; the new for names of provinces, most people, and new things like dazibao (big character poster).

The system is very simple. All vowel sounds are pronounced "pure," as they are in Latin. For instance, *ao* is pronounced to rhyme with "cow," *ai* to rhyme with "high," *ou* to rhyme with "throw." The consonants at the beginning of Chinese words are also, in general, just as they are given: *sh* as in "ship," *ch* as in "chew," *b* as in "boy." There are some variants, however:

IN CHINESE, THE SOUND	IS PRONOUNCED LIKE ENGLISH	IN THE ENGLISH WORD
e	*o*	am*o*ng (close to "uh")
iu	*yo*	*yo*-yo
si	*ss*	hi*ss*
c	*ts*	ha*ts*
z	*ds*	a*ds*
x	*sh**	*sh*eet (tongue touches top of teeth)
sh	*sh**	*sh*ock (tongue touches bottom of teeth)

---

*These sounds are different in Chinese but are represented by the same letters in English.

IN CHINESE, THE SOUND	IS PRONOUNCED LIKE ENGLISH	IN THE ENGLISH WORD
j	*j**	*j*iffy (slight *y* sound after *j*)
zh	*j**	*j*aunt (no *y* sound; purse lips)
ch	*ch**	*ch*unk (no *y* sound; purse lips)
q	*ch**	*ch*ew (*y* sound after *ch*)
u (after *b, d, f, p, r, s, w*)	*oo**	f*oo*l same as in English
u (after other letters, usually)	*ü*	no equivalent English sound; like German *ü*
i (after *ch* or *sh*)	*r*	mi*r*acle

CHINESE UNITS OF MEASUREMENT

mu	approx. 1/6 acre
yuan	approx. 40¢ U.S.
fen	approx. 0.4¢ U.S.
catty	approx. 1⅓ pounds

Itinerary

Wednesday, June 23, 1971. Shumchun, Canton

Morning: Traveled by Kowloon-Canton Railway from Kowloon to border. Walked across border to town of Shumchun in the People's Republic of China!

Afternoon: Train to Canton after lunch.

Arrived in Canton, went immediately to Dongfang (East) Hotel.

Spent rest of afternoon discussing itinerary in China.

Evening: Guests of honor at banquet held by members of

Canton Municipal Revolutionary Committee, CATT, and CPAFFC (China Administration for Travel and Tourism; Chinese People's Association for Friendship with Foreign Countries).

Thursday, June 24. Canton

Morning: Full day's visit to the Huadong People's Commune, north of Canton.

Evening: After-dinner discussions with Chinese friends about the origin and development of the Committee of Concerned Asian Scholars.

Later, were joined by Dorothy and Frank Kehl who arrived by car from Macao.

Friday, June 25. Canton, Shanghai

Morning: Sat in on classes at Canton City Deaf-Mute School. Acupuncture is used to treat and cure the handicapped children.

Afternoon: Rode and walked around the midtown area of Canton.

Took a three-and-a-half-hour flight to Shanghai. Went straight to Heping (Peace) Hotel. Later went walking through the back streets of the city.

Saturday, June 26. Shanghai

Morning: Spent first full day in Shanghai on the Hongqiao (Rainbow Bridge) People's Commune.

Afternoon: Shared lunch made from produce of the commune with peasants. Spent time with them discussing life in the United States.

Evening: Invitation to special showing of three film documentaries. One on Premier Chou En-lai's recent visit to Hanoi; another on the battle for Highway no. 9 in Indochina in early 1971; the third, *Learn from Tachai*, on China's foremost model in agricultural production.

Sunday, June 27. Shanghai

Morning: Toured the Shanghai Industrial Exhibition. Saw

heavy and precision machinery and browsed in sections for pharmaceuticals, medical supplies, construction machines, metallurgy, toys, and musical instruments, to name a few. Kay Johnson took the new "Shanghai" model automobile for a test drive.

Afternoon: Attended forum on the nature of the Great Proletarian Cultural Revolution in Shanghai, followed by a banquet in our honor given by members of the Shanghai Municipal Revolutionary Committee and CATT.

Monday, June 28. Shanghai

Morning: Split into two groups. One visited the Shanghai Machine Tool Factory which employs over six thousand workers. Joined the workers for lunch in their dining hall. The other group visited a huge settlement of worker's housing, Chaoyang Workers' New Village, giving special attention to the children's nursery and kindergarten which allows both husband and wife to work full time. Had discussion with members of the neighborhood committee.

Afternoon: The women met with several women cadres and workers including Yang Fujen, a woman member of the Central Committee of the Communist party of China who is also a textile worker in Shanghai. Discussed the women's liberation movement in the U.S.A. and the position of women in China.

The men met with a group of young people to discuss social conditions in the U.S.A. and the youth and antiwar movements.

Tuesday, June 29. Soochow

Morning: Arrived at Soochow Hotel after short train ride from Shanghai. Visited the first branch of the Soochow Embroidery Factory. Afterward strolled through the Common Man's Garden, built during the Ming dynasty.

Afternoon: Visited the East Wind People's Hospital, Discussed the role of traditional Chinese medicine in modern society with members of the medical staff. Walked through the wards, which can accommodate two hundred patients.

Evening: Attended a cultural performance put on by local schoolchildren.

Wednesday, June 30. Soochow

Morning: Met with Fang Xishi, leader of the Soochow Grain Store no. 57, and several other workers in the store.

Afternoon: Toured the Tiger Hill Pagoda and the West Garden which contains a Ch'ing dynasty Buddhist monastery and five hundred carved Buddhas.

Evening: Dined with members of the Soochow Revolutionary Committee.

Thursday, July 1. Nanking

Morning: Traveled to Nanking, arriving at noon.

Afternoon: Rode to site of Yangtze River Bridge, one of the major engineering feats of New China.

Evening: Attended performance of the modern ballet *Red Detachment of Women* put on by the Artistic Ensemble of Jiangsu Province to commemorate the fiftieth anniversary of the Chinese Communist party's founding.

Friday, July 2. Nanking

Morning: Visited Nanking's Chengxian Primary School. We sat in on classes, toured workshops and gardens, and had discussions with the students.

Afternoon: Toured the Nanking Film Projector Factory.

Evening: Attended a banquet hosted by the Jiangsu Provincial Revolutionary Committee. Afterward we enjoyed an artistic performance by a group of Little Red Soldiers and then participated ourselves in a songfest.

Saturday, July 3. Nanking

Morning: Drove to countryside to observe ground maneuvers of a unit of the Nanking People's Militia. Later, traveled to East Wind Park.

Afternoon: Walked around the Sun Yat-sen Mausoleum. On return to hotel stopped for a swim with Chinese friends at the Wutaishan municipal swimming pool.

Sunday, July 4. Nanking

Morning: Met with staff of the Nanking Astronomical Observatory.

Afternoon: Continued our discussion with the scientists at the Nanking People's Park.

Monday, July 5. Peking

Morning: Arrived in Peking. Ambled around Tiananmen Square and toured extensively through the grounds of the Summer Palace.

Evening: Were dinner guests of the CATT and CPAFFC at the Peking Roast Duck Restaurant. Later, met with young Cubans visiting Peking.

Tuesday, July 6. Peking

Morning: Extensive visit at Peking University.

Afternoon: Toured the libraries and dormitories. Had lunch in the student cafeteria.

Evening: Began overnight train trip to Tachai Commune in Shanxi Province.

Wednesday, July 7. Tachai Commune

Morning: Arrived Tachai Production Brigade of Tachai Commune. Were greeted by Chen Yonggui, well-known leader of Tachai, and a member of the Central Committee of the Communist party of China. After a preliminary discussion he took us for a long walk through the terraced hills of Tachai.

Afternoon: Traveled to nearby Houjuang Production Brigade of Tachai Commune.

Evening: Returned to Tachai Production Brigade. Saw a

film about the history of Tachai called *Fields of Tachai.*

Thursday, July 8. Tachai Commune

Morning: Visited the Xigubi Brigade of nearby Jiedu People's Commune.

Afternoon: Had long discussion with Chen Yonggui at Tachai.

Evening: Broke into small groups to have supper in homes of the local peasants.

Afterward, boarded a train for overnight trip to Taiyuan, capital of Shanxi Province.

Friday, July 9. Taiyuan, Sian

Morning: Arrived in Taiyuan. Attended a surprise morning banquet. Had fast tour of the Taiyuan Heavy Machinery Factory where more than ten thousand workers produce mining excavators, heavy cranes, and steel rolling machines.

Afternoon: Flew to Sian on an Ilyushin 14. Visited the five-thousand-year-old archaeological site Panpo Village—a neolithic village which has been excavated and made into a national museum.

Evening: Saw a production of the ballet *White-haired Girl* performed by the Provincial Ballet Troupe of Shenxi Province.

Saturday, July 10. Sian

Morning: Toured the Textile Mill of Northwest China no. 1 and met another woman member of the Central Committee, Wu Kuixian.

Afternoon: Visited the school for the Sian Municipal Red Guard Cultural Troupe which specializes in modern ballet and Western symphonic music. Attended rehearsals.

Evening: Banquet. Watched a performance which included a puppet show, comedy routines, and acrobatics.

Sunday, July 11. Yenan

Morning:	Arrived in Yenan by air.
Afternoon:	Saw Fenghuangshan (Phoenix Hill), the first Yenan home of Mao Tse-tung. At a memorial hall at the site we were given an account of the Communist movement in China from 1921.
Evening:	Watched a Yenan cultural troupe perform folk dances, as well as some dramatic sketches first put on in the guerrilla base area in the late 1930s.

Monday, July 12. Yenan

Morning:	The group visited Mao Tse-tung's second Yenan home at Yangjialing. Walked by the caves where members of the Central Committee had lived. Went to the historic Anti-Japanese Imperialism University (Kangda), an inspirational model from the War of Resistance Against Japan for present-day educational experiments at Peking University.
Afternoon:	Visited Mao Tse-tung's cave dwellings at both Caoyuan (Date Garden) and Wangjiaping and caves formerly occupied by Premier Chou En-lai and Vice-Chairman Lin Piao. Met two old peasants who told us stories about the old days at Yenan.
Evening:	The Yenan District Revolutionary Committee gave an evening banquet for the group.

Tuesday, July 13. Yenan, Peking

Morning:	Visited Liulin People's Commune to talk with intellectual youth from Peking who had come to settle down in the countryside where the labor force was still too small.
Afternoon:	Flew back to Peking and spent the afternoon walking through the Imperial Palace.

Wednesday, July 14. Peking

Morning:	Wandered through the Jiaoyang Vegetable Market and shopped along Wangfu Street.

Met with a delegation from the embassy of the
Democratic People's Republic of Korea.

Afternoon: Most of the afternoon spent in a long meeting
we had requested at the embassy of the Provisional Revolutionary Government of the Republic of South Vietnam.

Thursday, July 15. Peking

Morning: Activities related to people's diplomacy were
continued when the CCAS group met for several hours with Prince Norodom Sihanouk and
other representatives of the Cambodian people.

Afternoon: Visited Peking Middle School no. 31.

Evening: Joined Swedish and Italian visitors at a hotel
showing of the color film *Red Detachment of
Women.*

Friday, July 16. Peking

Morning: Witnessed four operations at Hospital no. 3
attached to the Peking Medical College.

Afternoon: Some members of the group visited the old
Peking home of Lu Hsun, one of the greatest
literary figures of twentieth-century China.
Some members made a quick visit to the Peking
City Zoo. Others took the opportunity to stroll
through the streets.

First word of Kissinger visit.

Evening: Long session held at embassy of the Democratic
Republic of Vietnam. Were later invited to
watch two Vietnamese films.

Saturday, July 17. Peking

Morning: Spent day at a May 7 cadre school located in
the rural area east of Peking.

Evening: The group was hosted by members of the
embassy of the Democratic People's Republic
of Korea at an evening dinner party. Watched
the feature-length color film *Maidens of Diamond Mountain.*

Sunday, July 18. Peking

Morning: Full day visit to the February 7 Rolling Stock Plant, one of Peking's oldest factories. Joined some of the workers for lunch in the dining hall.

Afternoon: Listened to Hang Baohua, a retired worker, who told stories about his involvement in the great labor strikes which swept China from 1921 to 1923.

Monday, July 19. Peking

Morning: Gave three seminars at the hotel for the benefit of Chinese friends.

Noon: Were told during lunch not to leave the hotel during the afternoon because a very special meeting was being set up.

Evening: After supper we were told to get ready for a meeting with Premier Chou En-lai. Upon arriving at the Great Hall of the People we were again surprised to see that Premier Chou had been joined by Yao Wen-yuan and Chang Ch'un-ch'iao, both members of the Political Bureau of the Communist party of China. We presented Premier Chou with group photographs and CCAS buttons for himself and Chairman Mao Tse-tung.

Tuesday, July 20. Peking

Morning: Made the long trip through the mountains north of Peking to the Great Wall of China.

Afternoon: On the way back to Peking we stopped for a couple of hours to visit the Ming Tombs.

Evening: Some of us went to see a Japanese film, *Yamamoto 56,* which Yao Wen-yuan had spoken of the previous evening as glorifying the revival of Japanese militarism. Others met with Peking city planners to talk about urban problems.

Wednesday, July 21. Peking

Morning: A six-member subcommittee held a lengthy

meeting with representatives of the CATT and the Chinese People's Association for Friendship with Foreign Countries. During the meeting we were presented with three films made in China: *Red Detachment of Women, Red Flag Canal,* and *Nanking Yangtze River Bridge.*

Other members of the group visited a mosque in Peking, while still another group were given a tour of the Great Hall of the People.

Afternoon: Visited Tsinghua University at the request of Premier Chou En-lai.

Evening: A farewell party held in our honor at the International Club.

Thursday, July 22. Peking

Morning: Typhoon in the Canton area. Scheduled departure postponed for one day. Visited the Peking subway. We went out during the day in groups of two and three to walk the back streets.

Evening: Were taken to a Mongolian restaurant by an American resident of Peking.

Friday, July 23. Canton

Morning: Flew from Peking to Canton during the morning.

Afternoon: Held a summing-up meeting with the Chinese friends who had been with us for the duration of the trip.

Evening: Enjoyed a Cantonese banquet.

Saturday, July 24. Canton, Shumchun

Morning: Rode the bus for the last time through Canton. Boarded the train for Shumchun.

Midday: Walked across the border bridge to Hong Kong.

1. YEARS OF BITTERNESS

One day as we wandered through the streets of Yenan, we noticed a cluster of children staring at a billboard, their small faces sober and sad. On the board, there was a display of photographs—China, past and present. But it was the photographs of old China which held them. We could see the shock in their eyes as they stared at pictures of faces shrunken with hunger or the bodies of their massacred countrymen lying in a ditch, watched over by a Japanese soldier. They also saw children their own age doing dangerous work in crowded, dirty factories, and small girls being sold on the streets. Quietly we walked away, but in the days after that we began to notice that similar displays were common in other places we visited.

This is China's generation gap. Chinese children have never had to face the hardships their parents knew. They have never experienced the misery of years of warfare, or the natural calamities, or the agony of being driven from their homes by landlords, nor have they wandered aimlessly—landless and homeless—through a barren China.

Today in China this gulf is bridged by teaching children the "bitter remembrances." Visually, verbally, and through reenactment of their experiences, China's old people become living museums for the young.

A "meal of bitter remembrances" is one way in which the old people keep these memories alive. On certain days of the year, the leaves and bark of trees and the bitter herbs that many Chinese were forced to eat during times of famine are cooked and served while a grandmother or grandfather, father or mother tells tales of the past. A young girl in Tachai, red-cheeked and obviously well fed, told us, "I am saddest when I recall that my parents had to eat grass and leaves while the granaries of the landlords were full." When the Chinese we met spoke of such things, it was always with a solemnity which made us sense the depth of their feelings.

Peasants and old people even visit schools and study-classes in the residential areas. They show the young people the tattered rags which were their only clothes in pre-Liberation days and tell of brothers and sisters who had to be sold into slavery or who died from starvation.

In Shanghai, when we visited Chaoyang Xincun, a workers' residential area, one old woman told us just such a story. We had been invited to go inside the apartment house and talk to the residents. Inside her apartment, sitting on her bed, the woman told us how she had been treated by the people to whom her parents sold her. "The animals of the household got their choice of the leftover food before I did," she said. "Illness was no excuse for rest. I was beaten at whim." As she recounted her story, tears flowed down her face. All of us were truly moved.

Even in art, the young people of China are confronted with the past. One example is the *Rent Collection Courtyard*. This famous group of statues portrays the real-life sufferings of the peasant tenants of one landlord in Sechuan Province. The landlord sits in cruel splendor apart from everyone else. To one side, an old peasant enters, staggering under the burden of rice he has brought to the landlord as taxes. His eyes gaze sadly out over the scene—the landlord's henchmen fixing the weights, beating a debtor, and demanding a daughter in payment. The sculptors have made us, the viewers, look at all this through the eyes of the old peasant. The original sculpture has been placed in the actual courtyard where the peasants used to pay their rents, but we saw copies throughout China. Pictures of this work of art, with the story that inspired the statues, are reproduced in paperback children's books. In Nanking an excerpt from the story and illustrations of the statues were included in a new textbook we saw being used in the primary schools. The bitter remembrances are not meant to be merely gothic horror stories from the past. They aim to show Chinese of all ages the reasons the greater part of their people lived in chronic poverty and misery for so many years. From these tales, everybody becomes more aware that the natural disasters and private tragedies which plagued them were intensified by the social organization of Chinese society. Their discussions of these old experiences reflect such an awareness.

Whenever Chinese talk about the past, five topics they are certain to mention repeatedly are the recurring pattern of natural disasters; the foreign invasions which dominated much of nineteenth- and twentieth-century Chinese life; the semifeudal rural landlords; the especially severe oppression of women; and finally the Kuomintang rule under Chiang Kai-shek—for them, the symbol of all that was backward, corrupt, and reactionary in Chinese society. These categories can be easily separated on paper, but not in the minds of the people; for all five combined to make their lives in the old China lives of misery.

The Natural Disasters

Before 1949, drought and flood, one frequently on the heels of the other, were the most common forms of natural disaster in China. The massive famines which followed, in this period of general economic collapse, left the peasants helpless. Even the old systems of dikes and irrigation works had fallen into total disrepair under "warlord" and then Kuomintang rule. Not only did the social system fail to provide relief or assistance during these perpetual disasters but it allowed the few privileged members of society to take full advantage of these calamities to accumulate more land. In *Red Star over China,* Edgar Snow vividly described the effects of natural disasters in one area of China during the 1930s:

> I saw fresh corpses on the streets of Saratsi, and in the villages I saw shallow graves where the victims of famine and disease were laid by the dozens. But these were not the most shocking things after all. The shocking thing was that in many of these towns there were still rich men, rice-hoarders, wheat-hoarders, money-lenders, and landlords, with armed guards to defend them, while they profiteered enormously. The shocking thing was that in the cities . . . there was grain and food, and had been for months; that in Peking and Tientsin and elsewhere were

thousands of tons of wheat and millet, collected (mostly by contributions from abroad) by the Famine Commission, but which could not be shipped to the starving. . . .

While this famine raged the Commission decided to build a big canal (with American funds) to help flood some of the lands baked by drought. The officials gave them every cooperation—and promptly began to buy for a few cents an acre all the lands to be irrigated. A flock of vultures descended on this benighted country, and purchased from the starving farmers thousands of acres for the taxes in arrears, or for a few coppers, and held it to await tenants and rainy days.[1]

This was hardly an isolated instance. In 1927–28, famine engulfed the provinces of Henan, Anhui, Shenxi, Gansu, Sechuan, and Guijou. In some places up to 75 percent of the population starved to death. In 1941–43 over one million people died in a famine which hit north China. A firsthand account by an American reporter gives a picture of the extent of human degradation in the Kuomintang-held areas during this time:

Women exchanged their babies, saying, "You eat mine, I'll eat yours." When a man was going to die, he dug a pit and sat inside and asked neighbors to fill in the earth when he was dead. Afterward, however, no one could be found to fill in the pits for all were either dead or too weak to shovel earth. Men sold their children first, then their wives.[2]

The natural disasters ruined crops, while unimpeded erosion destroyed the soil. The peasants were left without food, housing, and work. Physically weak, they were unable to undertake the massive collective work on dikes and irrigation systems necessary to guard against natural calamities. As they streamed into the cities, the urban situation steadily deteriorated.

---

[1](New York: Grove Press, 1961).

[2]Jack Belden, *China Shakes the World* (New York: Monthly Review Press, 1971).

Foreign Domination

For nearly two centuries foreign troops, businessmen, and missionaries asserted their right to do as they pleased on Chinese territory. They defended that claim with military might. Foreign businessmen rushed to get in on what they believed to be a limitless Chinese market and an endless supply of cheap industrial labor. This foreign business "invasion" had such a severe impact that a modern Chinese business class never fully developed. There was, however, a "comprador" class of Chinese who worked with the foreign business community, serving primarily as profiteering middlemen. In this exploitative role—along with the foreign businesses and large- and small-scale Chinese landlords—they helped to destroy the Chinese economy. As foreign textiles, lamp oil, industrial products, and tools flooded in, village handicrafts—an important source of livelihood for millions of peasants—were undersold and wiped out. Yet, while the peasants and workers starved, urban shops overflowed with foreign luxury products for the rich. And the landlords and compradors who bought in these shops used money squeezed from the peasants and workers.

On the military front, China fought contingents from almost every major European country during the hundred years before 1949. The first defeat came in the Opium War of 1840, in which the British army intervened to force China to allow the importation of huge quantities of Indian opium on British ships, for British profits. In 1860, an Anglo-French military force occupied the capital city, Peking. In 1884, a French army took Annam from the Chinese. By the turn of the century, through use or threat of force, Russia, Germany, Japan, France, and Great Britain had all carved territorial "spheres of influence" out of the Chinese empire. In 1900, an international expeditionary force, including a contingent of U.S. Marines, captured Peking, putting down the Boxer Rebellion, a popular uprising against foreigners. Throughout this period, foreign troops stationed in China intervened in Chinese civil affairs, massacred Chinese demonstrators, and defended the right of Chinese Christian converts to ignore China's laws.

But the most brutal of all foreign attacks on China began in 1931, when the Japanese invaded Manchuria. During the fourteen years of war that followed, until they were defeated in 1945, the Japanese earned the intense enmity of the Chinese people. At first the people were totally unprepared to resist the aggressors. Attacks by isolated resistance groups on the Japanese forces in north China were met with the Japanese "three-all" policy, "Burn all, kill all, loot all," which wiped out entire villages and drove thousands into the hills. It was only after many years of struggle and experience that the Communist-led armies began to drive the Japanese back, to carve out pockets of safety, and to build the rural areas which became the nucleus of the future People's Republic.

The Landlords

Frequently on the brink of destitution and often on the brink of starvation, most peasants were lucky to own a small scrap of land. Those owning too little land to support a family had to rent land from a local and frequently absentee landlord. Rents, already high, continued to rise until 1949. In parts of Guangdong Province they ranged up to 75 percent, even 90 percent of the crop; 50 percent was common. In every province they were too high to allow an ordinary peasant to achieve financial security. In good times he could raise enough to pay the rent, save some seed, and feed his family meagerly until the next harvest. But rent had to be paid first. In bad times, what was left after rent rarely lasted the year. Then, to feed his family, he was forced to borrow from the same landlord. In the end, he got back his own rent grain, at inflated prices with usurious interest rates. For collateral, he had only land to offer. Finally, unable to repay the loan, he and all his family would be driven off. In the 1920s and 1930s the plains of north China were filled with such wandering families, many forced to sell their children (to give the children a home and food as much as to bring in money), and all searching, endlessly, for the security of land to till.

If the peasant were not broken by rents, he might be by

the never-ending taxation. In the last years of Kuomintang rule, taxes covered nearly every possible good, service, or movement across the land. Edgar Snow related a story told him by one missionary who followed a pig from the seller to the buyer—all this within a few miles' radius, with the pig sold alive—and observed six separate taxes being paid. In many cases the local tax collector was a landlord. Since the government required only a lump sum from him, he was free to squeeze as much as possible from the families in his jurisdiction. At times, in fact, he would invent his own taxes, for there was no one to question him. Expectably, landlord households paid little or nothing. The rest had to come from the empty pockets of the peasants. Objections invited reprisals and confiscation. Appeals to higher authorities fell on deaf ears, for the local magistrate was probably of the same mind, if not of the same family, as the tax collector. Moreover, he would receive his own share of taxes collected.

As Snow's description of famine-time profiteering makes clear, the less scrupulous landlord benefited even more from calamitous times than he did from just plain bad times. There is no question that at the time of Liberation in 1949 the greatest amount of bitterness was directed against the landlords, because the vast majority of the people had suffered under their domination for as long as their families could remember.

Yet direct oppression by the landlord and his friends was not the only factor contributing to the misery of the Chinese peasant. He lived also with the knowledge that his poverty was self-perpetuating. Advancement for his children was nearly impossible, and became more so every year. In the early twentieth century peasant youths had been able to travel to the city, work in factories for several years or seasonally, and bring home enough money to buy land for the family. But increasing unemployment in the cities soon closed that alternative. Village schools existed, but only for the sons of the rich. The poor peasants could not have spared their children from fieldwork even had education been free. Western medicine was unheard of in the villages, and traditional doctors charged so much that, after a serious illness in the family, even a rich peasant might find himself back on the bottom rung of the economic ladder. The much-vaunted cultural life of old China belonged to the landlords and the rich in the cities, who had leisure time in which to learn the difficult writing system and the intricacies of literary Chinese. In the decay of village society which resulted from these decades of economic collapse, recurrent wars, displacement of population, and severe political vigilance by the Kuomintang, people kept more and more to themselves and the old folk songs, dances, and folk arts began to die out. Mao Tse-tung's description of China's peasants then as "poor and blank" may seem strange to Westerners, but the miserable state of hundreds of millions of her peasants would have easily fit that description.

Women

These tragedies struck everyone who was poor in China. But they did happen more to men than to women, for large numbers of women did not live to experience them. Women constituted a good deal less than half of the Chinese population, and many of the reasons for this were not natural. Girls were often killed at birth by parents who were too poor to support them and their brothers, who were valued as harder workers for the fields. Women were the first to be sold into slavery, the last to have a doctor called for them in times of illness, and the last to get food when food ran scarce. These dehumanizing conditions made the position of women particularly miserable in an already miserable society.

Tradition taught that women were by nature inferior to men. Arranged marriages prevailed, and stories of young girls committing suicide the night before the wedding were common. But those who took the path of suicide were, perhaps, better off than those who entrusted themselves to fate. Married women were subject not only to their husbands, but also to fathers-in-law, mothers-in-law, brothers-in-law, and the wives of their husbands' elder brothers. Custom forbade their venturing out of the home, and women who dared to do so invited public censure. Yet without a man, the Chinese widow was faced with an even more desperate condition, vulnerable and unable to make her way.

Men sometimes indirectly suffered the effects of the oppression of women too, for there were not enough women to go around, and at times the poorer peasant men could not afford marriage partners. Some resorted to the expedient system of "little daughters-in-law," in which the parents of a boy would arrange with another poor family to take in their daughter while she was still a child, and to marry the two when they reached adolescence. In practice the adoptive family did its best to get its money's worth out of the girl, and she occupied a position of virtual slavery in the household.

Some women were fortunate enough to have parents who looked carefully before choosing a husband for them. However, many peasants were not sophisticated enough to apply their own experiences to the best advantage. If the mother or the older sister had had an unhappy marriage with a husband of about the same age, the mother might press the next time to choose a much older man for a girl of marriageable age. Or the parents might choose a man whose mother was dead, thinking to avoid the problem of the mother-in-law, and end up instead subjecting the girl to a marriage where she had to cope with a vicious father-in-law. Moreover, marriages generally were arranged between people from different villages, with a go-between doing the negotiations with both sides, and not bothering to do justice to the truth. Women were of course expected to do all the adjusting in the marriage, and their happiness was not a matter of importance.

In addition to the problems for women inherent in marriage, women also suffered more from twists of fate than men. When the Kuomintang or Japanese armies garrisoned in a village, the prettiest women were rounded up from their homes and taken off to entertain the visiting troops. When famine hit or the taxes went up, a daughter or wife was sold into slavery, to the highest bidder, who might easily just be another peasant who would work the woman literally to death. A more attractive woman closer to a large town might be fortunate enough to be sold to a wealthy man, who could keep her or give her over to his son for use. A lucky woman might even advance to the position of concubine, although here she would have not only in-laws but also senior wives to cope with.

The difficult position of Chinese women was not so immediate and sweeping as a famine in which millions starve in a matter of months. It was not like a battle in which thousands die in one day; nor was it even like being able to see physically how much grain or how much land a landlord or a tax collector confiscates. It was much more than that, for the women suffered as much as the men in all those things, and still, day in and day out, from birth to death, they had to bow down to those put above them by custom, they had to bite their tongues and never answer back, they had to suffer treatment a donkey would not take, and still give only sweet words to their men. All this they did, not hoping for things ever to get better, but only believing that it was their lot in life.

Kuomintang Rule

Chiang Kai-shek's Kuomintang made no serious attempt to solve any of these problems. Usually they simply collaborated with those causing the problems to worsen the situation. This was particularly the case with the landlords and the foreign incursions. Chiang after 1927 turned completely away from the peasants, urban workers, and smaller businessmen who were looking to him to carry out the promise of improvements held out by the Kuomintang after the 1911 revolution. Instead, to achieve political control of China, he joined with the landed and business interests in an alliance to wring money out of the country. Chiang ignored the urgent need for land reform and concentrated his rural efforts in controlling the peasants and extracting as much from them as possible.

Peasants especially hated the Kuomintang revival of the old baojia system, in which one man was made a guarantor of the good behavior of a number of families under him. In practice, the Kuomintang baojia head was usually a local landlord, and he could rid himself of any upstart peasant simply by refusing to guarantee him to the government. Moreover, in order to spot "trouble-makers," the bao head employed henchmen who could spy on the peasants, and peasants who had tidbits of information to offer against a fellow villager could receive payment. The peasant himself was subject at any moment to arbitrary arrest. This method of control worked quite effectively in the villages under Kuomintang control. It turned villager against villager and created an atmosphere of fear and suspicion in village society. The collusion of the Kuomintang officials with the local landlords was the last straw for millions of peasants. Despite its proclamations of the principle of the "people's livelihood," the Kuomintang did nothing to curtail the exorbitantly high rent rates; nor did it police the tax collection system. And without these controls, it put into positions of power those most likely to take advantage of their power, the landlords, who obviously would not tax their own money or curb their own sources of profit.

Chiang's policies in the cities were no more progressive. He encouraged foreign capital to invest and exploit; his urban Chinese base of power was the comprador class, who had the most to gain from increased foreign presence in China. Chiang's treatment of the worker rebellion in Shanghai in 1927 gives eloquent testimony of the side he took. The Shanghai workers had armed themselves and carried out a rebellion in the city, which resulted in their brief seizure of power in order to prepare for the arrival of the Kuomintang Army. Chiang, however, decided not to let this experience of power go to the workers' heads and had his armies round up and execute thousands of the workers who had participated in seizure of the city.

In the war with Japan, the Kuomintang armies were thoroughly defeated in the campaigns of the first few years. While some of Chiang's soldiers fought well, most were demoralized early in the war, and once Chiang withdrew to the isolated city of Chungking, there were only scattered attempts to engage the Japanese, leaving the Communist guerrilla forces to do most of the fighting.

The American entry into the war against Japan brought Chiang huge amounts of military aid. Much of it never found its way into battle, being siphoned off by Kuomintang officials along the way. What did go into battle before 1945 went into battle not against the Japanese but against the Communists, who were at the time the only force willing to organize national resistance. But this was not just war against a Communist army. It was a war on the Chinese people, for in the areas not under resistance or Japanese control, the Kuomintang soaked the urban workers and peasant farmers for money to pay the army. Even after the Japanese surrender, Chiang was able to get millions in American aid by pointing to the red peril, and this alone kept him going.

And Now?

When Mao Tse-tung proclaimed the establishment of the People's Republic of China in Peking in 1949, the Chinese were reminded that the struggle was only beginning. Those who made the victory fought for it knowing what the old society was like, and they believe that it should not be forgotten. Susan asked an old peasant in north China if he felt there were personal freedoms and civil rights in China today. As though the images of the past were flashing through his mind, he replied, "Yes, now we have the right to love. We are free to work full-time, to have a secure home, to eat enough food, to have complete medical care, to receive education and culture —and free to take our future in our hands. Yes, we're free to do all these things for the first time in our lives."

2. THE SPIRIT OF YENAN

A trip to Yenan is a visit to China's Valley Forge, Boston, and Yorktown—all wrapped into one city. We arrived there in summer, when Yenan is hot and dry, and fine yellow loose dust blows in from the arid surrounding hills. Yet the city is very neat, tidy, like a museum with the wax figures replaced by live people and all the exhibits still in use.

We wandered through the hall, now reconstructed, where Mao had delivered his famous talks in 1942 during the Yenan Forum on Literature and Art. Small clusters of people strolled about, examining the exhibits and reading the signs. A short distance away was Mao's cave house. The windows were covered with oiled white paper as they had been thirty years ago, but now the paper is stretched over wooden lattices, and some of the furniture is newly made from old models.

It was Yenan, a remote provincial town, that Mao and his comrades made their capital in 1936. For the next ten years of struggle against the Japanese and the Kuomintang, Yenan served as their base. Here Mao and the other guerrillas shaped the Communist party of China, and in their fight to free China, molded the basic principles of their leadership.

Today part of the city is a museum, but it also is the source of a vital living tradition. Everywhere, the people we met talked of Yenan. Why does this barren, wind-blown city hold such an important place in the everyday lives of millions of Chinese? What is the spirit of Yenan?

The Communist guerrillas had arrived in northwest China in 1935, decimated and bitterly exhausted, at the end of the six-thousand-mile "Long March." Fleeing the Kuomintang armies, with their original bases to the southeast destroyed, 130,000 men and women had begun the trek. Now, 370 days later, in October 1935, they numbered only 20,000. On the Long March they had trekked through eleven of China's provinces, in a vast loop west and then north, passing through swamps and snowcapped mountains and hauling with them guns, a printing press, and other equipment.

But they were not yet secure. Chiang Kai-shek's armies had also pushed north into the area—more committed to defeating the Communists than defeating the Japanese. Because of this, a number of the other Kuomintang-allied commanders in the region grew increasingly critical of Chiang; and in December 1936, on a visit to the city of Sian, Chiang was captured by the troops of Chang Hsueh-liang. Representatives of the Communist forces pressed for Chiang's release, and after several weeks of negotiations, a new united front was formed in January 1937 between the Kuomintang and the Communists on the principle of cooperation against the Japanese.

Although that united front only lasted a few years, and often appeared to be more a matter of fiction than fact, it did allow the Communists a respite in which they could turn their full attention to the Japanese. Mao and the party leaders moved to the city of Yenan and established it as their capital. For the first time, Mao was the acknowledged leader of the entire Communist party. There were still challenges to his ideas, but in this period the party and the government of the liberated zone were most concerned with analyzing the mistakes of the past and determining how best to successfully lead the revolution.

This meant most of all "going among the masses." For their war was a guerrilla war, and to survive and succeed, they had to depend entirely on the support of the people they lived among. They were, Mao said, like the fish in the water, the party among the people. It was not difficult to understand the determination of the people to fight the Japanese, or their needs for food, homes, and freedom from landlords and local officials. But in real terms, how should these be achieved? How important was land reform if it would alienate small landowners who might join the fight against the Japanese? Where should the people be encouraged to stand and fight against the Japanese, and where were they too weak, where should they withdraw into the hills, or prepare traps in the villages? All of these questions—vital questions on which the survival not only of the party, but of the people, depended—were answered in practice, slowly and over time, at Yenan.

It was not enough, however, simply to recognize the needs of the people and help them to achieve them. The Communists soon learned that they also had to be able to protect the people. When they arrived in the northwest, they discovered that the local party organizers had concentrated their efforts in the area around Sian, but were having difficulties persuading the people of the area to openly support them. After some investigation, it became apparent that the people, while they were very sympathetic to the social and economic reforms the party proposed, were simply afraid. With strong Kuomintang garrisons right in the Sian area, they were skeptical of the ability of the Communists to protect them against reprisals from the garrisons. And in fact the Communists could not at that point.

By moving north to Yenan, the party established a base area they could protect, and the liberated zone began to grow. During these years the population of the zone grew, too, for thousands of Chinese youths, especially those of the large cities, streamed to Yenan to join the resistance against Japan and to see the new government for themselves. One of these young people was an actress from Shanghai, a determined woman named Chang Ch'ing, who later married Mao.

As young intellectuals, they must have found life there hard at first. For the Communists insisted that they should not be a burden on the people. The base area supplied all its own food and fuel needs. They would have no more food, no better clothing, even simpler cave houses, than the people they were fighting with. Here students of Kangda, the "Anti-Japanese Imperialism University," lived together in cave dormitories, studying part of the time but also farming and helping to make the base self-sufficient. The students fashioned their pens of chicken quills, made abacuses by stringing peach pits on wires, and used shallow boxes of sand for practicing writing characters. This was a whole new style in leadership for China and it stood out in sharp contrast with that of the Kuomintang.

Throughout the struggle the Communists were constantly compared with the Kuomintang. The sharpest contrasts were in the way the armies of both sides behaved, and here the Red Army demonstrated most clearly of all that the party was "of, by, and for the people." Consisting both of formal fighting divisions and small guerrilla groups in the hills, the army followed the three main rules and the eight points. The three main rules were to obey orders in all actions, to take not even a single needle or piece of thread from the peasants, and to turn in everything captured. The eight points were: (1) Speak politely; (2) Pay fairly for what you buy; (3) Return everything you borrow; (4) Pay for anything you damage; (5) Don't hit or swear at people; (6) Don't damage crops; (7) Don't take liberties with women; and (8) Don't ill-treat captives.

For centuries, the Chinese peasants regarded all armies as a form of natural disaster that descended on an area like a plague of locusts. Marching from village to village, they ate up stores of grain, carried off women or abused them in their own homes, tortured captives and killed any villagers who protested. Most of the Kuomintang troops, poorly led and knowing they were being used not to fight the Japanese, but to suppress a revolt among their own countrymen, fit this traditional image closely. For the millions of Chinese peasants who saw or knew of their pillaging and arrogance, the Communist armies were a revelation. Villagers asked to join—there was no conscription—and members of the eighth route and other red armies were respected everywhere. Even without conscription, social pressure was strong on young men to join these armies, for peasant families considered it embarrassing to have a healthy son at home when he could be in the people's armies. They also knew that if their sons left, the party would organize help for them among the villagers and from the party cadres to make up the difference in labor power.

The cadres were the backbone of the party, the local workers who had either left their village, been trained in Yenan and returned, or who had come from training at Yenan to another village. It was their responsibility to organize the people, maintain communications with the guerrilla units, and promote reforms. The army, too, had cadres who helped to teach the soldiers about the history of the struggle, what the present situation was, and how the army should relate to the people.

It was in the armies that many of these young peasant soldiers first learned to read. We heard about how it was done: as a group of soldiers or peasants helping a transport unit marched along, each would have a piece of paper or cloth pinned on his back with a Chinese character written on it. The man behind him could study the character, memorizing it and discussing it with the men around him. After a while, the lines would become scrambled and everyone would be walking behind a new word. In this way the young men of the liberated zone learned to read—an ambition few of them would have dreamed of before.

It was in this spartan, struggling but successful period that Mao and his comrades worked together at Yenan. And in these years, Mao produced most of his famous writings.

The Foolish Old Man Who Removed the Mountains

There was an old man who lived in northern China long ago and was known as the foolish old man of North Mountain. His house faced south and beyond his doorway stood the two great peaks, Taihang and Wangwu, obstructing the way. He called his sons, and hoe in hand they began to dig up these mountains with great determination. Another graybeard, known as the wise old man, saw them and said derisively, "How silly of you to do this! It is quite impossible for you few to dig up these two huge mountains." The foolish old man replied, "When I die, my sons will carry on; when they die, there will be my grandsons, and then their sons and grandsons, and so on to infinity. High as they are, the mountains cannot grow any higher and with every bit we dig, they will be that much lower. Why can't we clear them away?" Having refuted the wise old man, he went on digging every day, unshaken in his conviction. God was moved by this, and he sent down two angels, who carried the mountains away on their backs.

This is an ancient Chinese fable, quoted by Mao Tse-tung in a speech in 1945. Mao was talking to members of the Communist party, and he said, "Our god is none other than the masses of the Chinese people. If they stand up and dig together with us, why can't these two mountains (of imperialism and feudalism) be cleared away?" Today, this fable and Mao's use of it are quoted all over China as examples of the great determination and patience required of those who want to bring change and progress.

"The Foolish Old Man Who Removed the Mountains" is one of the three old favorite articles, selections from Mao's *Collected Works* which are read and studied, and whose ideas are constantly referred to. Each, though simple and straightforward, leads to a number of other basic ideas and eventually to action.

At the Xigubi Production Brigade, the people are reclaiming a large piece of land from the bed of the rambling river (see chap. 5, "Communes"). When they undertook this project, they said, some of the people of Xigubi thought the effort was useless. For centuries the river had followed its course. Maybe the People's Liberation Army, with lots of machinery, could do something. But how could they change things? Their grandfathers and grandmothers had had to live with little plots of land, and they probably would too. Even if they could change the course of the river this season, could they be sure that a flood would not wipe out all their work? Others, however, quoted the "Foolish Old Man" story, and said that if they did not try, who would change anything? Certainly the national government did not have money and technicians to help them right away—would they just wait helplessly forever?

Now, although it will take them another year of hard work to finish breaking a channel through the mountain for the diverted water, they are well on their way to having twice the land they had before. This is their idea of how the "Foolish Old Man" story helped to make them self-reliant. The story is not very different from the American saying "Where there's a will, there's a way." Because they did not have sophisticated machines to dig and transport the earth that they were trying to clear from the new channel, the peasants of Xigubi devised a system of pumping water to a small reservoir above the proposed channel, loosening the soil with dynamite, and then allowing the water to rush down carrying the loose soil into the river; by this method they were able to cut the channel in a few months, and the removed earth had been deposited in the old riverbed, helping to prepare it for the time when it could be planted.

The scientists of the Nanking Observatory were also talking about self-reliance when they explained their concept of the "Liu Shao-ch'i line" to us. Before the Cultural Revolution, they said, the observatory had closely followed Western development in science—so closely that scientists were discouraged from doing original research on one part of a project on solar explosions. This attitude was called "following behind at a snail's pace" and it meant that they could not try to solve the problem on their own. After the younger scientists protested, this policy was changed, and the observatory is now doing its own research. Self-reliance means not only not waiting for the government agencies to do something, it also means not waiting for the West to do it.

"The Foolish Old Man" is an Aesop's fable about the necessity of hard work and struggle. One old farmer we met at Houjuang said that Mao's teachings, and this story in particular, show that "it is necessary to struggle against nature, to struggle against class enemies, and to struggle against selfishness in our minds. We cannot assume an easygoing and comfortable style of life. The road to socialist construction is no peaceful journey, but one full of hard struggle."

It was already late afternoon near the Date Garden outside Yenan and the mountain air was beginning to be crisp and chill as three of us walked down a narrow dirt road. We came out on to a grassy field with a small platform raised at one end. Now cultural performances and speeches are given here for large groups, but its importance stems from another period when Mao delivered a memorial speech for a common worker accidentally killed at his job in 1944. Entitled "Serve the People," this speech has become another of the three old favorite articles, and in a sense it commemorates all those who gave their lives in service to the people.

As we walked back across the field one of the Chinese walking with us mentioned that many people who come to visit this place sit on the grass to reread the speech at the same spot where it was first given.

"We don't have a version of it with us, in English, or we could read it out for the group," said Ray. But of course Ray and others had been speaking in Chinese, so our companion said, "You understand Chinese, I'll read it for you," and he pulled a well-worn book from his pocket.

So, as Ray, Ken, and Susan walked slowly along with him, he read the words:

. . . All men must die, but death can vary in its significance. The ancient Chinese writer Ssuma Ch'ien said, "Though death befalls all men alike, it may be heavier than Mount Tai or lighter than a feather" . . . Comrade Chang Szu-teh died for the people, and his death is indeed heavier than Mount Tai.

If we have shortcomings, we are not afraid to have them pointed out and criticized, because we serve the people. Anyone, no matter who, may point out our shortcomings. If he is right, we will correct them. If what he proposes will benefit the people, we will act upon it . . .

In times of difficulty we must not lose sight of our achievements, we must see the bright future and must pluck up our courage. The Chinese people are suffering; it is our duty to save them and we must exert ourselves in struggle. Wherever there is struggle there is sacrifice, and death is a common occurrence. But we have the interests of the people and the sufferings of the great majority at heart, and when we die for the people it is a worthy death. Nevertheless, we should do our best to avoid unnecessary sacrifices. Our cadres must show concern for every soldier, and all people in the revolutionary ranks must care for each other, must love and help each other.

Mao concluded this speech by suggesting that each time a person died, his or her village hold a memorial meeting to discuss the ways in which that person contributed to the village. The message of this was both about equality —that everyone who contributes should be honored, and not forgotten—and about service to society. To serve the people is not an idealistic, hollow platitude. It is seen as the measure of an individual's worth. In judging one's fellow villagers, the old indicators of "worth"—money, position, and physical possessions—are no longer meaningful symbols. For everyone's share of money is likely to be roughly the same, their physical possessions of the same type and quantity, and "official" positions, such as brigade leader or treasurer, are held by persons elected by the village.

The idea that in serving the people you are serving your family and your village, as well as all China, is now clear to almost everyone. Having seen the results of cooperation and hard work, the people of China tend to return to these themes of self-reliance and service in solving new problems. To work hard for your village, factory, neighborhood, is to be respected and to find your place in the scheme of things.

During dinner at Tachai, Judy asked her hostess how Mao Tse-tung's writings and teachings have changed the lives of individuals. The woman—a short, motherly woman with a slow smile and a quiet face—thought for a while, trying to find an example which would tell us clearly. Then, nodding her head, she said, "Yes, the best example is the old man down there," pointing in the direction of the center of the village. "He is a cripple, and all his life he didn't work much, for the tasks around here mean a lot of walking up and down hills and hard labor. But two years ago, during the Cultural Revolution study classes, he decided he wanted to do something. So he gathered waste wood and bits of metal, and fashioned them into turnip graters. In northwest China, we all eat turnips—so in one year he made three thousand of these to sell for the collective. Before everyone had pitied him and called him useless, but now they say, 'A useless person took useless material and turned it into wealth.' Now he feels so much better."

Serving the people is thus seen as a way to fulfillment as an individual in China. It means to work hard, not for personal gain but for the advancement of everyone in your village or factory.

The most extreme case is to die for the people. Chen Yonggui told us of such a person at Tachai, the mule-team driver Jou Shaohe. When Tachai was rebuilding caves after the rains of 1963, the demands on the mule carts which haul stones were especially heavy. Jou insisted that he could handle a cart by himself, although usually each cart took two drivers to handle it. Other carts made four trips daily; Jou pushed his team and made seven, sometimes even nine trips a day. Everyone in the village asked him why he was working so hard. He told them that he was thinking of Norman Bethune, the Canadian doctor who died serving with the Red Army. If Bethune, a foreigner, could sacrifice himself for the Chinese people, then he—a Tachai man—would too. One day Jou was injured in a cart accident and died.

It was not coincidence that Jou talked of Bethune, or that Chen mentioned this incident to us; for the third of the three old favorite articles was written as a memorial for Bethune in December 1939:

> Every Communist must learn from him. There are not a few people who are irresponsible in their work, preferring the light and shirking the heavy, passing the burdensome tasks on to others and choosing the easy ones for themselves. At every turn they think of themselves before others. When they make some small contribution, they swell with pride and brag about it for fear that others will not know. They feel no warmth toward comrades and people but are cold, indifferent, and apathetic. In truth such people are not Communists, or at least cannot be counted as devoted Communists. No one who ever returned from the front failed to express admiration for Bethune whenever his name was mentioned, and none remained unmoved by his spirit.

When Bethune came to China, he had the opportunity to be a one-man wonder, to perform complicated operations and save individual lives. Instead, he set up field hospitals, trained doctors and nurses, and designed battle-field transfusion equipment, always as patterns which other units could study and emulate, and always with the idea of "phasing out" his own participation.

Thus today the Chinese say that doctors who go out to the rural areas should not complain because conditions are not good, or feel like celebrities because they are needed. They should seek to ensure that after they leave their loss will be felt as little as possible. To do this they will have to pay close attention to the local conditions, the needs of the peasantry, and redesign their ideas of medical care so they can contribute effectively.

This is the other side of the coin of self-reliance. For if the Chinese people want to become self-reliant, but the skilled technicians of her society don't want to share their skills and don't listen to the people, then progress will be difficult and class distinctions will persist.

The Chinese recognize that even the most devoted leader will often begin to define the "needs of the people" as he sees them, and will begin to think of himself as a "father" who guides the people because they cannot help themselves. Very early in his career—in 1927, in Hunan —Mao Tse-tung began to develop the idea of investigation as a way to combat these problems. The technique is simple, but has remained one of the basic principles of Communist party doctrine: Before you attempt to devise the solution for a problem you should go to the people who live with that problem to investigate. Is this really the problem, or is there some other factor which should be attacked first? How do the people define the problem? How much of a problem is it? Do they have any solutions to propose? Are they interested in working to solve it if a solution can be found? Who are they willing to work with?

Chairman Mao

The barren hills of Shanxi, where people lived poverty-stricken in loess caves, sold their children in order to survive, and eked out a miserable existence as hired laborers, have been transformed into innumerable terraces of green corn, orchards, vegetable plots, and rows of solid granite-block houses.

"This happened because of Chairman Mao's leadership," said Chen Yonggui to us the afternoon we walked around the hills above Tachai. "Chairman Mao has high prestige all over China. The people, all of us, have great love for him. Why? Because in the past China was mistreated by foreigners. We will never forget the atrocities committed by the Japanese imperialists here. The landlords oppressed and exploited us; and Chairman Mao also led us to defeat them. We achieved our liberation under his leadership. Both in political and economic aspects, Chairman Mao led us to win liberation and emancipation. That is why we love Chairman Mao and follow him. It isn't that Chairman Mao asked us to love him; this is the people's spontaneous reaction to his leadership in all these struggles."

Life has changed tremendously for the people of China, and it is not surprising that they love and respect the man who led them then and leads them today. They read his writings, and put pictures of him on their walls, identifying with him as the one who best symbolizes the new road that China has taken.

During the Cultural Revolution, there was a tremendous increase in the amount of attention paid to Mao. In the years since the Great Leap Forward, pictures of him had been on the walls and much had been done in his name, but his actual writings and even some of his more recent ideas were often suppressed by the "Liuist" faction in the party and governmental bureaucracies. The Cultural Revolution revived study of his works, and the Chinese people say that most of the bursts of innovation and reorganization which began then were the result of their going back to the ideas of self-reliance, serving the people, and the spirit of the "Foolish Old Man."

But certain practices which sprang up during the Cultural Revolution are now seen as excessive. With the assurance that Mao's writings and ideas will not be suppressed, the people (and Mao) feel that continuing to post quotations everywhere and to chant slogans could easily become empty formalism. Mao himself has said that he did not like the "personality cult" aspects of this veneration, which he felt should be directed toward the ideas which he—with others in the party and the Chinese people—had developed over many years. Today this is happening in China. Some of the pictures and statues of Mao are coming down, and these cultist excesses of the Cultural Revolution are being reversed. Rather than the accomplishment of a genius, no matter how well motivated, the Chinese today stress in articles and posters: "The people, and only the people, are the motive force in world history."

A Pocket Guide to Revolution

The three old favorite articles are constantly quoted and referred to, but they are not as ubiquitous as the world-famous little red book. That phenonenon is one of the most difficult for us, as Westerners living outside China, to understand, even after studying China for years. This summer was our opportunity to see how these small, red-plastic-covered books are actually used.

The books are actually entitled *Quotations of Chairman Mao Tse-tung,* since that is what the Chinese call them. They are not original works. Rather, their purpose is to provide a boiled-down summary of all the experiences of the last fifty years in China. There are sections on women, on the role of the party, on all kinds of topics, and each section contains a number of quotes from Mao's writings, some only one or two sentences long. It is a kind of pocket guide to the revolutions of the past, and because of that it is also, the Chinese say, a very practical guide for a revolutionary approach today.

The *Quotations* have also served another purpose, especially for the many old people in China who can now read, but still find it difficult and time-consuming on top of long hours in the fields. How can these basic ideas be presented to them in a simple, direct form? The answer of course is this small book of "Aesop's fables." There is now a common political culture which all of China has read and heard about, and which encourages the people to go on and read more.

Mao himself has warned against taking these books, or any set of ideas, as a dogma. They should be a way of judging situations and deciding how to act in a general sense. The Chinese are no less pragmatic than any other people, and they have found that the *Quotations* have a practical usefulness for the solution of all kinds of problems.

This is what the Chinese mean when they say "this happened because of Chairman Mao," or "I was able to do that because I read Chairman Mao's writings." "This" or "that" really did happen because of Chairman Mao, or because the person studied Chairman Mao's writings, but not because Chairman Mao is a good doctor, or garage mechanic, or irrigation expert—only because Mao talked about self-reliance when the people were discouraged, about serving the people when fear of failure made them think cooperation impossible. Because in China's darkest hour, Mao and the party led the people to what still seems an amazing victory.

Who Leads, Who Follows?

In China, a leader is said to be a man or woman who comes from and is completely in the service of the Chinese people. The American government is said to be a "government of the people, by the people, for the people." In practice, the Chinese and American forms of government share little if anything in common. What are the differences? How does government work in China? What are their leaders really like?

What makes Chen Yonggui, for example, a "model" cadre? Why is he, a brigade leader of Tachai, so respected everywhere in China? What is it *about* Chen that is admired?

We enjoyed his easygoing style, his pleased grins displaying newly acquired teeth, but we were quite sure that this homey appearance was not the basis of his great reputation. That, we were told at other communes, in Shanghai and in the factories of the northwest provinces, is his relationship with the people of Tachai. He is talked about as an example of something which is now common everywhere in China—representatives—who spend several months each year working at home among the people they represent during the rest of the year. Even local leaders who never see the capital are constantly reminded by their own constituents that too much time in an office, away from the daily life and work of the people, is the quickest route to becoming insensitive, self-seeking, and bureaucratic politicians.

Chen, like Wu Kuixian of Sian's textile mill, is a member of the party's Central Committee—and like Wu, he lives very much like everyone else around him. His cave house stands in a row next to his neighbors' and the only material difference we saw between Chen's home and those of the other villagers was a telephone in his room. Of course, the opportunity to travel to Taiyuan and Peking on official business, while not materially rewarding, is an exciting difference. Perhaps a better measure is a lower-level leader like Chen's neighbor, the brigade leader of Houjuang. This old pipe-smoking man has a personality much more garrulous and ruminative than Chen's, but it seemed to us that he had much of the same leadership style. He too worked part-time (actually, most of the time) in the fields, and his relationship with the other villagers seemed relaxed and close, not the back-slapping display which often passes for intimacy in American politics.

In addition to Chen, Wu, Yang Fujen, Premier Chou En-lai, and Chang Ch'un-ch'iao and Yao Wen-yuan of the Political Bureau, we talked to several members of provincial and municipal revolutionary committees and a great number of "lower-level" leaders, ranging from primary school directors to production team leaders.

Our overwhelming impression was that in China political power is not a transferable commodity. Everyone has it, and everyone is supposed to be involved in using it, in constant discussions and meetings and projects. Political power is not simply handed over to an official, with the implication of "Go ahead, we trust you, so go ahead and do your best for us," much less the more familiar attitude of "Well, you were the best of a poor lot, and let's see what you can do for us." Instead, a leader is chosen largely because he is already an effective leader within his home community, and is expected to devote more of his time to local activities.

Very few leaders ever leave their communities, except perhaps to journey into a nearby town or city to meet with representatives of the next-higher organization such as a county revolutionary committee. If the community—

commune, brigade, factory, or school—is going to be self-reliant, then a leader is not primarily a negotiator with the state government or some outside agency. He is someone who can help organize the people within his community to achieve more within their own limits, a person who can tap everyone's special talents and make things happen. Obviously, he is not going to be able to do this unless he knows the community well and is closely in touch with it. In *Fanshen,* William Hinton's retelling of the revolution in a Chinese village, we had read of a proverb which was invented to describe this situation: "Under the Kuomintang, a plague of taxes; under the Communists, a plague of meetings."

This situation seems to generate a feeling of common effort to meet common goals, rather than a "manager-worker" relationship where the leader can tell the other members of the commune or factory what to do or how to do it. Some of this may be due to the fact that China—still a poor country—must set certain national plans for its economy and thus give quotas to lower economic units. In this way, the leader is never responsible alone for telling the people how much they must produce: either it is a quota in a general range set outside their community, which he and the workers discuss and then respond to, or it is a project generated within the community, like the Xigubi river-diversion scheme or the subsidiary factories at the rolling-stock plant, and has therefore been agreed to by everyone in the community. With the goal set, the problem becomes how to achieve that goal, and here again, everyone participates. The leader has been chosen because he encourages innovation, sharing of responsibility and cooperation.

What *is* a leader, though? Is he a representative in government? Or a factory manager? Or a school director? Or an organizer of spare-time study groups? In China, he or she is all of these things. This is the most startling fact about the structure of China's government—there is no division into things "political" and "nonpolitical." Leadership structures are essentially the same for factories, hospitals, communes, schools, government offices, and agencies; everyone is a politician and no one is *only* a politician.

Revolutionary Committees and Party Committees

While we were in China, we visited thirty-one different local organizations, an average of one daily. They included factories, rural communes, hospitals, schools, local governments, housing settlements, retail stores, and research units. In each case, we were invited to observe the organization in some detail, and we were given an extended verbal presentation with plenty of time for questions.

Some of our questions stemmed from that of "Who leads, who follows." We were interested in the actual structures of these administrative and governing organizations. Everywhere, there are two basic committees: the party committee and the revolutionary committee. Why are there so many committees in China? How are group decisions made? Can a factory really be run like a commune, a hospital like an army unit?

The answer was an enthusiastic yes—enthusiastic because the Chinese we talked to had just spent a great deal of energy in the Cultural Revolution to establish that fact. The basic idea, they said, is that the people of the factory should run their factory, and the people of the hospital should run their hospital; thus the governing structures can be essentially the same although the actual tasks are very different. And the only way to ensure that the people are actually running things is to have a leadership group which includes all the important groups in the factory or commune. And yes, committee deliberations take time, but the result is very much worth it.

What do these similar political structures look like? All share the system of party and revolutionary committees; there is no separation between what we call the "public" and "private" sectors. In all of China, we saw only a few departures from this, at the production team and production brigade levels of some rural communes where the pre-Cultural Revolution "administrative committees" still exist instead of revolutionary committees (but greatly resemble them).

The relationship between the party committees and the revolutionary committees has an interesting history. We had come suspecting that in fact the party committees would tend to control everything. After all, China is a Communist country, and by its own statements this is the period of the dictatorship of the party of the proletariat, the Communist party. But we found that the revolutionary committees seem to have a great deal more prestige and influence within the communities we visited. This was partly the case because during the Cultural Revolution, the party committees were for the most part shut down and completely overhauled, while the revolutionary committees were developed to function in their place. The revolutionary committees are based on the "three-in-one" pattern; which three segments are represented varies somewhat from unit to unit, but basically they consist of party members, People's Liberation Army members, and representatives of the factory or other unit. Often during the Cultural Revolution it was these revolutionary committees which coordinated the criticism and rectification of the party committees. Now the revolutionary committees have a watchdog heritage, which party committees evidently keep in mind.

The major change for party workers, called cadre in China, has been the great emphasis on the "mass line." This is a particularly strong version of the idea of "investigation" mentioned before. Because party cadres, in contrast to other types of leaders, are often asked to work in new areas or to work for periods of time in bureaucratic posts, there is a greater need for them to consciously "go down to the local level" where other local leaders already are working. This they now do regularly for large parts of each year, working on the assembly lines or in the fields, listening to the ideas and complaints of the workers.

Some of this was done before the Cultural Revolution, and the changes since may have been more quantitative than qualitative. But in combination with the revolutionary committee checks on them, the party committees have been made to feel more responsible than in the past.

Lost Among the Masses?

What is the role of the individual in all this? Has all the talk of cooperation and serving the people selflessly created a bland society—successful economically but boring in every other way? Hardly. It was quite obvious to us that in China socialism does not blur personalities, but in fact the contrary seemed true—we constantly saw tremendous encouragement of individual initiative. The rewards are not remunerative, usually. But achievements are written about and respected, and the pride these people shared with the others of their factory or commune or hospital was very evident. This sharing of pride and accomplishments, while it does not deny the achievement of the individual, is different from our sense of personal distinction. The roots of the Chinese attitude, however, go back further than 1949. For traditionally the social unit has been the family—and a very large "extended" family, sometimes a whole lineage—rather than a single person. Now the most important social unit is the production team, or a comparable small unit.

The individual has an outlet not only for positive accomplishments but also for criticism of leadership. This is the very important custom of "criticism–self-criticism," a process carried on in open meetings where workers and cadres come together to discuss a particular problem in terms of the people or person working on it. The person is asked to attempt to analyze his own successes and failures, particularly paying attention to what he might correct in the future. After he has finished, others talk with him, offering collective support for his efforts to change and criticisms of aspects he has not mentioned. In this way, a person making mistakes is not simply ignored or ostracized, but instead is given an opportunity to understand what his mistakes are and to demonstrate his desire to change. The assumption is that problems must be solved not by isolating the difficulty (for example, by locking the individual up in a prison), but by dealing with it in a way which will reintegrate the person into society, so that he will be both accepted and personally satisfied.

We saw all kinds of people in China engage in "criticism–self-criticism," from Premier Chou En-lai, who criticized himself for his lack of firmness and experience at the 1954 Geneva Conference, to the People's Liberation Army official showing us through a factory complex: he told one young woman to hide a urinating child from our sight. A young man standing with her challenged him immediately, asking why such a natural act should be hidden from the eyes of guests, and why the PLA officer should make such demands in the first place. The reaction: the PLA officer admitted he had been wrong for making such an order.

As we went through the Soochow Grain Store no. 57, several of the workers referred to criticism–self-criticism as a good method for handling problems. Later, in our "discussion session," we asked what they meant. A young worker, her cheeks almost as red as her hair ribbons, gave a few examples: they had felt they were not "serving the people" enough, so they worked out a system of delivering some of their goods to the blind and handicapped people of their section of the city; they kept the store open longer for workers on odd shifts and set up a twenty-four-hour service schedule for special needs; and they continually asked their customers for criticisms. She finished by telling us that she had recently criticized herself for being irritated and snapping at a customer over the telephone.

But this didn't really answer our question. This was the "self-criticism" side of criticism—and was a way of preventing problems of complacency or bad relations with customers. How did they use this method to solve problems that had already come up? What if someone from outside the store criticized them first?

This time the grain-store workers told us about a dispute they had had with a factory several blocks away. The grain store processes flour and rice into wrappers for varieties of Chinese "dumplings"—small paper-thin skins of dough which are wrapped around chopped stuffings of meat, spices, and vegetables. These are sold at the store and are also made to order in larger amounts. One afternoon the month before, someone called from the factory cafeteria to order a large number of one kind of dumpling wrapper to be ready by three p.m. They were made, but by five that afternoon no one had come to collect them. Meanwhile the regular supplies of dumpling wrappers had been sold out and customers were asking for them. It was too late to make any more that day, so the grain-store workers sold the wrappers; and of course the factory workers appeared soon after.

"There were some hard feelings," one man from the grain store told us. "But we talked it over and decided that it was our fault—the factory workers had been involved in a long meeting and they couldn't get away to call us. If we had called them, we would have found out the reason and kept the wrappers or maybe even taken them over to the factory. In any case, some of us volunteered to go over and talk to the people at the factory, and the factory workers thought this was a generous attitude for us to take, so they began to offer criticisms of themselves. By the time we finished talking, everything was all right again—and we really had learned something. After that we would call before we sold out an order!"

This "happy ending" was a practical working arrangement, and it also demonstrated one advantage of group discussions: a single person might be very unwilling to blame himself in order to solve the problems with the factory cafeteria; but when the whole grain store discussed the issue and took responsibility as a group, criticism was seen as a constructive step toward better business practices within the store and led to a new procedure for dealing with the problem, not to mention a sense of increased solidarity with the factory workers.

A "Social" Disease

No flies in China? Well, there are some—but not very many, and certainly far fewer than the swarming, buzzing masses of them we were all used to elsewhere in Asia. This was the result of one of the "four-pest" campaigns to eliminate mosquitoes, rats, bedbugs, and flies, all carriers of disease. To attack the flies, everyone was urged to swat ten a day—and soon China's people, 700 million strong, defeated its flies.

This is a famous example of how mass campaigns have solved problems in China. Another example—one which we were especially interested in as Americans—is how China solved the problem of venereal disease. In the United States, this disease is now officially an epidemic: the rate of incidence of gonorrhea is 285 per 100,000 and that of syphilis is 44 per 100,000, or a total of about 0.3 percent. In China at Liberation, the rate of syphilis alone (the much more serious form of venereal disease) ranged from 3 percent in the countryside to 5 percent in the cities, more than 10 percent in the minority areas, and 20 percent in the Kuomintang Army. Today active venereal disease has been completely eradicated from most areas and completely controlled throughout China, an amazing accomplishment which has been corroborated by many Western doctors who have traveled or lived in China, including Dr. Joshua Horn, the British surgeon who practiced in China from 1954 to 1969. Several CCAS members heard Dr. Horn discuss the process of curing VD in China, and found his discussion supported by our own talks with physicians and other health workers in China.

This cure was effected while malaria, schistosomiasis, TB, kala azar, hookworm, leprosy, and opium addiction were all competing with venereal disease for the attention of the small handful of trained technicians and doctors. How did they do it? How could China, a poor struggling nation facing all of these crises, cure in twenty years a disease which America, rich and with a highly advanced medical technology, has not? The answer everywhere, from everyone, was the same: that the strength of China is that of its people, and when its people organize themselves to attack a problem, they win.

Most problems, the Chinese say, are in fact political and social at root. Even so-called "medical problems" are political in nature, for once the technical means of curing a disease is found, it is a *political* decision not to organize the energy, time, and money to cure it. In such situations the continued existence of any disease is a sign of social decay—and makes any disease a "social disease."

The cure of syphilis was known. What stood in the way of a complete cure for China? First, the position of women. Women still were the chattels of men. The brothels were closed—but that was not enough. Just a few months after Liberation, the Marriage Law of 1950 was passed—a law which in one stroke ended the legal oppression Chinese women had endured for centuries.

Women were declared equal to men, with equal rights to divorce, to take jobs, to own material possessions, and to raise children. Forced marriages were abolished. With their status as women drastically changed, the prostitutes leaving the brothels could rejoin society, not as outcasts but as rehabilitated victims of old China.

Second, poverty. Without enough to eat and with wretchedly poor clothing and housing, all other health problems for the Chinese people remained secondary. Inflation was ended in the first year, and everyone was given what they lacked to meet the basic requirements of a decent life. This also provided the physical strength needed for recovery from diseases.

Third, ignorance. Most of China's peasants knew nothing of how disease is spread and how it is cured. Because the peasants were illiterate, the process of spreading this information was doubly difficult.

But what resources did China have—what weapons with which to wage the battle against venereal disease? Here the slogan "Rely on the masses" took on a new meaning for health work. For at first it appeared that the resources were few. It was relatively simple to manufacture greater amounts of medicine—but how to manufacture greater numbers of personnel to discover venereal disease and administer the medicine?

After long discussions and arguments, two positions became clear. One faction believed that only doctors and nurses trained by the established medical training programs were qualified to undertake this work, and that therefore the process of curing venereal disease could only proceed as fast as new people could be trained in the old ways. The most important step according to this view was to expand the present training programs.

Other people—these were the same people who said that medical problems could have political solutions—said that new campaigns against venereal disease should be developed, training new kinds of "paramedical" workers specially for the task and relying on the involvement of thousands of unskilled workers to help spread the campaign. Slowly they began to convince the more traditional thinkers that only a program as broad in scope as this—one that was essentially political—would have a chance to solve the enormous problem of venereal disease in China.

Traveling in China then, one would have seen teams of young men and women in the remotest villages putting on plays, reading stories, giving demonstrations and tests, and setting up treatment days. On their arrival in a village, the youths would hold a meeting to explain their purpose. Using simple posters and illustrated signboards, they described the symptoms and cure of the disease. In the next few days, they would perform one-act plays and talk about venereal disease in the marketplace, and begin to introduce the questionnaire form for diagnosing venereal disease. The questionnaire had been developed after intensive testing, and it asked the peasants to answer ten questions. A "yes" to any of them meant a person might have venereal disease, and ought to be checked with a blood test.

At first, of course, many—most—of the people were embarrassed to fill out the forms, and tried to disguise any symptoms they had. More talks were given and sometimes persons who had used the test and were being treated talked, too, explaining how they had hesitated and finally decided to take the test . . . it sounds a little like a medicine show out of the old West, doesn't it? But this time the content is no patent medicine but a real cure for a very real disease—one which in some villages, especially in the minority areas, meant the slow depopulation and extinction of a whole segment of the population. And because all these "testimonies" came from people they knew or could trust, the people began to see the reason to cooperate. A final and convincing argument offered by the young people was that of national pride. China had just achieved Liberation and was beginning to build socialism. Could it take this rotten disease with it?

Slowly at first, but then in a steady stream, people came forward to take the tests and receive treatment. Prejudices blocking the way to treatment had been broken down, and the principal sources of the disease's spread—rampaging armies, prostitution, and ignorance—had been abolished. By the end of the second decade, cases of active venereal disease have become so rare that is is impossible today for the medical schools in Peking to find examples for their students.

The Inheritors: The People's Liberation Army

Again our bus rolled through the outskirts of Canton toward the countryside—yesterday we had left the city to visit Huadong Commune, but today we headed in a new direction. We were invited to spend most of the day at the Canton Deaf-Mute School. Although the school has for many years taught deaf children to read, write, and speak, it has recently become well known for its experimental use of acupuncture to treat deafness.

This new program is an innovation begun by the People's Liberation Army members working on the school staff, so our visit was not only to see the school, but to find out what the PLA was doing in a school for the deaf. As we arrived, we could see through our windows the small cluster of staff there to greet us. One of the women wore a PLA uniform—the only one in sight.

The campus was simple and pleasing, with whitewashed three-story buildings set amid willow trees and plots of vegetables, surrounded by fields of corn. Inside the main hall, a few more students and staff met us and we all filed into a small sunny room for the first talk. The discussion was very short, for we had thought the briefing at Huadong too long, and asked our guides if the initial talks could be curtailed—it was much more useful to discuss the commune, or school, after we had actually seen most of it. So one of the teachers, with the PLA woman, outlined the function of the school.

The most important work of the school continues to be that of teaching the children to read, write, and speak. The program of acupuncture treatment has been expanding because of its initial successes, but not all the students respond to it equally well. Each child is treated according to the severity of his or her physical impairment. Some children in the area are too severely handicapped to come to the school easily, and would rather live at home, so the school staff goes to them. There are live-in students at the school, but students whose families live in the city or close by usually stay at home.

Now we would see the school in progress. Classes had already started, and we could look in through the open doors to see classes in session. The whole school echoed with the sound of lessons read aloud and the students' enthusiastic singing. Bright posters were stuck on the walls and sunshine streamed in through high windows. The teachers all appeared to be very young, and we saw many of them in People's Liberation Army uniforms. Some were helping individual children or walking hand in hand with them through the corridors.

We stopped at one room and the teacher invited us in. Here about twenty children were reciting songs and poems —the teacher, like others we had seen, had been shouting at the top of her lungs. "It helps them learn," she said, smiling, "and it makes them feel bold enough to try, too." How advanced were the students, we asked. "These students are still 'beginners'—we try to differentiate between stages in the students' treatment. Early classroom drill consists of rote recitation like this and 'creative work,' usually singing." We could hear many classrooms singing, now that this one had stopped, perhaps a bit off key, but with great gusto! "Later on, as treatment progresses, they learn to read newspapers as well as *Quotations of Chairman Mao Tse-tung*. The usual time for learning the necessary number of characters for reading is about two years. We use tape recorders to check on the progress students are making."

We also asked how rapidly most students respond to treatment for their handicaps; and one of the girls showing us around answered, her speech halting but clear. When she came to the school she had not been able to speak or hear. Now she has achieved partial speech, and can hear voices at a distance of up to about sixty yards. With a proud and very determined air, she said that when she is finally cured, "I will be better able to serve the people." Serving the people is the foundation of relations between students in the school and society at large, a PLA member said. Everything that they learn must be useful to them either within the school, or in the place they will go to after they leave. The basis of all active motivation for recuperation from illness is to be able to "serve the people" better. In accord with this, the curriculum for all students consists of Chinese language, music, arithmetic, physical education, and manual labor.

After our brief tour, our guides brought us to the school auditorium, a high-ceilinged, bright room with tall windows and a green-painted floor. Several teachers left the room to reappear a minute later ushering in small groups of giggling students. They were not shy, but a little embarrassed, we thought—they proceeded to sing several songs and perform a longer skit skillfully, smiling and not too self-conscious. Then one of the PLA members watching with us said that—since we most probably wanted to see their methods of acupuncture—part of the day's treatment would be given there. She, it turned out, was one of the medical workers, and she went out to pick up the equipment.

A young boy sat down in one of the empty chairs, and we turned to watch the process. First the PLA worker showed us the needle—it was long, thin, and silvery in color. She showed us where the needle would be inserted, pointing to the area directly in front of her ear. She had good reason to be familiar with the location of the proper point on her own ear, because PLA acupuncture teams work with the motto, "One thousand needles on oneself before one needle on a patient." Then, bending over the student, she inserted the needle to a depth of about one-and-a-half inches, rotating it gently. The boy sat quietly, his eyes open and his face calm, until the needle was withdrawn. Then he smiled, stretched his neck as though he had been holding it too rigidly, and walked back to join the other students sitting beside us.

"How does it work?" we asked. But the medical team told us that they didn't really know. Experiments are being conducted to find out how acupuncture actually works, but for the present it is simply a method which gets results. Most of the students are treated once or twice a day for two weeks at a time, and then rest for a week.

Our next question was difficult to put. "Why is the People's Liberation Army here?" The answer took quite a while, and generated a good deal of discussion among the staff, children, and medical workers, each explaining it from a personal point of view. The woman PLA member who had met us at the gate began by telling us about the time when the PLA first came, in 1968. "At that time the PLA was encouraged to form teams, and go into every unit—communes, hospitals, schools alike. We were a new addition of people with revolutionary enthusiasm, and the desire to overturn old methods and devise new solutions to everything we could. So when we came to the school, we already knew some acupuncture and we wanted to cure the students. Although we had no deep knowledge, and had to study the conditions here in detail, we learned a great deal and eventually we began to use acupuncture in these new ways. Now we are just an ordinary part of the staff."

The PLA had played two significant roles at the school in addition to their introduction of the new acupuncture treatment. The first had been to implement the general medical principle of involving the patient in his own cure —to create active participation and trust on the part of the students. The students watched the PLA members practicing acupuncture on themselves, and talked to them about "what it feels like," and how best to handle the occasional pain. "How bad is the pain," Susan asked. At first they tried to explain it to us, then they offered to let us try it ourselves. Not everyone was eager to, but finally Tony volunteered. They cleaned a needle of medium length—like the other, silvery and very thin—and slowly slipped it into his hand between his thumb and forefinger. Tony watched them, his brow wrinkled, but when they had inserted the needle almost two inches and had moved it several times he looked up and reported, "I can't feel it, almost nothing." They laughed with us, and the PLA member slipped the needle out again, saying, "You felt nothing, it seems, but sometimes the acupuncture needles do hurt, or actually just make the patient uncomfortable and want it over with. So it was very important for us to show the students we could use the needles on ourselves, and since they think the PLA soldiers are very brave, they want to be like us." This is an important ingredient in the PLA's contribution everywhere—for the PLA is greatly admired for its courage and determination. If PLA members urge students, factory or commune workers, or hospital staffs to try to devise new ways of solving problems, to be determined to do it themselves, this has a powerful influence on the situation.

In addition to this, the PLA members spotted another difficulty at the school: although the students were helped to adjust to the school routine, and were taught many basic skills in addition to reading, writing, and speaking, there was too little preparation and encouragement for the students' eventual return to regular society. "This 'school learning,'" they said, "will not be enough when the students go out into the real world. To really serve the students, the school should do everything it can to prepare them for that adjustment."

The school now has more than three hundred students, and since 1968 there have been about two hundred graduates. After they graduate, the students go to work as regular members of factories or farms, and the school tries to help them find a situation which will allow them to participate fully with the least problems. To find ways of preparing the students, the PLA, schoolteachers and students all talked together at great length, and students who had graduated came back to offer their ideas. Now the school has started the vegetable plots we saw as we came in, since this is an activity the students will participate in whether they live in the cities or the countryside. At harvesttime almost the whole school goes out to help. There are also more programs to teach the students new skills and give them experience in a wider range of experiences. The transition from the school to society at large has been made easier, and now the students are eager to learn and leave.

We had had a fairly good answer to our question about the PLA's presence in a school for the deaf. Although we continued to ask about the PLA's role in other units we visited, and often found considerable variation in the activities of PLA members, their contributions seemed everywhere to be very similar.

The Good Guerrilla Soldier

"What do you want to be when you grow up?" In China, the answer is most likely to be, "I want to join the PLA." At Peking's Middle School no. 31, the teachers complained to us of their difficulties in placing graduates, because so many of the students want to join the PLA. This does not sound like our American experience at all, nor that of other countries. What is the People's Liberation Army?

The answer, simply, is that the PLA are the heroes and heroines of China. As an army, the PLA is unique in the world. First, the soldiers of the PLA are the inheritors of the Yenan legacy . . . a legacy only slightly more than two decades old. Most Chinese look back on the war years and Liberation as the most momentous events of the century. The PLA was born in these years, created by the Communist party from the men and women of the villages of China. The army lived and fought among the people—as "fish in water"—and there was never the distinction of an institutionally separate army, segregated on bases and independent of the community.

Another side of the Yenan legacy is that the army tried to support itself. When they were not actually fighting, the PLA soldiers would help to work the fields or make repairs in the peasants' homes. They learned how to read, and taught the people of the villages. If they offended the villagers, they could be—and were—reprimanded by the village leaders. Village boys and girls regularly volunteered to join the PLA, and when they could not (for instance, only sons could not join the regular army because if they were killed their family line would die out) they were just as disappointed as the graduates of Peking Middle School no. 31 today.

Second, the PLA is a domestic, defensive force. The People's Republic of China has no military bases in *any* foreign country. Born as a guerrilla army to defend the people of China in the wars against Japanese invaders and Kuomintang repression, the PLA remains at home and occupies itself with a domestic role in Chinese society.

Third, the PLA is only one part of China's defense preparations. The Chinese say that the responsibility of defending their country falls on all the people, and that the PLA is just the most "professional" level. Far more Chinese are in the local militias than in the PLA; after seeing them in action, we are convinced that the local militias are the backbone of China's strength.

Nanking: The People's Militia

The morning was hot and muggy and dismally overcast as we left our hotel in Nanking, riding out toward the hills beyond the city. After about thirty or forty minutes, we arrived at one side of a very large field with a structure something like a section of a small football stadium on the near side. This was the reviewing stand, and we were about to see one of Nanking's militia units practicing. To one side, a large group of people of all ages, young men and women, girls and boys, and a few older adults, perhaps in their forties or fifties, were lugging around pieces of military equipment and setting them up in position for the exercises.

Some of the Nanking CATT staff had come out with us, and they now led us toward the reviewing stands. We climbed up onto the simple platform, and found long wooden benches facing out with another wooden table bench running the length of the platform in front of us. It was covered with a cloth and—even here—there were thermos flasks of hot water and plenty of tea. Stretching out before us was the full length of the green field with a small stream running down the middle from right to left, and in the distance a sharp slope up into the hills and a low ridge of hills still further on.

The men and women of the militia group were practicing first. One of the members of their unit came up to talk with us. The militia is entirely voluntary, he said, and they practice two or three times a week for a few hours. Today they would speed up their practice and run through most of their basic training so we would get a good idea of what the militia is. The women (there were almost as many women as men on the field) were wearing dark pants and light pastel or white blouses with ammunition belts strapped over their shoulders. The men had on old dark work clothes, with rifles and ammunition belts as the women had. All of them appeared to be sure of what they were doing, from long practice, but they did not look particularly military in these outfits. Most of them were fairly young, in their twenties or early thirties, except for a few older members. We asked their representative sitting with us what the age requirements were, and he said that anyone can join and they are allowed to stay in the militia until an unspecified retirement age, but he told us that most of the people who join are young; looking at the group in front of us, we speculated that members must tend to drop out as they get older.

With professional assurance, the militia unit fired rifles (like our M-1s) using tracer bullets at targets about one hundred yards away. Ken asked how big the bull's eye was, and the representative told him it was three inches across; we thought this very impressive, but Ken assured us it is the standard marksmanship range and target—he remembered it from his Boy Scout days in Ohio. Their skill, however, impressed even Ken, because they brought their targets up to show us. All had hit at least 30 bull's-eyes out of 40 shots, and one very young man had shot 40. After this, they lobbed light and heavy mortars at white stone rings on the hillsides across the field, with fairly good accuracy, and fired bazookas and 50-caliber machine guns (the kind set up on tripods, with three people needed to operate it) at cardboard tanks.

Then the younger children—some seemed only about ten or eleven—came forward to take their turns. The boys were dressed like the older men in simple dark pants and shirts, but the girls had on skirts of all different colors and most of them wore ribbons in their hair, lending an unlikely air of festivity to the firing line. They practiced marksmanship, shooting at large cardboard "paper tigers" (taken from Mao's remark that U.S. imperialism and the atom bomb are "paper tigers"), which were set up so that when one of the tigers was hit, it would topple over and reveal another sign with a large Chinese character on it—and when, with fair accuracy, the tigers were all down, we could spell out "Defeat the U.S. aggressors and all their running dogs."

This was the end of the demonstration, and we stood up to thank them. But a young woman, after some urging from the others, came up to the stand and asked our guides if they could talk with us. They understood that we were Americans, and they wanted to speak with us just for a few minutes. We went down onto the field and found that she had been joined by a man from the group and one of the older children, as a "team" of spokesmen. "We wanted to tell you that although we are in the militia to defend China, we are not enemies of the American people. The U.S. government's policies in Asia threaten us, and we must prepare to defend ourselves well. But we know you, and most Americans, do not support the U.S. government's policies, and we want to be friends, not enemies. We feel no hostility for the American people."

Moved by their speech, we were momentarily at a loss, then Frank began to talk. "In our first week in China," he said, "we have heard a good deal about China's determination never to be conquered by an invading force. This kind of preparation makes sense, and we admire you for it. We hope that the U.S. government policies, which we do not support, will be changed to prevent hostilities between the U.S. government and the people of China."

The speech by the militia members in Nanking stayed on our minds through all the rest of our time in China. Especially in north China, where the people had faced and fought the Japanese invasion, this determination was stated again and again. Almost every family we spoke with had lost someone in that war, and the people said that if ever a foreign country tried to invade China, she would become a "sea of guerrillas."

Everywhere, too, the people of China made the same distinction between our group, as representatives of the American people, and the U.S. government. They believe firmly that the American people do not condone what is being done in Indochina, that the U.S. policies of encircling China with hostile bases, and financial and military aid propping up the Chiang Kai-shek regime on Taiwan, are not supported by the American people. Because of this there was no hesitation on their part in offering us their full friendship—everywhere, without question, the Chinese were warm, open, and quick to accept us. Only once, in Sian, did an old woman, hearing that we were Americans, look doubtful. Her brow knitted, and she seemed to be drawing herself up to say something to us when her daughter-in-law quickly interceded, saying, "No, they're Americans, but they are different—they're not the government. Remember, they are from the people; we shouldn't be angry with them." The woman's face cleared, and she bobbed her head, but did not seem entirely convinced.

Certainly, a part of the freedom the Chinese feel is based on the knowledge that they are strong enough to remain independent. That knowledge depends both on the PLA and the militia—the regular army and their own "national guard."

The People's Liberation Army in the Cultural Revolution

At the peak of the Cultural Revolution in Canton, the People's Liberation Army was called out to help restore order. But instead of riding tanks into town, they came walking down the streets in small groups, and they were totally unarmed. Calmly, they walked up to clusters of people and started to talk with them; they went to the university campuses and talked with the students, to the factories to talk with the workers, and to the offices to talk to the bureaucrats. When they were done talking, and listening, the angry factions had begun to work together again. Eventually "revolutionary committees" were formed from these discussions to implement the new ideas and be the new governing bodies.

In the city of Harbin at the same time (this was in early 1967), the whole city had come to a standstill as though everyone had gone on strike and spent all day every day arguing. The Red Guards (mostly high-school and university students) were the most active, and in Harbin, as elsewhere, each group waved the red flag against the others' red flag, claiming that its position was more "Maoist." When the PLA entered such scenes, they always said they were doing so "in the name of the revolutionary forces"; but with delicate political tact, they refrained from saying exactly *which* revolutionary forces. Here they announced that they had formed an alliance with Red Guards, but since there were many factions even among the Red Guards, this had the same effect.

The PLA units were not sent into local level units with any final message of what leadership organizations should look like. Their most important function was to "support the left": to bring people together to discuss and review the experiences of the last year or so, to determine who were those with a genuine proletarian outlook, and to begin to consider possible new forms of government.

The situation during and immediately after the height of the Cultural Revolution was unique because of the depth and intensity of the division within the Chinese Communist party. The party itself had been the normal source of outside leadership during local crises, but now in many locations it was not functioning at all. At this point the government, the party, and most production units were in various states of disarray. The PLA was the only national organization still capable of providing experienced and respected leadership, restoring some semblance of order, and getting production moving again.

An example of this happened during construction of the Nanking Yangtze River Bridge. In June and July 1967, factional disputes had halted construction work. The PLA was asked to intervene, and by August an "alliance" had been formed among the bridge workers and construction was resumed. Out of the alliance, the bridge revolutionary committee was formed in March 1968, including PLA members in addition to party cadres, workers, and technical personnel. In many other cases PLA representatives stayed on in the revolutionary committees after initial settlements had been reached.

In all, we visited thirty-one organizations. Some of them had no PLA members on their revolutionary committees, but most of them had several—on an average, the PLA constituted less than 10 percent of the committee memberships. The rural communes had a particularly low PLA representation. In many of the factories, hospitals, and schools we visited we were told that the role of the PLA has been decreasing in the last year or so. The PLA representatives have also become more and more integrated into their new environments, for PLA members who go into managerial positions outside of regular army units are expected to give up their active-duty status. They are subject to recall for active duty, and when their usefulness to the civilian organization comes to an end they can return to regular army status.

Training programs within the People's Liberation Army have been designed to maximize contact with and respect for civilian working people. PLA members, while they are still in the regular army, participate in the daily work of the community around them. They help till the fields, work in factories, and are most often found helping in large construction projects. They helped build the Nanking Yangtze River Bridge (before, during, and after the factional dispute which they helped to resolve) and they help routinely with the construction of irrigation networks and road systems. In Yenan we saw soldiers helping at the city produce market, and every day in the cities, great truckloads of soldiers passed us on their way to some nearby farm or project.

This integration of military and civilian work raises morale among the soldiers, reduces boredom, and contributes to a sense of continuity with everyday life. It eases alienation between the soldiers and civilians, and helps to reduce authoritarian attitudes within the military. "Serve the people" is the ethic of the Chinese soldiers, one which preserves their identity as a "people's army"— and the Yenan heritage.

3. THE GREAT PROLETARIAN CULTURAL REVOLUTION

> I hold it, that a little rebellion, now and then, is a good thing, and as necessary to the political world as storms in the physical.
>
> —Thomas Jefferson

> Men by their constitutions are naturally divided into two parties: (1) Those who fear and distrust the people, and wish to draw all powers from them into the hands of the higher classes. (2) Those who identify themselves with the people, have confidence in them, cherish and consider them as the most honest and safe, although not the most wise depository of the public interests.
>
> —Thomas Jefferson

The Cultural Revolution is the deepest political struggle the People's Republic has experienced since Liberation. Today the Chinese people date many aspects of their lives as "pre-" and "post-Cultural Revolution," just as they continue to speak in terms of pre- and post-Liberation. The Cultural Revolution began in 1966 and still continues, although it has passed the peak of open demonstrations and struggle in the streets. It touched everyone, at every level of organization in the factories, schools, communes, in the government, and in the Communist party itself.

Why? Certainly no one watching from without predicted the Great Proletarian Cultural Revolution. By the mid-sixties China was seen to be the most revolutionary socialist nation in the world, and its accomplishments did indeed seem miraculous. In the fifteen years since Liberation, inflation had been halted and prices continued to fall; everyone had adequate housing and clothing and an abundance of food; rent cost only 3 to 5 percent of the average income and there was no income tax; education was the right of all and illiteracy was rapidly disappearing. There was full employment and no national debt abroad or at home; the industrial growth rate was rising and China's strength and pride rose with it.

Where in all this was there room for discontent—discontent on a scale which shook China and reverberated around the world? It lay in the possibility of ultimate failure: loss of the revolutionary goals in the material success of modernization and death of the Yenan spirit in the birth of a new class hierarchy.

The struggle which emerged between the new elites and the Maoists centered on the question of ends and means. China was building socialism—but how? Was it possible to preserve the revolutionary spirit, *after* the revolution, to rely on the masses for active participation, leadership, innovation, and decision making, as had been true in Yenan and the years before Liberation? Or must the party temporarily separate and elevate itself, leading the people for their own good in directions the party chose? These were the "two lines." The Great Proletarian Cultural Revolution was the process of defining these lines and discovering who supported which line, and it was the struggle to determine which line China would follow.

During the course of the Cultural Revolution, two men came to symbolize these lines: Mao Tse-tung and Liu Shao-ch'i. Liu, an old comrade-in-arms of Mao from the Yenan period, had assumed the role of the "organization man" concerned with administrative problems in the party and the government. He represented a strong sentiment within the party and government bureaucracies, best summed up in his statement that "in China, the question of which wins out, socialism or capitalism, is already solved." From Liu's point of view, the revolution had been won. Now the task was simply to proceed with economic development—and there was no reason not to adopt the Western or at least the Soviet model, with their emphases on technology and specialization, for this development.

Mao represented another sentiment, one which he himself acknowledged was not the strongest in the beginning. He warned that the revolution had not been finished: "The question of which will win out, socialism or capitalism, is still not really settled. The class struggle . . . will continue to be long and tortuous and at times will even become very acute." It *was* possible for the revolution to change direction, even to reverse itself and turn back along the road to capitalism. The only check against this was to rely on the revolutionary wisdom of the masses.

This idea of relying on the masses stood in direct opposition to the developmental model Liu and others proposed, for that model depended upon the relative freedom of a small group of planners—technicians and party officers—to decide China's course with a minimum of interference from its people. It increased the distance between the leaders and the people, emphasizing the manipulative character of expertise. By the mid-sixties, this new elite had emerged in strength. High party cadres used their positions to win special educational privileges for their children, special privileges for their families, and to entrench themselves in power at almost every level of the party and state hierarchies.

The Western model was followed in other ways: health, educational, and cultural facilities were concentrated in the cities; the urban population grew and industrialization concentrated increasingly in a few major centers. The countryside lagged far behind, beginning to resemble again the contrasting third-world pattern of modern cities and impoverished, exploited agricultural regions. During the Great Leap Forward in the late fifties the Soviet model had been rejected and attempts made to devise an alternative Chinese model. But problems inherent in this first new model, compounded by the Soviet withdrawal of technical and other forms of aid and a series of natural disasters (the worst of the century) resulted in the "three hard years" of 1959–62. In the process of righting the damage to the economy, political considerations had been relaxed. Material incentives and private plots were encouraged, free markets flourished, and the path seemed to veer ever more sharply right—back toward Western and Soviet models, toward an abandonment of revolutionary ideals, and toward the "capitalist road."

Every society contains the seeds of personal selfishness, of the bureaucratic mentality, and of the desire on the part of some to dominate and rise above others. Traditional Chinese society, like every other, had a long tradition of noncooperation, inequality, and exploitation. The traditional Chinese landed gentry was among the deadliest. The urban capitalist class, although small, was among the most rapacious. Fifteen years after liberation, despite major economic, social, and political progress, the Chinese found that the revolution could be lost . . .

The Years Before

In the fall of 1962 Mao warned of the serious danger of a "capitalist restoration" in China. This was the occasion for the launching of the socialist education movement, designed in theory to cause the people (and especially the party cadres) to rethink present policies in terms of this danger. In practice, however, many of the socialist education movement programs were watered down or ignored. Mao's influence was at a low ebb, and the Peking newspapers carried long articles debating and criticizing his ideas.

By spring 1963, however, there was enough support for Mao to launch a new attack on the party cadres who formed part of the new elite. Criticism was to be directed at cadres who "indulge in idleness and hate work, eat too much and own too much, strive for status, act like officials, put on bureaucratic airs, pay no heed to the plight of the people, and care nothing about the interests of the state."

The real debate, as it emerged, seemed to be over why this elite of lazy, aristocratic party workers had developed. Mao, as part of his insistence on reliance on the masses, accused the higher party officials of setting a bad example and encouraging the lower cadres to aspire to high positions immune from criticism. The only way to reverse this trend would be to call on the masses—the people in each school, factory, or other unit—to help reform their own cadre.

But Liu insisted that the fault lay with the masses themselves. It was their own uneducated and unsophisticated ideas which had led the cadre astray; and the cadre could only be reformed within the party, by the party. As a part of this policy Liu set up teams of higher party cadre to go out to the countryside to "cleanse and strengthen" the rural party workers. It was at this point, Mao later said, that he first began to doubt Liu.

Meanwhile two other campaigns had been started in an effort to find some way of shaking up the complacency of the bureaucrats and "new class." One was to "emulate the People's Liberation Army"—the clearest indication of how closely Mao and his supporters identified their vision of society with the spirit of Yenan, and how much they felt the PLA were really the inheritors of that tradition. All the people were encouraged to study and learn from the PLA's examples of courage, dedication, hard work, and independence. The second campaign was exclusively directed at popular culture and education, reflecting a concern that culture was again becoming the property of an intellectual elite, and that the educational system was failing to pass on revolutionary values. It was called the Cultural Revolution campaign—in some ways a forerunner of what later was called the Great Proletarian Cultural Revolution (and what is commonly called *the* Cultural Revolution).

By 1965, when U.S. escalation of the Vietnam War suddenly brought everything to a halt, three important issues had been raised and were being hotly debated. First, should the then rather limited Cultural Revolution be continued on an expanded and deeper scale? Second, was criticism and change necessary throughout the Party at all levels, and who should carry it out? Third, what was the proper response to the increasing threat of U.S. military invasion in Indochina? After the Tonkin Gulf incident (which China claimed was a U.S. fabrication and which we now know *was* a fabrication) intensive U.S. bombing came very close to the Chinese border. China began to prepare for the possibility of war.

One group of China's military leaders wanted to withdraw the PLA from its normal civilian duties of helping in agriculture, construction, and opening new land. They urged that China reshape its military forces to resemble the Soviet armies, with a more rigid ranking system and greater dependence on sophisticated military weaponry. But Lin Piao (who had replaced P'eng Teh-huai as defense minister in 1959 when P'eng did not approve of or cooperate with the Great Leap Forward) argued that the strength of the Chinese army was its guerrilla heritage, its closeness to the people, and the very fact that it did *not* rely mostly on technology, but rather on the masses, for its support. A bitter debate ensued. By September 1965 Lin and Mao had won enough support for Lin to make his now-famous speech, "Long Live the Victory of the People's War." The issue had been resolved in favor of the guerrilla tradition, and Lin's speech predicted the victory of people's liberation armies fighting guerrilla wars against imperialist powers.

The military issue had been resolved, but the fate of the Cultural Revolution and the need for struggle at all levels in the party and bureaucracy had not.

The Beginnings

The Cultural Revolution, although it was still largely limited to higher educational and cultural institutions, had begun to make waves in the intellectual circles of Peking. In 1961 a play had been written by the deputy mayor of Peking, Wu Han, called *Hai Jui Dismissed from Office*. At the time it had caused a stir because of its very un-Maoist ideas; now the play was being quietly attacked as anti-Maoist, and was accused of being a thinly veiled defense of the ousted Defense Minister P'eng Teh-huai.

Mao asked the mayor of Peking, P'eng Chen, to work with four others to investigate and report on the controversy. In retrospect, Mao said this request was a kind of "test" for P'eng. It was reasonable to assume that P'eng was closely linked with Wu Han, his immediate subordinate, and this was an opportunity for P'eng to speak out and take a stand for or against the ideas of the play. While this investigation was going on, a major newspaper in Shanghai published a critique of *Hai Jui* . . . this was the first open attack and the reaction was tumultuous—but still confined largely to the universities and upper circles of the intelligentsia.

In February 1966 P'eng issued his report. It avoided the real issues at stake, and treated the controversy as an academic debate over the historical validity of the play in question. P'eng had failed the test; he had identified himself as part of the faction more interested in protecting their own power than struggling over the ideas and politics of the issue. In May P'eng was ousted and his report criticized severely. This criticism was the beginning of the next stage of the Cultural Revolution.

The first dazibao went up at Peking University. The battle was on—overnight, dazibao multiplied and became the symbol of the new Great Proletarian Cultural Revolution. These were the "everyman's newspaper" of China, great strips of paper filled with contending ideas and pasted on walls, posts, and kiosks all over the country. Anyone could post one, and everyone else was free to respond, to scribble their remarks on a poster already up, or to write their own dazibao and post them beside the others. Everywhere clusters of people gathered in the streets to read and debate the posters; inside buildings the dining rooms and hallways would be covered with these "big character posters." ("Character" is the term for a Chinese "word"—a better translation might be "big handwritten posters.")

Within a week, Mao had seen copies of the first poster at Peking University and ordered it broadcast over the national radio. Word of the new stage of the Cultural Revolution—open struggle with higher officials—went out and the students of China were the first to respond. In the heat of the ensuing struggles the schools were closed for six months.

The Red Guards formed that summer. They were young —the first group began in the universities and almost all were middle-school or university students. They were ardent—they did not hesitate to attack anyone and everyone they considered an enemy, heckling them, embarrassing them, even in the height of the first summer dragging people out of their houses to face criticism from their neighbors. Impetuous and determined, the Red Guards were the first shock troops of the new revolution.

By now, as the revolution spread and Mao realized the support it had gained, he seems to have encouraged the students to call into question *all* power holders, debate everything, criticize everything. That which survived the test of the masses would be worth preserving—that which fell would have been shown to be elitist and dangerous. He withdrew to Hangchow, going into seclusion, seeming to watch and wait for the results of this new stage.

While Mao was gone from Peking, Liu Shao-ch'i and other high party officials formed work teams to go into the universities and middle schools to try to calm down the students. They offered the students minor concessions: the firing of a few educational leaders, a curriculum reform, and more independence. Liu, like P'eng before him, tried to avoid or ignore the real reason for the students' discontent, and to buy them off with minimal reforms.

The students balked, and the struggle became more intense. Mao returned to Peking (after his famous swim in the Yangtze River) and in August criticized the work teams sharply for "suppressing revolutionary students." The "sixteen points" were issued, supporting the Cultural Revolution and urging the masses to criticize all power holders. Liu's position was somewhat weakened within the party Political Bureau, but he continued to work in Peking.

Again, Mao brought his prestige and influence to bear on the situation. The Red Guards, who until this point had been an unofficial organization, were formally recognized and encouraged. Mao gave a speech, calling on them to "bombard the headquarters" of "party power holders who take the capitalist road." The Red Guards fanned out over the country, traveling out to the countryside, from and to Peking, undertaking "long marches" in the fashion of the historic 1935 trek to Yenan, "exchanging revolutionary experiences" with the peasantry and the workers, with students of other areas, and with revolutionary (pro-Cultural Revolution) party cadres.

But in a different sense from that of P'eng and Liu, the Red Guards also "failed" their test. They failed because they split and split again into warring factions, and because they were so convinced of their own revolutionary wisdom that they failed to respect that of the workers and the peasants and the People's Liberation Army. So that October Mao expressed his concern as well as his support. He was amazed at the growth of the Cultural Revolution;

it seemed a sudden tidal wave had been unleashed. But he believed that this was all necessary, that the cadres and officials under attack should bear with it and take the process seriously. He said that he could understand how difficult it would be for them, but expressed his confidence that they would pass the test. He reminded them of warnings in 1962 about the dangers of a capitalist restoration; these had been ignored. Now, under the impact of this tidal wave, "minds which have not thought in years will think for the first time." But Mao also warned against the use of armed violence, and indicated that resistance must be met by discussion and criticism, not violence.

The Red Guards were in fact meeting tough resistance, especially from some of the higher party cadres. By November Mao apparently was finally convinced: all power holders must be criticized, and in order to do so, they must be deprived of power. Liu was removed from his offices and sent to a thought reform school; the revolutionary masses were urged to seize power.

In January, the revolutionary masses (students from the Red Guards, workers, and PLA) seized power in Shanghai in the "January revolution." Mao supported this power seizure and ordered Lin Piao and the PLA to support the "revolutionary rebels." In Heilungkiang Province a first "revolutionary committee" was set up, composed of veteran cadres, rebel leaders, and PLA representatives in a "three-way alliance." In February, Shanghai's government established its own revolutionary committee and became the model for the whole country.

As we flew into Shanghai from Canton, the pig-tailed stewardess announced that we were arriving in "Shanghai, the revolutionary city . . ."

While we were in Shanghai, we met with a member of the Shanghai municipal revolutionary committee to discuss the course of the Cultural Revolution in his city.

Zhu Yongjia: The Story of the Cultural Revolution in Shanghai

It was early afternoon. We had just come back from the Shanghai Industrial Exhibit that morning, and now after lunch we went upstairs to the cavernous old ball-room of our hotel. The Peace Hotel, ex-Cathay, was built well before Liberation, by the British, and in the high-ceilinged, ornately plastered ballroom it was easy to imagine silver cutlery, liveried Chinese servants, and toasts to the king's health on his birthday. Today, how-ever, it is simply furnished and our footsteps echoed on the wooden floor as we filed in. A group was waiting for us, sitting around two long double tables in the center of the room—Zhu Yongjia, a standing member of the Shanghai municipal revolutionary committee, several of the researchers from Fudan University who had accom-panied us in the morning, and many of our guides and hosts from the CATT in Shanghai (for they were very interested in this discussion, too).

We shook hands all around and Zhu said a few words of welcome. His smile was boyish, and even for a Chinese leader his style was extraordinarily relaxed: his socks drooped at the ankles, his bermuda shorts bagged slightly, and his shirt crumpled over a pudgy frame. He must have been roughly in his early forties, but like many Chinese men he looked younger.

First, he said, he would tell the story of the Cultural Revolution and afterward ask for our questions. Though his voice was soft and reserved, he seemed quite used to public speaking—later we learned that he had been a Ming history professor at Fudan University before the Cultural Revolution. He would talk about the four stages of the Great Proletarian Cultural Revolution in Shanghai: the first was the creation of public opinion (September 1965–May 1966); the second, exposure and criticism of the "capitalist roaders" in the party (May 1966–January 1967); the third, seizure of power and formation of revolutionary committees (January 1967–September 1968); and the fourth, the period of "struggle, criticism, and transformation," which is still going on.

Zhu's Chinese was clear and easy for us to follow, but as in most of our more formal meetings an interpreter translated all of his remarks. At first we had protested, or rather questioned the practice, but we soon learned that the pause for translation gave us time to write down what we had been hearing and to compose questions. Here during the translations we could whisper questions or remarks to the Fudan researchers and guides sitting next to us, and sometimes they volunteered remarks to us, such as one who told Frank proudly that she had been there at a particularly important mass struggle session.

"The Cultural Revolution here," Zhu began, "was accomplished by relying on Chairman Mao and the party." This was our first surprise; for most Western observers have discussed the Cultural Revolution in terms of an attack on the party. Here, however, Zhu seemed to feel that the party had been an important source of support—from the discussion he presented, it was clear that there were factions within the party and that some of the party officials had been severely criticized and removed from power. Nevertheless, the main body of the party cadres and leaders seem to have been active proponents of the Cultural Revolution.

"After the founding of our country in 1949, there was still class struggle." But Zhu went on to explain that this class struggle had been increasingly ignored. Most dangerous of all, he said, "it even seemed to us that a skeleton shape of the old class structure was beginning to reemerge." This meant that China was in fact going *backward*—toward capitalism. It was this realization which had provided the impetus for a total reorganization of leadership, government, and even the party itself. The rebels came to feel that the only permanent insurance against renewed elitism ("revisionism") among those in leadership positions was a careful top-to-bottom overhaul of the structure of government and production.

A bureaucratic pattern of organization, Zhu went on, is built like a pyramid, with lines of power extending upward through an endless series of offices and officials. It is certain to lead to individual abuses and official privileges. Collective leadership, especially in the three-in-one alliance form of the present Revolutionary Committees, would make it more difficult for leadership to be twisted toward the realization of personal ends, or to ignore public needs.

The First Stage: Mobilization of the Workers and Testing Public Opinion

After the Great Leap Forward, the Soviet pullout, and the three hard years, both the capitalist countries abroad and the capitalist roaders at home had said that China could not make it on its own if it continued to follow a revolutionary line. Liu and other capitalist roaders argued that the revolution was over, class struggle had died out, and the focus should be on economic production; what was good for economic production was revolutionary. Mao and those who remained faithful to the revolutionary spirit argued that the reverse was true—that what was revolutionary would be good for production.

Zhu told us that in 1965, when Mao and other revolutionary leaders were becoming more and more worried about the revisionists' activities, Mao suggested that someone in Peking write an article criticizing the play *Hai Jui Dismissed from Office*. But because Mayor P'eng was in league with his deputy mayor Wu Han, the author of the play, none of the Peking newspapers dared to print such an article. At this time Chang Ch'ing (Mao's wife, and a leader in the cultural aspects of the Great Proletarian Cultural Revolution), together with Chang Ch'un-ch'iao and Yao Wen-yuan (two members of the Political Bureau whom we later met during our interview with Premier Chou) decided to write a critique. They worked on it over a period of almost eight months, knowing the stir it would cause. Finally in November 1965 the critique was published in the Shanghai newspaper *Wenwei Bao*.

Here Zhu digressed temporarily to fill us in on some of the history of Shanghai politics. Until 1964, he said, Shanghai had had a pro-Maoist mayor named Ke. There had been a struggle in the Shanghai municipal party committee between Ke and two others: the party secretary, Chen Baixian (who had served with Liu Shao-ch'i in the New Fourth Army before Liberation); and the deputy mayor, Chao Tijou. In 1964 Ke fell sick, and Chen and Chao took power, and then in April 1965 Ke died. Chao became mayor and Chen became first secretary of the party. They consolidated their power. It was under these conditions that the criticism of *Hai Jui* first appeared that November.

At first there was no response to the critique of the play. So several days later, the three authors arranged to have it published in the *Liberation Daily,* another big paper in Shanghai. They reprinted it in pamphlet form. The mayor of Peking, P'eng Chen, refused to allow the pamphlet to be brought into his city. He tried to find out who had written it, and finally he was told by Chen. But at the same time Chou En-lai read the pamphlet and suggested it be published in the *Liberation Army Daily* (the PLA newspaper). In this way it was read all over China.

The country was shocked, Zhu said. Everywhere people discussed the article, but there were two kinds of discussion. Some of them saw it as an academic debate over history (this idea was supported by P'eng and others who did not like the political ideas of the critique); many other people launched into a full discussion of all the issues raised. In February P'eng's report on the controversy was published. Zhu told us that it is now known that P'eng had written the report with the help of Liu—that the rough draft had actually been written in Liu's house. (He smiled at our surprised expressions. These events, which we had studied as a series of speeches and articles, began to come alive . . . It was almost like a detective story, as Zhu pieced together the complex lines relating leaders within each faction and the ideas they fought for.)

After his report was published, P'eng and the four others who had worked on it with him took off for a vacation near Kunming in Yunnan Province. This was a mistake, because while they were gone Mao called a meeting of party leaders and as a result of that meeting, the May 16 repudiation of P'eng's report was issued. In that repudiation the Cultural Revolution was explained to party members and they were warned to beware of "Khrushchev-type people." However, this repudiation was not made entirely public until a year later. Meanwhile, Mao asked for more studies to be made, investigating the questions which P'eng had avoided.

The Second Stage: Exposure and Criticism of the Capitalist Roaders

In late spring 1966, just as the first dazibao appeared on the Peking campuses, the student movement quickly spread to Shanghai and Liu's work teams were sent out to try to smooth over the problems. Liu's counterattack, Zhu said, is referred to as the "fifty days" or the "white terror." In August Mao posted his own dazibao in Peking calling on the Red Guards to "bombard the headquarters" of the power holders taking the capitalist road, and from all over China 130 million Red Guards came to Peking to see Mao . . . eight times Mao received them, speaking to masses of students in Tiananmen Square, giving them encouragement and urging them to return and carry out the Cultural Revolution.

As they left Peking, the Red Guards brought with them word of the "bombard the headquarters" dazibao. When they reached Shanghai they found that Chen and Chao had blocked circulation of the poster; incensed, they pasted it up in the city, openly defying the established heads of the city party and governmental bureaucracies. When the Shanghai party cadres found out about this, Zhu said, their confidence in Chen and Chao plummeted, and the credibility of the municipal party committee was seriously undermined.

The Red Guards attacked the municipal party committee in poster after poster, exposing their suppression of news of the national revolution. Chen and Chao defended themselves saying that because the first critique of *Hai Jui* had been published in a Shanghai newspaper (when it had not been allowed in Peking) they obviously were revolutionary.

In August one segment of the workers began to organize, encouraged by the example of the Red Guards and increasingly distrustful of city officials. During September and October they formed an integrated force with the Red Guards (this was the period of "exchanging revolutionary experiences"). The workers criticized the factory managers for trying to buy them off with bonuses and wage increases, demanding to know "who is behind this policy."

In early November the workers of seventeen large factories met to set up the Shanghai revolutionary rebels' general headquarters (afterwards called the workers' headquarters). They marched together, ten thousand strong, and demanded that Chen and Chao meet them at a large theater, the Friendship Cinema.

Chen and Chao responded with the "three nos" policy: no recognition, no participation, and no support for the workers' headquarters. In accord with their policy, the two leaders did not show up at the Friendship Cinema. So from the cinema the workers marched to the railroad station and thousands boarded a train for Peking. If the Red Guards could travel to Peking, they would too, bringing with them their complaint against Chen and Chao.

But Chen and Chao had control of the railroads and stopped the train at Anjing station, not far from the city suburbs. There they organized groups to go among the workers, trying to dissuade them and offering them bread. The workers replied that they would either walk to Peking on foot or block all other railroad traffic from Shanghai to Peking, but they would not give in.

Word of the situation had reached Peking, and Mao sent Chang Ch'un-ch'iao (one of the authors of the original critique of *Hai Jui*) to investigate the workers' demands. Chang camped out at the railroad station with the rebel workers and talked with them; finally he sent back a report saying that the workers' demands were reasonable. Mao replied that the workers' headquarters should be recognized as a legal revolutionary mass organization.

With this victory, the workers returned to Shanghai. In their absence the municipal committee had put up posters attacking Chang Ch'un-ch'iao for his interference; the struggle intensified and on December 25 culminated in the *"Liberation Daily* incident." This newspaper was well known as an organ of the Liuist faction, and the Red Guards had started their own paper in opposition to it. Now they were demanding that their paper be circulated with the *Liberation Daily* (a demand for "equal time"). The revolutionary workers came to the street on which the *Liberation Daily* stood and joined with the Red Guards, while the Liuists organized the masses to come and shout "We want to read the *Daily*." Again word of the situation reached Peking, and this time Chou En-lai responded, saying that the Red Guard demand was justified and should be granted.

At this point in Zhu's talk one of the researchers from Fudan leaned over and said to Frank, "This is where we began to understand who the reactionaries were. Before this we were very confused, but now it became clear." The lines were beginning to emerge and in the struggle the people—both the leaders and the masses—began to think about the issues deeply and to decide which side they supported. In the beginning the Maoists among the workers had been very few, only 10,000 in all, while the Liuists had been able to organize as many as 800,000 people to form a counterorganization, the Chiwei Dui (Scarlet Guards). To do this the Liuists stressed economic benefits and promised a slack hand in economic affairs.

But at this juncture the Central Committee of the party (in Peking) did not support or recognize the Chiwei Dui as a legal mass revolutionary organization. In this way they exposed Chen and Chao to the workers, for Chen and Chao immediately attempted to dump the Chiwei Dui. The Chiwei Dui marched to the Shanghai municipal committee offices to find Chao. Talking about this, Zhu used the phrase "on the pretext of," saying that the Chiwei Dui had invaded the municipal committee offices on the pretext of criticizing Chao. Presumably he was underscoring the fact that while the Chiwei Dui had begun to catch on to Chao's cupidities, they were not yet criticizing him from a revolutionary perspective.

Hearing of the Chiwei Dui actions, thirty thousand workers from the workers' headquarters marched to the offices to announce that they would either go to Peking as they had originally threatened to, or they would shut down the city. At this point Chao and Chen evidently felt it was better to be rid of them, and offered money for the trip to Peking. Some of them (primarily the dock workers) accepted the money and left; but most decided to stay and battle it out. The workers' headquarters published a statement calling on the people of Shanghai to oppose this "economist"—using economic means to fudge political issues—counterattack of the capitalist roaders.

Events between then and January 4 moved rapidly.

More and more workers joined the attack on the economist party leaders; there was great confusion in the city.
The workers' headquarters, now growing by thousands
every day, attempted to get the city moving again but the
impetus of the revolution could not be stopped or controlled. Chang Ch'un-ch'iao was sent again by Mao (this
time with Yao Wen-yuan) to support the revolutionary
forces, and on January 4 the revolutionary masses seized
power.

This was the January revolution. First the *Wenwei
Bao,* then the *Liberation Daily* were seized. After this,
thirty-one mass organizations sent an "urgent notice" to
Peking; Mao broadcast the notice throughout China and
the Central Committee sent a telegram congratulating the
workers on their revolutionary actions. On January 6
Chao and Chen were removed from office, and Chao was
paraded through the streets of the city in a great cele-
bration of the victory of the workers.

Stage Three: Seizure of Power and Formation of Revolutionary Committees

In January and February the government, party, and
production organizations were totally dismantled and
replaced with revolutionary committees. These were "three-
in-one alliances" of revolutionary (pro-Cultural Revolution) party cadres, People's Liberation Army representatives, and revolutionary masses. Zhu smiled and said,
"But there were some people and organizations who
wanted 'me first' and opposed the great alliance of all the
masses. For instance there were more than thirty-one mass
organizations, but the Red Guards felt that only four
would be enough for a great alliance; just representatives
of the workers' headquarters, the office workers, the peasants, and the Red Guards. So they stole the seals of the
other organizations. Of course this was criticized by the
other mass organizations . . . in the last part of January
the Red Guards retaliated, putting up dazibao, holding
meetings, spreading rumors, and trying to coerce the people, criticizing Chang Ch'un-ch'iao and other revolutionary leaders and demanding that their own ideas be followed. But the Central Committee sent another telegram

saying that these actions of the Red Guards (stealing the seals and coercing people) were wrong. So finally on February 5 the new Shanghai revolutionary committee was established. The other mass organizations would not allow the Red Guards to attend because they were 'ultra-leftists,' i.e., 'those who made themselves out to be more revolutionary than the revolutionaries.' " Zhu criticized this attitude as being "du wo dzo"—"The only leftist is me!"

"There were other ultraleft tendencies during the following summer. In July one small group announced that they would direct the spearhead against the army. And in the Shanghai Diesel Engine Factory the workers attacked the Shanghai municipal revolutionary committee. The other revolutionary mass organizations criticized them, but they beat one of their own factory workers and ran down some pedestrians with their trucks . . . this was coercion on a mass scale. On August 4 thousands of workers rushed to the Diesel Engine Factory and pulled out these bad elements. There were some other smaller struggles in the country, and some of them were violent.

"But over the six months from February to August the revolutionary committees for all units in the counties around Shanghai were set up, and during the same time revolutionary committees were being established all over China as well."

The Fourth Stage: Struggle, Criticism, and Transformation

The last stage is still going on, Zhu said. Now they are going through the process of struggle, criticism, and transformation. In the months after the January revolution great mass meetings were held in the football stadiums and televised so that all the people of the city could watch. The meetings criticized Liu, Chen, Chao, and other capitalist roaders. This has been the period of consolidating the party, "getting rid of the stale and taking in the fresh." Administrative structures have been tremendously simplified; the number of bureaucratic positions has been reduced by 80 to 90 percent in the city.

Many useless rules have been eliminated and the worst party officials have been removed from power.

Unlike our hosts at many of the rural communes we visited, Zhu and the other Shanghai citizens with whom we talked did not give us long lists of the technological innovations or changes in production methods resulting from the Cultural Revolution. Although Zhu did tell us that industrial production in Shanghai from 1965 to 1970 jumped 66 percent over that of the five years before, he said that the most important changes had been in the people's thinking.

This change came out in his long answer to a question about the class background of the workers. We wanted to know why so many workers had supported Chen and Chao at first, but were now considered "revolutionary masses" without prejudice. Zhu's answer was very detailed, and it was clear that he felt this a very important point. "The advance forces," he said, "always are small at the beginning. At first the workers' headquarters had only about two thousand textile workers, dockers, and steelworkers, but between early November and the January revolution that number increased to eight hundred thousand. In Shanghai there are more than one million industrial workers; in the beginning there were almost eight hundred thousand in the Chiwei Dui, but in the end the workers' headquarters had eight hundred thousand."

Everything was changing very rapidly. It was important, Zhu said, not to blame the backward workers, for they often hit back harder at the class enemy when they understood the struggle. He compared them to the Kuomintang soldiers in the war for liberation. When Kuomintang soldiers were captured by the People's Liberation Army, they were treated well and urged to discuss their experiences in the Kuomintang. Because they knew the Kuomintang so well, as soon as they began to think about it with open eyes they hated it far more passionately than those who had never shared their experiences. (We later discussed with our guides another comparison—the American GIs who, now that so many are opposed to the Indochina War, are by far the most effective forces opposed to it.)

Our meeting was over. After a brief rest, we met again in the hotel lobby and went into the dining room for dinner.

Zhu's Own Story

This was our opportunity to ask in a more informal setting about Zhu's own role in the Cultural Revolution . . . but it would have been easy to suspect the hotel cooks of plotting against our best efforts, for they brought in a steady stream of delicacies to tempt our thoughts away from such concerns: dishes of food in the shape of chickens, ducks, and other animals; tiny baskets woven of thin noodles and holding sauced shrimps; whole winter melons, carved in the manner of a scroll painting on the outside and filled with chunks of melon, meat, and vegetables in a thick soup; plates of meat sliced in intricate patterns . . . but through it all, a glimpse of Zhu himself.

When he was at Fudan before the Cultural Revolution began, Zhu said, he had been involved in preparing the critique of *Hai Jui* with Yao Wen-yuan. Several others from Fudan had worked with them, and this was how he knew that the entire critique had been worked on for eight months. At the time they were working on the critique, however, none of them had realized that Wu Han was actually backed by the Peking committee or by Liu himself. Later in the first heat of the Red Guard attacks, he had been opposed to the Red Guards and had even stood guard between them and the offices of the old municipal committee. When the Red Guards posted Mao's "bombard the headquarters" dazibao, he was not sure what to think; was it really Mao's? It had not been published by the Shanghai party committee—how could it be? It was not until the *Liberation Daily* incident that he and many others began to realize what was going on and who was behind what.

Would there be any more cultural revolutions in the future? "Well, not in the next few years," Zhu said. "But in ten or twenty years from now if two lines develop, of course. Perhaps there will be many great proletarian cultural revolutions before communism is achieved . . ."

What Are the Revolutionary Committees Today?

The revolutionary committees were almost all formed by fall 1968. It has taken much longer to form the new party committees, because the strongest opposition to the Cultural Revolution—as well as the strongest support—came from within the party. While we were in China, we talked extensively with representatives of twelve revolutionary committees, almost all of them various combinations of party cadres, People's Liberation Army representatives, and representatives of the revolutionary masses.

Ordinary workers formed an average of 45 percent of the committees. This is as if half the board of directors of General Motors was composed of outstanding assembly-line workers, floor sweepers, and test drivers, and the other half of more managerial types. The revolutionary cadre contingent was an average of 36 percent, and the People's Liberation Army representation averaged 14 percent. The "management" members—leadership cadres with advanced education and paperwork skills—are required to spend a portion of their time working in the workshops and fields.

Following the formation of a revolutionary committee, usually about a year later, the party committees were re-formed. From what we could tell, the party committees were seen by the workers as more detached from the day-to-day activities of a plant or commune than the revolutionary committees. The party committee maintains ultimate control over the affairs of the organization through a membership overlap with the revolutionary committee. Zhu told us that the two committees in Shanghai are really one administrative organ—"in this way we exercise unified leadership." Formerly there were two separate apparatuses, "but now with this system the leadership of the parts has been strengthened." About 50 percent or more of the membership of revolutionary committees is composed of party committee members. This virtually ensures a voting majority for the party in day-to-day administrative decisions. In addition, standing committee members, chairmen, and deputy chairmen of the revolutionary committees are likely to be members of the party committee.

Elections

Everywhere we went in China, we were told that revolutionary committee members were elected at large from among all members of their respective organizations. Finally at New Peking University we asked how these revolutionary committee elections take place.

The answer to our questions was that an election at the local level is a process of mutual discussion and consensus (taolun), rather than a process of competitive electioneering. The original election of revolutionary committee members took place in mass meetings of each organization. The political struggles of the Cultural Revolution had created factional divisions in a great number of these local organizations. In some cases where these factional differences developed to a serious level an outside group, such as a "workers' Mao Tse-tung thought propaganda team" or a local unit of the PLA—or both—was sent into the factory or school to resolve the conflict. The function of these outsiders was to support the left, to restore and maintain order, to get the unit reopened for business, and to set up the revolutionary committees.

At some point in this process of reconciliation, revolutionary committees were elected to head each organization on a more permanent basis, with elections taking place, we were told, in this fashion: representatives were first nominated at large, with each major faction and subgroup (including party membership) submitting a list of suggested nominees. These nominees were then screened by the mediating group—such as the PLA—and discussed at length by the entire membership of the organization, both privately and in mass meetings. It was implied that any candidate who failed to gain the approval of both the outside mediators and the general membership of the organization was dropped from the list. In this manner the list was pared down to a manageable size, no doubt along the rough guidelines (the "three-way alliance") suggested in the national press. We were told that the presence of outsiders in leadership positions has been gradually reduced, and this process is expected to continue, making local organizations increasingly dependent on their own memberships for leadership.

Since most of the revolutionary committees were set up only a few years ago, reelection has not yet taken place, and we could not tell from our conversations whether there is a regular period of office.

Making Decisions

Once elected, the revolutionary committees continue to function on a basis of democratic centralism. Important issues are raised with the whole committee in attendance, discussed at length, and put to a verbal vote. As a rule, votes are not taken by secret ballot or even by the raising of hands. Rather, after an issue has been discussed thoroughly, a proposal is placed on the floor which seems to reflect the general consensus. On serious issues, each member is then asked in turn to state his opinion of the proposal, and the committee then attempts to reach a full agreement. In several groups (for example, the February 7 Rolling Stock Plant), we were told that if a consensus cannot be reached after reasonable discussion, the position with a majority of votes is followed. The types of issues which were cited as likely to cause a division of opinion were production quotas, wage levels, the introduction of new products, and curriculum innovation—all clearly important issues. If a decision is made by majority rule, then the position reached is considered less permanent and more subject to review than a decision based on full consensus.

Decisions on important or particularly divisive issues may be referred to discussion and a vote of the entire membership of the organization. For example, we were told at the Shanghai Municipal Machine Tool Factory that last year the revolutionary committee had had a difficult time deciding on a production quota for the year. The committee couldn't make up its mind between 1,500 and 1,200 lathes. The question was referred to the whole membership of the factory—some ten thousand workers —who decided after discussion to limit the quota to

1,200 lathes. This figure was then adopted by the revolutionary committee as the year's production quota.

The party committee also functions as a referral team for important decisions, or for crisis situations. At such times joint sessions of the two committees are held to resolve the issue. The party committee is expected to know about any national policies which would bear on important administrative decisions, particularly on those issues which are likely to divide the revolutionary committee.

A Westerner viewing this open and democratic process should not make the mistake of thinking that China is following the road to New England democracy. Many of our Chinese friends simply scoffed at the Western election process, with its corruption and huge campaign contributions by special interests. To them, the very mention of elections and political corruption brings back the foul aftertaste of their experiences under Chiang Kai-shek. They remember vividly how he paid lip service to constitutional democracy while bleeding China dry with corruption and installing his personal cronies in high positions.

Instead, they say that the collective leadership of the revolutionary committees promotes real democracy and the inclusion of all groups in each unit. It depends on open discussion, criticism, and consensus agreements. Because the committees were forged in periods of great struggle, they represent a unity of purpose which the Chinese say will help them to preserve their openness and democratic nature for longer than more superficial structures.

The Violent Summers

During the two years after the January revolution revolutionary committees were set up throughout China. In the course of the seizures of power and in the attempt to unite all factions fierce struggles were waged. Attacks and counterattacks in the dazibao, in marches, demonstrations, and mass meetings were part of a very real revolution, but this revolution culminated in physical armed violence only sporadically, and then almost exclusively in a few large cities. In these cases the People's

Liberation Army, as the more disciplined force in the Maoist coalition of revolutionary groups, was usually asked to bring the situation under control.

Some of the most intense struggles were against the ultraleftists, especially against factions within the Red Guards. The most extreme of these called themselves the "May 16" group in honor of Mao's original circular repudiating P'eng's report. In June and July 1966, in the first summer of the Cultural Revolution, Red Guard groups had organized and certain of them opposed Chou En-lai in policy debates in Peking. When the Red Guards left Peking to travel at the end of the summer, groups of students in Canton responded to the message they brought and an extremist contingent formed there as well. Almost all the "May 16" groups were students—only one workers' group has ever been publicly identified as a part of that faction. In January 1967 the most extreme groups attacked Chou again, and on January 5 a dazibao went up at the Peking Foreign Languages Institute criticizing him. Throughout that year, as Mao and Chou and other revolutionary leaders supported the Cultural Revolution, they warned increasingly of the dangers of anarchism or ultraleft factionalism. In September of that year Mao denounced such factionalism as "counterrevolutionary." By January 1968, the PLA was instructed to "support the left but not any particular faction." In the late spring the extreme left regained the initiative and that summer again the violent "May 16" attacks escalated. Finally in August 1968 things came to a head.

Tsinghua University in Peking had been a center of some of the most recalcitrant Red Guard factionalists. Fighting on the campus during the summer had become increasingly violent, and finally Mao asked a delegation of the Red Guards to come to see him. They talked but evidently reached no agreement, for on July 28 there were renewed outbreaks of fighting. A few days later, five of the student leaders representing the various factions came again to see Mao. In an incident which became famous all over China, Mao met them with tears in his eyes and told them, "You have let me down, and what is more, you have disappointed the workers, peasants, and soldiers of China." Within forty-eight hours, a "Mao Tse-tung thought propaganda team" was dispatched to the campus to invoke discipline.

When we were at Tsinghua the students told us their story of what happened. Two of the students we talked with had been members of different factions during the time of the struggles. The thought propaganda teams, they said, were made up of workers from the Peking area who had already gone through the "seizure of power" stage in their own factories, had established their own revolutionary committees, and were now going out to try to help other units. The teams came in great numbers, with members of the PLA as well, to the campus to hold a mass meeting and try to restore peace. The students by then had divided into two main factions, and both factions told the "interlopers" that "we don't need you to make our revolution. We'll make our own. Stay away."

Despite this the workers and PLA came on campus, in the face of bomb threats and warnings that the lawns had been mined with home-made devices. The students opened fire with small arms and crude automatic weapons, even from university trucks which they had turned into armored cars. When there were not enough weapons to go around, the students used tiles from the roofs of the campus buildings . . . not unnaturally, some of the workers and PLA soldiers wanted to return fire. But by far the greater number of them opposed this, saying that the Red Guards were basically revolutionary, that they were simply being misled by extremists, and it was a wrong line to fight fire with fire when the Red Guards were being misled by only a handful who were the responsible ones. Meanwhile five of their own workers had been killed. Slowly this pacifist technique impressed the students; the workers and soldiers were able to talk with them and restore peace and the rudiments of order.

By the third day the workers and soldiers began to meet with the students to analyze what had happened and discuss the future. The students explaining this to us said that these discussions had been rather different from what they had expected. Instead of apportioning blame and lecturing them, the workers and soldiers simply asked questions and more questions, until in the end the students themselves decided that their differences were more a matter of factional jealousies than real disagreements, and that they could work together. At this point mass meetings were held to present the results of their discussions and criticize factionalism. The workers and soldiers sent representatives with reports of the situation to see Mao. In gratitude for their help, Mao gave them some mangoes which a Pakistani delegation had given him . . . when they returned to Tsinghua, the representatives worked with the students to preserve the mangoes in formaldehyde!

There were other struggles in addition to those with ultraleft Red Guards. In February 1967 a number of high party officials in big cities had "seized power" in the name of, but without the participation of, the revolutionary rebels. Since they obviously were only following the form of the revolutionary committees and could not provide the content, the workers and students and People's Liberation Army continued to struggle with them. In July of the same year there was a fierce battle in the industrial and transportation center of Wuhan (a cluster of three cities at the confluence of the Han and Yangtze rivers). This was perhaps the most violent confrontation of the Cultural Revolution—the struggle was complex, with elements of regionalism, ultraleftism, and severe factionalism. Finally the PLA had to come up the river to restore order and high government representatives were sent from Peking to negotiate a settlement. In August the anti-Chou Red Guards seized the Foreign Ministry, and then invaded and burned the British Embassy.

By fall, things seem to have calmed down somewhat, but when this calm encouraged counterrevolutionary forces the party issued a statement saying that only "bourgeois factionalism" was to be opposed. Since the ultraleftists did not consider themselves in that category, they took this as encouragement to renew their attacks on capitalist roaders and other factions . . . so in the summer of 1968, violence was on the rise again. This time the criticisms from Peking were much sharper, propaganda teams were dispatched to work with the students, and in September the extremist students were denounced as "petty-bourgeois intellectuals." By that October most of the still dissident Red Guards had been sent to work in the factories or countryside to be "reeducated" by the workers and peasants, and revolutionary committees had been established by three-in-one alliances in almost every part of the country.

So two years after the Cultural Revolution had begun, the most intense struggles had been waged and won by the revolutionary forces. Armed violence had occurred, but had been both sporadic and limited to a few large cities. The struggle had been for the minds of the people, to change their way of thinking . . . and because of this, the Cultural Revolution was different from any other revolution. The real "enemy" had been a way of thinking. The Revolution of 1949, as Liu argued, had defeated the bourgeois classes and seized power for the proletariat. But he had not been correct in assuming that the revolution had been won for good, that the class struggle was over. Instead, Mao and his supporters argued that even after the first revolution, there would be opposition to the ideas of reliance on the masses and serving the people. There would still be those who would betray the spirit of Yenan.

Some would do so wittingly, having actually decided that the spirit of Yenan was no longer useful for growth and progress. These, the "small handful" of intransigent capitalist roaders, were class enemies and would put up a desperate struggle. But the vast majority of those guilty of elitism did so unwittingly and unthinkingly. For them it was enough to join the struggles of the Cultural Revolution, to debate the issues and begin to think about them . . . then, as had happened with the eight hundred thousand workers of Shanghai, the great mass of them would begin to understand what was at stake, "who is behind this policy."

For the others, the "small handful," it was necessary to deprive them of power because they were harmful. But these people were not physically liquidated as in Soviet purges. In most cases they were not even imprisoned . . . instead, they were called upon to engage in public self-criticism, to be "struggled against" in huge mass meetings, to bear the brunt of public disapproval, and to realize the extent of their crimes. During this period (the first years of the Cultural Revolution) they were generally held in house arrest. Later they were either demoted to lower positions within the party or sent to factories and farms for "reeducation" at the hands of their fellow workers. Many also spent from several months to a year or more in a May 7 school where they studied Marxism-Leninism and Mao's thought and worked at ordinary jobs in agriculture and rural industries along with other cadres who had not been criticized during the Cultural Revolution.

Mao explained this policy with a comparison to medicine, saying that the purpose is "like that of a doctor treating an illness . . . to cure the illness in order to save the patient." In the last year or two, some of the leaders removed from office during the Cultural Revolution have returned from periods of reeducation and resumed their former positions on a probationary basis.

Why Should Bureaucrats Plant Corn?

When we were asked about our ideas for an itinerary on that first afternoon in Canton, a visit to a cadre school had high priority. What were they like? Reports from the sensationalist newspapers of Hong Kong had created an impression of labor camps like those described by Solzhenitsyn. But after spending a day at the Peking Eastern District May 7 Cadre School, an hour out of the city in the suburban farmland, this impression was completely changed.

First of all, to spend a period of time at a May 7 cadre school is not a form of punishment. While enrolled at the school, bureaucrats receive their regular salaries from their work units. They are also free to make weekly visits to see their families in the city; a few cadres bring their families to live with them at the school.

Although some cadres came right after the Cultural Revolution began and stayed for one or two years, now there is a system of six-month "terms." All government officials, even schoolteachers, will spend six months at a cadre school. Each office and school sends a few cadres at a time, and the goal is eventually to have everyone go. Officials told us that the schools will be on the Chinese scene for a long time, so possibly each cadre will go to a school several times over the years—a revolutionary sabbatical.

One good indication that May 7 cadre schools are for all cadres, and are not punishment for those who have done wrong or for political outcasts, is that all four of our guide interpreters from CATT had spent approximately a year each in a cadre school. Traveling with Americans is an important political responsibility, and no cadre with serious political problems would be chosen for the job.

Why is a stint at a cadre school seen as so important? What do bureaucrats do during these six months away from their offices?

The May 7 cadre school run by the eastern district of Peking is first of all a place where officials can get away from the pressures of bureaucratic life, do political study, and reexamine themselves. Through such study and discussion, individuals take a critical look at their own work habits, life-style, and political attitudes and set about changing themselves. For example, the director of transportation in the district told the CCAS group how he had tried to run his department singlehandedly, would rarely consult subordinates, and stayed in his office to avoid dealing with ordinary people. Moreover, he did not encourage either subordinates or ordinary citizens to criticize him, and whenever he was criticized, he resented and ignored it. But after a period of work, study, and self-examination at the cadre school, he was determined to rid himself of these bureaucratic attitudes and habits.

The cadre students devote as much time to work as to study. The May 7 cadre schools are essentially farms, set up on previously uncultivated wasteland, and are always away from the cities. The cadres work on the farm and in the small factories attached to it. Although many of the officials in the beginning didn't like to dirty their hands in this menial work and were awkward and unskilled at agricultural tasks, many of them told us that after a few months they became quite accomplished farmers.

Why should bureaucrats plant corn? The idea is that they learn to respect and understand the vast majority of Chinese people who do manual labor, break down their own attitudes of white-collar superiority, and become more physically fit through labor. Cadres at the Eastern District School spoke with pride of how their school-farm was now producing enough to be self-sufficient, but they always emphasized that they did farmwork primarily because of its impact on their attitudes.

It is also important that cadres of all ranks from various district offices and schools are mixed together at the Eastern District May 7 Cadre School. Differences in seniority and status are irrelevant in this context. In addition, while at the school bureaucrats are sometimes sent back for a day to their offices in the city to do the most menial tasks, e.g., cleaning the toilets. The goal is for officials to purge themselves of status consciousness and arrogance and to learn to treat coworkers like equals rather than subordinates.

Before the Cultural Revolution cadres were often sent down (xiafang) to rural areas to reform their attitudes. In small groups or as individuals they would live for long periods among ordinary peasants in the countryside. The cadre schools have supplemented this "xiafang" system. The advantages of the new system of reeducation are that it is a regular system which can enroll more cadres than the old system, and since each school is a self-contained and even sometimes economically self-sufficient unit, there is less disruption of regular agricultural production than under the old system. But one disadvantage is that bureaucrats have less contact with ordinary peasants than under the old system.

We debated among ourselves the long-range significance of the May 7 cadre schools. Some of us thought that a stint at one might become a routinized experience or even "the thing" for bureaucrats to do. But in spite of these reservations, all of us agreed that May 7 cadre schools were an important, exciting experiment in attacking the universal problem of bureaucratic stagnation. As Susan said, "At least the Chinese are conscious of the problem and are trying to solve it in a systematic way. Compare this with the bureaucratic elitism of the Soviet Union and Eastern Europe. And can you imagine bureaucrats who administer the American government's poverty program ever leaving their isolation in Washington and going to live for even a few months in Appalachia?"

The Cultural Revolution and the Future

The May 7 schools follow logically from the resolution of a basic issue in the Cultural Revolution, that of whether or not China should "rely on the masses." To rely on the masses, it is necessary to know them, to live their life-style, experience their work, and talk with them—ulti-mately, for each leader to identify himself as thoroughly as possible *with* the masses.

In October 1968, talking about the Cultural Revolution, Chairman Mao Tse-tung said, "We have won a great vic-tory. But the defeated class will still struggle. These peo-ple are still around and this class still exists. Therefore, we cannot speak of final victory. Not even for decades. We must not lose our vigilance."

Many of the goals of the Cultural Revolution can be expressed in terms familiar to us:

Equality. This means breaking down elitism, bridging the gap between the people and their leaders, and struc-turing leadership collectively so that it will represent as many groups as possible. In the admissions criteria and work-study programs in education we can see these ideas take shape in new policies. In health work, too, the bare-foot doctors and greatly increased emphasis on traditional medicine are concrete results of the Cultural Revolution. Perhaps the impact is most clear in the field of culture itself, where for the first time everyone can participate, sing, dance, act . . . and does, with enthusiasm!

Community. The changes since the Cultural Revolu-tion have worked to build integrated and self-reliant local communities. Education, production, culture, medicine—in every area there has been a real decentralization, not only of structures but of power. By relying on the masses as well as on guidance from the party, the government, and the technical experts, fascinating innovations have been made and experiments are underway all over China. In each unit, we would be shown a new textbook or machine or skit and told, "This is just experimental.

Wait until you return—we will have changed again and progressed much further."

Independence. The tremendous spirit with which the Chinese people work, their determination and confidence, stem from a new belief in their ability to independently solve their own problems. The slogan of zili gengsheng—self-reliance—expresses a faith in man's power to determine his own destiny which flies in the face of two thousand years of Chinese history. Today the Chinese say that neither nature in the form of terrible natural disasters, nor man in the form of class enemies will divert them from their revolutionary path.

The Generation gap. How could Chinese parents, who had fought throughout their lives to free China and then to build a new China, be sure that their children would carry on the revolution? These children had not lived under or fought against the Kuomintang or the Japanese, had never known aching poverty, disease, and the death of whole villages of relatives . . . how could China avoid falling into the same stultified and bureaucratized patterns that other revolutionary movements—especially that of the Soviet Union—had adopted over time? The partial answer to this was that new generations have to experience the process of revolution themselves, to think through for themselves what kind of society they want, who opposes that vision, and how to struggle against them. In the *Quotations*—the "little red book"—which Lin Piao compiled, this selection was included from an essay Mao wrote at Yenan in 1937:

Whoever wants to know a thing has no way of doing so except by coming into contact with it, that is, by living (practicing) in its environment . . . If you want knowledge, you must take part in the practice of changing reality. If you want to know the taste of a pear, you must change the pear by eating it yourself . . . If you want to know the theory and methods of revolution, you must take part in revolution. All genuine knowledge originates in direct experience.

4. CITIES

The Chinese say they are attempting to resolve one of the most important contradictions in the history of the world, a driving force which Marx himself said summarizes all other contradictions: that between town and countryside. The Chinese have broken this down into three further contradictions which they call the "three great differences": between urban and rural areas, industry and agriculture, and intellectual and manual labor. Their goal, they say, is to totally integrate the cities into the countryside.

As early as the 1920s, there were disagreements within the newly formed Chinese Communist party about the relative roles of the city and the countryside in China's revolution. Official doctrine from Moscow, supported by a majority of the young party members, stated that revolution would come only when the proletariat (the industrial workers in the cities) led it. Mao and others differed, and Mao broke with Moscow through the establishment of a rural-based revolutionary political organization. He began in Hunan Province in 1925, but from that time until Liberation in 1949 there were only slight changes of tactics. Mao never advocated abandoning the urban areas completely, and he depended heavily on people of urban origin for positions of responsibility within the organization. But generally the pre-1949 period is characterized by emphasis on rural areas. The concrete issue involved was one of political power: where would the revolution come from—the city or the countryside?

It came from the rural areas. Though many of the leaders were from the city, the strength of the party was in its ability to speak to and for the needs of the peasants, and to organize them into an effective fighting force first against the Japanese and then against the Kuomintang.

With Liberation, China's leaders faced a difficult problem. Could they continue to emphasize the rural areas? In the period of guerrilla warfare, the countryside had been the principal focus for revolutionary work and the cities had been targets of encirclement. Now in the post-Liberation period, national reconstruction was the highest priority.

This new priority resulted in a significant change in the role of urban areas, largely because of the concrete difficulties of rapid industrialization. The Chinese implemented the Soviet model, which recognized the city as the central source of social and political power, and concentrated industrial expansion in urban areas. Increasing differences developed between conditions in city and countryside, ones which Mao and some of the party veterans found difficult to tolerate. The cities had become bureaucratic industrial centers for the nation, and their urban intellectuals so dominated the priorities and development of China that in 1957 Mao said: "It seems as if Marxism that was once the rage is not so fashionable now."

Mao, and others who agreed with his criticisms, undertook to reverse this trend. The process actually began with the Eighth Party Congress in 1956, when the xiafang movement was initiated. Xiafang means to "go down to the countryside." Large numbers of cadre were sent to the agricultural areas and administrative staffs were significantly reduced. The campaign climaxed in the Great Leap Forward in 1958, which reaffirmed the importance of the rural areas and of manual work.

The years after this were dominated by the tension between urban and rural alternatives. The need for a high rate of industrial growth—while remaining independent of foreign investment and control—limited the options. And many of China's leaders believed that it could not industrialize at the same time that it sought to integrate the cities with the countryside. Industry on rural communes was thought to be an impossible dream. It seemed that China might well take the road followed by other developing nations, one that ignores the rural regions and leads to the creation of huge, unwieldy, and cramped industrial cities.

The Cultural Revolution brought a dramatic change of direction. The Chinese hope to create urban areas which are basically self-sufficient, serving the needs of the countryside through effective integration with it. This means that although there will continue to be urban industrialization, there is conscious emphasis on rural industrial development. City-based factories are urged to engage in agriculture, while mechanization of farming and the construction of small machine-tool industries on rural communes are encouraged.

In terms of urban development the importance of this strategy is obvious. It means decentralization and reduction of administrative apparatus. More local control of agricultural mechanization will reduce the financial and political dependence of the countryside on the cities and permit sustained rural growth through development of local industries. The intellectual and cultural gulf separating the urban and rural areas will be narrowed by the peasantry's mastery of modern technology, and the city will no longer constitute an intellectual and administrative elite controlling, but divorced from, the process of production.

These changes are good examples of the link between theory and practice which the Chinese Commmunists have always emphasized.

The Chinese did not realize the effect large-scale industrialization and bureaucratization in the cities would have until they tried that path. Thus the present policies are the result of experience in the past. The Chinese have seen that a rural strategy is valuable for building highly politicized and creative qualities in their society, but that it also creates problems for traditional methods of increasing agricultural and industrial production. They know too that a policy of highly centralized, urban industrialization can increase material production, but can also act as an obstacle to individual development. The present strategy should be seen then not as the dominance of the countryside over the city, but rather as a new unity combining and using the best aspects of the two.

We had all, particularly the "urbanologists" among us, read about this phenomenon, but had found it difficult to imagine what it might mean in real terms. In China we found that "real terms" varied tremendously from city to city. In each city, the program of integration was an ideal that guided planning, but concrete plans were adapted to an individual city, each with its particular problems. This single goal has not yielded look-alike cities—there is no danger of mistaking a Peking suburb for Nanking, or Soochow for Shanghai.

Almost all the cities we saw were alike in one way: they were green. Peking was lush, verdant—Paris, but with still wider boulevards and even more trees. Soochow has supplemented its famous Ming dynasty gardens with trees planted during the Great Leap Forward. Only Shanghai of all the cities we saw would be recognized by an American, because so much of it was built by foreigners before 1949. Even there thousands of trees have been planted, partly disguising the heavy style of the British banks and Soviet architecture of the fifties. The impression is suburban, although the physical layout and land use are definitely urban.

Municipal Bus No. 7, Canton

As we emerged from the train station in Canton on June 23, the atmosphere was almost a physical shock. After Hong Kong—noisy, pushy, and crowded—the busy streets of Canton seemed gentle by comparison. People almost sauntered, their pace purposeful but relaxed. Everyone looked healthy, no one wore rags, or begged, or jammed an elbow into you if you stood a moment too long in one place. We heard people chattering and laughing, bicycles ringing, occasional buses, and a few whispered comments and giggles at the sight of us. But no raucous horns or street vendors shouting vainly for a sale.

First we saw the people. Only later, after we had climbed into the bus for the hotel, did we begin to look at the city itself. Our first impression was of a continuous series of small towns. Each area had its own streets of shops, noodle stands, and playgrounds, with no apparent "center" of the city. From a rise looking out over the city, the rooftops seemed all of equal height, undulating with the curves of the land rather than jutting up from it. There were no skyscrapers. Because the city is spread out, as our bus rolled through the streets we saw only a gradual change from the more concentrated inner city to the suburbs.

Our hotel, built for the large foreign population which comes for the trade fairs, was a large red brick structure set well back on a curved driveway—hardly like the bustling tourist hotels we had left behind. Teacups clinked, and we heard soft footsteps on the red carpeting of the lounge as we came in the door. The hotel manager, a round, middle-aged man with a broad Cantonese face, welcomed us warmly and showed us to our rooms. Following him down the corridors, we realized suddenly that every year many people come to China. It is only the Americans who have isolated themselves. What was new for us was a common occurrence for the man who led us through the halls—indeed, it was his business. Curious, we looked around for other guests; later, we met a few foreigners in the lobby, some of whom we knew from Hong Kong, but July seemed to be off-season. In October and April each year at the Canton Trade Fair hundreds of businessmen from Japan, Eastern Europe, West Germany, France, Britain, and Africa pour into the city for a month of exhibits and bargaining—presumably enough to fill the hotel, and justify its current existence.

By that evening, after an afternoon of itinerary discussion and a huge banquet in the hotel dining room, we were impatient to explore the city. The hotel manager told us which number bus to take, and five minutes later we were bumping along on municipal bus no. 7 toward what we hoped would be the center of Canton.

We never did find gay night life in Canton, or anything that would have satisfied the sophisticated tastes of Hong Kong. Instead, we wandered happily along the streets, eating ice-cream bars and trying bowls of noodles, watching the shops close up for the night and talking with the people on the roadsides. The streets were lined with trees, tall and dusky green in the light of the streetlamps, and underneath them men and women played cards and smoked. The buildings were similar to those of

Macao or Hong Kong's older sections, two or three stories high, with the second and third stories projecting over the sidewalks supported by round posts. In the lee of the upper stories the sidewalks had room for small tables, and there were often children sleeping on benches that had been dragged outdoors in the warm air. An earnest young man on a bicycle stopped, sure we were lost, and then decided to take us to an amusement park a few blocks away. But it was closed—it was 9:30 by then—and we walked back to our bus stop. Almost all the shops were shut now, and on the streets fewer bicycle bells rang as people seemed to be heading home. Families still lingered outside their houses, there were a few last customers at the noodle stands, and we climbed back on no. 7.

Canton is an old city, moist and warm, set on the banks of the Pearl River in one of the most fertile regions of China. Parts of it, and some of the villages we saw on our way out to Huadong Commune the next day, are centuries old. Like Peking, Canton is proof of the urban societies China supported while most of the world's people knew only villages. Today excavations have revealed elsewhere in China the complex capitals of the Shang dynasty, a thousand years before Christ, with bronze workers living in segregated suburbs around the wealthy core of aristocrats and emperor. These cities, and those which grew up in the next 2,900 years, were of one basic type: they were administrative centers, living off the agricultural produce of the people, contributing nothing in return but their autocratic rule. This wealth, taxed from the peasants, supported the arts, comforts, and amusements of China's rulers.

By the end of the Sung dynasty (960–1276) this form had been highly developed, and China was probably the most urbanized country in the world. It was the cities of this period, with their fabulous merchants and cultured elite, that amazed Marco Polo and Father Ricci. After the Mongol invasion had been finally defeated (1279–1368), the cities grew still larger, until in 1800—when the West stood at the threshold of industrialization—almost half the people in the world who lived in cities were Chinese.

Throughout these centuries, however, the cities remained linked to the countryside; with the coming of Westerners, new cities were developed within the old and called "treaty ports." Here, foreign-owned industries reaped profits from cheap Chinese labor; floods of foreign imports that ruined the native industries followed. The sudden influx of laborers to Canton expanded the city's population far beyond its ability to provide shelter, sanitation, or food for all. Instead these necessities went to those who could afford them; and the slums of Canton filled with those who could not.

Today there are no slums in Canton. The city still looks poor to us, as Americans, but when we contrasted it with Hong Kong and other Asian cities it seemed relatively rich. For example, there were no open sewers, a drastic health problem in Hong Kong refugee settlements, and Canton had clean water, swept streets, and clean, sturdy housing. But we had no opportunity in Canton to find out how these changes had been made.

China's New York, Shanghai

From our hotel in Canton, we again boarded the China Travel Service bus and headed for the airport. The airport was another surprise, for it was a strange flashback to some of the small American city airports we had left behind. There was one simple passenger building with a colorful mural on the large wall inside, and from the door we walked out across the asphalt directly to the aircraft, up the staircase, and into the British-made propeller plane. The plane held about forty people, and was nearly full. For three-and-a-half hours we flew northward to the Yangtze River Valley.

Shanghai airport was slightly larger, but also had the small-town feeling of Canton airport. Here, too, we took a bus, but this time the ride into the city was very different.

Like Canton, Shanghai was a treaty port. But rather than being an expansion of an older city, Shanghai grew almost overnight in the middle of the nineteenth century from a small fishing village to the largest city in China. There had been no stimulus from the Chinese economy for a city to exist there—it was entirely the creation of foreign investment. It did share one characteristic with the older cities, however, in that it too did not produce wealth to exchange with the countryside, but drained the countryside and reserved this wealth for foreign profit. A Chinese sociologist of the 1930s described these treaty ports as "economic ratholes" which dribbled away the wealth of China.

Such treaty ports were not only economically but also sometimes politically separate from the surrounding territory. Foreign "concessions" were sectioned off and given to French, Japanese, British, and other national interests. Here foreign residents created small societies as similar to Europe or Japan as they could. To ensure their control of some cities they demanded the right to govern them entirely. Although Shanghai was legally a part of China, it was partly governed by a foreign municipal council until long after the 1911 revolution. There were, of course, Chinese who collaborated with these foreigners to exploit their own countrymen, the "compradors." But the net effect was to divorce the city from the countryside and to create squatter settlements housing a population of the poor in a "no-man's-land" between China and the West.

Since Liberation, all that has changed. The shanty-towns have been torn down, and the older buildings which are still sound have been renovated and now provide housing for many people. In addition, much new housing has been constructed on the perimeter of the city. We saw examples of all these areas, and spent part of a day at one of the older housing units built since 1949.

When we arrived in Shanghai, however, we drove directly into the heart of the city. Here the streets bristled with activity, bells clanged and buses trundled by, people streamed in and out of the buildings—Shanghai is more like our cities than any other Chinese city we saw, complete with a faint touch of air pollution. And it has much more of the frenetic pace we associate with city living, at least in the downtown area, so that after walking through the streets we were glad to return to our hotel to rest. As it was everywhere we went in China, the weather was hot in Shanghai, and the tall buildings shut out the breezes so that the trees along the streets stood motionless, green and a little dusty.

Only when we came down to the Bund itself did the

harbor breezes begin to reach us. The Bund is the old waterfront section where foreign businesses had had their offices and warehouses, and where the hotels, shops, and restaurants of the rich had been located. It faces on the Whangpoo—Shanghai sits at the confluence of the Whangpoo and Soochow rivers—and the avenues intersect the waterfront. The Bund itself looks like Wall Street must have in 1920, before giant skyscrapers began to be built. No building is taller than twenty-odd stories; all are thick, solid, and look like banks. The hotel we stayed in must have been well known to the foreign residents of the Bund, but then it was the Cathay, not the Peace Hotel. It too is an enormous block, with baroque ornamentation, and there were many more guests than in the Eastern Hotel in Canton.

Foreigners no longer run Shanghai, and the beggars and prostitutes are gone. But in the harbor ships still crowd the quay, for Shanghai is one of the largest ports in the world, a funnel for products coming down from the rich Yangtze Valley and chief harbor for China's trade with the world. Its total population is six million, ranking with New York, Tokyo, and London among the major cities of the world. Shanghai has grown rapidly (almost 6.5 percent each year) and disproportionately to the countryside, where the average annual growth is only 1.5 percent. Shanghai is China's largest city, and in many ways presented the worst problems for China's planners after Liberation.

By contrast with Peking, Shanghai has been an industrial city for decades. Most of the large-scale industries before 1949 were foreign-owned, and working conditions as well as living conditions outside the factories were calculated to extract the most labor for the least cost. As a result, most of the workers lived in crude shantytowns. As the city expanded, new industries competed with the workers for this land, which was a particular problem in Shanghai, where the river basin is soggy and wet, floods easily, and encourages disease. Industries occupied the higher lands and the workers were driven into the bottomlands.

National planning priorities after Liberation emphasized the need to locate workers' housing near industries and shops. In Shanghai, however, this was difficult. So much industry had already been built within the city environs, without space for housing, that a new solution was devised: the workers' villages.

What does an ordinary Chinese home look like? In Shanghai, we visited two workers' apartments in Chaoyang Workers' New Village—a low-rise, parklike housing development on the edge of Shanghai's urban area, about twenty-five minutes from the downtown area. Chaoyang was the first such workers' housing estate built in Shanghai.

Some statistics on the estate first: its first phase was completed in 1952 at which time there were 1,200 households living in what were mostly two-story blocks. 1959 was the last year of construction and the high tide of people moving in occurred that year and the year before. (10,000 families moved in, in 1958–59. The total then was 12,000–13,000 families.) Now at Chaoyang there are 15,000 families with 68,000 people. We were told that this population was about average for such estates in Shanghai. As with other estates, the original two-story blocks were found to be too wasteful a use of urban land. Therefore five-story blocks became the norm—the blocks don't have elevators—and earlier blocks with strong foundations had one or two extra stories built on top. The one we visited had been left unchanged at three stories.

The estate houses mostly industrial workers, usually those working in Shanghai's many textile factories. In addition to the housing blocks it also has shops, markets, clinics, a cinema and culture hall with reading rooms, a park and swimming pool, and schools. From the statistics on schools, it is probably safe to assume that all the school-age children residents in the estate can go to class within the estate. There were no factories within the estate. Nor was there a hospital, but residents could use the one in the surrounding Putu District of Shanghai. We learned that of Shanghai's six million urban population, one million were housed in workers' new villages like Chaoyang.

One of them was Zao Aiying, a slight, smiling, extroverted woman of fifty. She lived in a corner apartment on the ground floor with her husband, who was a worker in an auto repair factory, a son, who worked in a radio equipment factory, and a daughter, who was an apprentice in a leather factory. The apartment consisted of two rooms about ten by fourteen feet each, a lavatory, and a kitchen. (There was a public bathhouse for every several housing blocks.) Electricity and water cost the Zaos 1.50 yuan per month (about sixty cents U.S.), and the rent ran to all of 4.90 yuan a month. (Rents in the estate are calculated by the number of square yards in an apartment with slight adjustments for quality. The rate was generally about 0.20 yuan the square yard and families paid from 2.50 to 5 yuan a month for an apartment, indicating that the Zaos' apartment was probably one of the larger units.[1])

We sat in the room that doubled as a living-dining room and bedroom, where Mrs. Zao served us tea poured from an ever-ready thermos into ordinary glasses. About a third of the room was taken up by a double bed in the corner opposite a wall with two windows. Between the windows was a table that could be opened out. There were four small closet wardrobes with four suitcases on top arranged neatly along the wall from the windows to the head of the bed. On either side of the table, in front of the windows, was a chair, and eight other chairs and stools stood along the remaining wall opposite the wardrobes. The floor was cement and the walls were whitewashed. Decoration consisted of simple curtains, snapshots of the family mounted behind glass and hung on the wall above the stools, and several revolutionary posters frequently seen in Chinese bookstores. One was a picture of Mao waving from Tiananmen. The overall impression was of snug neatness, not nearly so cramped and overflowing as the average working family's flat in Hong Kong —where double bunk beds are de rigueur in order to conserve space—but obviously nowhere near as roomy as

---

[1] The room-size estimate was our own. The rent figure was supplied by Mrs. Zao. The estate's square-yard rent rate was given by the chairwoman of the estate's revolutionary committee during a different meeting. All figures jibe.

a working-class apartment in some New York City housing project. The only consumer durable in sight was an old sewing machine.

When we asked Mrs. Zao about where she had lived before moving to Chaoyang, she started by describing life in a squatter shack in pre-Liberation Shanghai. After several sentences, her smiling face began slowly to cloud over and she had to daub her eyes with a handkerchief. (Only twice did any of the Chinese we met cry. Both were women. The other was a primary-school teacher in Nanking. She was temporarily overcome while describing landlord oppression and exploitation in the old society. About Kuomintang or Japanese depredations, for example, they remained stoically calm.) This was Mrs. Zao's story:

Her father died when she was ten. Since there were a son and daughter younger still, Mrs. Zao was given to another family as a child bride. In her father-in-law's home things were very difficult for her. "In those times we women didn't have the right to say anything in the home. I wasn't even supposed to look directly at my father-in-law."

Then gonggong (father-in-law) died on the job while repairing a streetlamp. Her mother-in-law blamed her for the family's bad fate and things became even rougher for her in her new home. She had to go out to work as child labor in a factory. During this period, before Liberation, they were all living in a small, leaky one-room straw hut in a slum and paying five yuan for it—or slightly more than she was currently paying in the Chaoyang estate.

Then came Liberation. Shortly after, they moved to Chaoyang. She had children by then; the mother-in-law died subsequently. Their life here was just so much better than before. Several times she asked, as much to herself as to us: "In the old society, who would look up to us?"

Where did the changes in the new society come from, we asked. From Chairman Mao and the Communist party, she said. To show her gratitude to them, since 1958 she had been taking an active part in neighborhood work. She first performed in cultural performances along with other housewives and retired workers in the estate. (She confessed that she had a good singing voice.) Later, she helped organize the performances.

We asked if she was a member of the Communist party. She replied enthusiastically that the greatest joy of her life was when she joined the party last May 30, "on the 'eve' of the party's fiftieth anniversary." (The anniversary was several days away when we spoke to her.) We wondered why a person like herself, so active in neighborhood affairs, had only just entered the party. She told us that she had applied some ten years ago, but since she was cocky about her role in the neighborhood recreation group, the comrades advised her to be modest; only then could she make progress.

Her daily schedule was filled with hygiene work—she sweeps the grounds—and "propaganda" work, i.e., organizing and singing with the estate's old and retired workers' cultural group. With so many outside responsibilities, we asked if her husband ever complained about her neglecting housework. In the new society, men and women were equal. If she comes home late as a result of her neighborhood work, her husband cooks. It's the same every Sunday when she works. Likewise, they share the washing; but it is the husband who does the sewing and mending. We asked her to relate for us her activities of the preceding day, from rising to going to bed. She said that that day was exceptional but gave us the rundown nonetheless:

5:00   Rise; wash and clean up; clean house; do marketing.

6:30   Meet at estate movie house for cultural group rehearsal.

7:00   After breakfast take a charter bus to downtown Shanghai with the other old and retired workers.

11:00   Rehearsal for day's performance over; rest and lunch.

2:00   Give their performance in a cultural show for the people of Shanghai. (They were nineteenth on the program of performances.)

4:00   Arrive back home; do washing; take bath; have
to   supper—husband cooked. Over supper, talk with
5:00   husband and children about the performances

and the audience reaction. Told them the audience really enjoyed the performance by the old and retired workers. Told children they should learn from old and retired workers.

9:00 Finish talking and retire.

(The day she described was a Sunday, the day of the week most Chinese workers have off.)

Even though our time was growing short, we asked if it would be possible to make a short visit to some other neighbors in the building. She told us that most of the other residents were at work, but that there was a retired worker on the next floor, just above, who was probably in. We all went up, and found him in. We were greeted with the same cordial enthusiasm, and again served tea from a thermos—this one had a picture of China's earth satellite on its side with several bars of "The East Is Red" emanating from it.

The old gentleman's name was Yuan Chengsu. He was seventy-five years old and his motions were slow but firm. His Ningpo accent was so thick that one of our friends from the Travel Service had to interpret into Mandarin for us. His family consisted of himself, his wife, and three children. None of the children currently lived at home. One son was in the People's Liberation Army— in the navy—a daughter had emigrated to the Sinkiang border area. The youngest son had just graduated from middle school and was doing labor and studying agricultural knowledge. The apartment was laid out exactly like Mrs. Zao's downstairs, except that Mr. Yuan had two electric lights in the room instead of one, and fewer "wardrobes" but more trunks. The decorations naturally were different and in addition to those on the walls, there were also family snapshots under a glass covering the tabletop.

Mr. Yuan's memory for dates was not altogether accurate, but he filled us in on his life history. Until retirement, he had been a textile worker all his life. That work life had started when he was twelve. In his time he had worked in Japanese, Chinese, and American mills. Before Liberation they were all pretty much the same. If you got sick, you were fired—or if a woman became pregnant, she was fired. He had rarely held a job for more than one year in any one mill. He always worried about being unemployed. He was fifty-four—or was it fifty-six?—at Liberation. For the first time in his life, work was steady: he worked for ten years after Liberation in one factory; employment was guaranteed. When he was sixty-five—or was it sixty-four?—he retired, and since then he has been drawing a pension, the same amount he was making at his retirement. (China's currency, the renminbi, has not become inflated over the years, so his pension was not eroded.) He was proud of his children, proud that they had gotten an education he never did; proud especially of the son in the PLA. His neighbors often complimented him on having a son in the PLA.

Although Mr. Yuan's apartment now housed only two (it was originally meant for five), there would be no attempt to have him move to a smaller one. The policy of the revolutionary committee in the estate favored continuity of tenancy. From newlywed couple through young family back to aged couple, there would be little or no switching of apartments within the estate.

We were falling behind in our schedule, so we began to leave. Mr. Yuan shook our hands warmly as we left. We urged him not to see us downstairs. Mrs. Zao would see us out. No need to descend the stairs and remount again. After a little persuasion, he accepted.

As we were going down the stairs and out into the yard, Mrs. Zao, still beaming with pride and enthusiasm, told us again: "In the old society, who would respect us ordinary working people? When could we have had foreign guests come and visit us in our homes? In a straw hut? There wasn't even room to sit down. It's all because of Chairman Mao and the Communist party. In the old society, who would have considered us as having any worth?"

Mrs. Zao was a neighborhood activist and an unpaid party member who came up through, and now helped organize, a neighborhood "mass organization," the old and retired workers' cultural group. What did the organization of community groups, especially revolutionary committees, look like in Chaoyang Workers' New Village?

At Chaoyang, there are two types of revolutionary committee. The first is for the whole of Chaoyang; it is a state organ, with paid personnel, legal responsibility, and is a part of the administrative hierarchy of Shanghai's Putu District, to which Chaoyang belongs. There are nine standing members of the committee, and twenty-one members in all: of the nine standing members, four are retired workers, one is from the People's Liberation Army, two are veteran cadres (one of these is a woman and the chairman of the committee), and two are representatives of the people at large. The other type of committee is the neighborhood revolutionary committee. Positions there are not paid, and the committees are totally independent, not answerable to the higher governmental authorities. These groups are concerned with political, ideological, and arbitration work primarily, within a small neighborhood. In Chaoyang there were twelve neighborhood revolutionary committees, each composed of thirty members, ten of whom are "core leaders."

We asked how much control each body had, and at what level. The answer was given using the Chaoyang primary and middle schools as an example. Teachers for all the schools are assigned by the education division of the Shanghai municipal revolutionary committee; since they were assigned, many of the Chaoyang teachers have moved to live within the housing area. The neighborhood revolutionary committees are responsible for the primary schools, and the Chaoyang revolutionary committee administers the middle schools. What happens if you get bad teachers, we asked. "We would help them with their shortcomings."

In all of China's cities, there are three general varieties of housing. In addition to the workers' new villages we had just seen, there is the pre-Liberation housing (which has been renovated or to which amenities have been added, such as electricity, water, and closing of sewers), and housing built around factories as a part of a complex designed to provide all necessary services in a single area. Each factory complex is run by the factory's revolutionary committee. The workers' new villages and the pre-Liberation housing, however, are managed by a housing board called the "house management office." For example, if a couple plan to marry and they are looking for an apartment, they will apply to this office—and will get housing almost immediately. (We asked this question in many ways, everywhere, and always got the same answer; that housing comes through immediately.) This is evidently true only when a couple marries and sets up a household, for when they begin to add to their family it is unlikely that they will be able to get a new apartment, at least in a short period of time. This was very different from our own American pattern, where families move frequently and over great distances. But it is important to remember that traditionally the Chinese have placed great value on being able to stay for generations in one locale—if possible, in the same house—to be forced to move one's family was considered a great tragedy. While this pattern is beginning to change with large groups of young people moving to the agricultural and border regions, the housing policy explained above is less restrictive than it might seem at first.

As we left Chaoyang and drove back into the city, we could see the physical layout of the region in terms of various functions. A rough diagram of the urban area appears opposite.

Back in the city that night, we went out to explore. A few of us wandered off from the others, trying to avoid the huge crowds which gathered every time we slowed down, but it was hard to become anonymous even in those busy streets. Here people sat out at night as they did in Canton, but played a special table game, something like backgammon. We noticed many more couples out strolling in Shanghai than in the other cities we visited. As in Canton, though, the atmosphere was low-key, friendly, and completely relaxed.

The cities of China wake up early, and by six-thirty each morning the shops are open. For breakfast in Peking and Shanghai they sell doujiang, a milky soup of soybeans made sweet with sugar or sour with pickles to taste, and youtiao or xiaobing, long thin doughnut sticks or sesame rolls encasing them. Some of the shops have been open all night, for in each neighborhood some stay open for workers coming home from odd shifts. We got

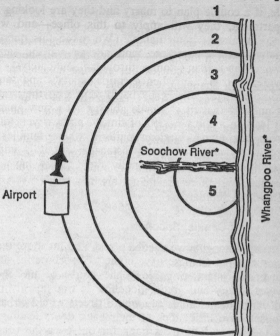

1 vegetable communes shading outward to rice communes

2 belt of vegetable communes and airport

3 mixed workers' new villages and factories

4 mixed factories, pre-Liberation housing, shops, etc.

5 central business district—the Wall Streetlike ex-foreign concessions

*The Soochow River—or creek—is narrow and has many bridges across it. The Whangpoo is wide, has no bridges, and serves to interrupt what would otherwise be a neat set of concentric circles.

the impression that this was arranged on a rotating basis. For the rest of the day, shoppers come and go. We never saw long lines except before the watermelon stands—understandable in the heat!—or inside the cloth shops.

It is difficult to convey our growing amazement as we explored in Shanghai. China has overcome almost all the tragic problems of Asia's cities. It has eliminated its worst slum housing, and renovated or built housing for all those tenants as well as for the tremendous population growth within its cities. It has provided water, public latrines, electricity and transportation, covered sewage systems, and is continuing to build. The problems that are left, and there are many, are not tragic by Asian *or* American standards.

Trees and Canals, Soochow

After Shanghai we needed a rest, and for more than five centuries the Chinese have come to Soochow for just that purpose. Meandering along the banks of the Soochow River, shady and green, Soochow is traditionally famous for its beauty. Canals run where streets would be, and the houses have little steps at their back doors leading down to the water. The trees hang far out over the roadways, and the houses are set behind long walls to keep out the heat of the summer days. The buildings are small, reminding many of us of the architecture in Kyoto, Japan's ancient capital. We mentioned this, saying that it must have been due to the strong influence China has historically had on its smaller neighbor. Our hosts in Soochow diplomatically assured us that the influence had been mutual. And despite the fact that Soochow so often lends itself to comparisons with Venice, Kyoto, and the scroll paintings of China's heritage, it is also distinctly a city of modern China.

Soochow is developing modern industry. These new factories stand on the outskirts of the city, and we could only see the wisps of smoke from their chimineys. But Soochow is not large. The population is only slightly over 600,000, and to say the city is industrializing is not to say that it will soon take on the look of Peking or Shanghai. The only factory we visited in our stay there was the

Soochow Embroidery Factory, which, though definitely mechanized and modern, was gaily decorated with pieces of its own work and surrounded by lovely gardens. It seemed somehow less convincing as a factory than those we saw elsewhere.

Soochow, from traditional times, was compact and planned. The streets we drove through were narrow, wide enough for two small buses. With the small houses and overhanging trees, the effect is almost that of a city drawn to two-thirds, or three-fourths scale. Yet the gardens are calculated to give the impression of vast spaces in their carefully planned acres. We spent our first afternoon in a garden which had been designed and finished during the Ming dynasty, five hundred years ago, and has now been renamed the "Common Man's Garden." But the park remains the same, the graceful landscape and ancient pavilions unchanged. It is the people in the park who have changed, for today everyone in Soochow is welcome, and the park which used to be only for the upper classes now belongs to everyone in the city.

"The canals have not always been so beautiful," said one of the older women among the Soochow friends we made. "I can remember when they were heaped with refuse, until in the wet season the dirty water would run up to the threshold of my house and the garbage of months before passed by. The canals were so filthy no one believed they could ever be clean; and everyone tossed in his garbage too. After Liberation, though, we began to learn about the importance of sanitation to health, and we decided for our own sake to do something about it. Now, of course, we are proud of their wonderful beauty, but you should remember that clean canal water is important for other things too, and that we have not always had it."

So Soochow, too, has changed greatly in the last two decades. We found out that all those trees, which we had assumed were also from the Ming dynasty, or at least the Ch'ing dynasty, had actually been planted in the Great Leap Forward, just fifteen years ago. The people of the city are very anxious to preserve its reputation for grace and beauty, and we left thinking that perhaps with its smaller population and fertile environs, Soochow might have an easier time of it in the future than Shanghai.

Bicycles and Trucks, Nanking

We arrived in Nanking at midday on July 1, 1971, the fiftieth anniversary of the founding of the Communist party in China. There were no great parades, however, only small groups of people sitting before their houses and shops, talking and reading together. They were discussing the history of the party over the last fifty years, the Nanking CATT told us. It seemed an appropriate way to celebrate this event. The Communist party in China has a long and fascinating history in this century. It has undergone many changes, and, through them, led the people to the exciting new China we saw this summer.

Nanking, like Canton, is one of China's older cities. Today the old city walls still stand, giving the green city inside a parklike atmosphere. The pride of Nanking is a modern creation, however: the magnificent Yangtze River Bridge, which, with its double rail vehicular levels, is one of the most impressive achievements of China. Almost everywhere in China the people know the story of the building of the bridge, and, in fact, a film has been made of it. People quote its dimensions, describe the dangers of its construction, and marvel at the fact that China did it all on its own. The bridge has changed the life of Nanking, and transportation from the north to the south of China, drastically. Before, only ferries crossed the river, carrying trains, trucks, carts, and passengers alike. Now more than a hundred trains can cross every day, and thousands of motor vehicles, carts, and pedestrians use it regularly. It also has become a "Sunday outing" place, where families come to watch the river traffic, and we saw students in clusters singing as they hiked across the bridge.

Forms of transportation in China are widely varied. In Nanking we began to pay attention to the carts especially. In the north of China, north of the Yangtze, we would find animal-drawn vehicles in profusion. But here in the south tricycle carts, carts with people pulling them, trucks, and small, three-wheeled truck carts predominated.

Chinese trucks are medium to large in size, not pick-ups, and are used both for cartage and passenger transportation. Passengers are usually groups of people being taken from one specific location to another; for example, from their homes in a worker's village to the factory they all work in. They often ride standing up and several times when we saw them they waved and cheered at us. The three-wheeled trucks are very much like Italian Lambrettas, but stronger looking. There are almost no passenger cars. The only place we saw them in any number was Peking (generally Polish-made compact sedans)—where they were usually connected with a hotel or embassy for the use of foreigners. There are no privately owned cars in China. We did see a Chinese-made car in the Industrial Exhibition at Shanghai, and looked for it on the streets, but we saw one in use only in Sian, where some streets are so narrow that buses cannot get through. The Chinese have no plans for increasing the production of passenger cars, except possibly for taxis to be used by groups.

We asked about the many carts pulled by people. The answer, from a young Chinese official in the city, was very straightforward: "You can interpret this in one of two ways: first, in a hostile fashion, you could see it as exploitation of the people. But secondly, in a more favorable light, you could say that our society is modern and backward at the same time, and that people don't throw up their hands because industrialism hasn't reached them yet. We call this 'walking on two legs,' to proceed using both old and new means until we get where we want." Indeed, most of the Chinese people we met did not seem to find these human-drawn carts particularly embarrassing, and seemed to take it merely as a sign of industrial backwardness in some areas. We tried to calculate roughly the ratio between cargo carried by motor vehicles and by people-drawn carts, and from our own observations it was approximately half and half in the south. There are usually three people to a small cart, holding on to the shafts and pulling on lines. In the north of China, we saw only animal-drawn carts, however; this evidently is the traditional pattern in north and south. Northern draft animals are a strange assortment: mules, donkeys, and horses, sometimes one of each yoked together before a large cart, with complicated harnessing arrangements.

Without passenger cars, the most important forms of transportation for the people of China are buses, trolleys, and bikes. Buses come in all sizes and conditions, but are invariably clean. The first one we rode was the no. 7 we caught outside our hotel in Canton, which held about forty passengers, some straphangers, others using wooden seats. It turned out to be fairly typical of the other buses we saw, although those provided specially for us by the China Travel Service would have passed for the most modern Greyhound.

With the profusion of buses, there is good reason to have conductors to advise passengers and facilitate their seating and ticketing. These conductors are usually young women, helpful and also very determinedly political. They lead their riders in reciting quotations by Mao, singing revolutionary songs, and calling out slogans. All this is done as they walk up and down the aisles, selling tickets at one fen a stop (in Peking; at this rate a very long ride would cost only approximately six cents in U.S. currency). Each bus stop has a metal map of the routes with all transfer points, very similar to those in the New York subways.

In every city there seemed to be as many people on bicycles as on buses. Indeed, if there are any traffic problems in China, they must all be the result of the welter of bicycle commuters. More and more of these commuters every year are, proportionately, the office workers in the central-city offices, because so much workers' housing is being built close to the factories and shops. Ultimately the hope is to have everyone living within easy distance of their work, but that will take a long time and may never be totally possible in the cities built up before 1949.

The bicycles were fairly expensive. We saw so many teen-agers and young adults on them that we asked about prices, and how high they were in relation to the average salary. The price range is from 150 to 165 yuan (about $65). Since the average salary of a young worker is 60 yuan a month, a bicycle is a big investment. If they are so expensive, how can so many people buy them? One reason, evidently, is that many of the young single workers live in dormitories at their factories, paying almost no rent.

A Visit to a Police Station

One good way to find out about a country's government is to get arrested . . . but no, that is *not* what happened, although everyone back at our hotel in Nanking had decided it was. Frank tried to explain: "Dorothy and I just went out shopping. We were walking along, stopping at some of the stands to buy lemonade and ice cream because it was so hot. Dorothy got ahead of me at one point, and I paused to take a picture of an old cobbler by the side of the road. He grinned at me, embarrassed, but stood still while I adjusted the lens and got ready to shoot. Then he started to adjust the straps of his two kits, hanging from either end a pole over his shoulders, so I waited. Then, just as I was about to take the picture, a young man in a bright blue-and-white-striped T-shirt came by. He saw me, looked at the cobbler, and frowned. Shaking his head, he put his hand over the lens to show me that I shouldn't take the picture. Surprised, I turned to look at him—we had never had any trouble before taking pictures of anything in China. He shook his head apologetically but firmly, his expression serious. He couldn't have been more than twenty-one or twenty-two years old. 'Why not?' I asked.

" 'You're in new China, you shouldn't take pictures of him. He's old, that's a picture of old China. Take pictures of the Nanking Bridge, not him,' said the young man.

" 'I have lots of pictures of the bridge, but we should take pictures of everything, especially everything to do with the life of the people,' I replied.

"But he was not convinced. I put away my camera, and he relaxed; we continued to discuss the question. By now the usual small crowd had gathered and another man stepped forward. He was slightly older than the first, and he was wearing the uniform of a People's Liberation Army veteran (a PLA uniform without insignia on the cap or lapels, and without a belt). He seemed to take charge of the situation, unobtrusively, and at first I thought he might be a policeman, since they too wear PLA-like uniforms. But policemen have insignia different from those of the PLA, so this man without insignia could have been either. In any case he was curious and a little concerned about what was happening on his street.

"We talked for a while longer. I was concerned because I didn't want them to think that I—or any other visiting American—was hostile and trying to take pictures that would damage China's image. On the other hand, they were equally determined to convince me that I should only take inspiring pictures. I tried to point out that if I returned to America with only glowing descriptions and perfect pictures, no one would believe me, but they didn't accept this. They said that the people of America would know that the pictures were of new China, and would believe them.

"Finally, because the crowd was continuing to grow, I invited the second young man back to our hotel to talk there (by now the first fellow, slightly embarrassed, had withdrawn). So we set off, with groups of children walking in front and behind, laughing and staring. One little boy was walking backward in front of us, his mouth gaping open, listening as hard as he could to our conversation—and he backed smack into a telephone pole. At this the other children broke up laughing, for they had been staring just as hard, and he blushed furiously and melted back into the crowd.

"Dorothy was still oblivious to what had happened and by now she was far ahead and almost out of sight. At the next corner we came to a trolley stop and the fellow in the uniform suggested that we go somewhere else besides the hotel. I agreed so we got on a trolley, he paying our fares, and rode for a few blocks. When we got off, he took me across the street and turned into a shady courtyard. There didn't seem to be anyone around; we went inside the small office building and climbed to the second floor. Here we could hear people talking and laughing. He showed me into a small office, going off himself to fetch someone. I looked around. There was only a large desk, several chairs, and against the back wall a bookcase filled with census reports. Although I had seen no sign, this must have been some sort of neighborhood security station.

"A few minutes later my new friend came back in, bringing with him a man about ten years older than he was, in the same casual clothing and with a long crew cut. He seemed very relaxed, immediately sitting down and offering me tea and cigarettes. 'What happened?' he wanted to know. My friend nodded good-bye and left the room.

"I explained briefly what had taken place and who I was. While we talked, men and women would wander in from other offices, listen a while or leave something on the desk, and go out again. It was all very relaxed and cordial. My concern still was to explain why I had been taking the picture—for this man, though he didn't push the point, also seemed to feel it was unnecessary to take pictures of the remnants of old China. During all this, I felt my ability to speak Chinese deteriorating rapidly.

"While we were talking, someone must have made a phone call to the Nanking hotel to check on me. After all, I could hardly blame the young man who had invited me to come with him—foreigners are still a rare sight and especially foreigners who speak Chinese and try to strike up a conversation. In any case, the man sitting before me finally came to the end of his questions and our discussion, and suggested that if I didn't know the way back to the hotel he could take me. I did know the way, so I declined the offer and left, still feeling vaguely frustrated and unsure I had convinced anyone.

"On the way back, I met Dorothy and one of our guides who had come to find me after getting the phone call at the hotel. We talked briefly and came back—that was all."

So Frank outlined his story for us. We all talked for a while among ourselves and then asked our hosts what they thought. Both the CATT guides and our Nanking CATT office hosts apologized; they assured us that the government's policy was very open—we could take pictures of anything we wished. But they explained that since foreigners are still so rare, many of the people we met might not realize that there is any policy at all, much less such an open one. Their pride and suspicions were quite understandable, and our hosts hoped we would not take offense.

Lao Xi assured us that our personal security while on the streets was something we didn't have to worry about. Ray, who's lived in New York City, assured Lao Xi in turn that he had never felt more secure in the streets than on this trip to China. The people were extremely courteous and friendly.

We went on to talk with Lao Xi and our other Chinese friends about differences between the approaches in China and America to law and the police. Frank was struck by how informal the situation was at the "neighborhood security station." In China, the emphasis is clearly on public persuasion as the first means of mediating a dispute—arrests and trials are resorted to only when other attempts to negotiate have failed.

Traditionally, the Chinese views on law have been very different from our Western ideas. Face-to-face resolutions of differences have always been preferred to court decisions or trials, and this attitude has carried over into present-day China. Courts do exist, but they seem to handle primarily divorces and serious criminal cases. They do not devote much time or thought to petty traffic cases and damage suits, because these problems are solved in the community by neighborhood revolutionary committees.

There is no tradition in Chinese law of juridical decisions resting on previous cases of a similar nature, as in the American system of precedents. Instead, politics has long been and apparently still is accepted as a natural influence on the law. Chinese law and courts today, we were told, follow the "mass line," seeking to conform to an idea of justice that is both political and based on the community's opinions.

As it has in many other areas, the People's Liberation Army has been active on police forces since the Cultural Revolution. One reason for this army involvement in police duties, our guides said, was that before the Cultural Revolution the police were politically unreliable. Some of the police in the cities were close to local party bureaucrats and many were said to have opposed the Cultural Revolution. Thus one purpose in the PLA taking over police functions was to oust police in areas where they resisted the new movement for reform and to challenge established local bureaucrats. Now many policemen are PLA veterans. But with the role of the police more clearly defined, the PLA today exerts much less direct control.

As our discussion with the guides at the hotel ended, we mused about one important impression that had stayed with all of us throughout our visit in China. Our hosts had asked us if we felt comfortable on the streets. Certainly everyone had been friendly . . . we mentally compared the great difference between the streets of China and America. Here we really *were* safe to walk the streets at night or during the day. No one was going to mug us—and not just because we were foreigners, though that's hardly a protection for foreigners who visit the United States. Even Dorothy, who is Chinese, encountered no problems whatever, and we all noticed the freedom with which young bicyclists and families passed through the dark evening streets of China's cities.

Astronomy and Politics, Nanking

Before we left Nanking, we rode out to the Nanking Astronomical Observatory on a high hill above the city. Since our return to America there has been a great deal of interest in this visit, because the Hong Kong press described the observatory as a "satellite-tracking station." While it is true that one of the functions of the observatory is to track China's satellites, it is only a small part of the purpose of the observatory and definitely, in the eyes of the scientists we talked with there, not the most important part.

It was a relief to drive up into the hills outside Nanking that day. The city was sweltering under a fierce sun, and as we passed beyond the city wall we could almost feel the air grow cooler. For a while we wound gently up the wooded hillsides until we came out into a level area where six buildings stood apart from each other, partly hidden by the trees but identifiable by the domed tops rising above them.

We stopped in front of the most modern building, and several of the staff came out to greet us. On the grass in front of the observatory, and scattered over the lawns between it and the other buildings, were strange objects of bronze, iron, and steel. These were armillary spheres, astrolabes, and other reconstructions of ancient astronomical instruments. The largest one was a set of iron rings, each as tall as a man, set at angles inside each other, with dragons and other animals decorating it. It was based on a design from the Han dynasty (200 B.C. –200 A.D.). In the observatory itself, some of the staff took us through the lower rooms and then up to the top of the observatory, into a room nearly filled by a giant telescope. With great pride, the workers pointed out the factory label on the side of the telescope: "The Zujinshan telescope, made in China." We crowded in and tried looking into it, then followed the workers back downstairs. There we found that several of the astronomers had decided to take us to the People's Park to talk rather than remain in the observatory, where, it being Sunday, the staff had the day off.

Just before we reached the city gates, the bus turned off and followed the road a few yards before pulling into a parking area. We had arrived at the People's Park, a spectacularly beautiful, lush, and rambling park not far from the old city walls. There were ponds with man-made islands, arched bridges, streams crisscrossing the green lawns, and even a teahouse, where we sat down together to talk.

In the observatory our chief guide had been a middle-aged woman, described to us as one of the staff. For our talk in the park, we were with three of the research scientists, also middle-aged and very earnest in appearance. The Nanking Observatory is one of three schools of astronomy in China, they told us. The others are at Peking University and Peking Normal University. The one in Nanking is the old Qilu School, moved there from Shandong Province. There are also three other observatories in China, in Shanghai, Peking, and "the west"—being security sensitive, they preferred to leave the exact location vague.

We asked the scientists where they had been trained, referring to the belief, common in America, that all of China's science had been brought from the West since

1949. We mentioned Hsien Hsueh-shen, the scientist trained at California Institute of Technology who left America for China after Liberation, and the credit he had received in the United States for much of China's achievements. The question was obviously one with which they were familiar, and although they answered us quietly and well, they were as incensed as one could expect a polite Chinese to be.

"All of us have been trained in China. We are from Qilu, and he is from Nanking University," said the scientist on our left, a tall thin man with thinning hair. "None of us were taught by foreigners. At Qilu we had no foreign-trained teachers at all. At Nanking, there was only one, trained in the Soviet Union." They went on to explain that modern science is far too complex for any one man, or small group of individuals, to be the source of knowledge and innovation. Scientific advances demand cooperative action with other related departments, and with a wide range of scientists and workers, all of whom reject the domination of the field by "important persons."

Before 1949, the observatory had been rather small. Now it is one of the largest in China, and in addition to carrying on research it has produced a number of innovations in technique and equipment. Earlier, the common practice had been for the scientific staff to design the materials they needed and then give these plans to the production staff for completion. Now the people of the observatory work together. They have found that if the scientific staff explains to the production workers exactly what they hope to achieve and what they need from the equipment, the workers will be able to create the designs themselves and often do a better job of it. In one case we were told about, they made a significant improvement in the design of an instrument after rejecting the overly complex design done by the scientific staff.

How far does this practice go, we asked. Does this method cover your research plans as well? There are channels in two directions on the planning of observatory projects. No individual research is done. "We feel that the worth of any individual—no matter how clever—is limited," they said. "For instance, during the eclipse of the sun in 1968, the scientists wanted to observe this in

Sinkiang Province far to the west. But the single observatory they first planned to use could not do everything necessary alone. Instead, amateurs, the People's Liberation Army, and other scientific personnel in the area planned the undertaking together, and it was a success. In accordance with this principle, all our research plans are discussed by the group as a whole and decided upon. Then we divide up the labor involved, each taking a share. Part of these plans are submitted to us from the planning bodies higher up, and part of them are projects which we have devised and proposed to them." We asked who the scientists of the observatory are responsible to, and were told that the chief administrative and planning organ is the Academy of Sciences, the Kexueyuan.

Their answers to some questions were cryptic. We asked them about China's satellites. Why spend money on them when China needs all its resources? "The purposes [of the satellites] are in line with the needs of the people." On other topics, however, they were very willing to answer our questions in as much detail as we requested. Do they undertake "pure" research as well as that with practical applications? Yes, they are engaged at present in the investigation of solar explosions and their effect on radio and geophysics. Before the Cultural Revolution, this research had gone on, but official policy had tended to discourage it on the basis of the failure of other scientists in the world to solve the problems. This kind of policy, which looks to the West to see what is possible and does not try to push ahead, is what is commonly referred to as the "Liuist line" in science (associated with Liu Shao-ch'i). It is also called "lagging behind at a snail's pace," a very graphic picture of the frustration many of China's scientific workers felt under these restrictions. At the time of the early Cultural Revolution, the young graduates of the scientific departments and research institutes called this the "comprador mentality," comparing it to the servile attitudes of the Chinese who collaborated with Western imperialists before 1949. The Liuists were accused of believing that what foreigners have not done, the Chinese can't possibly do; and being unwilling—for fear of loss of reputation—to try to solve difficult problems. Obviously, China's advances in science did not all begin after the Cultural Revolution. But the spirit of these challenges found a target, for the scientists themselves feel that their work, and China's science, has improved with this new attitude.

At the Nanking Observatory we asked as usual about the wage scale, and here we were given the highest figure for an individual wage we heard of in China. The monthly salary for the chief astronomer of the observatory, who had been an astronomer forty years ago and who also works as a professor at Nanking University, is 330 yuan (about $130). Of course we asked about the wages for the others, both scientists and workers. In all, there are a total of 230 people employed by the observatory. Of these 30 percent are women; the average wage for the entire group of employees is 60 yuan a month. We questioned the men sitting with us more closely about themselves.

The first to answer was the most highly paid, 130 yuan a month. He looked like a character from one of the Chinese heroic posters, with a slight five o'clock shadow to make him real. He is the son of a poor peasant, and a member of the revolutionary committee of the observatory. The other scientist from a poor peasant class background was also a man in his forties. He wore glasses and talked very proudly about his five children. It obviously meant a great deal to him, especially with his background, that all his children were in school, and he emphasized this point. He earns 70 yuan a month and is also on the revolutionary committee. The last to speak was the balding man who had earlier answered the charge about science imported from the West; he makes 100 yuan monthly. He is not of peasant background—his family were landlords before 1949—and he can speak some English; he is not a member of the revolutionary committee, but is a party member. Frank asked what the policy was with regard to party membership and class background. Could a landlord easily be a party member? "Sure," said the man wearing glasses, "it all depends on his thinking and attitude toward the people."

The high salary of the observatory's chief astronomer is an interesting extreme of a phenomenon we found everywhere in China: seniority multiplies wages fantastically.

Often we would discover that the salary of an old, barely literate factory worker was higher than the salary of his factory manager. In response to our surprise at the particularly generous wages paid the chief astronomer, his fellow scientists said that it was simply in proportion to his work for the nation. He had worked energetically for forty years, and his contribution to the country's progress could not be measured easily in money terms. But they all seemed quite genuinely to feel that it was justified, and equitable in proportion to their own salaries.

All of the employees of the observatory, scientists and workers alike, spend one to one-and-a-half months each year in the fields doing manual labor. The times of these work periods are arranged to coincide with harvesttime, and there is no pretense that the work being done is related directly or even partly to scientific research. Nevertheless, the three men talking with us said that they felt there had been major changes at the observatory because of this policy. The case they offered in point was that of the woman who had shown us around the observatory when we first arrived. When she came to work here, they said, she was only a middle-school graduate, and simply carried out time measurements as she was told. Now, because of their own experience, both in the observatory—with innovations introduced by the production workers—and in the fields—because of the tremendous spirit of self-reliance, they had become convinced that "reliance on the masses" was a good policy and she had been given increasing responsibility. Now she conducts her own research on methods of time measurement, and they said they were all proud of her accomplishments.

By now the day was nearly over, and the people leaving the park formed a steady flow of children, families, and young couples. The roller-skating rink was almost empty and all the rowboats were off the lake. We walked slowly to our bus and said good-bye. From there we went to the hotel, and on to the train station where we boarded the "little blue car," an overnight sleeper which seemed to accompany us everywhere in China. We were on our way to Peking!

As our train pulled out of the station and headed

for the river, we realized that we would be crossing the Yangtze River Bridge in just a few minutes. Out came our cameras, up went the windows, and we all hung out, squinting into the setting sun and shooting backward at Nanking. The river is wide, like the Mississippi in some parts, and the ride across was breathtaking. Then, coming off the bridge, we began to roll northward through rice paddies. The first major station we reached was Chuxien, and Frank began taking pictures in great number. This was the same town his adviser at Columbia had done research in before 1949. Again we realized how lucky we were. . . .

Day became night and the train pushed on, stopping very rarely. About ten or eleven that night it did stop briefly at what seemed to be a small station. Everyone piled out of the train, though, so we did too. Up near the front of the train, against the wall of the station, there were long lines of sinks and faucets. Each passenger carried his own soap and hand towel, and waited patiently for his turn to wash up. With some difficulty we refused first place in line, and waited our turn. The water was freezing and after a few splashes we began to walk back toward our car at the rear of the train. A young man walking next to us began to ask us about our trip, and we talked for a while with his small son, a very bold and happy boy two or three years old. Then, as always, a crowd began to gather. The boy suddenly, seeing all the people, began to cry. His father shushed him and smiled apologetically, and we assured him we had learned by then not to be too embarrassed at the reactions we got from children.

Back on the train, we fell asleep. When we woke up we were in the north of China—an entirely different terrain and color from the south we had left behind us. Rain swept down from a low sky, and instead of rice, the fields were full of corn. Soon we reached Tientsin, the industrial port city for Peking. It was morning rush hour as we passed through the outskirts of town, and at the crossings swarms of bicyclers waited for us to go by, or pedaled under the underpasses. From Tientsin it was only a short ride to Peking.

Peking

The train came into Peking's East Station. As we climbed down from the "little blue car" onto the platform, we must have seemed dazed, a little distracted. Finally, after years of reading about Peking, talking about Peking, dreaming of it, we were here!

From the station our bus turned west, toward the center of the city. Peking—the older part, at least—is a giant square, and the heart of it is Tiananmen Square, the Gate of Heavenly Peace. Our bus passed by the edge of the square and then turned south; our hotel, the Xinqiao, was only about ten minutes from Tiananmen. The Xinqiao is a huge old building, and well known to foreigners, for this is where most visiting diplomats, newsmen, and guests are housed. During our stay there we met Eastern Europeans, Cubans, Swedes, Canadians, Swiss, Vietnamese, and whole Japanese families, their children tricycling back and forth in front of the hotel. One Italian couple was living there permanently with their three small children; the children had the run of the hotel and used it to good advantage.

Our first afternoon was spent wandering around the Tiananmen area and then on an extensive tour of the Summer Palace. Here the subject of the old society came up again. Our guides told us that before Liberation the Summer Palace was almost never visited by the people of the city because transportation was difficult and the price of admission was relatively high. Now excellent transportation has been provided and the admission charge is five fen (about two cents U.S.), a part of the idea that the city should belong to all the people in it, they said. We asked how they felt, seeing the huge marble boat which the empress dowager had built with money earmarked for fighting the Western invaders. The answer was very much like that of some blacks in America—yes, the Chinese people were exploited, but all the same it was Chinese work, and without the people it would not have existed; it was they who built the country.

After a day at Peking University, we left the city, but returned a week later. This time we stayed longer, and had an opportunity to visit the February 7 Rolling Stock Plant. This factory has a very long history, and is discussed in detail in chapter 6. But while we were there, we also were taken to see the housing built on the grounds for the workers, part of a great change taking place in the city of Peking. The February 7 Rolling Stock Plant is essentially a self-sufficient unit; it combines both industry and agriculture in productive work and has integrated housing, schools, factory, health centers, and farming into one area. The rolling-stock factory itself employs some nine thousand workers. In addition to that, however, there are several subsidiary factories worked mainly by the dependents of those who work in the rolling-stock factory, or by workers retired from the heavier labor there.

As we drove out to the factory, there were no visual clashes between the urban, suburban, and semirural areas. Unlike Shanghai, Peking was not heavily industrialized before 1949, and the city planners were largely able to realize the goal of housing workers next to their factories, especially in the southeastern section of the city, where most of the factories have been built in the post-Liberation period. Of the two kinds of new housing, workers' villages and factory-grounds housing, the first is slightly closer to the center of the city on the southeastern side, and the factory housing complexes are set further out in the same direction.

The rolling-stock factory was about a half-hour drive from our hotel. The area it occupies is very large. Unfortunately we did not get any statistics for the actual total. The main factory is surrounded by a number of subsidiary factories and cottage-type industries. These secondary production units are important, not only to ensure that all materials are used thoroughly (that is also handled by selling scraps to other factories), but also to provide work for the residents of the complex who are not employed in the main factory. In this way the factory complex is seen as much more desirable than the workers' villages, where residents do not live close by their work.

The factory owns a large amount of farmland, also worked by residents of the complex. There is apparently some degree of supervision by experienced peasants and most of the work is done by the factory workers' dependents. The factory itself is state-owned, but the subsidiary factories and farmlands are collectively owned. That is, they are owned not by the state, but by the factory workers and their families. These subsidiary factories receive a small investment of capital from the state, through the rolling-stock factory, but mostly operate by utilizing waste materials from the factory. We saw them using waste metal to produce links and chains, and they were working with the wood of the old railroad boxcars as well.

This type of complex is the direction Peking's industrialization will take, to the extent that it develops within its urban areas. There is also an immense amount of industrialization taking place in the countryside, with the eventual goal of creating a network of partly or wholly self-sufficient units across the countryside. But this has not always been the goal. China's thinking about cities and industrialization has gone through several stages.

In the Streets and Alleys of Peking

We spent more time in Peking than in any other city, and every day we went exploring. Sometimes, when we had a few hours, we would take buses to other parts of the city. More often we stayed within walking distance of our hotel. The sounds of Peking are a cacophony of horns honking: truck horns, bus horns, and bicycle horns, with bicycle bells ringing shrilly above them. There is almost never a real traffic jam, but the closest thing to it, congestion during rush hour, is the result of streams of bicycles, not of cars. The buses are full almost all day, but run so frequently we almost never saw long lines at the stops.

All along the streets are vegetable markets, fruit piled high on the wide sidewalks, with baskets of apples and tomatoes and small heaps of coal for sale. One day we decided to price the food in a large market and found immediately a great difference from Hong Kong and other Asian cities: no bargaining! Standard prices are marked plainly, and the market workers weighed everything scrupulously. All of the stores, even the smallest sidewalk stands, were impeccably clean. Everywhere there were great heaps of vegetables, barrels of rice and flour, chickens and ducks (with their feet still attached—the feet are the best part, the Chinese say!), sides of pork and beef, and boxes of fresh garlic, mushrooms, and beans. Prices are measured in fen per catty (where 5 fen = 2 cents U.S. and 1 catty = about 1⅓ pounds).

At the fish seller's we saw the widest price ranges—here the most common fish were only 27 fen per catty (about 8 cents U.S. per pound), and the very best delicacies were 86 fen per catty. Chicken, by comparison, ranged from 66 fen to 1 yuan (40 cents U.S.) per catty, and pork from 71 to 95 fen per catty. Eggs were 90, beans 8½, plums 18, peaches 24, and watermelon 3 fen per catty. Tomatoes were less than 1 fen per catty. There were only three rationed goods: blue cotton cloth, of which each person may buy 6 yards a year; rice, which is rationed according to the work done (a worker in heavy industry may buy 50 catties a month; a baby is allotted 9). We asked why these goods were rationed, and some of the older Chinese we spoke with said that the rationing was not so much to limit consumption as it was to prevent hoarding. Traditionally, they said, because of the frequent famines and the great poverty, the custom was to hoard as much as one could buy as insurance against future disasters. Now that is not necessary, but some people might still want to, and this way everyone can have an equal amount without depleting the amount available.

Life in Peking is less sophisticated than in Shanghai, according to Chinese stories. Certainly it shuts down earlier. We found everything closed tight at nine thirty each night, and even the families were inside, not sitting out in front of their homes. It is a northern city, and in the summer it bakes in the heat until the ground becomes a fine layer of dusty earth. The trees planted since Liberation have helped to hold down the dust and prevent the great winds from sweeping through the city. There are limits now on the number of people allowed to move to Peking each year, in an attempt to hold down the population. Our first day we noticed small four-by-six-inch handbills on many of the lampposts. Dorothy investigated and announced that they were requests for a special kind of exchange—the people writing the handbills had obtained permission to transfer jobs and would like to trade jobs with someone in Peking.

Often small groups of people would pass us walking in files, two by two. Many of them were either very old or very young; and each group was led by someone of the appropriate age. The older people were usually on an outing, going to see a cultural performance in one of the city's halls, and the children were usually on their way to school. Their school playgrounds were wonderful. In Peking's Tiantan Park they had the most innovative play equipment we had ever seen. There were jungle gyms which gave three or four alternative means of going up and down; ropes, ladders, chinning bars, and other ways to get up; and firemen's poles, chutes, and slides for the trip down.

As we had in Shanghai and other cities, we asked about the pre-Liberation slums of Peking. Again, Peking turned out to be very different from Shanghai. There were no squatter settlements. Frank speculated that this might be because of the climate (winter in Peking is bitter cold, and in Shanghai is merely uncomfortable). Because it was not heavily industrialized, there had not been the sudden influx of workers before 1949 either, although it was already a large city of 1,800,000 people. The slums of Peking had been built of brick, and were solid structures. They were slums because of the lack of water, latrines, sewage disposal, lighting, or heat, and because of severe overcrowding.

Today some of that has been torn down, either because it had been built in low-lying areas, where dampness and occasional flooding was a problem, or because the buildings were no longer structurally sound. We asked to see one of these areas, they told us where it was, and the next day we went on our own for a look at the Goldfish Pond. This area had been famous before Liberation as one of the worst slums in Peking, with no running water, electricity, or hospital. Then it was called Dragon-Beard Ditch. Today the area has changed as much as its name. The older houses, made of the typical blackish brick of Peking, stood one or one-and-a-half stories high along the narrow streets and alleys. They had obviously been cleaned and restored, and now vines grew up over the doorways of many of them. Beside the older housing still standing, new housing had been built for the residents of torn-down buildings. These units were generally four stories high, and they were set much closer together than housing in the rest of the city. The whole area was swept clean and looked well kept, but it definitely was not of the same quality as the workers' villages or the factory complexes. Nevertheless, it was still a distinct improvement over most of the slum housing we had known in Hong Kong. Frank had lived in the squatter settlements of Hong Kong while he conducted his research, so he was well prepared to make the comparison. Most impressive to him was the absence of open sewers. Throughout Asia open sewers breed disease, foul the air, and are an ever-present danger to children playing nearby. Even Tokyo has only recently finished closing over the great part of its sewers, and this is a major aspect of sanitation work. In addition, there were fresh-water spigots placed frequently along the streets and clean concrete and brick public latrines (again, in profusion compared to Hong Kong).

Goldfish Pond, in addition to the new and renovated housing, also has a theater, a workers' club, a stadium, and a hospital. Yet it exists as a temporary solution, an improvement over the past waiting for a better future. Even in the workers' villages and factory complexes, it was obvious that housing in China is still tight. It is better than in Hong Kong and many Asian cities, but it is not yet what either the Chinese—or we—would consider a problem solved.

A Conversation in Peking

Four days before we left China, five of us spent an evening talking with Wang Yijen and Qian Ming, two of Peking's city planners. We had asked particularly for this opportunity because of the questions we still had about urban planning. Our interest had been stimulated not only by what we had seen, but by some intriguing comments our China Travel Service interpreters and guides had made as well. One of them, a young man in his thirties, had questioned us about our description of city planning in Hong Kong and the United States, and the difficulties of carrying out plans. He said, "Why are you concerned about these things? You must have political power first, and no piecemeal, secondary approach will cure the symptoms." We had also been told of the garden plots given the China Travel Service staff to maintain. It allowed them to be nearly self-sufficient in fresh vegetables, and they beamed with pride in their accomplishments.

Wang Yijen and Qian Ming came to a reception room in our hotel and we sat in a small circle with tea before us. Wang, a smiling, round, and very relaxed man, did most of the talking, smoking a lot, making us relax, too. But as Uldis said later, he did know what he was talking about—he came very well prepared and went systematically through a great deal of material. In contrast, Qian was quiet, mild, slightly built, and a little shy. Wang, fifty, and Qian, forty, are "responsible people" from the city planning management group of Peking's highest political organ, the Peking municipal revolutionary committee.

The people of Peking had a saying about the city, referring to its unpaved roads and absence of trees, "In rainy weather, [muddy] like a Chinese inkstand; in windy weather, [dusty] like an incense burner." This was Peking in the old days, before Liberation, Wang told us. Peking was a consumer city. By this they meant that Peking took from the countryside but produced nothing for it in return. There was some handicraft industry, but its machine industry could only repair, not produce, and new machines had to be imported from foreign countries: the iron smelting plant couldn't smelt steel. The city was industrially backward. Splendid urban facilities served the ruling class—and were concentrated where they lived—while the vast majority of the people lived in the lower areas, damp and susceptible to flash flooding.

With Liberation many of these aspects of the old semifeudal, semicolonial society were swept away, including some 200,000 tons of garbage—some of it dating from the Ming dynasty. Mao Tse-tung asked the question, "Whom do we serve?" The answer of course was, "The people." In urban planning the slogan became, "Facilitate production; facilitate the livelihood of the people." What this meant in practical terms is that priorities in urban development, in a city such as Peking, fell into three categories: the construction of government offices, the building of productive facilities such as factories and work shops, and the creation of residential areas, with workers' housing, schools, nurseries, hospitals, and markets.

The first step was to get the production that had existed running again, and to end the runaway inflation induced by the Kuomintang fiscal policy. Only when that problem was solved could the Communist party consolidate political power in the cities. And only then could the cities be changed from consumers to producers. For the ability to plan for any society depends upon political power.

Production was restored and developed. Peking's industry diversified, and the city became a center of production. The Shijingshan complex, for example, has become a major producer of both iron and high-quality steel. Development was rapid, and now Peking has metallurgy, machine, computer, construction, instrumentation, textile, chemical, and many light industries.

The planners allotted space in the eastern sector of the city for the construction of these new factories. This move was calculated with the environment in mind; for the east is leeward of the prevailing winds and downstream of Peking's waterways. In the large suburban factories, dependents of workers ran good-sized farms to supply their own agricultural needs. As the city expanded, the planners continued to preserve cultivated suburban land that had high vegetable yield, and in this way they assured the city of a readily accessible fresh vegetable supply, a matter of very great importance to the Chinese. In turn, the city provided manure and electricity for the suburban and rural areas.

The problem of industrial pollution was attacked not from the perspective of aesthetics, nor even from a concern for health—pollution in China is still quite rare— but out of a socialist concern for "comprehensively utilizing the three wastes—waste water, gas, and dregs—changing the harmful into useful, waste into treasure."

Wang told us of a Peking pharmaceutical factory whose waste water polluted an adjacent river, thus influencing irrigation and preventing use of the river water by factories downstream. The leadership of the offending factory organized the people to extract chemicals such as phosphates and potassium chloride from the waste, and obtained three thousand tons of useful products each year, improving the river and saving money at the same time.

While this was going on near the city's growing edge, things were happening in the city proper. Peking's population expanded from 1,800,000 in 1949 to 4,000,000 in 1966–67. Roads were being paved, trees planted, and housing built. We were provided statistics on each:

Between 1949 and 1970 the surface of paved roads went from about 250,000 square yards to 1,400,000, an increase of 460 percent. Buses and trolley buses on those roads increased from 164 in 1949 to over 2,000 by 1971.

Responding to Mao's call to make the whole country green, some 500,000–600,000 new trees have been planted every year in Peking and environs. There are now 20,000,000 trees—and it was the "broad masses" of Peking rather than a municipal department who were largely responsible for them, actively participating in the tree planting program twice each year. The professional department handled only the public gardens and the nurture of saplings. The city's inhabitants care for the rest.

This program has also greatly diminished the effects of one of Peking's most serious natural problems, the constant dust storms which blow in from the desert areas to the north. We were told that the great quantity of trees has even changed the climate of Peking, making it several degrees cooler in the summer.

Again, all is not limited to aesthetics; large numbers of pepper, walnut, and apple trees have been planted so that Peking is now self-sufficient in apples, which before 1949 had all been imported from distant Shandong and Liaoning provinces.

Tremendous efforts have been made to house adequately all of the people of Peking. In pre-Liberation Peking the total floor space of all buildings was 20 million square yards. Since then, another 50 million square yards have been built, including 22 million square yards of living quarters. As monumental as these construction efforts have been, they could not keep pace with immigration and natural population increase in the city. People were living better. The new housing had electricity, running water, sometimes even gas; old housing was electrified and public latrines and bathhouses were supplied. But before the Cultural Revolution, housing density was rising. Wang attributed this growth in urban population to the influence of the "Liu Shao-ch'i line"—that sector of the planning bureaucracies which had tended to imitate Western, and capitalist, solutions to China's problems. The "best" of intellectual, cultural, medical, and industrial life had gravitated to the cities, and the "three great differences" were becoming greater every year. This form of development was fine with the planners following Liu's line; but those supporting Mao looked upon it differently.

In Peking, the north and northwestern suburbs had been given over to universities and institutes such as Peking University and Peking Medical College. As Qian explained it, this concentration of institutes had two drawbacks. First, it separated intellectuals from the working people. Second, it was not conducive to the integration of education with productive labor. And certain institutes, those concerned with mining or agronomy for instance, had no business being in the city at all.

After the Cultural Revolution, things began to change. Mining schools were moved to mining areas where students and faculty could combine theory and practice and work together in productive labor, learn from the mine workers, and provide them with theoretical knowledge.

For those institutes that did not move from Peking, factories and farms were started right on campus. We had earlier seen a student-staff-built pharmaceutical factory on the Peking University campus. Several days later we saw farmlands within the Tsinghua University campus. Here again, the idea was to integrate theory with practice and to strive for self-sufficiency. Peking University sold the insulin and antibiotics it produced as would any other state enterprise; Tsinghua consumed its own vegetables.

It was the planners' opinion that Peking University had entirely too much space, even with factory and farm. This they attributed in part to the work style of previous designers. Before the Cultural Revolution they were separated from the people. They did their designing in their offices but rarely went out to participate in the implementation of their designs.

They did not specifically make the point in this context, but the planners might have added that the post-Cultural Revolution institution of May 7 cadre schools, such as the one we visited in the eastern suburbs of Peking, was geared to just such problems of armchair designers. These half-work, half-study schools for urban leaders, bureaucrats, and teachers are built from scratch on suburban or rural wastelands. The cadre engage in basic agricultural or industrial labor. The "school" becomes economically self-sufficient in a relatively short while. The cadre reexperience the value of physical labor. When they return six months later to their white-collar jobs in the city, the cadres—and any designers among them—have a thoroughly renewed sense of the pragmatic and utilitarian.

What the May 7 schools do for cadres, Mao's call, "There's a vast horizon in the countryside," does for urban middle-school graduates ("intellectual youth"). The reason that Peking's population has hovered around four million ever since the start of the Cultural Revolution four years ago is that many of Peking's youth—those in their late teens—have gone to settle down in rural and border areas. That reduces the urban population and its strain on facilities, while infusing the communes with "cultural delegates"—intellectual youth bringing their educations to leaven the countryside.

There was still another parallel in health care. Urban hospitals such as the Peking Hospital no. 3 attached to the Peking Medical School might have their staffs reduced by as much as one-third, in order to free medical personnel for roles in field hospitals that rove the countryside providing medical care in isolated areas. At an even more basic level, educated youth, sometimes from the city, will be given training as medics and then live in communes as "barefoot doctors" serving the day-to-day, but very real, health needs of the peasants.

It is not that China's cities have been abandoned. On the contrary, Wang and Qian noted with pride how hospitals, schools, and theaters had been designed for and built in districts of Peking that previously had had none. More specifically, Mr. Wang cited the example of old Peking's most notorious slum, Dragon-Beard Ditch. These were districts which the ruling class of pre-Liberation days never set foot in or cared about; districts that housed most of Peking's laboring people. But now the ruling class are the laboring people and the Great Proletarian Cultural Revolution has confirmed their rule.

As the two planners explained, "Due to our socialist system, we work not for profit but for the benefit of the people. This is our advantage."

5. COMMUNES

Chapter 1 describes the meagerness and poverty of village life in old China. Harvest failures, floods, dynastic wars, and uprisings all meant disaster for the villagers, and famines took millions of lives. But in the years since Liberation sweeping changes have transformed the countryside. Now, even in hard years, everyone eats.

The people of China say they have done in twenty years what two thousand years of emperors and feudal landlords could not accomplish. How? Is this really true? What is a commune like? Has progress been made because of, or in spite of, the communes? Eagerly, we leaned forward in our seats, staring out the windows of our bus as we drove into Huadong Commune. It was our first full day in China, and we had come to see for ourselves . . .

We visited parts of five communes. The first was Huadong Commune in a rice-growing area north of Canton. This was the largest commune we saw, with a population of 56,390 people living on 48,000 acres, of which 71,110 mu (about 12,000 acres) were cultivated. The second was Hongqiao (Rainbow Bridge) Commune, which produces vegetables for China's largest city, Shanghai; here 26,649 people worked 32,000 acres. The third was Tachai Commune, where we visited both the Tachai Brigade (438 people, 796 mu of cultivated land) and the Houjuang Brigade (500 people, 800 mu of cultivated land). In the same area—the dry hills of Shanxi—we spent a morning at the Xigubi Brigade of Jiedu Commune, an area of 1,100 mu worked by 640 people. The last, Liulin Brigade, was in China's northwest near Yenan, onetime center of the revolution and the war against Japan. In this rugged part of China, 770 people tilled

2,618 mu of land. Each of these five communes was different. Yet we came away with the feeling that in the most basic changes they had experienced, they were also very similar.

Huadong: What Is a Commune?

As we climbed down off the bus, a wiry young man walked up. Like everyone else we could see, he wore trousers and a simple short-sleeved white shirt, with plastic sandals on his feet. Under a rough crew cut, his face was tanned, lined and wreathed in smiles. He pumped our hands enthusiastically and introduced himself: this was the head of the commune revolutionary committee, Comrade Xu. He seemed to be in his mid-thirties, and we looked around, curiously, at the others present. Here was a great change already, for in old China men in important positions were always aged, and a leader of fifty or sixty years was considered young. We followed Comrade Xu into the main meeting hall of the commune where we would receive a short briefing.

Comrade Xu began to describe the Huadong area before 1949. He talked of the plagues of drought, pests, and typhoons, and quoted an old Cantonese saying, "Three days of drought stops the waterwheel; one day of rain begins a flood." Here, 80 percent of the land had been subject to drought and 20 percent to flooding. Sixty-nine percent of the land had been owned by 4 percent of the people. Natural disasters could be survived only by borrowing from the landlords at usurious rates, and there had been much begging, selling of children, and emigration abroad.

The process of transformation began in 1949 with land reform. In each village, families were classified according to their economic position. The landlord family lived off rent and taxes exacted from others; the rich peasant family worked, but also hired help; the middle peasant worked all his own land; the poor peasant worked for others. Using this classification, the landlords' land, draft animals, farm implements, surplus grain, and houses were distributed among the poor and landless. Criminal landlords were executed, but by far the majority stayed on to work in greatly reduced circumstances. At Huadong Commune approximately seven hundred landlords remain. About half are considered "reformed" now and have been given full commune member status. The other half are still considered "recalcitrant" and are carefully supervised. We also asked about this at Hongqiao Commune neaɪ Shanghai and were told that of forty former landlords twenty had been successfully reeducated and were therefore "reclassed." There undoubtedly were many excesses in the heat of the land-reform fervor, but these appear to have been held down by the efforts of the local Communist party leaders and by the satisfaction the people found in carrying out the long-wished-for revolution in land tenure.

The problem of feeding a growing population on limited arable land was immense. It soon became obvious that with land alone many of the peasants still could not make an adequate living. They lacked tools, animals, and money to invest. In the West, family farms have gradually disappeared, to be replaced by huge "agribusiness" enterprises. In China the same logic of combining land and pooling resources lay behind the collectivization of agriculture, but with one important difference. Instead of being gradually squeezed out, the families join together and are all owners of the larger farm. This road to collectivization was marked by several stages. The first step, *mutual-aid teams,* meant limited sharing of manpower, tools, and animals. By 1956 nearly all areas had put *cooperatives* into effect. Land was still held privately, but was worked cooperatively, and profits paid out in shares. In the *collective farms* which followed, the land itself was owned by the people in common rather than individually. By 1958 collective farms were being amalgamated into the *communes,* physically larger and with even greater administrative integration.

The communes as originally set up in 1958 were unworkable. The people, having witnessed the benefits of increasing degrees of collectivization in the past, enthusiastically followed the original directive from Mao, and diligent Communist party cadres encouraged them. Almost overnight, new administrative—and sometimes physical—structures blossomed. But the people, and the party, soon learned that while the commune might be the right-size unit for some responsibilities, it was not for others. For example the communes were effective units for planning and organizing water-control projects, building schools, and taking in the harvest. But they were much too large to handle the daily details of agricultural production and sometimes tended to multiply red tape without equivalent increases in productivity. Because of this, a reorganization evolved over the following three years which resulted in a three-level system. This three-tier organization remains today.

The *production team* is the smallest unit, consisting of about thirty families. The team leadership is responsible for the day-to-day planning of farming and for distribution of profits. It appears to be the real social unit—people who live close to each other, and indeed are often related to each other. The *production brigade* contains several teams, and organizes land for special use, such as planting of trees. It may also provide facilities for grinding and storage of grain, and for transportation. The *commune* includes ten to thirty production brigades and primarily concerns itself with overall planning: small factories, registration of births, deaths, marriages, and education and health services. It serves as a link between the small natural village groupings and the larger county and provincial administrations.

We have heard Americans ask, "Do Chinese still live in villages?" The answer is very much, "Yes!" The Chinese peasant still works primarily within the confines of his village, as he has always done. He will also work on larger projects, such as flood control and irrigation. The commune plays an important role in these tasks which require large-scale planning and effort, encouraging efficiency and self-reliance and freeing labor time for industrial production. But the Chinese village does live on, if in a transformed way.

What has changed? A great deal—now there is plenty of food, warm clothes, and electricity, sanitation, education, health care for all. But more than that, the basic spirit of the villages has changed—for the people of Huadong know that these changes are their own work, and that self-reliance will bring them even greater improvement in the future.

After our briefing with Comrade Xu, he and several other commune leaders suggested that we ride out on our bus to look at the new hydroelectric station on the river. This station is a part of the huge network of irrigation and flood control he had shown us on maps in the meeting hall—it has all been built as a cooperative project by Huadong with two other neighboring communes. Now there are three large dams, each with its own small hydroelectric station serving a part of the total area.

As we rode through the rice paddies, we noticed on one side that the rice shoots had been replaced by another plant growing close to the ground. These were peanut plants—another aspect of Huadong's program of self-reliance. For peanut oil is a basic cooking ingredient in Chinese cuisine, and by supplying their own oil to the homes of the villagers, the commune avoids spending money in town. Later we ate litchis off trees in their orchards, planted with the same goal of self-sufficiency; and for lunch that day we had a magnificent meal cooked entirely of produce grown or raised at Huadong . . . great varieties of vegetables, heaps of fruit, dishes of pork and beef and fish from a hatchery they have started. We were also told that the commune now grows winter wheat. This seemed a strange crop for hot and humid Guangdong Province. But the commune members explained to us that several years earlier they had begun to plant small quantities of the wheat, and that when a bad series of typhoons hit them two years ago—destroying their rice harvest—it was the winter wheat that saved them; in fact, they had been able to plant enough in the aftermath of the storm to more than equal their expected grain harvest.

We were surprised to find out that Huadong also has a coal mine, worked by the commune members and supplying them with fuel for their kitchen stoves and for sale to the railroads. We did not visit the mine, but it was obvious that on this huge commune a great deal was going on, all designed to make Huadong far more than a simple rice-producing agricultural unit.

Coming back from the river, we stopped to look at

the machine-tool industry recently developed at Huadong. Here expansion had come directly as a result of the Cultural Revolution. The villagers had for many years had a tool-repair shop employing ten or twelve men; but when news of the Cultural Revolution reached them, with its stress on self-reliance and moving industry to the countryside, the people of Huadong decided they could participate too. Further workshops were made out of converted farm buildings (the ones we saw were square brick buildings, with large windows for good lighting and packed-dirt floors). Designs for a common form of hand-powered threshing machine were reworked until the commune members felt they had achieved the best plan, and blowtorches, lathes, and metal-working tools were bought or more often constructed right in the shops. By the time we visited Huadong, these original workshops had increased in number until now there are three large clusters of workshops, each with more than one hundred workers; the threshing machines are supplied to all the commune villages and also sold on a limited scale to neighboring communes.

During the Cultural Revolution there was another injunction which Huadong acted upon: waste nothing, use all. This became the basis of one of the most fascinating small-scale industries we saw in China—the processing of cassava plants. The plant roots are used in several stages. First, they are ground and used to produce a type of starch for cooking very much like cornstarch. The residue of this process is then further treated to produce chemicals for industrial use. Finally, the residue of that process becomes fodder for the livestock (mainly pigs) of the commune. We were impressed. But that was not all—the leaves, too, are used. Huadong has developed a breed of silkworm which will eat cassava leaves instead of mulberry leaves!

Despite all of this, Huadong is not entirely self-sufficient yet. And although the improvements in village life were immediately striking—especially in comparison with what we knew of pre-Liberation conditions—Huadong was still one of the poorer communes we saw. At one point as we walked through a village on the commune, Ken, Ann, and some of the other members of our delegation were invited into one of the houses. This, like the other homes of Huadong, was a simple construction of gray-black brick with a high-pitched tile roof. Because it was not whitewashed inside, the color of the brick and few windows made the four large rooms inside very dark. The furniture was roughly made of wood, just a few stools and benches and a small table in the main room. On the walls were bright posters of the revolutionary operas. In front of the door outside was a small low brick enclosure, like a tiny courtyard, with a well in the center. Beyond the house we could see the common latrine which this family used with several others; it was a simple brick building with separate doors for men and women. Most of the family were out in the fields, but the grandparents were there, dressed in the traditional black silk "pajamas" of China's peasantry. Wizened and bent with age, the grandmother smiled and poured hot water for us as we looked around. She began to explain to us where her family had gone—but this was a back-country accent of the Cantonese dialect, and even Rhea, who understands Cantonese, was having problems understanding her. We turned to ask Lao Shi for help, and then realized that our four companions were very embarrassed—they were having trouble understanding too! Only one of them spoke Cantonese well, and he was slowly repeating her comments in "standard" Cantonese, then translating into the national language; a laborious process. We realized how difficult it must be for those who visit China not knowing any Chinese!

At Tachai: The New Men and Women of China

Mao Tse-tung believes that economic progress in China's countryside depends on change in the values of her peasants. China is trying to move from socialism, where each receives according to his work, to communism, where each receives according to his needs and gives according to his ability. Communism will demand a much greater productivity and desire to work for society. This necessary new man is one who struggles to overcome all difficulties and takes initiative boldly. He is ready to give his all, taking only what he really needs. The Chinese say they can approximate these values only by studying the writings of Mao Tse-tung and trying to apply them in their daily lives.

Nowhere did we see this spirit as clearly as in the nationally famous Tachai Production Brigade. Tachai has served as a "model village" since 1964. All over China there are signs urging, "Learn from Tachai!" What has happened there, to make this out-of-the-way Shanxi village a model for emulation by the whole rural population? Who are the Tachai people? What have they done?

Our overnight train headed west from Peking through sunset and then into darkness . . . nine hours later, just as the sun was rising, we arrived at the Shanxi Province station of Yangquan. Standing on the platform was a short old peasant, his breath cloudy in the sharp morning air. His head was shaved clean and his skin burned dark and ruddy by the sun; like the peasants of Huadong, he wore simple cotton clothes and a big smile. He had come from Tachai to meet us and to accompany us for the ride out from Yangquan. This meant he had had to get up at 2:00 A.M., we estimated, since it was at least a two-and-a-half-hour ride; but he was in great spirits and chuckled and talked as he helped us pile our things onto the bus. His teeth were dark and stained—a condition we learned is typical of this part of China, though we never found out the reason. On the trip back to Tachai, our new friend pointed out cornstalks pushed over by the severe rainstorm the night before, and talked about the problems of flash flooding in mountainous Shanxi. He wanted to know all about American agriculture, and we ransacked our memories for answers to questions about methods of water control, crop rotation, and the size of farms. Our answers were not very satisfactory . . . Through the windows of our bus, we looked out at the terraced crops. In spite of yesterday's rainstorm, they lay lush and green in the early light next to barren hillsides not yet tackled by the peasants.

On arriving at Tachai we put our suitcases in our rooms and went to the brigade room "to rest." There we were welcomed with the ubiquitous Chinese cups of tea, and damp cool towels for our faces. In walked Chen Yonggui, now the deputy director of the Shanxi Province revolutionary committee and a member of the Chinese Communist party Central Committee. This weather-beaten, stubbly-bearded man had been an illiterate peasant. An orphan, he had been left to fend for himself as a child. Since before Liberation he has worked at Tachai. Today he is well known as a "model leader." Posters of him, his head wrapped in the common worker's towel, decorate homes and factories all over China. But we remember Chen vividly for another characteristic, too; his very unusual way of smoking. As he talked with us, he smoked constantly, and as each cigarette burned down he would take out another, loosen the tobacco in one end, and fit the old cigarette into it; then he would begin to smoke this "double-decker," having wasted nothing and smoking nonstop through it all. He grinned often.

"Welcome, my American friends," he said. "You must be tired. We have eighty-three households in our brigade, and our families would like to have you visit them. We want to show you how we have changed the face of the land. But first," he added, smiling to show his beautiful new false teeth, "since man is the most important thing in the world, we must eat."

And eat we did! Breads and noodles made from corn, millet, wheat, and soybeans. Garden-fresh tomatoes, green peppers, and squash along with pork and chicken. This brigade of 430 people, which twenty years ago could not support half their population, has transformed the eroded hills into fertile terraced land. Washed-out gullies now grow corn as tall as that in Iowa. Rivers have been diverted, saving the land from the scourge of floods and providing valuable irrigation water; about 100,000 cubic yards of rock were moved to build stone walls enclosing the fields. Mechanization is as yet minimal. "The creative power of the people—this is the strength of Tachai and China," says Chen Yonggui.

In Tachai, as in much of northwest China, people have traditionally lived in caves cut into the loess hills. Dark and damp, these caves sometimes collapsed during torrential rains. This happened in 1963: Tachai was deluged with rain and virtually the whole village lost their homes. Families were housed temporarily in an old boiler factory while the people began to discuss what was to be done. They rejected one possibility immediately. They would not ask the state for disaster aid. But there wasn't enough money in the brigade's funds to build new, more permanent homes for everyone. After taking a careful inventory of the wealth of the village, it was found that by having individuals loan their own savings to the brigade, new homes could be built for all without having to ask the state for help.

Now the average family lives in two "cave" rooms, each one twelve by twenty feet in size. No longer cut into the hillsides, they are constructed of heavy stones and covered with packed earth. In this way they are as well insulated as the old caves but far more sturdy. Warm and snug in winter, the cavelike homes are equally well protected against the summer heat. The homes are owned collectively by the brigade; families pay five yuan (about two dollars) rent per year.

The second evening of our stay in Tachai we split into groups of three, each group joining families for dinner. Dorothy, Uldis, and Kay went off with a very short wiry man, who seemed rather pleased to be taking a part in our visit but who was not talkative at all.

Inside his home, he seated us and called to his oldest son, who looked about sixteen, to begin bringing the food from the kitchen. Over our bowls of noodles, we struggled with his very thick Shanxi accent. Dorothy asked him if he had always lived in Tachai. Yes, he had, though before Liberation he and his family had lived in the old mud-style caves, the kind which were not reinforced with brick and collapsed easily in heavy rains. Had he been here when the Japanese came? Yes—that was when he was about twelve. His family had been so poor he had just acquired his first pair of real pants then . . . The first time the Japanese came, they just took a few chickens. Then a few days later they came back, and finally there was nothing left for them to take away but one old chicken. It was very agile and ran away each time. Then a Japanese soldier ordered the young boy to catch it. But he was so weak from hunger he couldn't; the soldier slapped him on the head and he fell down. Today the memory still lingers, and in telling of it his voice was low and strained.

Uldis asked him if he had ever left Tachai. He shrugged and said, "Just once, for a few days, to Peking. It was an experience, but I got uneasy after a while. You just sit around, you don't do any work. I wanted to come home. If you sit around in the city too long you'll get sick. Here if you get a little sick you don't have to take any medicine, just go to the fields and hoe a few rows; you'll start to sweat and then you'll get well." Had he ever been sick? Yes, once—a cold.

After dinner we walked to the door into the kitchen and thanked his wife. She was very shy, and a little un-sure of herself, but she smiled and said softly to come again, please come to see us again.

By contrast, Mrs. Guo—who came to take Rhea, Ray, and Paul to her home—was much more outspoken. Her family was also a good deal larger; besides Mrs. Guo, aged thirty-four, the family members included her hus-band, thirty-eight, sons aged twelve, seven, and four, and Mr. Guo's mother. That morning Mrs. Guo had worked from seven to eleven in the fields hoeing corn. Mr. Guo had become a truck driver for the brigade two years ago when the brigade got its first medium-sized truck. He had learned to drive during his stint in the army (1957–61), and from 1967 until 1969 had been a mule-team driver. The grandmother helped with the household chores.

We sat cross-legged on the blanket-covered "kang" eat-ing our meal. The kang is the northern Chinese bed, really a brick platform raised off the floor so that a fire can be built underneath it during the cold winter. A large wooden box placed in the middle of the kang served as our table. Five different varieties of cornbread graced the table—ranging from a flat, tortillalike round pan-cake to a raised sweet raisin cake. A large platter of fresh tomatoes to be dipped in sugar, sour cabbage, boiled millet, and huge bowls of soup noodles laced with string beans, pork, and garlic completed the meal. The three boys had been fed earlier. The older two served as their mother's helpers. The youngest, perhaps somewhat shy of his strange house guests, pestered his mother to sit on her lap until he fell asleep in her arms and was moved to his bed in the family's other room.

The old grandmother told of her life in the past. "My husband died in 1942, leaving me with five children. The two oldest daughters were quickly married off, but our tiny plot of land was insufficient to support me and my three sons. They scavenged coal and traded it for a little wheat, enough to feed us. But one of my children had a chance to go to school. Now," she added proudly, "all of them have learned to read and write during the last fifteen years." This sort of remembrance of the past is seen as an important part of educating young people so that they will not lapse into complacency. The Guos told us how within their family they celebrate the "meal of bitter remembrances" on New Year's Eve or New Year's Day, or even more often. On those nights, because she is the oldest member of the family, Grandmother Guo retells the story of her past. Then dinner is served—husks mixed with herbs or bitter wild vegetable soup. There were accounts of occasions when educated youths newly arrived in the countryside went to the home of a simple villager for dinner, and much chuckling about the vivid lesson in class education these new commune members had had.

"What is life like now?" Rhea asked Mrs. Guo. "Tell us what you do, what did you do today?"

"Well, you know, you've come to Tachai in early July, the busiest season of our year. Right now the corn is growing on the terraces and it's already about four feet high. You would think there is nothing to do now but wait for the corn to be ready to harvest, but you're wrong. Any day now the summer rains will begin, and we get almost all our yearly rainfall in these three months from July to September. Once the rains start, there's little we can do to protect the terraces, but before they begin we can do a lot. We've developed a system for holding the water around each plant and allowing it to sink in slowly. Right now we plow between the rows of corn, making little holes to hold the water like tiny reservoirs. This prevents the flood waters from washing too quickly over the soil and carrying away all the plants, fertilizer, and terrace walls.

"To finish this job we must all work from dawn till dark every day. Everyone gets up at about 4:30 A.M. While grandmother watches the babies or young children, I build a charcoal fire in the stove for breakfast. Then for the whole family I prepare a hearty breakfast of rice or millet gruel with sugar, cornbread, and some fruit or meat.

"Meanwhile the men and all the teen-age children, boys and girls, go out to the fields to work from 5:00 to 7:00 A.M. They return at 7:00 for breakfast until 8:00. From that time until noon, babies are left with older women in the commune nurseries, and school-age children are all in the brigade school. The men, women, and all unmarried older children who still live with their families go to the fields to work. Of course, if the mother has a tiny baby, she can leave the fields whenever necessary to nurse the baby.

"At noon I come home to build the charcoal fire again, and prepare lunch. All this cooking takes a long time; the fire takes a good part of an hour to get ready, and for lunch grandmother and I must make fresh corn or wheat noodles for noodle and vegetable soup. While we're cooking, the children come home; then when lunch is ready, the men and older children come home from the fields to eat. After lunch, we all rest till 3:30, because it's too hot in the fields out in the sun. I may not have time to rest, however, because lunchtime is a good time to wash the family clothes and hang them out to dry.

"At 3:30 everyone goes out again to work or school till 7:00 P.M., when I come home an hour earlier than everybody else to cook supper and watch the children. The meal is after 8:00 at night; and then there are usually brigade activities for an hour or so. Sometimes these are leadership meetings, study classes for literacy or Mao Tse-tung thought, cultural performances, or just sitting around talking with friends. Unfortunately it is still easier for the men to attend these functions than the women, because we have the children to care for and put to bed. Everyone goes to sleep at about 10:00, and we get up each morning at 4:30.

"Of course, we do not have to follow such a rigorous

work schedule all year. In the winter we get up much later in the morning, skip the nap after lunch and work straight through till a lot earlier in the evenings. During the long winter evenings we can have several hours of political, cultural, and leisure activities."

The Guo family lives a spartan but secure life. Six tall earthenware crocks filled with grain lined one wall of the stone cave. Smaller jars stacked on top held a variety of dried foods. The family had a sewing machine and a radio. The room was liberally decorated with pictures of family and friends as well as three pictures of Chairman Mao. Mr. Guo told us that their total annual cash income was about four hundred yuan, of which they could save approximately half. When grandmother Guo had a serious stomach operation at the county hospital last year, her three sons paid the hospital forty yuan. If they could not have afforded to do so, the operation would have been free, he said.

Like all children in Tachai, the young Guos go to school for nine years beginning at the age of seven. In the upper levels of the school, the students study math, Chinese, physics and chemistry, basic agriculture, Mao Tse-tung thought, art, and culture and take part in productive labor when necessary. Usually this is one half day a week, but they also help with spring planting and fall harvesting.

For the children younger than seven there is a nursery. Young mothers, unless in ill health, are expected to work outside the home. When one adds making breads and noodles, and washing and cooking to the time spent in the fields, the woman's day is full. Men are not as likely to share in the household chores in the countryside as in the urban areas. A party leader in Canton's Huadong Commune reflected the rural view when he said, "Women do more housework. After all it is natural. They have the children and are at home more. It just works out that way."

The Spirit of Tachai

How has this village gone from being poor and food-deficient to having a secure if simple life and a spirit of persistent hard work filled with confidence and hope? First of all, the people of Tachai say, they have studied and tried to put into practice the teachings of Mao Tsetung. They have learned to put the needs of the collective first, to work together (as they have in transforming the land and building their homes), and not to fear hardship or death.

The people of Tachai say that life is not a peaceful journey. They speak of struggle—of struggle against the forces of nature, of struggle against the spirit of selfishness which reappears again and again in individuals and society and must constantly be guarded against. "To learn from Tachai," said peasants at another commune, means to be prepared to struggle on with confidence that man will win against nature and that the spirit of working for the whole of society will prevail.

"Learning from Tachai" also means self-reliance. Chen Yonggui said that this had been a cardinal principle at Tachai from the early days of the mutual-aid teams. The decision not to ask for state aid after the 1963 disasters, when nearly all the villagers' homes were destroyed, is an example of this. Self-reliance means relying on local resources and the initiative of the people. When people tackle problems themselves, hidden resources and strength are discovered.

The feeling of confidence this has brought to Tachai was very evident to us one afternoon. Chen Yonggui had taken us for a walk to see the terracing and some of the newer irrigation projects, and—winded by the climb—we had stopped to rest on a hillside. Dorothy sat down next to a young woman, perhaps twenty-five or -six years old, who had been walking with us for a while. Her braids were long and thick, and she looked very competent and strong and also very gentle. Dorothy was wearing a Chinese-style jacket (what we would call a "Mao jacket") against the chill breeze, and the woman asked her if she had bought it in China. No, Dorothy said, she had made it herself in Hong Kong. "Very good!" smiled the young woman, "I make my own clothes too. I have a sewing machine. I made this blouse." It was a soft pink color, very well made, with long sleeves rolled partway up her arms. But in the cool air her exposed arms had goose bumps. Dorothy asked if she wanted to borrow a sweater. "Since we are tender foreigners," said Dorothy, "we were all warned to wear long pants and take sweaters for our climb!" The other woman looked at the sky and remarked that it was unusually cold for noontime in that area. Perhaps it would hail today. Surprised, Dorothy thought of the several "bad years" and the hailstorm we had been told of which destroyed nearly all the crops at Tachai in 1962. But this young woman discussed the prospect matter-of-factly, obviously confident that whatever nature brought, the brigade would be able to deal with. A great change, indeed, since the times when nature was a capricious enemy, feared and placated with offerings to the gods!

To an American Tachai still looks poor. The people live simply, but their spirit is impressive. Tachai serves as a model for the rural areas of China, particularly for those who are most poor. Yet it cannot just be copied. The important thing is that looking at Tachai, other parts of China can see a great change. If Tachai can do it, so can they.

Experiments like Tachai have appeared in many places. In Guangdong's Huadong Commune, Comrade Xu took us to visit a production team where barefoot peasants showed us the marginal land they had reclaimed by removing huge boulders. Now women and young girls were hoeing in that field. The team leader scooped up the soft dirt in his hands and looked at it fondly. "We are learning from Tachai," he said. "We can build ourselves into a Tachai in three years. We can do it."

Tachai's neighbors, especially, have thought of themselves and their work in terms of Tachai's influence. We visited two other brigades in that region. The first, Houjuang, is itself a part of the larger Tachai Commune. To get there, our bus wound up into the hillsides for about half an hour, following a narrow road with hairpin turns so sharp that the bus had to back up and turn around in a cleared area at the end of each turn before beginning upward again. Finally, we came out into a level area. Houjuang was obviously a good deal richer than Tachai, and had roughly the same number of people. Their cave-style new brick homes stood in rows in the hill slope above us, the woodwork of the windows in simple patterns and bamboo shades hanging at the doors. At the other end of the village we could see the new middle school being built.

Here Houjuang's brigade leader greeted us, and gave us our short briefing in a spare meeting room with a packed-earth floor, furnished with rough-hewn benches arranged around a long table covered with oilcloth. Stocky and middle-aged, he had a broad, wrinkled face and his eyes almost disappeared when he smiled. His teeth, like most everyone else's, were stained brown and he smoked an old long Chinese pipe with a tiny bowl at the end. As he talked, the words came out in regular bursts, followed by noisy sighs and "hmmms." His presentation was impressive, with long lists of statistics reeled off to explain to us the nature of the projects Houjuang was undertaking. He said that until recently, Houjuang had studied Tachai but their yield had not increased significantly—then they realized that they had merely adopted the mechanical techniques which Tachai used, and they had not adopted the "spirit of Tachai." Now, knowing that hard work is the most essential ingredient in Tachai's success, they have been successful too. In conclusion, he apologized for his presentation. He was still illiterate, and felt that it had been too simple and displayed his ignorance. Amazed by this, we protested that we had been surprised at his command of the facts with no notes at all. He didn't seem entirely convinced, but we set off together to look around.

The other brigade we visited was the Xigubi Brigade of Jiedu Commune, also about one hour's ride from Tachai. Xigubi was a good deal larger than either Tachai or Houjuang, but it had only a few more people. The purpose of our visit was to see a waterworks project in process.

In the past, not much of the land of Xigubi could be used because, although it was a great expanse on paper, a good portion of it lay under a river for part of each year. In dry seasons the riverbed still could not be tilled, for each year the water deposited huge boulders in its path. The brigade often could not feed its own people and badly needed to increase food production. They decided that the best solution would be to increase the tilled acreage, and with this in mind the water-control project was born.

The process of diverting water from part of the river-bed has been designed to accomplish two aims. Working during the dry season, a wall is being built down the center of the riverbed. Then the water is shunted to one side of the wall at a point upstream. In this way a large portion of the riverbed is freed for cultivation. At the same time, a part of the river—which now in peak seasons would overflow its narrowed channel—is directed through a nearby mountain gorge so that it irrigates the back side of the mountain. This area has never been irrigated before, and opens a whole second piece of land to cultivation. The work of digging through the gorge is being done largely by the people of the commune, with hand tools, but they have also borrowed a bulldozer from the county; they will be finished in about a year or so, and in two years from now they will reap a harvest from twice the land they had before.

Tachai's example of always working collectively to strive for success is even used as a model in regions without great natural obstacles. People living in relatively good conditions are exhorted to never relax, but to strive harder in production for the good of the country and the "revolution."

Work Points at Hongqiao

Hongqiao Commune is about half the size of Huadong. It supplies about three hundred tons of vegetables to Shanghai each day, enough to feed half a million people! The land is fertile, and the major problem, flooding, is controlled by an elaborate underground water-control system. Substantial tile-roofed, two-story homes are privately owned. These houses are much bigger than those of Huadong or Tachai, and some have many rooms. The floors are of unfinished wood, and the "living rooms"—which uniformly display a radio and often a sewing machine—have mirrors, good furniture manufactured in Shanghai, and bright bedcovers and curtains, all of which are evidence that the people of Hongqiao have more money to spend than those of other communes we saw.

The fields looked almost manicured as we walked through them. In addition to the new irrigation system, which is already built, the commune is working on its own electrification system. We passed an area where tomatoes were being picked—could we try our hands in the fields? Our "guide," the commune leader—a tall thin crew-cut man with an angular face and warm eyes—grinned at us. No, no, we couldn't be serious. Guests never work. But he went into conference with Lao Shi and Xiao Li . . . We could imagine our CATT friends telling him, "Look, these people have been bugging us to let them try working on a commune. Just let them work on a few rows, please?" . . . Anyway, he conceded, and—still grinning—called over some of the people in the fields to show us how. We picked tomatoes for about twenty minutes, predictably snapping the vines and squashing as many as we picked, until we had a few baskets full. These we were promptly given, much to our dismay; but the next stop was the commune nursery, where we managed to give away most of our tomatoes to the children. Delighted with the unexpected break, they happily ate the tomatoes, red juice dripping down their white aprons, as we looked apologetically at the teachers. But they were very pleasant and after a short tour of the school, we went on.

While we were in the fields, the commune leader also talked about Tachai, saying that it had taken them a while to decide how they might apply Tachai's example to their much wealthier commune. Finally they decided that since they have plenty themselves, they ought to be more concerned for the needs of the city people they supply vegetables to. For example, they could investigate what kinds of vegetables city people like; they went to the city and asked, and now their production has increased from 80 to 168 varieties.

Hongqiao also follows Tachai's system for determining wages. Under the "Tachai system" peasants work together on tasks determined by the team leaders. Meetings are held at regular intervals in which peasants evaluate their own work and suggest a work-point rating for themselves. Then other peasants discuss the ratings and adjust them if necessary. The factors considered in determining work points for each person are first that person's attitude toward work and then his or her level of skill and degree of strength. Chen Yonggui said, "High skills, and abundance of enthusiasm for work, support from the community, honesty, and a high degree of class consciousness are important. A man's ability or labor power may be great or small. But if he works with heart and soul for the good of everyone he is respected and we will ensure him a secure life even if his labor power is limited." Some of us felt that this seemed to be given more weight at Tachai than at other communes now following the "Tachai system."

At Hongqiao the highest number of work points per eight-hour day is 10, with a middle level of 7 and a low for the aged or beginners of 4. Every season (three months) the production team evaluates the work of each member and the figures can be readjusted. Because a large factor in work points is the amount of strength (more work, more pay) men tend to have higher work-point averages than women. At Hongqiao old experienced men average 5.5 work points, very old women 5.0. The highest figures for women range from 8 to 8.5 whereas men often have more than 9 points. The political factor can cause a person's work-point figure to vary as much as two points, the Hongqiao people say.

The value of the work point is figured on the annual income of the production brigade (at Tachai) or team (at Hongqiao or Huadong). The total number of work points is divided into the income left after all other expenses are met. In Hongqiao, for example, 60 percent of the total income is distributed to the workers; 5 percent goes to the state for tax; 7 percent for capital improvements of the commune; 3 percent to a fund for public benefit (medical services, social welfare for the aged and disabled, nurseries, and schools); and the remaining 25 percent meets the costs of production.

Several people mentioned the problem of inequality between different production teams and the need to equalize resources. At present, fairly wide differences exist. Among Shanghai vegetable communes, per capita incomes vary from 150 yuan to 230 yuan annually. At Hongqiao the average per capita income was said to be 180 yuan, that of each working person 500–600 yuan a year. This figure does not include income from private plots or side occupations. At Huadong Commune annual household income was reported to average 454 yuan plus another 25 percent earned from private plots. This seems significantly lower than the Shanghai commune, although 80 percent of the Huadong families had savings in the bank. Each household had at least one bicycle and every other home had a sewing machine. Family income in Tachai was reported at 1000 yuan exclusive of grain, firewood, vegetables, and housing; housing was roughly 10 yuan a year. Some families said they could save about half their cash income. With statistics given in such different ways it is difficult to analyze the degree of variation between one area and another, but it is obvious that differences do exist.

Peasants also maintain small private plots to grow vegetables for their own consumption. Government policy has never been to completely abolish these small bits of land which the peasants till in addition to their work for the collective. In Huadong each family head is allowed ⅛ mu. In addition some raise their own hogs, ducks, and chickens. Twenty-five percent of the families' income was said to come in this way.

Down to the Countryside: Intellectual Youth

At Hongqiao Commune we saw a small part of another important movement in China: that of educated young people leaving the cities to settle in the countryside. Campaigns to send educated youth to the rural areas occurred long before the Cultural Revolution. But since 1968 the movement has been extended to call for permanent resettlement of intellectual youths in the countryside. ("Intellectual youth" is a term used to include anyone who has finished a middle-school education, in other words approximately nine to twelve years of schooling.)

Jung Zhiguan from Shanghai was a middle-school graduate who went to the Hongqiao Commune in April 1968. "My father is a worker. I never thought of becoming a peasant. Naturally I knew life in the countryside was more difficult than in the city. In school I thought that my education would be useless in the country. I thought peasants simply worked with mud, that they had no future.

"When I was inspired by Chairman Mao's call to young people to go to the countryside, my parents were worried. There would be no future for me in a commune. But in the three years I have been here I have learned that I *can* use my talents in the countryside. In fact, the countryside is the base for the development of the whole national economy. I can learn from the peasants. In the relatively hard conditions in the countryside I can temper myself and develop myself.

"Of course life here has been a struggle. When I first came I didn't know how to work at all. But the peasants were concerned about me; they treated me warmly. They also told of their past suffering so that I could appreciate their happiness of today. Now I am also very happy here. I am determined to stay here all my life."

Millions of young people have moved to rural areas. We were told that in Shanghai alone, 730,000 youths were sent to the countryside from the beginning of the Cultural Revolution until the summer of 1971. Huadong Commune, with a population of 56,000 people, had 273 young intellectuals. The whole county in which Tachai Brigade was located had 800.

Jung Zhiguan seemed typical of the youth we met. A few of them may have the opportunity to return to the city for university education after a few years of practical experience. But by far the majority expect to live their lives in the countryside, becoming peasants and making their contribution to China there.

Mechanization—Industry on the Commune

People still talk of a labor shortage in certain rural areas. Before 1949 the village of Tachai could not even support its population of 190, but now it could support many more than its present 430. With the development of commune industries even more people can be used. Would the intellectual youths help, we asked Chen. "Yes, they are a partial solution. But they cannot basically solve the problem. Even ten times these eight hundred youth wouldn't solve this problem."

The peasants realize that progress so far has depended heavily on manpower—building retaining walls and terraces, clearing rocks, constructing irrigation systems. They see the next phase as moving into mechanization, necessary because of the labor shortage. Many communes would like to develop new land, like the county farm near Jiedu Commune, and to construct factories in the countryside. In Tachai, with the production brigades doing well and the standard of living increasing, peasants do not want to leave their brigades to open new areas or work in factories. Now they are beginning to link together hillside terraces so that small-size farm machinery can be used, and to consolidate the low-lying plots for use of medium-sized equipment. Isolated plots of arable land are being turned into orchards and other types of farming that require less labor.

During the Cultural Revolution the campaign to build small factories on rural and suburban communes accelerated. At Huadong Commune, we visited the factory where threshing machines are made for their own and neighboring communes. We also saw a mechanized system for cutting and chopping grain stalks and other products for pig feed. This makeshift project uses bicycle wheels, gears made of wood, and other hand-wrought parts, powered by an electric motor. A sophisticated farmer from the United States might view this as primitive, but through such labor-saving devices productivity is increasing, and traditional-minded peasants have begun to gain confidence and mechanical ability. They recognize that this is only a beginning. It has, however, shown the peasants the advantages of mechanization and has opened the way for future advances.

At Hongqiao, the affluent commune near Shanghai, leaders mentioned mechanization and industrialization as matters of high priority. They had built five small-scale farm-implement factories, were processing their own fodder, and had twenty-six insecticide producing stations.

At Tachai we remarked that we had seen little industrialization in the brigade. "It's true that in our commune, industry is comparatively backward," Chen Yonggui said, "but during the past four years in our Xiyang county we have worked on this. We have built a cement factory which can supply the county's needs. There is also a chemical fertilizer plant. We have a small blast furnace with a daily output of fifteen tons of iron. All these were built in the course of the Great Proletarian Cultural Revolution. Before the Cultural Revolution there was a handicraft co-op which repaired farm implements; now we make our own grain processors, grinding implements, garden tractors, and electric generators.

"Chairman Mao says that the basic path for agriculture is that of mechanization. We educate people to study Mao's thought in a living and creative way; this is a revolution in ideology which will guide the mechanization of agriculture. We call this 'revolution to lead mechanization.'"

We had walked several hours along the small terraced fields separated by rock boulders. Susan asked, "What will Tachai look like as you move toward mechanization? It would seem there will need to be changes."

"Of course, we are preparing for mechanization," replied Chen. "We are trying new ways of linking up the plots. Since our land is so mountainous, this is often difficult. Sometimes we need to blow up hills in between the small plots to link them. We could never use large-size planting or cultivating machines. But forty percent of our fields can use medium-sized machines, and the terraces, another forty percent, can use garden tractors and small-sized harvestors. The remaining twenty percent of the land will be used to develop orchards and for reforestation. Gradually more and more people will be liberated from agriculture so that they can develop such things as cattle breeding. We will create a many-sided wealth. This requires the support of industry for agriculture and of course agriculture supports the growth of industry.

"You must understand that this mechanization of agriculture will not mean a migration to the towns as I understand happened in some other countries," continued Chen. "We have rich resources in our countryside and can use many more hands. We have a bright future ahead of us!"

6. FACTORIES

Textile Mill of Northwest China no. 1, outside Sian, is a large compound of factory buildings and two-story dormitories, all constructed of coarse earthen bricks and surrounded by tall trees. We were taken for a guided tour of the factory by Wu Kuixian, a woman worker at the textile mill and also a member of the Central Committee of the Communist party of China. Like most of the women we saw in China's factories, she wore dark pants and a simple blouse, and her hair was caught back in two long braids. Although she is already thirty-four, Wu was married only two years ago, to a university graduate, and she has just had her first child. She seemed a little tired as we walked through the rows of spindles and past the large textile weaving machines. At one point, as we reached the end of a long aisle of machines, Wu noticed a broken spool of thread on a spindle. She stopped to fix it, quickly, expertly, and unobtrusively, and walked on with us, smiling as she noticed our interest.

Before leaving Textile Mill no 1, we asked Wu Kuixian to sign her name in one of our notebooks. She complained, with obvious embarrassment, that her handwriting was not very good, but finally agreed. Taking a ballpoint pen, she wrote the three characters of her name crudely but correctly. Afterward, we learned the reason for her hesitancy: Wu had not been able to finish middle school and was ashamed that she had trouble writing.

China is surely one of the few countries in the world where a high party official works almost full-time in a textile mill and has only recently learned to write. But we learned that this is not at all rare. Several other members of the Central Committee were nearly full-time workers or farmers in their native regions. But while there are "genuine" workers on the governing body of the Communist party of China, including fifteen women, is it really true that the workers rule China? Has the liberation of China from a feudal landlord system and foreign control of its cities and industries also resulted in the liberation of its workers as well? What role do the workers actually play in China today?

These questions were on our minds as we visited six different factories in China—representing heavy and light industries and handicraft production. When we left China, much remained unanswered, but we had also received strong impressions about the role played by workers in building China's new society.

The Past and the Present

Before Liberation the Chinese worker went to his job in an undernourished state and possessed few resources even for minimal health care. He was then expected to work between twelve and sixteen hours a day, seven days a week, in crowded, damp, poorly lit shops, with machinery often dangerous to operate. The combination of undernourishment, fatigue, and unsafe equipment led to a high incidence of sickness, injury, and even death. In pre-Liberation China, life in a factory was hazardous indeed. In the factories we visited all that has been changed.

Health care is no longer a problem. There were small clinics in all the factories we visited, Red Medical Teams (the factory equivalent of the barefoot doctors) assigned to the workshops to handle minor injuries, and at the Shanghai Machine Tool Plant we saw a clinic with a hundred beds and a medical staff of forty. This clinic provided bed space for extensive recuperation, as well as regular hospital treatment for its patients. Furthermore, health care for the workers in all these factories is free of charge. Unlike the old days, there are no economic reasons to prevent workers from getting complete medical care.

It was also clear to us that the workers from these six factories go to their jobs with full stomachs. Low food prices throughout China make it possible for all to eat well—for the first time in Chinese history. The convenient factory canteens serve inexpensive, wholesome meals. We ate at three of these canteens and the food was tasty and varied, with plenty of meat, vegetables, eggs, and rice.

Shanghai: Who Runs a Factory, and How?

The Shanghai Machine Tool Plant is a huge complex of workshops and factories in the middle of Shanghai. Its six thousand workers manufacture "mirror-surface" lathes, turning out over 2,500 in 1970, and surface grinders. These lathes are a vital link in the machine-tool industry, for they in turn make precision parts for other machines. These are parts so finely ground that you can see your face in their surfaces—hence the name "mirror-surface."

Walking from the factory gate to our briefing for the tour that followed, we passed an extraordinary assortment of old and new buildings. There were old workshops, built mostly by Western businessmen before 1949, with thin walls and rusting corrugated iron roofs, hot in summer and cold in winter. We also noticed a "culture palace," which looked like a very plain and unplush movie theater, with benches instead of fixed seats, and a workers' canteen. Our guide for the day was Xiu Guifu, chief engineer of the whole factory. Before Liberation, he had been a shepherd and had worked in the factory as a sweeper.

The questions we asked him, and many other people we met in factories throughout China, were ones to which we never really got complete or satisfactory answers. Who actually "runs" the factory? How much of a say do the workers have in fact? But here in Shanghai we received the most complete explanation.

At the Shanghai Machine Tool Plant, as in all other plants, the daily activities of the factory are under the direction of a revolutionary committee. Important issues are discussed by the party committee and then carried out by the revolutionary committee, over which the party committee had clear authority. For example, the production quota for the factory is discussed by the workers, decided by both committees, and is then implemented by the revolutionary committee. There is also an institution known as a workers' congress. This is the transformed labor union of the period from Liberation to the Cultural

Revolution. Most labor-union-type functions are covered by the workers on the revolutionary committee. Workers' congresses are mass organizations concerned mainly with political education now, though they do deal also with some grievance and welfare work. It's the factory revolutionary committee, however, that handles the big issues of salary, working conditions, etc.

The revolutionary committee is composed of representatives of the revolutionary cadres, technicians, and ordinary workers. Such a "three-in-one" combination guarantees, at least in theory, that the particular interests and knowledge of all the representatives are given fair evaluation by the entire committee. At the same time, it is difficult for any one viewpoint to dominate. In this way a system of checks and balances is built into the revolutionary committee. For example, the worker representatives can prevent a combination of technicians and revolutionary cadres, who might be overzealous about raising production levels, from disregarding the health and welfare of the workers. On the other hand, the revolutionary cadre can keep honest a technician-worker lineup arguing for easy quotas for the factory.

As a group, workers and staff participate in the consideration of the factory's quota and the plan of production. Differences of opinion are resolved through extensive discussion by all the workers. And very interestingly, each side of an argument must document the reason for its position. This apparently holds true for the representatives of the revolutionary committee, for the participants of a "mass airing," and for authors of dazibao (big character posters). Then the majority prevails, we were told; however, if practice proves the minority views correct, then a change of direction is made.

The individual factory worker has a number of ways of making his views known: the dazibao, the mass assembly, the "three-in-one" work team, the workers' congress, and the revolutionary committee. By making a dazibao a worker can write out any complaint or criticism he may have and paste it up for other workers and the factory leadership to see. We saw dazibao everywhere we went, at the workshops and throughout the factory grounds. At the mass assembly, workers can voice their opinions to the entire factory staff and thus be part of a democratic discussion. In the Shanghai Machine Tool Plant such assemblies seem to be informal and were referred to by the workers as "great debates" or "mass airings." Changes in the way the factory is run can flow from both the dazibao and the assembly.

As visitors briefly touring a huge plant, we could hardly tell how democratically these procedures would turn out in practice, but there certainly seemed to be a lot of give-and-take between all the workers, and none of the formal stiffness and everyday intimidation of boss-employee relations that Americans are used to.

Shanghai: When Factories Become Schools

Many Americans would wonder about workers actually running a factory. Isn't it possible, they might ask, that workers would not really know *how* to run a factory? This is a serious question, and one to which we turned as our tour of the Shanghai Machine Tool Plant continued.

Along with the active participation of large numbers of workers in the running of the factory's daily activities there is a new program which provides the background knowledge necessary for this type of participation to work. This new program is a series of schools and "universities" which were set up and are run *inside* the factory.

The schools are all relatively new, stemming from a 1968 directive by Mao Tse-tung, and are aimed at making qualified technicians of factory workers. In Shanghai there were four kinds of these schools:

1. *July 21 universities:* Fifty-two workers were selected in 1968 for the first session, and they will all graduate soon. All fifty-two were experienced workers, and had been recommended by their fellow workers and approved by the factory leaders. The average age of those enrolled was twenty-nine; average schooling was junior middle-school. After two-and-a-half years of training, the hope is that they will be technicians with good political consciousness.

Since 1953, the Shanghai Machine Tool Plant has trained more than three hundred technicians from the ranks of the factory workers. These technicians now make up half the present technical staff and are the backbone of the factory.

2. *Spare-time schools:* These began in 1969. More than six hundred workers are currently involved in this program of studying politics, technology, and culture in their spare time.

3. *Three-in-one designing groups:* This is a kind of on-the-job training program that places a worker in a designing team with a technician and a revolutionary cadre. In working with these two, it is hoped that the worker will learn from both. During the Cultural Revolution more than a hundred workers took part in such groups. The three-in-one work team operates the same way as the revolutionary committee, except that *individual* workers, technicians, and cadres are involved in a particular task—designing or producing. It is another way for an individual worker to express his viewpoint, because if the revolutionary committee has made a mistake, the work teams can correct it.

4. Some workers are sent to the *experimental departments at the factory,* where they receive direct training on the factory floor.

Politics, as well as technology, is stressed in all four of these training programs. The purpose of all four "schools" is to raise the educational level of as many workers as possible. Obviously some of the training is still available only to a few workers in the factory, but other types of training—especially the three-in-one design teams—seem to be spreading. We were told that these teams have been successful in stimulating workers' initiative. One result, we were told, was the design of the mirror-surface lathe.

Before Liberation the factory could only produce simple farm tools. Immediately after Liberation it was assigned the job of producing lathes, a task made difficult by the workers' lack of experience and by the Western embargo. Until the Great Leap period they were able only to imitate foreign models of lathes available in China. The workers we talked to said they were inspired by a visit to the factory by Mao Tse-tung in 1957. Mao had given a talk in which he discussed the need for zili gengsheng, "self-reliance"—a term we saw everywhere in China in posters and on walls. If Mao's emphasis on self-reliance did not have immediate effect, the Soviet withdrawal of all technical assistance in 1960 must have given his words greater weight.

In 1961 a student, a worker, and a technician from the factory pooled their efforts to design a mirror-surface lathe and achieved a significant breakthrough in its development by 1965. In other words, a student, a worker, and a technician were designing tools in a period when only the "expert" was supposed to do this sort of thing. It wasn't clear whether or not the trio were motivated by material incentives—a feature of factory life during the period of Russian influence—but the lathe was designed by a trio, two of whom were *not* experts.

The three-in-one design groups, Xiu Guifu told us, are a rejection of the previous emphasis placed on experts and material incentives.

Nanking: Making "Revolutionary" Film Projectors

We were totally unprepared for our visit to the Nanking Film Projector Factory. Instead of the plain gray appearance of most factories we had seen, the Nanking factory was set in a vast garden filled with flowers, trees, and a few small farms and vegetable plots. In fact, it all appeared to be quite rural, although we were inside the Nanking city limits.

The Film Projector Factory also has beautiful large stone statuary of mythical heroes dating from the Ming dynasty scattered randomly around the grounds. The main building of the factory resembles a small hospital, with a slightly antiseptic appearance. White-coated workers work in small, bright rooms that look more like science labs than workrooms. All of the factory buildings were well cared for, a far different picture from the dilapidated factories and garbage-strewn alleyways between them we had known in Hong Kong.

During our afternoon tour, we were taken through an immaculate, bright area where we watched workers grinding high-precision lenses for the projectors. The plant manager, officially called the "responsible person," then led us back out through the gardens and into the building where the final product—a lightweight portable film projector—was being assembled. Last year, the Nanking Film Projector Factory turned out 2,500 film projectors and 2,500 generators to go with them.

While a film projector factory might seem relatively insignificant to many Americans, in fact it is an example of how China's revolution has brought many small revolutions in virtually every phase of social life. Before Liberation, there was no film projector industry in China, and all projectors had to be imported. Production at this plant began in 1953, with only 40 workers (there are now 1,400).

At first, only repair work was done on foreign models, but the workers also began experimenting with them and slowly improved their skills. Later they started production of film projectors, but these were still based on the imported foreign models.

After the Cultural Revolution, we were told, three-in-one committees were set up at the Nanking factory. The first change they instituted was to send design teams to isolated and mountainous rural areas, to see if film projectors could be adapted to the needs of the peasants in those areas.

According to Wang Ligao, the chairman of the factory's revolutionary committee, these design teams investigated more than forty rural communes in three different counties. From their experiences in touring these areas, it became obvious to the teams that for most peasants the chance to see a movie—any movie at all—was an exceedingly rare luxury. Given the state of communications and roads, it was difficult and often impossible for most of China's peasants to travel the long distances to the cities; and their cultural life centered around home villages and market towns.

After showing movies in places where even books were scarce, the design teams returned to Nanking. In seventy days they designed a new 16-mm projector made of aluminum. The new projector comes in two pieces, with a small backpack for carrying, and weighs a total of 70 pounds (the old foreign models had four pieces and weighed 160 pounds).

The "illumination element" is 60 percent brighter, and a renovated generator was devised that weighs 60 pounds —only 40 percent of the weight of the old one (150 pounds). It, too, is portable in two backpacks, and uses aluminum in place of steel. This entire development, we were proudly told by the plant manager, was an illustration of the other main principle that is supposed to guide the workers, wei renmin fuwu, "serve the people."

While it is difficult to separate this from just plain ingenuity, and while 130 pounds for projector and generator is still fairly bulky, it did seem to us that the new portable projectors were indeed "serving the people," especially the peasants who had previously been almost totally isolated from all forms of culture.

As we left the Nanking Film Projector Factory, we began to realize what this meant, and images came into our heads of groups of young people climbing into the mountains with the four-piece projector and generator strapped to their backs. For many Chinese villagers, such a movie could easily be their first. And while children in the most isolated villages now learn to read, it is a long way to go for most of China's peasants to visit a city. As long as this is true, mobile movie teams made possible with the invention of the new Nanking projector will be their only link to China's new culture for many peasants.

Peking: A Railroad Worker's Story

At the gate of the gigantic Peking February 7 Rolling Stock Plant, we were met by Jia Ding, a dark-skinned man in his late forties, the director of the factory's revolutionary committee. Very relaxed, he wore a crumpled People's Liberation Army uniform almost nonchalantly and had the air of someone in authority who doesn't openly show his power. On the way to our briefing, we passed through one of the largest plants we had ever seen. The entire compound, divided into northern and southern districts, was so large we had to take buses from one side to the other.

Located about half an hour from Tiananmen, Peking's center, the rolling-stock plant is set among groves of trees and farm plots, but once we were inside there was no mistaking that this was a heavy-industry plant. The nine thousand workers here repair rolling stock for the Chinese national railways, and occasionally manufacture specialized locomotives and railroad cars. "Although these would probably be relegated to a museum in the U.S.," Jia said, pointing to large steam locomotives being serviced in the factory yard, "here in China they are still very important." But he said that the plant would soon begin production on a new internal-combustion diesel engine of six thousand horsepower, a considerable technological advance for the plant. (A several-hundred-mile test run of the prototype had just been completed the day of our visit, so we had a chance to climb into the cabs and inspect the engine compartment.) Inside the rolling-stock plant there are also many small farm plots, recreation buildings, living quarters, and an entire school system. The schools, we were told, have four thousand teachers and students, and the population of the whole factory area was an astounding forty thousand—all within the walls of the factory compound.

Our briefing included a thumbnail sketch of the plant's tumultuous history. The factory was built in 1901 by French and Belgian businessmen, had some workshops added later by the Japanese during their long occupation of the city and a few improvements built by the Kuomintang. In 1948, the rolling-stock plant was liberated. As one old machinist put it, the workers of this plant had had the dubious pleasure of being exploited by practically every nationality of foreign imperialism in China. Even today, equipment comes from more than ten countries, although much of it is now being manufactured in China.

The plant was a hotbed of labor agitation during the early 1920s, when not only Mao Tse-tung, but also Deng Zhengxia and Shi Wenbing of the Chinese Communist party were actively organizing inside the plant. As an important part of China's earliest railroad line, the maintenance shop for locomotives and cars was a natural focus for the efforts of the party to get a firm base among China's industrial workers.

After our lunch in the factory canteen, Hang Baohua— a veteran of the February 7 strike in 1923 for which the plant is named—sat down with us to tell his story. Now seventy-three years old, Hang worked in the factory for fifty-three years, and has recently retired. In all his childhood, he had had one year and two months of primary schooling, yet his syntax and diction were precise, almost professorial. We glanced at his hands, horny with the calluses of four decades of work.

As we listened intently he told us the story of one China's most important early labor struggles, in which he had been an active participant. Here is Hang's account:

"In 1918–19 Mao Tse-tung visited the factory and talked to us, the workers, about organizing ourselves. At that time our wages were seven to nine yuan a month, and we were expected to hand over gifts to the foremen and superintendents, usually amounting to about one-and-a-half yuan every month. Mao had come to spread the truth of Marxism-Leninism in this area. The organizing done here at the rolling-stock plant was some of the earliest done before the Chinese Communist party was founded in 1921.

"After the first contacts had been made, we all—workers in the plant—began to study in night schools run by Mao. There we learned about class struggle and revolution, and later we were the hard backbone of the party's strength in the plant.

"Workers in those days were looked down upon as dirty and were tightly controlled by the factory management. Even though there were four thousand workers, we had to organize very gradually. At the end of 1921 the workers' night school changed its name to the workers' club of the Peking-Hankow Railroad. We were not yet permitted to use the title 'trade union' and 'school' had too narrow a meaning. But workers were beginning to make advances."

Hang smiled, remarking that by this time they had acquired a certain amount of prestige and no longer had to take any abuse.

"Our strike in August 1922 was successful and we forced the company to accept our eight-point program—it included pay increases, improved working conditions, a shorter workday, and employment priority to workers' children. During this strike, we captured weapons from the police and soldiers and actually managed to stop railroad traffic on the Peking-Hankow line! We also drove away the French director of the factory, a man named Normand, after he interfered in our publicizing the names and pictures of scabs. During the strike we changed the name of our organization from 'workers' club' to 'trade union.' Other workers' clubs throughout China followed our example and for the first time the words 'trade union' were used openly.

"Another result of this strike was the feeling among many workers that labor was beginning to acquire real power. On February 1, 1923, the Communist party decided to hold a trade-union congress in the city of Zhengzhou. Five hundred delegates gathered there, coming from all parts of China. But while marching to the meeting hall for the first session, they were stopped by troops sent by the local warlord. The delegates broke through the cordon of soldiers and convened the meeting. Later that afternoon, police and soldiers stormed into the meeting hall, broke up the congress, and posted a notice closing the building. As a result of this incident, we called a great strike beginning on February 4, and twenty thousand workers on the Peking-Hankow Railroad left their jobs.

"By the evening of February 6, all the attempts at negotiations had failed, and suddenly the leaders of our trade union at the plant were arrested. So the next day, February 7, we were without our leaders, and our strike plans were in disorganization. When I went to the trade-union hall that morning, there were not many people there, and we were not sure what we should do.

"About ten in the morning though, we decided to march to the police station to demand the release of our leaders; in all there were two thousand workers. A platoon of soldiers faced us in the street and threatened to shoot. When we refused to move, the troops opened fire, killing four workers and wounding twenty.

"This massacre in Peking was the signal for a general attack throughout China on the young labor movement. Several hundred workers were killed or wounded, and after this the Communist party's organizing efforts were systematically wiped out."

As Hang himself concluded, this disaster marked a major defeat for the party, though a temporary one, after two years of strenuous work to organize China's factory workers. It also taught them an important lesson—that the Communist party had to broaden its base of support to include the Chinese peasants, who made up five-sixths of China's population. From then on, the focus of activity shifted to the countryside in the long fight to liberate China. The workers also decided that it was time to start arming themselves, and they set up small fighting groups in factories.

Hang was a worker in the rolling-stock plant and an active revolutionary for all these years, but he only joined the party in 1950. His life had spanned the periods of foreign invasion, Kuomintang repression, and finally the victory of the Communists. We left the briefing room with the feeling that we had been shown a panoramic view of twentieth-century Chinese history.

After this somber but fascinating story, we went out to look at the plant itself. The main part of the factory was devoted to the overhauling of locomotives, now an even more important industrial function as China's railroads begin to extend into the farthest mountain regions. In 1971, we were told, 215 engines had been overhauled through June versus the previous peak in a whole year of 209 (in 1966). This was one aspect of an impressive production increase at the rolling-stock plant since the Cultural Revolution. Jia credited this to the introduction of three-in-one teams and the consequent restructuring of much of the plant's activities.

The Peking factory included a fair number of other enterprises, including a "housewives' factory" (see chap. 10) and a shop which makes links and chains from scrap metal. Jia made a point of using these operations to illustrate how "self-reliance" was put into practice there. Old freight cars beyond repair are brought to the workshops and the wood from them is torn up and sold outside the factory to make new fiberboard.

This is an example of the near-total recycling process in China which not only is the result of a concern for the quality of China's environment, but also stems from the fact that China is still relatively poor—*everything* potentially reusable is saved. The subsidiary factories also provide employment and supplementary income for the families of the rolling-stock workers.

As we were about to board our buses for the trip back to Peking, Paul Pickowicz asked Comrade Jia his opinion of the Nixon visit. Jia shook his head and said, "Well, of course he'll be welcomed. Personally, I am not very enthusiastic about it. But you know I'm really glad you all came. I've really enjoyed showing you around, but if Nixon came here—well, I really couldn't get too excited about it."

Working Conditions

While the workers in China did seem to us to have an important role in running the factories they worked in, we were also curious about working conditions. It would not matter very much to have worker participation if conditions in the factories themselves were still poor.

In every factory we visited, the most noticeable physical characteristics were the clusters of trees, gardens, and vegetable plots on the factory grounds. This was the result of a massive tree-planting program in all Chinese cities and was also part of the general movement in China toward self-sufficiency. Thus, factory communities, in addition to repairing locomotives and manufacturing lathes, should also grow as many of the vegetables they need as possible.

Inside the factories we visited, the workshops were relatively neat and comfortable—though there was a noticeable difference between the heavy and light industries. The workshops in the heavy industries were generally large buildings, with very high ceilings that gave them a shedlike appearance—not too different from any large plant in America.

There was also plenty of space between the machines and we saw no evidence of crowding. In the Peking factory, for example, 9,000 workers in three shifts work in an area of about 140,000 square yards. The workshops were cool—there were many fans scattered around—and clean. It rained heavily the day we went through the Taiyuan Heavy Machinery Plant, yet the workshops we visited were completely dry. And these workshops were all well lighted for the work being done.

All the machinery we saw looked safe as well as clean. Movable parts that could catch fingers or clothing were all screened in some way. There seemed to be adequate equipment, such as cranes and mechanical pulleys, for lifting heavy items; we saw no workers tugging at lines to lift heavy goods, a common sight in the rest of Asia. All passageways, entrances, corridors, and staircases were clear, so that an accidental explosion or fire would not trap people. Time and again we had read in Hong Kong newspapers about workers being trapped in fires or leaping to their deaths because irresponsible factory owners were using the staircases as storage areas, so we were especially sensitive on this point.

For the most part, the workers seemed to be dressed very adequately for the work they performed. Face masks —for lint—were being used in the textile mill and welder's masks in the rolling-stock plant, although we did notice a lack of asbestos clothing at the Taiyuan Heavy Machinery Plant. Men working around the blast furnaces there had goggles, gloves, and asbestos "spats" to protect them from sparks and red-hot embers; it is standard in most Western steel mills for such workers to be clothed in asbestos suits. At the same time, however, we noticed that the workers at the Taiyuan Plant did their job slowly and with extreme care.

Finally, in none of the factories did we see any indication of "speedup." The workers seemed to be working at a reasonable pace. There were no conveyor belts mindlessly driving the workers to their tasks. The length of shifts worked also seemed to be reasonable. At the Shanghai Machine Tool Plant there were three shifts, one day and two nighttime:

day shift	8 hours
night shift no. 1	7½ hours
night shift no. 2	6½ hours

There is compensation for working nights, ranging from 30 to 60 fen a day.

Wages in the major factories are set according to national standards—this included all those we saw. The small subsidiary factories, however, which are owned collectively rather than by the state, set their own wage levels determined by the profits and earnings from sales by the collectives.

Thus there are obvious differences in wages, often inside the same factory. In Peking, for example, the dependents and women who work in the collectively owned metalworking subsidiary of the rolling-stock plant earn one yuan a day. Workers in the main, state-owned factory receive two yuan per day for similar work, of similar duration, effort, and difficulty.

Wages also vary between factories, based on the type of work done. These are the average wage scales at some of the places we visited:

	YUAN PER MONTH
Shanghai Machine Tool Plant	65
Nanking Film Projector Factory	45
Textile Mill of Northwest China no. 1	70
Soochow Embroidery Factory	40+
February 7 Rolling Stock Plant	60

Perhaps the greatest differences are those which result from increases given to workers with seniority. The size of this differential was surprisingly large. For example, at the Soochow Embroidery Factory the average wage is more than 40 yuan a month, but for workers with the most seniority, this rises as high as 90 yuan. From discussions we had at other plants this was not considered unusual.

But the wage level itself—which might seem low to an American—must be judged against other factors. Medical care in most places is free to workers and half price for families. Housing costs only a nominal amount, and most social services are provided cheaply. This includes child care, which is considered a vital necessity since the labor of women is needed in China. There was also maternity leave with pay for fifty-six days at the factories we visited.

Food is one of the few items in a worker's budget which must be planned for. Fortunately, food prices are quite low in markets, and there are canteens at every factory. These stay open twenty-four hours a day so that the workers on all three shifts can eat whenever they want or need to.

Canteen prices ranged from 25 fen (10 cents U.S.) for a plate of meat and vegetables down to 1 fen for a small roll. The average wage of the six factories we visited was approximately 55 yuan ($22) a month. At the Shanghai factory, where the average wage is 65 yuan a month, we were told that 12 yuan a month would cover the cost of three meals a day in the canteen. Workers who eat most or some of their meals at home spend less than this amount.

Most factories also contain large dormitories, usually for the unmarried workers but sometimes including living quarters for married couples and families. This is separate from the larger regular housing units for families. The dormitories we saw in Sian seemed to be typical. Two stories high, they are all made of brick and are surrounded by rows of trees. The dorms had a large common day-care center, obviously important at the Sian mill since 60 percent of the workers are women.

An average room in the dormitory is far from luxurious, but it is clean and adequate. The rooms we saw housed three people, perhaps a bit snugly but in comfort. In one room we saw, there were two tables, placed next to each other with thermoses, cups and sugar, several large clothing trunks, and plain wooden beds covered with colorful blankets and straw matting. Mosquito netting hung over the beds and under each was a porcelain washbasin. Small hand towels hung from racks near the windows. The walls were whitewashed concrete blocks, occasionally decorated with political posters. We were also told that there was no heat in the winter—a custom familiar to us from Taiwan. In short, the typical worker's room was quite simple—even spartan—but quite livable. Rent in Sian was 60 fen a month.

Soochow: Embroidery for Everyone

We walked past a woman designer putting the finishing touches on a painting which will be used by weavers at the Soochow Embroidery Factory as a model for a new piece of embroidery. From a distance the scene was very strange: she was bent over one end of the painting, putting a few strokes here and there; on the other end of her draftsman's table was a bolt-action rifle.

The woman was working on a new embroidery which was copied from a well-known North Vietnamese poster of a woman crawling through jungle grass with her rifle. To make absolutely certain that the rifle in the design looked like the real thing, the woman had brought a rifle to work and was using it as a model.

Around her in the designing room of the Soochow Embroidery Factory were eight other men and women, all equally absorbed in transforming a sketch, a poster, or an idea into a painting for a new embroidery design. Next we came to the thread selection room, which was filled from wall to wall with huge racks holding countless spools of thread in a wild rainbow of color. Workers would first come here to choose just the right shade needed for a particular embroidery pattern from the more than one thousand colors of thread.

Comrade Gu, a serious woman with short clipped hair, was our guide for the day. She took us to the tapestry room, where workers in teams of two were weaving large tapestries with the help of mirrors. Since the type of tapestries produced in Soochow had the same design sewn on both sides of the cloth, the only way to ensure accuracy in the sewing stage was for workers to do one side of the tapestry at a time, looking at the reverse side in the mirror to follow the pattern.

Finally, we came to the display room. Here we saw the full array of products made at the factory—screens, pillows, pictures, baby clothes, and even a rendering of the Battle of Pingxingguan, a revolutionary victory in 1937 in which Lin Piao's Eighth Route Army defeated the crack Japanese Fifth Division on a north China mountain road.

The embroidery factory was one of the most pleasant we visited in China. Every detail in the factory's layout and construction was well designed and seemed to be custom made for the eye-straining work involved in hand-sewn embroidery.

The factory's workrooms are longer than they are wide, with more windows than wall space along the sides, and large open doorways at either end. Since the building is constructed around a garden, the inside windows yield as much light as the outside ones. In addition, a solid line of thick-foliaged trees stands outside both sets of windows, far enough away from the building so that the shade doesn't darken the workrooms, but close enough and high enough to cut off the glare of the bright Soochow sky. When an embroiderer looks up from her needlework, done in bright, natural light, she looks out on a restful scene of neat footpaths and closely clipped lawns.

We were visiting the first branch of the Soochow Embroidery Factory, the section in which all handwork is done. There were three other branches and a total of 1,500 workers in the entire factory, of whom 80 percent are women. Four-fifths of the work done in the factory is done with machines, and of the factory's total output, half is exported.

Before Liberation, all embroidery work was done individually by a putting-out system in the workers' homes under very poor working conditions. There was usually inadequate light, and the embroiderers had to work long hours to meet unreasonable quotas. Many workers went blind from such eye-straining work.

Comrade Gu, now in her forties, had started doing embroidery at the age of thirteen, when she began learning the skill from her mother. Since her family was poor and there was no other work to do, she had been forced into full-time embroidery at an early age. Like many others, she worked from dawn to dusk. Liberation was one of the most important dates in her life.

"In the past we worked for a handful of people—emperors, scholars, generals," she said vigorously. "Now, with the same needle we can express many more themes, from the building of socialism to the struggle of the Vietnamese people." The older workers like herself, she said, were the ones who best realize the sharp contrast between the old and the new China.

Since 1949, all embroidery work is being done collectively in the Soochow factory, and working conditions have improved dramatically. As a result of bringing the embroiderers together, techniques have been improved and more varieties of embroidery are being done (from a dozen types to more than forty). The post-Liberation themes—revolutionary struggle and socialist construction —are much closer, she said, to the actual experiences of the people who make and buy the embroidery work. Old classical themes have been abandoned now in favor of pictures that illustrate episodes from the Chinese revolution and the revolutions in third-world countries. A particularly colorful example Comrade Gu showed us was a North Vietnamese antiaircraft team shooting down an American bomber.

The workers at the embroidery factory take the slogan "Serve the people" seriously and have come up with several novel ways of putting it into practice. One example arose during the designing of a large tapestry depicting the building of the extensive Red Flag Canal in Henan Province. They made initial drawings, went directly to the banks of the canal, and asked the workers who had built it to criticize the design.

An amusing example of this unique kind of opinion poll came when the embroiderers took a design of peasants transplanting rice out to a local commune. The embroidery, though attractively produced, showed two rows of peasants working from each end of the paddy toward the center, transplanting the young green rice shoots. The difficulty, as one peasant quickly pointed out, was that transplanting rice is done from one end of a paddy to the other, not from both ends simultaneously. It is now standard procedure at the Soochow Embroidery Factory to take designs out to ordinary people for their reactions on authenticity and accuracy of detail. In this way, modern ideas are incorporated into an art which has more than a thousand years of tradition behind it, ensuring its continuation and improvement.

Today and Tomorrow

Our visit to these Chinese factories left us with a number of very clear impressions. First, everyone in China— both men and women—works very hard. China is still a poor country, despite the changes it has undergone since

Liberation, and there is no question in anyone's mind there that in the future there will be more hard work to come for the Chinese people.

We talked with scores of workers. From what we saw and heard, it was evident that, in spite of the hard work, the Chinese people are enthusiastically participating in the development of their country. Why?

Conditions in the factories—certainly in every one we visited—have been vastly improved since Liberation. Work in China is no longer unnecessarily dangerous or unbearable. Gone, too, are the shantytowns, gambling halls, pawnshops, and opium dens that characterized the workers' districts before 1949—and are still problems to-day in Hong Kong.

Of equal importance, the worker in China is respected; she, or he, is no longer looked down upon, as was true in the past. Indeed, Chinese society now views the worker as its most important member. Along with this new respectability, the worker lives in a community both more secure and healthier than that of his Chinese counterpart before 1949 and his Western counterpart today. The factories we saw were communities, not company towns or ghettos.

The atmosphere in which the Chinese worker lives seems to be a healthy one, a place where a worker can grow and develop into a well-rounded, complete person. The key to this development is participation—the worker now has a solid sense of taking part actively in the daily activities of his society. There are also many cultural and educational outlets for workers—theatrical troupes, study classes, and opportunities to write. In all the workshops we visited, we saw blackboards covered with examples of workers' poetry, and at the textile mill in Sian we were shown an excellent performance put on by the workers from the factory. In the study classes, workers have a chance to discuss current events, study modern political writings like Mao Tse-tung's works, and —for some—the chance to learn to read for the first time.

In addition, China's "leftover people" are now fitted into the workers' communities. Old people and other adult dependents perform subsidiary, but important, roles in the factory community. They handle maintenance jobs, work the factory farms, and watch the children of the younger workers.

Working conditions are an important incentive in motivating workers, one that is especially meaningful to older workers who remember what work was like before Liberation. But perhaps more important still for the future, the Chinese have set out to break down some of the distinctions which make working in an American factory so unrewarding. The traditional and clear differences between "management" and "labor," for example, are being attacked in a variety of interesting ways.

The most obvious of these, and one which we saw everywhere in China, is the overwhelming and always visible emphasis on education and training—it sometimes even seemed to us that everyone in China was in school. The value of such programs is direct and has an immediate impact in the factories. Through training programs like the "July 21 universities" and the "spare-time schools," China is laying the groundwork for a future factory system in which everyone is equally educated—educated to a relatively high level.

In America, social inequality has been traditionally based on wealth, but it has also been accurately reflected in the availability and quality of education. Factory workers often ended up working in factories because they could not, financially or socially, get higher education, while the rich who become managers invariably went to college. The usefulness of a degree from an elite college is as great today as in the past.

But in China, while the overall level of education is still not as high as in America, the *need* for education as a means to a better job is far less important and becoming less so because of these new programs.

Another way of encouraging the active participation of workers is the "three-in-one" team. We learned about their creativeness and effectiveness in producing new technical advances in various areas of industry—the "mirror-surface" lathe in Shanghai and the new portable movie projector in Nanking. These teams, only recently formed in some places, should also gradually break down the differences between "management" and workers. Ideally, by allowing the worker on a three-in-one team an opportunity for full political expression and creativeness, the teams will prove that the worker can be just as "expert" as the technician and just as political as the Communist party cadre.

Of course, this is only what is hoped for, and we cannot say whether this will really happen. But from our trip it was clear that this new form of organization is spreading to factories and other units all over China, and there are already some concrete results of their success.

Foreign observers have noticed the Chinese penchant for hard work, and some have decided that China today has its own version of the American Puritan ethic—valuing hard work, and getting satisfaction from the very visible results. To us, that did not seem to be too far off the mark. There was another side of this, also familiar to us—a strong sense of the pioneering spirit in this new China. But here people didn't talk of working for fortune or fame; rather it was with "the needs of the revolution" in mind. The Chinese are not "going West" . . . they are staying at home and building China into a socialist nation.

7. EDUCATION

> Of course I never had a chance to go to school, so I was illiterate. The traditional rulers liked to keep us illiterate so that we would not demand our rights and make trouble for them. Now I have studied in literacy classes and can understand some articles in the newspaper. But still it is hard to learn when you are old. But all my grandchildren are students now. And, just imagine—one of my grandsons has gone to study at the university.
>
> —An old woman of Huadong Commune

The Old and the New

This is the old and the new in education, as described by an old woman in rural China. When the Chinese want to explain their ideas about education, they always contrast the present with the past. The past does not mean simply earlier in this century, for Chinese civilization is over two thousand years old. Throughout Chinese history, education has played a central role, as it does today. Here the similarities end, for in 1949, Liberation turned the old Chinese educational system on its head.

Education in traditional China was for the few and the rich; today it is for the many and especially the poor. In the old society most young people had to work; they had no time for school, and no money to pay their expenses. Only the sons of officials, landlords, and merchants could receive an education. The results were predictable. In 1949 about 80 percent of the Chinese people were illiterate, and these were the poor. Now priorities have been reversed. A lengthy literacy campaign has been successful, and only those people too old to learn cannot read Chinese newspapers. In place of a system that favored the rich, the Chinese have substituted one that gives extra support and encouragement to students from poor peasant and worker families.

Students under the old system were trained to be scholars, and this term had a very limited meaning. A scholar knew the history of the past; he was intimately familiar with Chinese literature and poetry; he often painted romantic landscapes; he could become a government bureaucrat. Most important, he didn't work with his hands, a fact emphasized by his long fingernails. In China today, intellectuals are taught to be completely unlike the scholar of the past. Practical skills are taught, skills that will help China develop economically and socially. Intellectuals do not merely sit in libraries. Long fingernails are not possible, for today's educated man or woman works on factories or on farms. Like some commonsense-oriented Americans, Mao Tse-tung believes that people cannot learn only from books, and the Chinese apply this theory in their educational system. A student learns theory, but also how to apply it. The student thus works with his hands, and learns to respect others who do, too.

In Old China those with education had power, as well as money. They used their power to rule China for their own profit. The purpose of the new education is just the opposite: the Chinese want to train leaders that will serve the interests of all the people, not just a few.

The Cultural Revolution

The Cultural Revolution, beginning in a university, brought the educational system to a complete standstill. Schools were closed in 1966, and some universities have not yet reopened. Throughout the Cultural Revolution there has been agreement about the aims of education. These are to train people with skills useful in solving China's economic and social problems, to motivate students to serve the people rather than to pursue their self-interest, and to expand educational opportunities for young people from poor peasant and working-class families.

The debates in the Cultural Revolution were thus about the methods of achieving these goals, not about the goals themselves. The Red Guards argued that school administrators were creating a new educated elite trained in abstract theory, not in practical skills. They felt that students were not doing enough practical labor, and consequently were too far removed from the people they were supposed to serve. Furthermore, and perhaps most important, the Red Guards believed that the educational system was producing students with "bourgeois" values. By this they meant that students were not interested in serving the needs of China, but in selfishly seeking material comfort and personal prestige.

The "three-door" graduate was the perfect example of what the Red Guards thought a Chinese intellectual should not be. The three-door graduate passed through only three doors in his life: from family to school, from school to university, and from university to office or laboratory. In the view of the Red Guards, such a person would have spent eighteen years learning theory, separated from real life, not contributing to production, and was thus a wasteful parasite.

Before we started visiting Chinese schools, we had many questions. What would the Cultural Revolution actually mean in the life of the students? Would the schools be drastically changed? Finally, we wondered, what would the Chinese children and young people be like?

Politics, Ping-Pong, and Guns

Like children everywhere, those of China are very curious, especially about Westerners. They have few inhibitions when it comes to giving their smiles and their friendship to foreigners. Wherever we traveled, children with bright, happy faces surrounded us and bombarded us with questions. A few would race, plastic shoes clicking, to tell their friends of our arrival in the neighborhood. The children would reach out to touch us and hold our hands. When they learned that we spoke Chinese, they were delighted. The first question was usually, "Where are you from?" Sometimes we would tease them, asking them to guess. "Are you Canadians?" "No." "Are you Albanians?" "No." "Are you Germans?" "No." After they had exhausted Europe, the amazing and unlikely possibility that we were from the United States would emerge in a small, dark head and would be hesitantly set forth. Many a child in China had his prestige raised immeasurably in the eyes of his peers for having correctly guessed our answer: "Yes, we are Americans."

Chinese children participate enthusiastically in sports. In China much emphasis is placed on good physical health, and early in the morning it is not uncommon to see Chinese adults doing traditional Chinese or modern Western forms of calisthenics. Schools all have strong physical exercise programs. Outside of school, favorite sports are basketball, swimming, and ping-pong. Youngsters sauntering down streets carrying ping-pong paddles were a common sight in China. In remote communes, it was not unusual to see nets strung across brick tables with concrete surfaces.

Just as children are the same everywhere, so are they different from one place to another. Chinese children grow up in a revolutionary country, one only recently wrenched from a semifeudal society. The history of this nation, its values, and its needs are passed on to the new children born since Liberation.

Learning about the old society is a major aspect of a child's education. Perhaps he has grandparents or other elderly relatives who speak of difficult days, when finding enough to eat was a major task. Children hear special testimonies in their schools about "bitter remembrances." Cultural events—photography exhibits, sculpture, ballet—all may tell of the old society, a world that must seem almost unbelievable to these youngsters.

Although the old society may seem distant, the awareness of the struggles that were necessary to overcome it becomes very real. The children learn and internalize the spirit of these struggles: self-sacrifice, respect for workers and peasants, and self-reliance in the face of hardship. As the leader of the forces which overthrew the old society, Mao Tse-tung is a model in word and deed for the children. They study his ideas and are constantly involved in efforts to implement them.

Chinese children have responsibilities that might seem difficult or dangerous to a Westerner. To learn about China's programs to industrialize, they participate in labor. To help defend their country, they join the people's militia. In Nanking we had the opportunity to observe local militia exercises. Children as well as young adults of both sexes participated. The little girls looked cheerful in long, bright print skirts with shorts underneath. The firing range was a collage of huge red bows and long shiny pigtails. We questioned the leader of the children's units about children being in the militia.

"China must be prepared," he said, and then went on to explain that China only became unified through a people's war. In this war for liberation, it had been necessary to mobilize every person in the society. Today the Chinese leaders are aware of possible war with the Soviet Union, and they also feel threatened by the many American bases surrounding China. As a result, Chinese children learn to be prepared for all situations. They work in factories, they work on agricultural communes, and they even learn to shoot guns.

Chengxian Road Primary School

On a rainy morning we visited the Chengxian Road Primary School in Nanking. The school is a collection of low gray-brick buildings surrounded by a wall of medium height; it is relatively new but very simple. On our arrival we were escorted into a large room where we met with representatives of the school revolutionary committee which oversees the operation of the school. There we listened to a brief history of the school and an outline of the curriculum. The school was described by our hosts as being slightly above average, but not one of the best primary schools. Four of the teachers—one man, balding and in his late forties, and three younger women—offered to show us through the buildings, and we visited several classrooms and the school workshops.

The classrooms are medium-sized, with large windows. Since this is a primary school, the students were from ages seven to thirteen, and were enrolled in grades one to six. Students sit on benches behind small desks in double rows. Each class has forty to fifty students, because there is a shortage of space and teachers.

The classroom atmosphere is extremely orderly. The

children who had been sitting with forearms crossed broke into clapping when we entered one room. The teacher called the students to order and the English class resumed. "Sunflower," said the teacher with a strong British accent. The class dutifully repeated "sunflower" after her. This continued until each word in the sentence was pronounced, and then the students read the sentence as a whole. Most of the classes we observed were conducted in a similar manner. The teacher lectured, and the students recited their lessons. In some classes, students asked questions and there was discussion.

Curriculum

The daily schedule in the Chengxian Road Primary School changes from summer to winter. In the summer, classes begin at 7:30 A.M. and end at 11:00. Everyone then sensibly takes a break from the heat. Classes resume later at 2:30, ending at 4:00 P.M. In winter, school begins at 8:00 A.M., lunch break is from 11:30 to 1:30, and school ends at 3:30 P.M. The classes themselves are forty minutes long, and there are ten-minute breaks between them. During one year, the students spend eight-and-one-half months in class work. One-and-one-half months are spent in some form of productive labor—either working in factories or on farms. The remaining two months are vacation.

The length of time spent in this primary school is being experimentally reduced from six to five years. Since this is a recent change, the students in the older grades began school on the old system. To deal with this problem, the classes in the school are divided into two sections. The first, second, and third grades are geared to the new five-year system, while the fourth, fifth, and sixth grades are still on the old six-year plan.

Textbooks, too, are being changed since the Cultural Revolution. Each district now writes its own textbooks, relating them to local conditions and problems. For example, the schoolchildren in Nanking had a story about the new Nanking Yangtze River Bridge, a local accomplishment. Each class had two textbooks, one for each semester of the school year. Even though these textbooks are newly written, they were not in final form. According to the teachers, the books will be used for a year; then they will be criticized by the students and rewritten.

What does a Chinese child at this Nanking primary school study? The younger children have five basic courses: politics, Chinese language, physical culture, math, and revolutionary art and culture. After a child reaches the fifth grade, English and "common knowledge" are added to the curriculum. The material studied in "common knowledge" varies during the year, but includes mechanics, agricultural studies, and natural science. The theory and methodology taught in this class are applied later in the school workshops and gardens.

Ideological education—teaching children to have the proper political and mental outlook—takes first priority in this school. We were surprised to find a sixth-grade reading class using as a text *Rent Collection Courtyard,* a series of articles about life in the old society. It was a new text, published during the Cultural Revolution. In a fourth-grade politics class, we heard the teacher discussing imperialism with her students. The lesson for the day was that United States imperialism was the leading enemy of Asian peoples and all peoples of the world. She gave an account of the Korean War and of two decades of American aggression in Southeast Asia. The stress in the entire class was on the ability of the Asian peoples to triumph over American imperialism.

Many students also attend Mao Tse-tung thought study classes after normal school hours. They have a choice between classes at the school and those in their neighborhoods. The classes at the school are made up of students, and are of two kinds: regular ongoing discussions and special meetings about significant events, such as a major policy announcement from the government. The neighborhood classes are organized differently; teachers from the school, street leaders, and parents are represented. These educational committees can also offer opinions on the administration of the schools.

Putting theory into practice is also a key part of ideological education. As in the middle schools and high schools, primary students do actual productive work using knowledge gained in the classroom.

Children at Work

In the first workshop we visited, a woman was busily showing a group of twelve fourth graders how to use metal files. Their task was to cut a grid on metal strips destined to become bus steps.

"How long will it take you to finish one step?" we asked.

"Two class periods," answered a boy in a blue and white striped T-shirt, "sometimes less."

We saw bus steps in all stages of completion around the room. One little girl, with pigtails tied together so that they wouldn't get in her way, was learning how to measure lines and put a pattern on the raw strips. Another boy was learning to make the strokes of his file even so that the depth of the cuts would not vary. Each child completed a bus step from start to finish.

"What if a child wants to do it differently from the teacher?" we asked, remembering the ways of American children.

"He's allowed to do it his way on scraps kept for that purpose," answered the worker-teacher. She went on to say that the students gradually learned to trust the years of experience that the teachers had.

Our guide, an eighteen-year-old teacher, led us into the next workshop. Here a group of older children were electroplating small metal parts to be used in the construction of oil filters. The girls wore long aprons over their blue pants. On the walls were safety posters concerning the dangers of working with electricity and acids. They had been made by the children themselves. A girl with a Little Red Guard armband explained that the equipment had been constructed by the students themselves under the guidance of a worker-teacher.

"This used to be a vegetable storage vat," she said, pointing to a large container of acid. Scraps and discards from nearby factories had contributed to the construction of the remainder of the equipment. The students in the workshop were also aware of important industrial considerations, such as quality control. They had established performance tests for each of the electroplated parts.

These same parts were utilized in the next workshop. There a pair of sixth graders were using a stamping machine to punch out metal components for the filters. Both of the little girls were careful to be very economical. The metal sheets were turned and turned to make it possible to make one more plate from each sheet. In the same room a group of children was assembling the final oil filters, using the electroplated parts from the other workshop. All the parts had been made in the school. Now the filters would go to a factory to be installed. For one week each term the younger classes and their teachers would go to this factory to work. The upper graders would spend one month in the factory each year.

Why is all this necessary? Why are the children put to work? Is China so poor that even the children must work? These were the questions in our mind. We asked a teacher.

"The reason is neither profits nor production," she explained. "Every child must know that the things he uses in life are made by the hands of the workers." She went on to explain that education should not create an educated elite separated from the rest of the people. Rather, education should help to build a society that could work together to serve everyone. Other teachers answered us by emphasizing that learning facts and theory in the classroom and applying them in the workshops helped the children to learn. It also brought out their creativity and problem-solving ability, as we saw later in Peking Middle School no. 31.

Turning a child into a responsible Chinese citizen also means he should have experience with farming techniques. Almost every school we visited had some kind of garden. In this region peasants from outside Nanking were asked to serve as teachers. Old peasants thus came into the educational system to provide instruction in farming. As the deputy director of the school told us, "Before the Cultural Revolution, many of the children thought that potatoes grew on trees. Now they know better from this experience."

How did these city children from Nanking respond to having an "uneducated" peasant for a teacher? Our guide told us that the children treated the peasant with disdain at first, until the "tomato experience" taught the children the reliability of the peasant's teachings:

The children had planted a large space in their garden with tomatoes. They were quite pleased when the plants grew green and tall. At this point the old peasant told the children that the plants had to be thinned out in order to grow properly. Small heads were put together and the children decided logically that more plants would give a greater yield. The peasant wisely let the children have their way. Four weeks later all the tomato plants were dead, having squeezed each other out. "Now the children have learned for themselves that the peasants are good teachers," said our guide.

Peking Middle School No. 31

Entering the small campus of Peking Middle School no. 31 right in the middle of Peking, we could see evidence immediately of the school's long history. It began as a missionary school, run by Westerners, and the architecture reflects their ideas of what a school should be. To one side there was a gothic chapel, now stripped of religious symbols but still used as part of the school. The rest of the buildings were set around three small courtyards, divided by low brick walls. In the first and largest area were the classrooms themselves; in the second and third areas, more buildings with ping-pong tables in the center, and a swimming pool.

We began as usual with a presentation by teachers, administrators, and students gathered in a small meeting room. The students and their teachers and administrators were not especially proud of the school's long history; instead, they wanted to talk about the changes made since the Cultural Revolution. First, they said we should see the classrooms and the factories. As we walked out of the room, one of the teachers began to talk with Paul. He looked young, and Paul asked how long he had been teaching at no. 31. Last year had been his first year of teaching, he said, and he had had a terrible time trying to discipline his students. They wouldn't sit still and they wouldn't do their work. He criticized them, but with no results. Then he had noticed that most of them enjoyed their work in the factories and in physical education much more than classroom work. They worked diligently and well using their hands in the factory tasks for which they were given responsibility. He began to praise them for doing well at these activities, and now he had a better relationship with his students.

We had come out behind the buildings into a large flat area. This was the playground, where in addition to sports and games the students do exercises together every morning. Today, however, knowing we would arrive later, they had postponed the exercises. Now they began to stream out of their classes, laughing and whispering about this strange group of waiguoren—foreigners—who had come to watch them. They formed more or less regular lines, and just as we had seen in many pictures of China, they proceeded to go through a precise and exhausting routine. It was very hot by now, and their cheeks flushed bright red—we felt a little guilty standing cool and still on the sidelines.

From there, we walked on into the enclosed swimming area. Here a class of girls in bright blue and red swimsuits were learning to dive. Shouting and giggling, some of them were helping friends, showing them how to duck their heads, but others were pushing each other in with no compunction at all about being seen by either their teacher or us. We turned away after a while, and began to walk back toward the school. One of the girls who was showing us around said to Dorothy, "You won't see too many classes actually in session now, because we're just summing up our experiences from this year. Summer vacation will start soon." "What will you do during the vacation?" Dorothy asked her. She looked a little disappointed as she said, "Well, most of the kids at the school will go to a village to work. But our school can't arrange for enough places, so some of us can't go. I'll have to stay in Peking. I'll stay home and take care of my brother. He's only a baby, and there will still be some activities at school."

We were back in the front courtyard, and a small group

of older girls were preparing to give us a cultural performance. As they began to sing, we could see groups of
boys and girls from the ping-pong area beyond come
up to the wall and lean over, watching the performance
as well as us. The girls were rather self-conscious, and
looked like they might break out giggling, but they did
very well. They were all Red Guards wearing People's
Liberation Army uniforms, and they pretended in a skit
to be Vietnamese people shooting down a U.S. plane.
Then with another chorus behind them, they sang a few
more songs and clapped with us at the end. Everywhere
in China it is the custom for the performers to applaud
as well as the audience, expressing the idea that the
audience and performers are struggling together, each
doing his share. It struck us as a wonderful notion!

The program over, we walked back to the meeting
hall for another discussion. This time we had many more
questions, especially about the effect of the educational
experiments made possible by the Cultural Revolution.

Admissions

First of all, we learned that the tall, healthy-looking
students who greeted us all lived in the neighborhood
where the school was located. Before the Cultural Revolution, primary-school graduates had to take entrance examinations to be admitted to middle school, and each
school could enroll students from various parts of the
city. The entrance examinations institutionalized a "tracking system"; a few schools in each city, called focal
schools, took the top primary-school graduates, those who
had the highest marks on the exams. Frequently they
were children from nonworking-class families. The schools
of average quality enrolled students who had middle-range
scores on the exams. Many primary-school graduates who
scored badly were not admitted to any middle schools
and were forced to leave school. The only exceptions to
this rule were children of high-ranking Communist party
members or government officials whose parents could
pull strings to get them into top schools, even if their
entrance examination results were mediocre.

Now entrance examinations and the tracking system

have been abolished, and primary-school graduates attend middle (secondary) schools in their own neighborhoods. This is an important change. First, each primary-school graduate should now be able to continue his education. Second, each middle school can have a heterogeneous mixture of students with different abilities and family backgrounds. In every city we visited we asked about these changes. In Canton, Shanghai, Nanking, and Sian officials said that students were admitted on the basis of residence, and entrance examinations were no longer used. In this way they hope to create a more egalitarian system of secondary education.

Length of Schooling

Middle School no. 31, like all other middle schools in Peking, has reduced the length of schooling from six years to five. Before the Cultural Revolution, the six years of secondary education were divided into three years of junior middle school (junior high school) and three years of senior middle school (senior high school). An additional entrance exam was required in order to pass from junior to senior middle school. Since most of the young workers we met at factories all over China had reached only the level of junior-middle-school graduates, it seemed that very few young people were able to enter senior middle school before the Cultural Revolution. Now the division between junior middle school and senior middle school has been abolished, and all students will complete the five years of middle-school education.

Through shortening the period of study, the Chinese hope to make it possible for every child to receive primary- and middle-school education. Primary schooling in Peking has also been reduced from six to five years. In the past, even in the cities, few students were able to complete the full twelve years of primary- and middle-school education. By cutting the twelve years down to ten, the Chinese can use their available teachers and resources to teach more children.

As we heard the administrators in Middle School no. 31 talk about the advantages of the ten-year system, we compared their program with those we had seen in other Chinese cities. Because this is a time of local experimentation throughout China, there is variation from city to city in the duration of schooling.

There is even more variety in the length of schooling and educational arrangements in the countryside. Before the Cultural Revolution not all peasant children could break away from their farming tasks to attend classes. Furthermore, they had to travel long distances to towns or cities to find a middle school at all. Since the Cultural Revolution more production brigades and communes have established their own middle schools or simply added two years of middle-school classes to their five-year primary schools. Two years of middle school is a severely abbreviated form of secondary education. Yet most peasant children have never had any middle-school education at all, so it is a large increase in the amount of schooling available to them.

Tachai Production Brigade, set in the rugged, arid hills of Shanxi Province in northwest China, now operates its own nine-year combined primary-middle school. The 438 people of this rural village have struggled long and hard to overcome their stubbornly difficult environment, and they have recently emerged the winners in their contest with eroded land and erratic weather. Recent increases in production have made it possible for the brigade to offer its children middle-school education. Before the Cultural Revolution, few people from Tachai managed to gain admission to the middle schools in the county seat. A beautiful young woman with ruddy complexion and long braids told us that she had only managed to graduate from six years of pimary school. She had few complaints about her life, for she was an official of the local Communist party committee, was married to another Tachai native, and had a small child. But she is glad that her child will be able to receive the middle-school education that she could not.

Several other villages near Tachai that we visited also had newly established middle schools or combined primary-middle schools. In making more education accessible to rural children, the Chinese are struggling to make the opportunities for education as broad in the countryside as they have been in the cities.

Curriculum

The students at Middle School no. 31 told us that twelve subjects were taught at the school, and that each year they take eight or nine of them. The available courses were: politics, Chinese language and literature, mathematics, English, physics, chemistry, fundamental agricultural knowledge, health and hygiene, history, geography, athletics and military training, and cultural performing.

In other places we visited, we found that the middle-school course offerings were similar: in Soochow, middle school students study Chinese language and literature, mathematics, basic agricultural and industrial knowledge, physical education and military training, culture, history-geography, politics, and foreign language. The thirty-seven middle-school students we met in Tachai study Mao Tse-tung thought and Marxism-Leninism, mathematics, Chinese, physics and chemistry, basic agricultural and industrial knowledge, military training and physical exercise, and revolutionary art and culture. The rural Tachai students didn't study any foreign language, while in the cities most students study English, and some schools offer Russian, French, Spanish, or German.

Since the liberation of China in 1949, classroom education has placed more stress on politics than does education in America. A new revolutionary society meant a new kind of education and a new set of attitudes. Thus the study of Mao Tse-tung thought (the writings of Chairman Mao) and of Marxism-Leninism has had an important place in the Chinese curriculum. Having a good political outlook was an important factor alongside grades in graduation and job seeking.

Our conversations with students and teachers at Middle School no. 31, and our visit to a primary school in Nanking, suggested that since the Cultural Revolution even more stress is being placed on politics in all classes. For example, the material studied in courses like English and Chinese literature would be about political matters.

The Red Guards, activists during the Cultural Revolution, felt that the schools had previously paid too little attention to the attitudes of students. Teachers at Middle

School no. 31 told us that they strive to produce students motivated to serve the people: "We try to teach the students 'for whom' they learn and study; we emphasize that they should use their training to help China develop rather than to promote their own selfish ambitions."

All the textbooks we saw in various schools throughout China were written and published during the Cultural Revolution by local teaching material research groups. During this period of local experimentation, there are no nationally standardized teaching materials; instead the students in each area are using, on a trial basis, the textbooks put together by the city or province in which they live. All indications are that, after examining the results of the local experimental teaching materials, the educational authorities in Peking will issue new national guidelines.

Working While Learning and Learning by Doing

Everyone at Peking Middle School no. 31, especially the young students, was very excited about the school workshops which they have started since the Cultural Revolution. In these workshops, they told us we would see the most dramatic and the most important innovation in Chinese education. In the past, they said, students' had little opportunity to learn by doing actual production work, in industry or in agriculture. Therefore their graduates were not enthusiastically welcomed by peasants or workers, since they were regarded as people who "knew farming only from the blackboard and could use a lathe only in their imaginations." In other words, they had lots of theory and little practical experience.

Now every middle-school student in Peking spends one month a year learning in a school workshop or in a factory outside the school, as well as one month a year participating in farm production in an agricultural brigade. In addition, the school frequently invites workers, peasants, and army men and women to speak to the students about their work experience. In this way, the schools believe they have strengthened the links between school and society, made education more concrete and less abstractly academic, and started to give students better preparation for their adult lives.

Mao: "The deeper the oppression, the greater the rebellion!" Sculpture of peasants overthrowing Ming Dynasty.

Inside the People's Republic

"Never forget the past."
Photos on exhibition in Yenan
streets. Left, Japanese
massacre of Nanking people in
World War II. Below,
"Girl for sale," common in
famines in old China.

A rare old photograph of Mao Tse-tung playing ping-pong.

Mao's cave at Yenan, from which he led guerrilla struggle.

American visitors with Chinese friends on the Great Wall.

Nanking youth, members of the People's Militia.

Kindergarten performance at textile factory school, Sian.

Local folk dance performed by cultural troupe at Yenan.

Textile workers present a concert at their factory, Sian.

Construction of a new hostel for visitors to Tachai.

Peasants cultivating vegetables at Hongqiao commune.

Peking bureaucrat working at a metal recycling factory.

A textile worker in Sian wearing a mask against the lint.

Trishaw driver taking afternoon siesta on Nanking street.

A group of peasants from Guangdong washing by the river.

A grandfather and his grandson window-shopping in Nanking

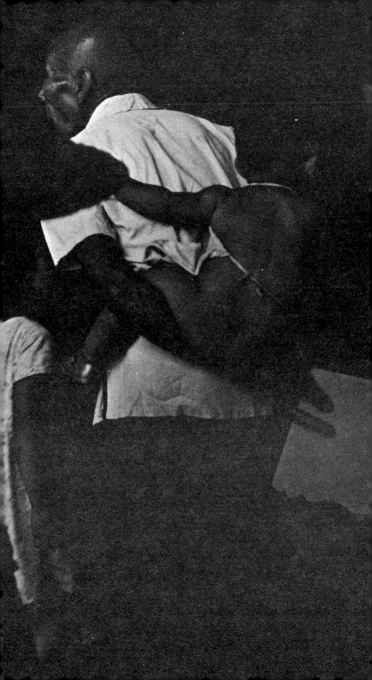

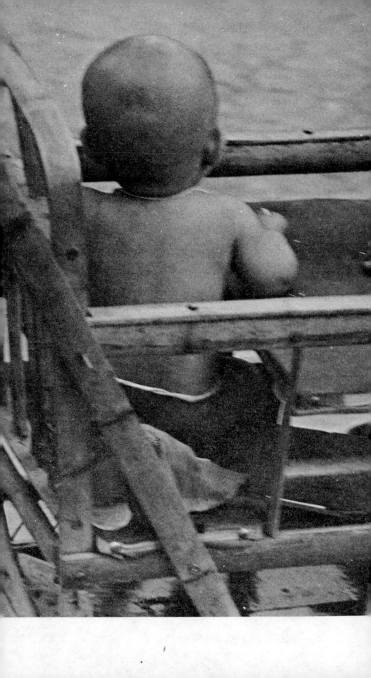

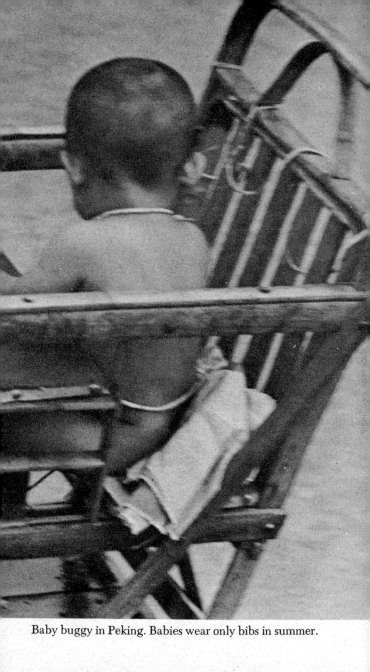

Baby buggy in Peking. Babies wear only bibs in summer.

A member of
Sian Red Guard
cultural
troupe rehearses
the ballet
White-haired Girl.

Day-care center welcomes visitors to Sian textile factory.

法 (珠笔结合)
37+14=
18+37=
26+29=
35+16=

Children working math problems in Nanking primary school.

School children after target practice in People's Militia.
Characters on targets:"Down with American Imperialism."

Peking middle school student assembling cables for trucks.

Mao quote in dormitory declares equality of the sexes.

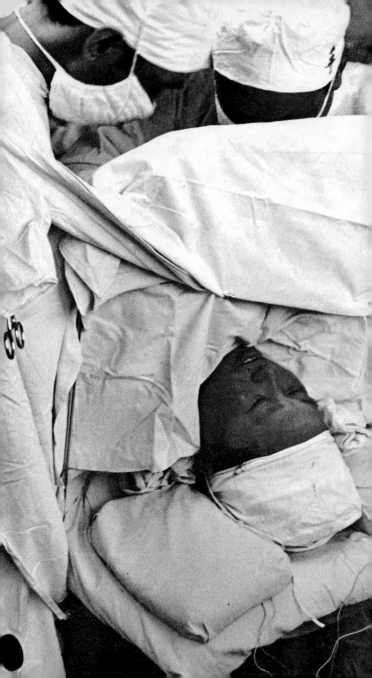

Removal of
thyroid cyst with
acupuncture
for anesthetic.
Right after
the surgery, the
patient is
up greeting the
Americans who
observed operation.

A Yenan peasant who was with Mao during guerrilla days.

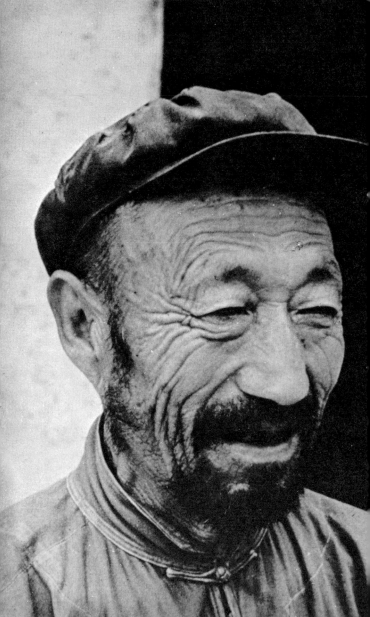

A dormitory in the day-care center at Sian textile factory.

Central Committee member speaks in factory where she works.

Red Guards performing on grounds of Peking middle school.

A Red Guard announces the performance to the audience.

Our group spent most of the afternoon exploring the school workshops and talking with the students and teachers working there. The school now has four small workshops, crowded into a rather dilapidated one-story building. Although some of the lighter equipment is new, most of the machines have been discarded by real factories as obsolete. In the spirit of self-reliance and frugality, nothing is wasted in China today. The school obtained these machines, the students and teachers repaired them, and now they are producing again in the school workshops.

In the United States, a very real objection to a socialist system is that creativity is lost. However, in the workshops we visited the opposite seemed to be the case, as children were presented with real problems to solve. In the United States creativity deals with artistic endeavors; in China, creativity extends to problems dealing with production.

The middle-school workshops, including a triode transistor assembly area, were full of innovations and inventions created by the students themselves. One of these was a camera for the production of negatives used in making printed circuits. "We found that a new camera would cost over a thousand yuan," said the girl workshop leader. To spend that amount of money would completely defeat the purpose of the workshop. Having learned the lessons of "self-reliance" well, the students found a secondhand lens for thirty yuan and constructed their own camera. It has been in use for over a year and is a source of pride for everyone.

Economy was the motivation for another innovation that we saw. The school made cables for automative wiring. This process required a great deal of work with a soldering iron. The soldering was very expensive since it required a 220-volt electrical source. It was also difficult to maintain quality control since the machine was so powerful that it often burned through the wires. Teachers, workers, and students invented a new set of soldering machines that only required a 6-volt power source. Quality increased since students learning weren't penalized by the use of a high-powered source. The safety record improved, and the occasional burn or shock was much less severe.

The students and teachers told us that the main purpose of the workshops is training and not high production or profit for the school, but they do arrange to supply outside factories with a certain quota of wiring and transistor parts. Thus, not only do the students learn technical skills, but what they make is actually used. The students said that this aspect of their work is important to them because they feel like productive members of society, playing a part in building up their country.

The students also learn a great deal about electricity and other technical aspects of their work. During their month in a factory or workshop, they stop attending other classes, but they read and discuss scientific books related to the work they are actually doing.

Some middle-school students spend one month a year working in a factory, rather than in the school workshops. When we visited a film projector factory in Nanking, we saw three young men working among the older workers. When we asked about them, the "responsible people" told us that they were from a middle school which had established a permanent link with this factory. The school sent its students and teachers in groups to spend a month working there. At the factory, the students change jobs every week so that they learn several different skills. They eat with the workers in the canteen, and often discuss the scientific and technical theories relating to their work. Apparently the middle schools in Nanking, like the schools in Peking, offer their students one month of factory work and one month of agricultural work every year.

The actual amount of time spent in work and the type of work arrangement varies from place to place. In Soochow a middle-school teacher said that students there do one month of productive work a year. In contrast, in Shanghai we were told that all students, during their final year of middle school, spend six months working: three months in a factory and three months in agricultural work. Rural youth may do their work more irregularly, in harmony with the rhythm of farming. For example, at Tachai a ninth-grade student said he works half a day per week, and helps out for a month at autumn harvest and for ten to twenty days during spring planting. However, our overall impression was that throughout the country, schools at all levels were implementing Mao's ideas of learning from both theory and practice, book learning and labor.

After Graduation

When we asked a rosy-cheeked girl of twelve at Peking Middle School no. 31 what she wanted to be when she grew up, she promptly replied: "I want to join the People's Liberation Army." We soon discovered that this girl was not unusual; most of the students we met at the school said that their first choice for work after graduation would be a place in the PLA.

Unfortunately the PLA cannot accommodate all these volunteers. Of no. 31's 1970 graduates, 60 percent went to work in factories, 30 percent settled down in farming communities, and much less than 10 percent joined the PLA. The others got jobs in commerce. The most striking aspect of these statistics is, of course, that none of the graduates went straight to a university.

This seems to be true all over China, though we were told in Shanghai that some universities might experiment with enrolling students directly from middle school. Young people now plan on going to work after middle-school graduation. Some of them may later be selected to study at universities after several years of work experience. But there are still so few places at universities that most young people will finish their formal education at middle-school graduation. They will, however, be able to attend an infinite variety of spare-time adult education classes.

This policy of sending all middle-school graduates immediately into productive jobs has been combined with an attempt to spread technical skills and manpower to the rural areas. Therefore, many urban middle-school graduates, from schools like Peking no. 31, will settle down in the countryside rather than take up factory jobs in the city. Last year 30 percent of this school's graduates went to the countryside. In Shanghai we were told that 730,000 of that city's youth have resettled in farming communities since the Cultural Revolution.

We met many of these "new peasants" when we visited communes in various parts of China. Some work in the new small factories run by communes, teach school, or work as "barefoot doctors," but a large number of these young people take up ordinary agricultural work.

We were unable to determine how urban middle-school graduates felt about being sent to the countryside to start new lives as farmers. The students at Peking Middle School no. 31 did tell us about one 1970 graduate named Chen Yuping. Her father wanted her to remain in the city after graduation, so he tried to pull strings to get her a factory job. But she refused to cooperate with him and requested a rural assignment because she wanted to serve where she was most needed. She later returned to her old school to tell her fellow students about her life in the countryside. The students said she had convinced many of them that there were ways to use their skills and talents in the rural areas. But the fact that many of them needed convincing, as well as the fact that the Chinese countryside is still less modern and more spartan than the cities, suggests that middle-school graduates may still be reluctant to settle down in rural areas.

As we left Peking Middle School no. 31 ourselves, we saw how the post-Cultural Revolution changes in secondary education fit together. Equal opportunities to enter middle schools, more educational facilities in the countryside, shorter period of schooling, integration of work in the curriculum—these are the big changes. All these policies are designed to produce a middle-school graduate who is not yet a high-level expert, but who has skills which can immediately be utilized to solve problems in factories and farms. He should be a graduate who has not lost touch with ordinary working people or with the pressing problems of his developing country, a graduate who respects people who work with their hands, and a graduate ready to serve the people in any way he can.

After a few years of work experience, a few of these graduates will be chosen to study at universities. How would they be selected? What would they study at the universities? To answer these questions we went to Peking University.

Peking University

Founded in 1898, Peking University quickly became the intellectual center of China, a role which it enjoys to this day. In the difficult years of disruption and disunity which marked China from 1911 to 1949, this university gave birth to many important political and intellectual movements. In 1919 the nationalist May 4 movement erupted from the activities of students here. Mao himself, while never a student, learned Marxist theory while an assistant at the university library. The Cultural Revolution began May 25, 1966, when students and young teaching assistants in the philosophy department of Peking University put up the first dazibao (big character poster), which attacked school administrators. Continuing this tradition, Peking University is now a model for the educational revolution in liberal arts institutions.

Peking University has a beautiful campus on the outskirts of the city. The buildings, many of which are in the attractive traditional Chinese architectural style, are spread over the large campus. Students walk or bike on paths which wind through groves of trees and flower gardens and pass over streams. It is certainly a lovely setting for an academic institution, but we saw that it would be easy there to settle down into a life of complacent academic isolation. Indeed, we were told that before the Cultural Revolution shook the school out of its quiet life, Peking University students did live an ivory-tower existence.

During the Cultural Revolution, from 1966 to 1970, there were no classes held at universities, and many pitched battles and vigorous debates occurred on campuses. Since 1970, Peking University and some other institutions of higher learning have started to enroll students and redesign university education. This process is only beginning; in many places we visited universities were still not operating. But everywhere people involved in university education are discussing and planning courses of study, enrollment procedures, and teaching materials. Rather than rushing to reopen all the universities, the Chinese leaders are encouraging people to make thorough preparation—debate, discuss, criticize the old, and then carefully redesign—before resuming classes.

Students have been admitted to Peking University since June 1970, and the beginnings are tentative and experimental. Although they plan to do so soon, at least two departments in the arts faculty, the law department and the library science department, still have not enrolled any students. The student body, now about 3,000, is much smaller than it was before the Cultural Revolution. Since the teaching staff remains about the same size as before, now numbering 2,133 employees, there are almost as many teachers as students. For example, the history department has 100 teachers and only 120 students. It was obvious that many more students would be enrolled in the future; what we were seeing was the very beginning of the new Peking University.

We compared these developments with what we had seen in Shanghai. We met several young men and women who were working in the economics department of Fudan University. Graduates of Fudan, they were helping research and write new teaching materials. They said the university enrolled its first class of 1,500 last year, and it was currently selecting the second class; but before the Cultural Revolution 6,000 young people were attending Fudan. Moreover, the economics teaching materials group is still designing the second-year courses for the department. Fudan, like Peking University, was only beginning to reconstruct its curriculum and student body.

We spent part of the morning attending classes. Looking at the students, we noticed that a few of them, both men and women, wore military uniforms. Later, on our way to the library, we fell in with a young freshman with short braids and a very serious—and innocent—expression. She was wearing a clean, unpressed People's Liberation Army uniform and Frank began to talk with her. Suddenly, out of the blue, she asked him, "Why has the Black Panther party split into two factions?" Astounded, Frank answered rather weakly. First, he said, he wasn't sure he could explain it well enough to help her . . . But secondly, where had she heard of this? "In the library," she said. "We have many English magazines and newspapers and I was reading the Black Panther paper."

Although disappointed in his answer, she went on to ask if we would like to write to her. She was also very concerned about the defects of the revolutionary ballet *Red Detachment of Women,* and asked our opinions of the performances we had seen.

Who were these new students at Peking University, with PLA uniforms and ardently political questions? What had they done before they came to the university and how did they happen to be selected to attend it?

Admissions

At lunch we spoke with three tall young women. All had long thick braids, and one wore an army uniform. While eating a hearty meal of eggplant, meat, and bread, we chatted away. The two women in ordinary pants and blouses were children of workers from Peking. They graduated from junior middle school (ninth grade) in 1964. From then until they were accepted into the biology department of Peking University in June 1970, they were ordinary workers in Peking factories. They were excited about being members of the first class at the new Peking University, and enjoyed telling us how they were beginning to develop new strains of vegetables to be grown in the countryside. The third woman had joined the People's Liberation Army after graduation from junior middle school in 1967. She also was a biology student. Not only did she seem proud of her uniform, but she returns to her PLA unit for training and drill whenever she can. Her father was also a worker in Peking.

Later in the day we found out how Peking University now selects new students. The national entrance examination, used as the chief method of choosing students before the Cultural Revolution, has been abolished. Each department at the university decides how many places it has, and the university "enrollment leading group" (like an admissions committee) then allots a number of vacancies to each of the provinces of China. In each province a special committee distributes these vacancies to the various factories, communes, and army units in the province. They decide how to distribute the slots after considering the manpower needs of the various units and of the province as a whole. Some units may get more than one vacancy. For example, the Hsinhua Printing Press has five students currently studying at the university.

After vacancies are assigned to various units, individuals working there who desire to enter the university apply. Then the people working in each unit decide which of the applicants to recommend. Finally, the recommended applicants must be approved by the Peking University enrollment leading group.

Behind this new administrative process is an important change in criteria for admissions from academic to non-academic qualifications. Previously, applicants had to survive a highly competitive examination. Now university authorities describe a different kind of new student. They must be activists in political study and have close ties with ordinary people like workers and peasants. They must at least be graduates of a junior middle school, and also have two or three years of work or army experience. They must be in good health, and with the exception of older, veteran workers, they should be about twenty years old.

The general rule is that no student is accepted directly after middle-school graduation. They all have been working in factories, farms, or the army long enough to have learned how to relate to ordinary working people. But perhaps most important, they have seen for themselves the immediate pressing problems of their society. Thus they come to the university with the intention to learn skills which can help solve these problems. The hope is that these individuals will be more mature, more broadly experienced, and more highly motivated people than their pre-Cultural Revolution predecessors at Peking University.

While visiting the mathematics department dormitory we met one of the veteran workers who had become a student once again; this definitely is a high-priority program in China. This broad-faced northerner was almost forty years old. He had a wife and two children who lived in Peking, so he could visit them frequently. But he said that if his family had lived in another part of the country, he would be given one month a year to visit them. He was pleased that he was being given this opportunity to resume his studies, and he was getting paid for it. All Peking University students get tuition, lodging, food, medical expenses, books, and pocket money paid by the state, but veteran workers who have worked at a factory for at least ten years continue to receive their salaries while attending school.

Not only do older workers come to the universities, but the universities also go to the workers. Some larger factories have established their own institutions of higher learning to train technicians and designers from among the ranks of ordinary workers. This is not a new idea; some factories have long sponsored primary and middle schools for workers wishing to study in their spare time. Running a university is a much more ambitious project. (See chap. 6.) Even more exciting is the belief that ordinary workers can be trained as technical experts.

Length of Schooling and Curriculum

Just as the course of study in primary and middle schools has been shortened, the curriculum at Peking University, too, will take less time to complete. Before the Cultural Revolution, students in the Arts Faculty spent five years in school, while science students graduated only after six years. But now the experimental plan in the new Peking University offers programs of only two or three years. The Red Guard urging was: "Cut irrelevant courses and get graduates out solving real problems as soon as possible."

Actual course offerings remain about the same. There are three faculties—arts, sciences, and languages. The arts faculty includes seven departments: Chinese literature, history, philosophy, international politics, economics, law, and library science. The science faculty offers programs of study in mathematics, physics, chemistry, biology, geology-geography, geophysics, radio and electronics. The languages faculty has three main departments: Oriental languages, Western languages, and Russian language.

First-year courses at the university are very general and centered around Mao Tse-tung thought and Marxist theory. However, discussions with students during our visit indicated that in the second year the students study their specialty (their "major") in a rigorous way. For example, a teacher in the Chinese literature department at Peking University said that his students will study a lot of traditional literature in their second-year courses. "Of course it is difficult to know how to creatively inherit our literary tradition," the teacher said. "But we must not neglect this rich literary tradition either."

Practical Knowledge

The teachers and students at Peking University frequently mentioned Kangda, the Anti-Japanese Imperialism University at Yenan. Situated in the rugged hills of northwest China, Yenan was the Communist headquarters in the war against the Japanese invasion of China, begun in 1937. In the late 1930s patriotic youths from all over China traveled to the rugged hills of Yenan. Kangda, open from 1936 to 1945, was established to educate these young men and women—train them to think, to work, and to fight. Kangda students built their own facilities, partly because of economic necessity, partly because they learned self-reliance and manual skills in such construction. In addition to studying from books, they also took part in military training and in production of crops and manufactured goods.

During our visit to Yenan, we saw pictures of the students, both men and women, sitting in rows on the ground, each beside a spinning wheel, learning from three peasant women how to spin cloth. We heard how they did sociological investigations and political education work among the people who lived in the area. This university was the first educational experiment which tried to carry out Mao Tse-tung's ideas about combining theory with practice.

The Kangda model has inspired Peking University, as well as other schools, to incorporate work in their courses of study. We had seen how successfully this was done at Middle School no. 31 in Peking, and now we were eager to see what was happening at the university level.

Students and teachers led us to the university pharmaceutical factory. Here students of organic chemistry and biochemistry specialties were experimenting with and producing medicines. All the equipment, including several large pieces, had been made and assembled by the students and teachers. The enterprise was sophisticated, well equipped, and even required a few full-time workers. Students are always there, too, working in shifts.

The students make anesthetics, antibiotics, insulin, and drugs to destroy intestinal parasites. Although the main purpose is training, the pharmaceutical products are sold and distributed to people outside the university. Thus students have the satisfaction of producing drugs which can help people suffering from illness.

The factory also runs a short course of two to three weeks for workers from Peking factories; when we were there, two hundred workers were enrolled. This is another way in which the university serves the community around it.

Peking University also has its own experimental farm, and the biology students we met said they worked in agriculture more than in industry. They went to the countryside three times this past year: once for three months from August to November 1970; later for one month; and then again on a ten-day trip. They also spend a half day each week in their department's vegetable plots on the campus. They were learning much about parasites and new plant strains, thus attacking two important agricultural problems.

For the students and teachers in the arts and languages departments, there was no obvious way to combine theory and practice, to relate their book learning to the practical needs of society. They said they wanted to follow Mao's instructions, but found it difficult to understand how to do it. For example, in 1964 Mao said: "But we cannot set up factories for arts—factories such as a literature factory, a history factory, an economics factory, or a novel factory. These faculties should regard the whole of society as their factory." But how should they go about using the whole society as a factory?

The work of the Chinese literature department at the February 7 Rolling Stock Plant in Peking was one attempt to answer this question. The factory was carrying on a campaign against waste and extravagance in its operations. The students participated by writing short comments or criticism, summaries of past work, and vivid descriptions of model workers. They were learning to use different styles and forms of political writing, as well as to do mass political education. This was good practice for their specialty, members of the other departments told us. In addition, the Chinese literature students taught the factory's workers and cadres how to carry out popular writing of literature. We saw evidence of such popular writing when we visited the rolling-stock plant a week later; the workers had composed their own poetry and had written it in colored chalk on blackboards in the factory workshop.

Teachers and students of the arts faculty feel that this is a promising experiment, but are uncertain about finding ways for other departments to learn through practice while contributing to the outside society. Library science students could set up mobile libraries for rural villages; history students could collect oral histories of life in the early twentieth century. But what could the students in the philosophy department do? Perhaps the only solution will be to have students travel outside the university to do ordinary labor in factories and farms, work which bears no relation to their studies. The purpose of such experience would be to broaden them as human beings, to guarantee that they are whole people rather than narrow specialists who know nothing about life other than abstractions in textbooks. That may be reason enough to get off the campus and into society.

Administration

The Cultural Revolution at Peking University brought about great changes in school administration. The professors and academic authorities no longer run the school alone. One of the basic arguments of the Red Guard attacks on the old educational system was that those who hold power in the schools will determine the schools' orientation toward society.

Soldiers and workers are assumed to have a good outlook toward society, while professors are suspected of lacking revolutionary fervor. Thus members of the People's Liberation Army and workers, along with ordinary students, play an active role in both the revolutionary committee, which administers the university, and the Communist party committee, which handles political issues in the school.

The workers and PLA soldiers first came to Peking University to reconcile warring Red Guard groups and restore order so that everyone could start building a new system of university education. At first there were over seven hundred workers who came from twelve Peking factories, but now there are only one hundred workers.

At Tsinghua University, later in our trip, we raised some questions about workers and soldiers in university administration. Why were they staying? What role could they play in the university?

The first answer was broad: workers and soldiers know more about concrete social, economic, and political problems than do professors. They also know what the actual needs of society are. Therefore they must stay to make sure that the university is oriented toward serving the people. When the professors and academic authorities held all the power in the school, only the selfish individual interests of students and teachers were served; their concerns were narrowly academic. Students studied in isolation from society and acquired knowledge which, in many cases, was useless and irrelevant to the immediate needs of the Chinese people. The workers and PLA soldiers are on hand to guarantee that this situation does not continue.

"But workers and soldiers don't know much about the subjects taught here," we insisted. "How can they help run an educational institution?"

Apparently there were some students and teachers who had asked the same question. One answer came from Comrade Xie, a vibrant young woman and PLA political officer who was an important person in the university. This thoroughly involved young woman explained to us:

"After the factional fighting calmed down, there were many people in the university who had doubts that the People's Liberation Army and workers could carry out the educational revolution. Sure they could handle politics and production work, but how could they manage education? Many professors and students were saying,

'Let the PLA seize the ship, but let us steer the ship.' But actually the PLA and workers play a crucial role in the educational revolution. For example, the PLA workers' team in the water conservation department of Tsinghua may not know much about the subject itself, but they do know its importance for serving agriculture. And the problem with this department was that before the Cultural Revolution they carried out their studies without understanding what water conservation problems there actually were in the countryside. For example, they designed a reservoir project for Wangjiayuan; but the designers only wanted to get a dissertation out of it and make a name for themselves. The dissertation was in print before the reservoir was finished. And the peasants found the reservoir almost useless. They ridiculed the reservoir in verse:

> It took eight thousand people's labor for half a year to build.
> It is shallow and is so small that it can only hold the urine of a cat.
> It can only be looked at; it cannot be used.

"The PLA men and workers have now organized the department to criticize this project as a negative model. And now the department investigates and designs in the rural areas so that the products will really solve people's problems. Also the department goes out of the school to train water conservation workers from among ordinary peasants so that peasants can build projects on their own as well."

Since we are students ourselves, we were happy to see that students, too, share in administrative power and responsibility at Peking University. In addition to serving on revolutionary and party committees, students help decide departmental issues, too. For example, in the philosophy department the new class of students helped design their own first-year curriculum.

Despite some resistance, students, soldiers, and workers actively have joined the ranks of university administrators. While professors and professional educators monopolized these positions before the Cultural Revolution, they must now share power with these other groups of "interested parties." The students feel they have a right to help make committee decisions because they should have a say about their own education. The PLA soldiers and workers who remain on campus believe they must play a key role because they represent the society which should be served by the university.

As we left new Peking University, we began to understand where the "new" came from: (1) a new admissions policy which means that students all have at least two years of work experience when they enter the university; (2) a new emphasis on learning through doing which means that students all leave the classroom to study actual problems of their society and help solve them, even before graduation; (3) a new system of administration which means that professional educators share responsibility with students, soldiers, and workers.

In primary schools, middle schools, and universities, the educational innovations of the Cultural Revolution all aim toward producing a graduate whose skills can immediately be used in solving society's problems—especially the development of the rural areas. The second and perhaps most important goal is to motivate young people to serve society with revolutionary enthusiasm. The third goal is to make Chinese society more egalitarian by providing more educational opportunities to working-class and peasant children. The innovations are drastic, and it will be difficult for the Chinese to succeed in accomplishing these goals. But we are more optimistic after seeing how carefully and thoroughly local schools experiment with the changes before national guidelines are institutionalized.

8. MEDICINE

The old woman flinched, then smiled at us weakly through the maze of hands and instruments. She said something, but it was muffled and we couldn't hear it, so we stood and watched them lift the cataract from her eye. Acupuncture needles protruded from the folds of her eyelids—no other anesthetic had been used. Yet, fully awake, she claimed to feel no pain. And she did look quite comfortable, despite moments of occasional anxiety. Much more comfortable, in fact, than we were—fifteen weakstomached, impressed strangers.

For a moment, we crossed the hall to another operating theater, where a much younger woman was having an ovarian cyst removed. Here we stayed longest, since this operation was easier to get a close look at than the delicate work of the cataract removal had been. We guessed the age of the patient to be roughly thirty-five. She seemed very confident, talking occasionally to the nurses and our guides, as the doctors slowly detached a cyst the size of a large fist from her abdomen. Now *we* were flinching rather than the patient. Each of the patients we saw had been anesthetized only twenty minutes before the operations began. How brave were the patients being, Kay asked a nurse. The doctor answered, assuring us there was no pain at all; but the nurse added that total anesthesia had still not been achieved. The patients do not feel pain, but many of them can feel something moving inside of them. That idea did not appeal to us. But acupuncture, the nurse said, is a good deal safer than the total anesthesia produced by drugs in Western-style medicine; the drugs themselves are often dangerous to the patients, and with acupuncture the recovery period is much shorter, roughly two weeks for serious operations.

In the next operating theater we came to, a middle-aged man was undergoing what many of us have faced: an appendectomy. But while we had all slept through our own operations in America, he was awake and very lively, chuckling at our discomfiture and assuring us excitedly that all was well, "It's nothing, it's nothing!" Looking into his abdomen, we found it hard to agree with him, but he was clearly not in pain. He seemed to know each step of the operation almost as well as the people working on him did, nodding his head with satisfaction each time the nurse told him of a new stage in his operation. "Does he work in the hospital?" Ken asked, turning to the young doctor beside us. "No, he just spent several sessions with these doctors and nurses and the acupuncture anesthetist, discussing the procedure and asking all the questions that bother him. Now he's not afraid because he knows what's going on." He certainly gave that impression; we wondered if this "team" approach might not produce patients who wanted to direct their own operations.

The last operation was spectacular—just as we arrived, the doctors were lifting a thyroid tumor from the throat of a young woman. Here, too, needles flashed in the high-powered lights, and small wires ran to some of them. Electric current, it seemed. In consternation we asked, "Are they giving her shocks?" Again our guess was wrong; the current is extremely small, comes from two ordinary flashlight batteries, and is used to stimulate the nerves more efficiently than having a nurse constantly agitate the needles with her fingers. We watched, fascinated; a nurse came in to speak to our guides. The first operation was almost finished, and we hurried back to that room.

The doctors and nurses were helping the old woman up. Without a sound, she turned and looked around the room, examining each face, each tile in the wall. Still smiling, she began to cry out of her other eye. "Chairman Mao has given me back my sight," she said, "now I can see again." Almost blind for twenty years, an illiterate peasant woman from the rough plains of North

China, she had received what never would have been
hers in the years before Liberation: sight. We could see
in her face what a miracle it seemed to her. Operated on
in a major hospital in Peking, with doctors, nurses, anesthetists, and staff attending—how had this happened?

China as the "Sick Man of Asia"

Honan Province, 1942:

The roads to the Taihang Mountains were soon filled
with corpses. In the spring of 1942, the buds of all trees
were eaten. The bark was stripped from every tree, so
that the trunks presented a strange white appearance like
people stripped of clothes. In some places, people ate the
feces of silkworms. In other places, they ate a queer white
earth. But such food could only stave off starvation for
a few days, and the victims quickly died . . .

Those who survived were getting weaker, and even in
those areas where there was rain, they were too weak to
plant or plow. This kind of famine is known in China as
successive famine.[1]

The body counts of that era were in the millions.
Famine went hand in hand with the ravages of foreign
armies and warlord troops. Jack Belden, an American
reporter, was describing the famine of 1942 in Henan
—but he could as well be describing the great northwest
famine of 1928–33, which took three million lives in
Shenxi Province alone, or dozens of similar plagues
which left tens of millions of Chinese dead in their wake.
Belden observed, too, the corruption of wealth and luxury growing fat on the misery of the Chinese people:

I was ashamed to go from one Kuomintang general to
another, eating delicacies from their well-laid tables,
while peasants were scraping the fields outside the *yamens*
for roots and wild grass to stuff into their griping stomachs. But I was more than ashamed—I was overcome
with a feeling of loathing—when I learned that these

---

[1]Jack Belden, *China Shakes the World* (New York: Monthly
Review Press, 1971).

same generals and Kuomintang officials were buying up land from starving peasants for arrears in taxes and were holding it to wait tenants and rainy days.[2]

Medical systems provide a sensitive barometer to the political and economic priorities of a society. Just a generation ago, China literally was "the sick man of Asia."

China's Health: The First Steps

How does a desperately poor, war-ravaged country heal the sick? How does a country encircled by hostile powers and committed to spending its resources on economic development confront such staggering health problems as famines, an acute shortage of doctors, and rampant disease? Surveying the health of the nation in 1949, the new Chinese government found hundreds of millions weak from malnutrition and the ravages of constant war; tens of millions more, victims of malaria, schistosomiasis, and venereal disease; millions of people, addicted to opium. It found TB, kala azar, hookworm, and leprosy unchecked.

Poverty and ignorance were reflected in a complete lack of sanitation, as a result of which fly and water-borne disease such as typhoid, cholera, and dysentery took a heavy toll. Worm infestation was practically universal, for untreated human and animal manure was the main and essential soil fertilizer. The people lived on the fringe of starvation, and this so lowered their resistance to disease that epidemics carried off thousands every year. The average life expectancy in China in 1935 was stated to be about twenty-eight years. Reliable health statistics for pre-Liberation China are hard to come by, but conservative estimates put the crude death rate in time of peace at between thirty and forty per thousand and the infantile mortality rate at between 160 and 170 per thousand live births. The plight of women and children was bad beyond description . . . The women . . . were so ill-nourished that by the time they reached middle age

---

[2]Ibid.

they were toothless and decrepit. Many adolescent girls, lacking calcium and vitamin D, developed softening and narrowing of the pelvic bones, so that normal childbirth became either impossible or so dangerous that six to eight per cent of all deaths among women were due to childbirth. Babies were breast-fed for three or four years for no other food was available. This threw a heavy strain on the mothers, and also resulted in child malnutrition and such vitamin deficiency diseases as rickets and scurvy. There were no preventive inoculations . . . Lice and poverty went hand in hand, and with them louse-born diseases such as typhus fever.[3]

William Y. Chen of the United States Public Health Service observed the total inadequacy of China's medical system prior to 1949:

Poverty and disease were prevalent over the entire country. There was only a handful of modern medical doctors. The total number of modern scientifically trained doctors was estimated at only 12,000 in 500 hospitals; the country was capable of producing only 500 medical graduates per year to serve an estimated population of 400,000,000!

China's first National Health Congress in August 1950 established basic health guidelines to draw on certain resources and inherited knowledge whose development eventually produced a distinctive Chinese health delivery system. These guidelines continue in effect two decades later:

1. Health work should primarily serve the masses of the laboring people, the workers, peasants, and soldiers.

2. The main emphasis should be placed on preventive medicine.

3. Close unity should be fostered between traditional and modern doctors.

4. Wherever possible, health work should be conducted by mass campaigns with active participation of medical workers.

Point (1) is an obvious one. Obvious, that is, until one

---

[3]Dr. Joshua Horn, *Away with All Pests* (New York: Monthly Review Press, 1969).

contrasts it with medical priorities in pre-Liberation China. China's medical system, and above all its modern, Western-trained medical sector, had served almost exclusively a narrow stratum of prosperous patients residing in the big cities. Setting out to serve the working people meant not only constructing a vast new health network, but cracking through barriers of ignorance and superstition among millions for whom the only doctors had been wandering herbalists.

The emphasis on preventive medicine was a response both to the immediate crisis, that of disease in epidemic proportions throughout China, and a long-range commitment to the health of all the people. Preventive medicine ranges from the most basic education in hygienic principles to the purification of night soil (excrement used as fertilizer) and water supplies to inoculations against disease, and it has been responsible for much of the tremendous advance of the past two decades.

The third guideline highlights one of the most distinctive features of health care in People's China. Mao's principle of "walking on two legs," of uniting and developing traditional and modern approaches through revolutionary practice, has been applied specifically to medical care since the early forties. During World War II, in a situation of acute scarcity of modern trained doctors, high mortality rates, and the pervasive influence of supersition, Mao called on modern-trained doctors to unite and work with their traditional counterparts:

Among the 1,500,000 people of the Shensi-Kansu-Ninghsia Border Region there are more than 1,000,000 illiterates, there are 2,000 practitioners of witchcraft, and the broad masses are still under the influence of superstitions . . . the human and animal mortality rates are both very high . . . In such circumstances to rely solely on modern doctors is no solution. Of course, if they do not concern themselves with the sufferings of the people, do not unite with the thousands and more doctors and veterinarians of the old type in the Border Region and do not help them to make progress, then they will actually be helping the witch doctors (and showing indifference to the high rate of mortality of men and cattle). There are two principles for the united front: The first is to unite, and the second is to criticize, educate, and transform. Our task is to unite with all the . . . doctors who come from the old society but are useful, and to help, educate, and transform them. They will welcome our help if only we act properly.[4]

Out of this unity—a unity combined with mutual criticism and mutual commitment to serving the Chinese people—would emerge a new and distinctive Chinese medical practice. China's health needs could not be postponed until hundreds of thousands of new modern doctors could be trained. Immediate efforts had to be made to utilize and improve medical care provided by traditional practitioners—and, moveover, to develop, systematize, and learn from the most positive aspects of their accumulated experience. Given the deep gulf in values and practices separating modern and traditional schools of medicine, especially given the deep-seated contempt of modern doctors for Chinese medicine, these tasks were enormous. Nevertheless, there is emerging in China today a health system which incorporates major features of traditional medicine with the most advanced scientific training.

To an extraordinary degree the health of the nation is no longer the exclusive prerogative of the medical profession. It has become the concern of the entire people through the introduction of popular campaigns to eradicate major diseases and improve hygiene. Within a matter of three to five years, China eliminated totally the world's most serious drug problem, involving millions of opium addicts. Venereal disease, which was particularly rampant in minority areas, affected tens of millions. Today, active venereal disease has been completely eliminated from most areas and completely controlled throughout China, and China is the first country in the world to do so. (See chap. 2.) The liver and intestinal disease schistosomiasis, one of the world's great scourges, affects some 250 million people in Asia and Africa.

---

[4]Mao Tse-tung, *The United Front in Cultural Work* (Peking: Foreign Language Press).

As late as 1955 it afflicted an estimated 10 million Chinese, mostly in the lower Yangtze area. Today, this disease has been brought under control in large areas of China and restricted everywhere. Malaria, which affected millions in south China, has been largely eliminated. Nor is it only diseases of epidemic proportions which have been affected. Through the popular health movement, initially directed toward the nationwide elimination of the "four pests" (flies, rats, bedbugs, mosquitoes), disease carriers of every variety have been attacked, and hygienic principles such as control of water and night soil have been introduced and implemented throughout China.[5] Most of these problems had been conquered by the time we traveled in the People's Republic, so we did not see the process at first hand. We have talked, in China and the West, with doctors and others who helped in these projects.

China in the mid-fifties had introduced comprehensive free health care for government and factory workers and university students in urban areas. Enrollment of medical and public-health students rose from 15,200 in 1949 to 49,100 in 1957. By the early 1960s, China was graduating more than 20,000 doctors and public-health workers annually.

But as late as 1965, despite immense strides in rural health care, urban facilities—particularly for privileged groups covered by state programs—remained vastly superior to rural facilities. Health resources were concentrated overwhelmingly in the cities. There was an elementary logic to this approach—a logic reinforced by the Rockefeller-financed Peking University Medical College training received by China's leading physicians prior to 1949 *and* the weight of medical experience in the Soviet Union. Newly trained doctors went to work in city hospitals where medical resources could be effectively concentrated. A network of county hospitals mushroomed outside the great metropolitan areas bringing hospital care to new areas, but remained centered in county

---

[5] This discussion of the development of health care in China has been drawn largely from an essay by a CCAS member, Mark Selden, which will be published by Pantheon.

seats. Eventually, Chinese planners reasoned, modern medical care would filter still further down to the communes and villages. Meanwhile, popular health campaigns would bring significant rural health gains even if doctors could not yet be permanently dispatched to the villages in significant numbers. Would not the alternatives—dispatching highly trained doctors to work in remote villages, or watering down medical education—create a hopelessly fragmented system, or impede the long-range development of quality medical care? The medical priorities of China's First Five-Year Plan for 1953–57 closely reflected overall priorities which emphasized development of heavy industries and the cities. Medicine was no exception:

> In developing health and medical services priorities must be given to improving the work in industrial areas, in areas where capital construction work is in progress, and in forest areas, and sanitation work in rural districts must be gradually improved.

The attacks on medical planning made during the Cultural Revolution should not blind us to the positive—indeed revolutionary—achievements of the health delivery system before 1965. But Mao and the Red Guards had directed their criticism at the right target. Health-care resources—physicians, hospital facilities, and money—were concentrated in the cities. This system could only perpetuate sharp differences between city and countryside, between prosperous and poor, between mental and manual laborers. It created a trained medical elite enjoying economic privileges and facing squarely toward the urban areas, toward the most privileged and prosperous elements of the society rather than the poorest and most disadvantaged; it left hundreds of millions of rural villagers with rudimentary medical care; and it impeded the flow of the most advanced medical knowledge back to the village by cutting off trained personnel from the rural areas.

China's Health: The Cultural Revolution and After

Early in 1965, Mao Tse-tung remarked that the Ministry of Health was the "Ministry of Health for Urban Overlords." This highlighted the crisis that had been developing in medicine for many years. As Chairman Mao put it then, "This question of 'for whom?' is fundamental; it is a question of principle." If health care in China was to be for the people, *all* the people, it must stress the countryside, where 80 percent of the Chinese population live. This new orientation was summarized by Mao in a sentence which became one of the chief slogans of the Cultural Revolution in health: "In medical and health work, put the stress on the rural areas."

With this new orientation, it became clear that rural medical work had been woefully inadequate and neglected. As a result, a second line in health work and medicine began to develop. This line embodied a model which was revolutionary in nature yet which could be adapted to fill the expanding health needs of the entire nation by relying on existing resources. This model made "Serve the people" its slogan and took as its highest example a foreigner named Norman Bethune. (Bethune, a Canadian doctor, died while serving with the Communist Eighth Route Army in the war against Japan.)

> Comrade Bethune's spirit, his utter devotion to others without any thought of self, was shown in his boundless sense of responsibility in his work and his boundless warm-heartedness toward all comrades and the people. Every Communist must learn from him. There are not a few people who are irresponsible in their work, preferring the light to the heavy, shoving the heavy loads onto others and choosing the easy ones for themselves. At every turn they think of themselves before others. Every Communist must learn this true Communist spirit from Comrade Bethune . . . Comrade Bethune was a doctor, the art of healing was his profession.[6]

At the Huadong Commune, outside Canton, we saw for the first time the practical results of this new emphasis on the countryside.

None of us are doctors. Other Americans, themselves

---

[6] Mao Tse-tung, "In Memory of Norman Bethune," *Selected Works of Mao Tse-tung* (Peking: Foreign Language Press, 1960).

doctors, have visited China and written about its sophisticated modern medicine. They have written about impeccable surgical techniques, the use of complex heart-lung machines and artificial kidneys, and the quantity of modern medicines such as polio vaccines. We are not qualified to write about many of these aspects of medicine —rather, we went to observe medicine in action. How had the new reorganization of medicine and health care affected the health of all China? How could political changes solve medical problems?

The staff of the Huadong hospital were eager to tell us. Like other communes, Huadong has a hospital which serves two purposes: as a treatment center for seriously ill patients and as a training center for midwives and for "barefoot doctors." More recently, Huadong has added a third function, the making of herbal medicines. The greatest changes to come out of the Cultural Revolution, we were told, have been the result of the new training programs.

"Barefoot Doctors" out in the Fields

Our delegation visited the hospital in the afternoon, while patients were being attended to. As we came in, small groups were waiting quietly. The building was simple, whitewashed and fresh, with an atmosphere of reassuring competence and uninstitutional friendliness. The hospital was small, with thirty-three beds and a staff of fifty. It was equipped with laboratory and X-ray facilities, but without a blood bank. (Should a patient require emergency operations that could not be handled at the commune hospital, the commune trucks are used as an ambulance service to transport him to the city hospitals.) After a short tour, we sat down to talk.

"Early in 1965 mobile medical teams of doctors, nurses, and health personnel from the large cities first began to appear in our villages. They came for periods ranging from six months to one year, and many of them have returned again." These roving teams, including some of China's most prominent physicians, nurses, and public-health workers, brought systematic health care to areas that had rarely seen a modern health worker.

But the direct treatment of patients was not their most important task. They were also there to train a new generation of rural youth who would carry on after their departure. Most important of these new medical workers are the "barefoot doctors." At Huadong, as elsewhere, they are members of the commune. They leave their brigades for an initial training course at the commune hospital, usually six months to a year, and then over the next two or three years return for follow-up courses during the slack farm season. When they return to their villages, these new doctors practice basic medical care and continue to learn from the roving medical teams. They still work half-time in the fields; at Huadong each brigade had about seventy barefoot doctors and three or four midwives.

In recent months, 180 barefoot doctors had been trained at Huadong. In a commune of 56,390 people, this is a significant increase. The tasks of the new doctors go far beyond the diagnosis and treatment of illness. They will see that every villager gets all his vaccinations, demonstrate the correct use of pesticides, improve sanitation methods, teach mothers about nutrition and child care, and give community lectures occasionally on the new ideas they are introducing. Through all of this, they will be farmers, teachers, or shopworkers as well as doctors. When they teach improved sanitation methods they will help to build new latrines. They will be using the pesticides in the fields, too, and in every case they treat they will be caring for friends and neighbors.

Barefoot doctors are integrated with their fellow villagers in one additional and highly significant way. They receive no special financial rewards for their medical care. Their incomes remain unchanged, calculated on the basis of work points like other villagers, and their hopes for the future lie not in the city or in "moving up" to higher medical positions in better facilities, but in advancing the interests of their entire brigade, village, and commune.

The training of midwives has probably had more effect on health at Huadong than we Westerners realize. It is hard to imagine the process of childbirth before Liberation, when superstition-ridden old women tended to the mothers. Since almost all rural women in China still bear their children at home, the training of competent midwives in the post-Liberation period has had high priority—especially since the Cultural Revolution. Part of the training enables the midwives to diagnose a difficult birth early enough to bring the mother to the commune hospital; now, for example, many caesarean sections are performed each year at Huadong—and this alone has saved the lives of countless women and children.

The financing of rural health has changed greatly with the advent of the barefoot doctors. In the past, the state had provided the salaries for tens of thousands of medical workers in roving teams and had, in effect, subsidized rural health. In China, that system could not go on indefinitely. Instead, emphasis on self-reliance and the integration of medical care with the working population formed the basis of the new cooperative system for health care.

Since late 1968, cooperative medical-care systems have been created throughout the Chinese countryside. Under this system each commune member pays an annual fee (equivalent to less than an American dollar). His production team will also pay for him, from its welfare fund, about five cents to the cooperative system. After that, each treatment costs about two-and-a-half cents (unless it is a chronic ailment), and medicines are free.

This system is an outgrowth of China's boldest and most revolutionary ideals. Run by and for the community, with minimal state involvement, predicated on principles of voluntary participation, self-reliance, thrift, non-specialization, local initiative, and service to the people, it has made medical care a basic right for hundreds of millions of Chinese peasants.

Traditional Medicine Revived

Huadong now grows much of its own medicine. "Grow medicine?" we asked. Yes—the herbs which, dried, ground, and mixed, are the basic source of simple medicine in China. We should remember, though, that the same is also true of many important medicines in the West. An American heart specialist, Dr. E. Grey Diamond, visited the People's Republic soon after we did, and commented on this in a newspaper account:

> Most of the people in that huge country still get most of their medical care from doctors who go out into the hills and make their own medicines from substances they've been using for 2000 years. I thought to myself, "By God, we in the West had to learn to use primitive herbs in digitalis, in ephedrine, and in the rauwolfia tranquilizers; there must be a lot of pharmacology the Chinese can teach us, too. I'd like to see us really test their medicines."

In every unit that we visited, even in mountainous Tachai, the commune or brigade set aside some of its arable land for the cultivation of herbs, or for alternate cultivation of herbs and other crops. Each unit also has a store with both herbal and other types of medicines. This is not merely a continuation of past patterns, it is part of a major attempt to improve the understanding and use of traditional medicines and to increase their supply.

After the Western penetration began with the Opium War of 1840, the traditional healing methods developed over the course of two thousand years quickly fell into disrepute. Chinese modernizers, influenced by the West, attempted to dispose of or discredit anything Chinese as being "superstition" or "unscientific." Unfortunately, this attitude carried over into the study of medicine as well, and the Kuomintang actually formulated a law making traditional medicine illegal. It is only since the People's Republic came to power that new efforts have been made to put these traditional forms of healing on a scientific basis.

Part of the work is being done at the Dongfeng Yiyuan, the East Wind Hospital outside Soochow, where we spent over three hours talking with the patients and staff in order to find out more about this side of medicine in China. The goal of the hospital as an experimental station is to combine Chinese and Western medicine into a practical system for treatment of illness; as a research station it is to put Chinese medicine on a scientific and standardized basis.

The East Wind Hospital was a good deal larger than the commune hospital at Huadong. It has two hundred beds, with three main departments: the inpatient, outpatient, and dispensary services. Before the Cultural Revolution, the East Wind administered only Chinese medicines; now it has facilities for Western medicines and treatments as well, and there were several doctors of both kinds on hand to answer our questions.

They pointed out that there are some 800,000 traditional doctors at work in rural China. Ignoring this resource, when Chinese medicine is respected and trusted by the people and when there is a shortage of doctors trained in Western medicine, would deny medical care to vast parts of China. But they emphasized the need for research, standardization, and education in the traditional methods.

The staff of East Wind has developed a unique machine to aid them in their work, one of which we saw but find difficult to describe. On one side of the large room were rows of shelves holding trays of raw herbal components. On the other side was a control board which activated chutes from the various trays leading to mixing pans. The contents of the mixing pans are then boiled and mixed to achieve the desired strength of brew. The original idea had been developed in Shanghai and then modified by the East Wind; it looked like a Rube Goldberg inspiration, but it obviously—as we watched its operation—worked smoothly and mixed the prescription ingredients properly.

Another contribution of traditional medicine frequently mentioned is the treatment of bone fractures. Western methods typically call for forcible realignment of the bones and a cast which holds the body area immobile. Chinese methods, on the other hand, use gradual pressure in flexible splints which, over time, will realign the bones. The Chinese methods avoid the use of anesthesia and reduce muscle wasting and joint stiffness. By the time the bones are in place, the limb or joint is often almost perfectly operative. In contrast, our Western techniques may show by X ray that the bone has mended but the patient may still take months before the limb can be used normally again.

Acupuncture

By far the most dramatic demonstrations of Chinese advances in medicine were the four operations we watched at Peking Medical College Hospital no. 3. The acupuncture techniques we had seen were evidently still considered somewhat experimental.

"In 1968," one doctor said, "we decided to display the 'dare to think, dare to do' spirit, and to try to use acupuncture for anesthetic purposes." Since that time, and after much testing and experimentation, most of it on themselves—the doctors and staff have increasingly used acupuncture to anesthetize patients. In some operations acupuncture could not be used because of the need to anesthetize more than one area at once. But, for a great many operations—more than 400,000 done in China since 1958—acupuncture has been the means of anesthesia.

Because acupuncture has been widely discussed in the American press since our return, we have simply described our experience in the East Wind and Peking no. 3 hospitals. It is worth pointing out, however, that acupuncture has been used and respected in a large number of Western countries for some time. Parkinsonism, skin ailments, rheumatoid arthritis, asthma, sciatica, migraines, and other illnesses have been treated successfully with acupuncture by German, French, Japanese, Swiss, and British doctors. Thus the skepticism with which acupuncture is treated in the United States is perhaps somewhat overdone.

Three-in-One at Peking Hospital No. 3

Other than the methods used in the operations we saw, the most interesting aspect of the Peking Hospital no. 3 was the way in which patients were prepared for the operations and for postoperation recovery. The patient and the doctors and staff concerned meet together before the operation to form a "three-in-one" combination. The operation is seen as a battle to be won, and the "three-in-one" combination as a combat team, composed of doctors and anesthetists, nurses, and patient. The idea is that the patient must declare war against his disease and take an active role in learning about it. During these meetings, the patient and his "three-in-one" team study the relevant Mao works and study the case in order to determine whether the operation is actually necessary, and if so what kind of anesthetic to use. If it is to be acupuncture, then the patient is told about the method in order to dispel any fears and to bring into play a positive attitude, rather than the negative feelings such as "I hate the hospital" or "I am not sure about my survival of the operation." This has the advantage of strengthening the patient psychologically to fight his disease or injury, and it speeds his recovery after the operation.

The doctors acknowledge that the person most concerned about an illness is the patient himself. So doctors and nurses talk to the patients, get their opinions and suggestions and cooperation, instead of taking the position of experts who know all. Of course, this has not all changed overnight. The doctor still has the final say, but his role now is as part of a team, and they treat the patient rather than the stomach or the big toe!

This team approach has been responsible for important innovations in operational procedure and medical techniques as well as medical equipment. During the cataract operation on the old peasant woman's eye, one of the nurses pointed out to us an instrument which had been adapted by the hospital from a more complicated Western model. The working principle of the instrument was very simple—that frozen objects tend to be adhesive. In this case, the cataract, after being cut from the eye, was stuck to the end of a probe which had been cooled with dry ice. After the insertion of the extremely cold probe, the cataract could be lifted simply from the eye, without discomfort.

After the Cultural Revolution

The training of doctors and medical staff at the hospital seemed to be the area that had undergone the most profound changes since the Cultural Revolution. Previously the course for doctors took six years; now the student is in school for three years. This is still experimental, according to the staff we talked with. After the three years of course work there is an apprenticeship of another one-and-a-half years before the student can begin performing operations. In the meantime, his training is preparing him, usually, to be a "generalist" rather than a "specialist." He is quite likely to spend a good part of his life in the countryside, either resettled there or as part of a mobile team, and a wide range of skills will be necessary.

There has been another innovation in the training program even more recent than the barefoot doctor program. This is the training of Red (health) Workers. They seem to be, in fact, an urban and industrial version of the barefoot doctors. An abbreviated basic course and recurrent follow-up sessions enable them to care for the health of fellow workers in the factories and to stimulate an awareness of health problems particular to industrial situations.

Although only two of us, Tony and Rhea, tried acupuncture (see Introduction), several of us had simple colds and fatigue and were treated by a number of different types of health workers. Our experience with the Red Workers came during a visit to Peking, where Paul began to cough violently:

"The factory worker sitting next to me asked if I wanted to see a doctor. I said that would be too much trouble and that I did not want to bother anyone. At that point, I began to cough again. He then got up from his chair and went out to find a doctor. He did not have to go far; it seems that three times every week a member of the factory clinic and one of the Red Worker medical team will visit each section of the factory. A member of this team was called, and I was led out of the meeting to a smaller room where my pulse, temperature, and blood pressure were taken. When I told the health worker I was sorry for bothering her, she said, 'Don't worry about it—I must.' I then said, 'Yes, but today is Sunday —isn't it a holiday for you? And am I not interrupting your day off?' She answered, 'Yes, it's a holiday for many people, but I have a day off when someone else is working, so now it is necessary for me to work. It's no trouble because I always make the rounds in the afternoon.' "

Paul was given a combination of Chinese and Western pills and by the time we were on our way back to Hong Kong several days later, the coughing was gone.

For barefoot doctors and Red Worker medical personnel, there are special classes in basic medicine. These classes run from three to six months with training given at the hospital. A great deal of emphasis was laid on the fact that the Peking Hospital no. 3 is a training hospital. As an experimental hospital attached to Peking Medical College, it had concentrated primarily on research before the Cultural Revolution. Today, medical research continues but is applied in practice. The great majority of doctors and medical staff at the hospital spend one-third of every year on one of the "four fronts" of greatest importance: the countryside, the factories and mines, the border regions, and finally, all major government and military units.

9. THE ARTS

The broadsword fight ended and the band started up again. The brightly dressed young actors began a skit based on part of the opera *White-haired Girl*. At the edges of the playground, the parents watched proudly and laughed with us . . . we were at the Hongqiao Commune, learning about culture in China. It was the same at every commune and school we visited—every unit has a cultural troupe of some sort—and this was the most impressive aspect of Chinese culture today.

It is a popular culture. For the first time in China's history, all the people are integrated into the cultural and artistic life of the nation. Everywhere, traditional forms of art and culture have been revived and with the help of modern technology spread throughout the country. Young people learn ballet and folk dancing, operatic singing and folk songs, as well as all the techniques necessary for putting on a stage performance before a large audience. Poetry and drawings appear on the walls and bulletin boards of all the factories. Many of the traditional arts and handicrafts are being manufactured on large scale, and these products (paintings, prints, embroideries, wood and stone carvings, porcelains) can be seen in most Chinese homes. To make certain that everyone has access to this new culture, factories produce equipment such as the high-quality portable movie projector, developed in Nanking, which comes with a small electric generator so that movies of the new operas and ballets can be shown in the rural areas which do not yet have electricity.

Two Cultures of the Past

Throughout China's history two levels of culture existed side by side. One of these, urban-centered, sophisticated, and highly literate, was the monopoly of the wealthy and leisured class. Only they had the time and resources to learn the varied and complex literary forms of classical Chinese. The arts which went along with literacy—calligraphy and brush painting, poetry and other forms of creative writing—were the contribution of this tradition to China's cultural heritage. But for the vast majority of peasants the harsh realities of everyday life put this culture beyond their reach. It remained the exclusive preserve of a tiny literate elite until well into the twentieth century. In fact this ruling few, by making literacy a major criterion for political and social advancement, managed to perpetuate their own control of the society by denying their culture to the peasants.

It is this "literate" tradition which is studied in the West as "Chinese culture." But through thousands of years of Chinese history, there was a second culture, for the peasants had their own rich and varied folk traditions. The forms of this folk culture (and there were distinct regional variations) were nonliterate: storytelling, puppet shows, small dramatic performances, drawing, singing, and dancing. This peasant culture was regarded by the mandarins in the cities with disdain and ignored, so what records remain from the distant past are rudimentary. Instead, the forms themselves have survived.

The tumultuous period before World War I produced a new generation of writers determined to revolutionize China's archaic culture and education. Though from the traditional cultural elite themselves, they advanced the idea that the spoken language of the average citizen—paihua—should be the basis of a new society. They demanded the elimination of requirements that government officials be well grounded in the classical language and culture, thus making possible the participation of millions of Chinese unable to obtain a classical education. In a proliferation of new magazines and pamphlets, they attempted to write for "the people"—but the people, by and large, could not read. Their efforts, because they remained concentrated within their own circles in the cities, failed to reach or influence the lives of most Chinese.

With the establishment of the People's Republic in 1949, all forms of culture underwent fundamental changes. The major emphasis was now put on making as many Chinese as possible literate. Educational campaigns to teach reading and writing were carried throughout the countryside. First attempts were also made to expand cultural and art forms that would be easily understood by the average person, and local folk-culture groups were encouraged. However, a wide gulf still separated the peasants from the cultural leaders, who were mostly writers and intellectuals. As this group became a solidly entrenched bureaucracy, once more the familiar distinctions between intellectuals in the cities and the newly educated peasantry arose.

The Cultural Revolution was an attack on all forms of privilege, including the status attained by intellectuals and writers. Significantly, some of the opening shots were fired at Peking University, the Harvard of China, and later developed into a full-scale attack on the elite in both government and education. As a result, virtually all the leaders of the post-Liberation culture movement were attacked for their backward policies. While the outcome of the Cultural Revolution is not yet clear, it is certain that there will be a totally new direction for cultural development. In China, we were able to catch a glimpse of these beginnings, just now becoming visible.

Everyone a Star

The broadsword fight at Hongqiao was very much like the performances we saw in other communes, and in factories and schools. The people of Hongqiao were tremendously proud of their children's accomplishments. They watched us as we sat down, smiling in anticipation —they had no doubts about our appreciation of the show. There was no feeling that because the performers were middle-school students in simple work clothes, their show was less valuable or enjoyable than one in Shanghai's great entertainment halls. And they were right.

We were all sitting on three sides of a flat cement threshing ground; directly opposite us, on the fourth side, was the school building with bright red tiles and wooden-lattice windows. The ubiquitous cold towels and hot tea appeared before us, with a few packs of cigarettes, and the audience quieted. Out came five or six girls—all from the middle school, judging by their appearance—with long pants, bright blouses in all colors, and their braids tied back in ribbons. The band welcomed them with a magnificent flourish of gongs and drums—during the show we also heard them play a kind of accordion, a Western-style violin, and the Chinese violin called an erwu; always very loud and with tremendous enthusiasm.

After the opening sword-fight dance (portraying the anti-Japanese struggles of the thirties and forties), one of the young girls stepped forward, waited for the band to begin, and sang an aria from *The Red Lantern*—beautifully. As she finished, another girl appeared to one side, rested a moment, and then danced onstage. It was a ballet sequence from the *White-haired Girl;* though she had only cloth shoes and could not go up on point, her dancing was so unstrained and confident it looked very professional.

There was a short break. "Where do they learn to dance and sing?" Judy asked the villagers of the commune. "Does the state send around teachers?" "No," said a pleasant woman who might have been the mother of one of the performers, "they see the movies of model operas like *The Red Lantern,* or ballets like *White-haired Girl,* and then they come home and practice. For the songs, there are the movies and also our radios, and they can buy records to listen to as well. They practice a lot together, and after a while they aren't bad at it." An understatement, we thought, but remembering the hours teen-agers spend at home learning to sing popular songs and practicing dance steps, this explanation was very convincing.

The final part of the program was a fascinating combination of songs and a short skit. The girls had woven hats of leaves and grasses to resemble the peasant hats of Vietnam; they played the role of guerrilla fighters, shooting down U.S. planes and working with the villagers to reconstruct bombed-out buildings and harvest rice. We found this theme of third-world people's struggles repeated in many of the amateur cultural presentations. In Nanking we saw a long and complicated dance skit about African workers. The young Chinese boys and girls wore dark brown tights and sweaters and makeup, and for music they had huge bongo drums and flutes. The story was of workers exploited on a plantation; the owner often beats his workers and one dies of a very severe beating. The others, enraged, rise up against the owner and drive him away. In this way the "fighting-back" spirit of the oppressed peoples is constantly portrayed and admired. When we saw an African drama very much like this in Soochow, we asked where the idea had come from. It turned out that there had been a group of Tanzanians who visited China and performed for cultural circles. The Chinese dancers learned the movements and rhythm, then popularized them. From this, each local group had developed its own variations on an African theme.

To our embarrassment, we found that the Tanzanians and other visitors before them had established another pattern—everywhere, we were asked to sing or perform something from America. Our junior-high music classes were far in the past, and we felt terribly inadequate. Even those of us who can sing passably are not used to doing so in front of others—and it was hard to explain that in America, performing is generally done by people paid for it, and others are embarrassed to try. No one really believed us in China. They would keep asking, smiling and urging us not to be shy, assuring us how much they wanted to hear American songs. Our solution was to sing a few standard songs—usually "I've Been Working on the Railroad" and "This Land Is Your Land," followed with our renditions of one or two Chinese songs. Since a good number of us weren't really singing, just mouthing the words, our sheepish performances were short and very unremarkable, but invariably loudly applauded.

What Is "Culture" Now?

The most surprising aspect of this new movement is the clear deemphasis and questioning of all the literary arts—novels, short stories, poetry, and other kinds of creative writing. Since the Cultural Revolution the writing of novels has almost stopped and other forms of creative writing have decreased markedly. Furthermore, the books written in the 1950s and the early 1960s are no longer to be found in bookstores anywhere. The new emphasis is on visual arts such as cinematic and theatrical productions, picture books, prints, posters, and sculptures. The reasoning behind this dramatic shift appears simple but is actually quite revolutionary: as long as there are millions of partly educated peasants and workers and some highly educated people at the top of a cultural and educational bureaucracy, a culture based on literature will continue to be an elite culture. In an attempt to deal with this problem, there is now a clear focus of attention on the forms of culture which can be enjoyed by anyone, literate or illiterate: the visual arts.

Primary examples of the new cultural works are the Peking-style operas on revolutionary themes, such as *The Red Lantern, Shachiapang, Taking Tiger Mountain by Strategy, Raid on the White Tiger Regiment,* and *On the Docks;* a ballet, *Red Detachment of Women;* a folktale made into a ballet, *White-haired Girl;* the symphony *Shachiapang;* and a group of clay sculptures called *Rent Collection Courtyard.* These particular works, which are known as "models" of the new cultural movement, are symbols of the new direction in art and culture since the Cultural Revolution.

Tremendous attempts have been made to popularize these new works in an effort to make culture accessible to even the poorest people. These works are performed live by cultural troupes in all the major cities and by provincial troupes in the smaller cities. They have been made into excellent color films and distributed throughout the country, and large color posters of scenes from them can now be found in almost every home in China. In addition, they are frequently broadcast over the radio. There are records, picture books, musical scores, postcards, wood-block prints, embroideries, and paintings depicting various scenes. Most of these items are quite inexpensive. Finally, songs and dances from them are learned throughout the country by children in many of the schools. The vast spread of these works indicates a thoroughgoing attempt to make them available to everyone and thereby break down the barriers which kept the literature of the 1950s out of the hands of many who could not yet read.

In addition to the model works, the new encouragement given to nonliterary culture has brought about a revival of folk arts in local and regional areas. Many amateur groups have resurrected almost forgotten songs and dances, and are engaged in creating new ones based on peasant and worker themes. In this area there is a great range of potential for development and the surface has only been scratched; there is reason to believe it will grow tremendously in the next few years.

Everyone a Singer, a Dancer, an Actor

The most important result of the spread of mass culture is that now almost everyone in China participates in some way in the cultural life of the country. One rather sophisticated example is that, in 1966, as a result of the new movement, the workers at the Dajing oilfield in northeast China wrote, produced, and acted in a full-length drama called *The Rising Sun*. It was the first such production ever created by workers and was obviously the result of the new emphasis on everyone's participating in cultural affairs. Most schoolchildren are now learning these skills as part of their education. Of course once the skills are taught, the door is opened for creativity from the grass roots, and now many works like *The Rising Sun* have been created by Chinese workers and peasants.

Naturally, the quality varies immensely. But the idea is that everyone is an artist—even if a bad one—and contributes in some way to the cultural life of the community. Thus there is a great development of "amateur" artistic and cultural activity. This kind of activity may be encouraged from above, but in the end the initiative must come from below, from individuals and local groups. This is now just in its beginning phase.

It does not mean, however, that cultural and artistic affairs are not coordinated at the national level by the leaders of the country. The model operas and ballets have all been carefully screened and revised, and are in agreement with the goals of the government's cultural program. As "models" of the values of New China they are meticulously performed as written, and few liberties are taken with any aspects of their production by the groups which perform them. In this way, then, the cultural movement is given direction by the government.

Nor does the goal of having everyone become somewhat of an amateur artist eliminate the need for professional companies or full-time specialists in cultural or artistic affairs. There are professional companies and schools throughout China for training cultural performers and artists. We visited one of these, the Sian Municipal Red Guard Cultural Troupe.

The cultural troupe had just emerged from several years of intensive change prompted by the Cultural Revolution. It was founded in 1959, but ten years later—in November 1969—the entire school had temporarily closed down and everyone had gone to work with the peasants in the mountains for eight months. Now they were back, and had spent the last year trying to put into practice what they felt they had learned from that experience. The most important results seemed to be a new emphasis on the idea of self-reliance, and their own attempts to "serve the people."

Self-reliance covered a wide range of innovations. Most obvious as we arrived at the school were their farming plots, but these were small and not the most important change. That we found in the shop, where the troupe now made their own ballet shoes, repaired musical instruments, and constructed sets. Before this new program the troupe had bought all of their ballet shoes from a factory at eight yuan a pair; now, making them themselves, they cost only three yuan, and could be supplied cheaply to amateur groups in the area. There had also been a great effort to simplify the sets and make them more easily portable because of the traveling the troupe had undertaken.

In the last six months the troupe had performed—taking orchestra, sets, and equipment with them—for 34 communes and factories and 12 units of the People's Liberation Army. Performances in Sian's city theaters for general admission had numbered only 42, and this represented a major shift in emphasis. After their stint in the mountains, the troupe had come back convinced that they could help brighten the lives of the peasants. They also realized, as they had not before, that they had a lot to learn from the peasants. The pleasure they gave could increase and their efforts would be appreciated more if they listened to their audience. What was important to them? What kind of character was admired, what kind only tolerated or despised? Were some situations simply not believable?

During this period no new members had been admitted to the troupe's school, but in the last year a second generation had enrolled. We visited them in a ballet training class, where we found two groups practicing in a large, high-ceilinged room lined with mirrors and bars. Against one wall, a group of teen-age boys were working on the parallel bars; their teacher walked among them, pushing up drooping legs and turning ankles in or out. The boys were in T-shirts and shorts; the girls, in the middle of the room, were wearing what looked like gym suits. The girls seemed to be somewhat younger, but no less skilled. The director of the school told us that the students have a full course load, including such subjects as Chinese language and literature, politics, and history, in addition to those directly related to the arts. All the students learn to perform ballets and dances, to play musical instruments, and to do the technical work (lighting, sets, props, etc.) necessary to putting on both ballets and local folk dances and music.

From the exercise room, we walked to the hall where the symphony orchestra was practicing. It was a full orchestra of Western instruments with a few traditional Chinese instruments as well. They were working on a section from the *White-haired Girl;* we were watching them when, at one point, they evidently began to get ahead of the dancers practicing with them—they grinned apologetically and started that section over again. Here we asked about wages, and were told that, as in most units we visited, the greatest range was a ratio of one to three, with a base pay of forty-five yuan a month.

Finally we were led into the central auditorium, a great airy room with a full stage. And here, as usual, we were offered refreshments. We groaned . . . we had just had a huge lunch at the Textile Mill of Northwest China no. 1 and now came tea, chishui (the Chinese "7-Up") and sherbet, then more ice cream and ice-cream bars. Obediently we ate, only to find empty dishes instantly replaced. Obviously, the solution was to leave a little; but by now, we had progressed to the ice-cream bars, and what we didn't eat would melt in our hands. Only desperate explanations forestalled another round, and the program began. First, there was a very professional performance of a scene from the *Red Detachment of Women,* and then a wonderful duet of a flute and a Chinese mouth organ, the melody carried by the flute with low, deep support from the mouth organ. The last part was a series of folk dances: a Tibetan dance with girls in heavy, long skirts, and an adaptation of a Mongolian theme. Finally, with a grand flourish of sound, the program—and our visit—came to an end.

The Sian Cultural Troupe had changed greatly, they felt, during the struggle against the "star" system and the desire for fame. The slogans of self-reliance and serve the people had led them to "engage in labor"—producing their own shoes—and to "go among the masses"—traveling to the factories and communes. The final goal is some day to have all cultural and art workers come from the working people, work with them, and perform entirely the kinds of things they appreciate. At the present time, however, this ambition is only in the beginning stage. Culture without the rise of some kind of cultural elite has rarely been achieved; it remains to be seen whether China can achieve such a state of cultural development.

Literary culture has always placed a great emphasis on individual creativity. Perhaps partly as a reaction to the old culture and partly as a result of the socialist value of cooperation, the Chinese have begun to put a great deal more emphasis on collective creativity and criticism. Many paintings, for example, are now done by whole groups of artists working together. *Taking Tiger Mountain by Strategy,* perhaps the best of the new operas, was a collective enterprise from start to finish. Members of the Peking Opera Theater of Shanghai wrote and revised the dialogue, music, and choreography many times. Together they arranged all production details of set design, costumes, and makeup, and they also wrote several critical reviews on theoretical and practical matters related to the production. This collective procedure was similarly carried out in the production of other model works.

The Chinese are also trying to get away from the "big name" in culture and art. There are few famous writers or star performers in the new movement. When the Sian Cultural Group performs the ballet *White-haired Girl* three dancers share the difficult lead role throughout the performance. Although there are excellent dancers there is no need for prima donnas. No one about to perform is introduced in the manner: "So and so will now sing such and such." It is always: "And now, such and such a song." They feel that if everyone participates, then it is elitist to headline one lead role—separating it at the start from the other actors and also from the audience.

What will the future hold for the new movement in culture and art in China? There seems to be little question that the movement is exciting, and that it is being well received among the Chinese people. Its excitement is generated in part by its lofty and egalitarian ideals. The Chinese seem to be saying that everyone has the right to demand active participation in cultural and artistic life, that it is part of being a whole person.

Yet this course is still relatively new. After 1949 it was believed that the movement for popular culture would accelerate, but in fact an old intellectual elite reaffirmed the predominance of the urban-based literary culture. Many Chinese think that even now there is danger that a cultural elite may spring from among those who are doing full-time cultural work. It is to provide a concrete alternative to this model that the present movement attempts to spread participation in cultural and artistic life.

New Forms, New Content

The new artistic and cultural works are in form a fascinating combination of the old and the new, the traditional Chinese and the Western, the realistic and the romantic. The total effect is something unique. On the one hand, old techniques are employed and in some cases even substantially improved. The Soochow embroiderers, for example, carry on a tradition dating back to the Sung dynasty (950 A.D.) but have now more than tripled the number of types of stitching and have produced thread in hundreds of different shades of color. The results have been to widen tremendously the visual variety and subtlety of lighting nuances and three-dimensional effects. Peking opera, too, is a highly developed traditional form, and the singing style and instrumentation are retained in the new operas. The technique of watercolor painting in the traditional style is still in use everywhere. And much of the folk culture now being revived has a long history.

On the other hand, many new techniques from the West are now in wide use. Oil painting is becoming increasingly popular; Western musical instruments are available everywhere and are used not only for adaptations of traditional pieces but also for ballet and other Western forms of music. There is a symphony, *Shachiapang,* and also a *Yellow River Piano Concerto,* both of which are quite popular. Of course, the ballet itself is a Western art form, and the Chinese have produced two beautiful fulllength works in this medium—*Red Detachment of Women* and *White-haired Girl.*

Combinations of Chinese and Western and old and new can be seen everywhere. For example, all the model works are scored for both Chinese and Western instruments, and oil paints are being used to paint traditional landscapes. The Chinese also point out that the model works combine what they call "socialist realism" and "revolutionary romanticism." That is to say, although the actors are real people, engaged in real activities, the heroes are portrayed as bigger than life to emphasize their virtue, and the villains are portrayed in sinister splendor to set off their iniquity. No one really believes that the People's Liberation Army troops wore spotless uniforms with white capes during the war against the Japanese, or that the "Internationale" was played by an orchestra at the death of martyrs for the revolution!

While the forms employed in artistic and cultural pieces

are drawn from both Chinese and Western traditions, the content is what is most strikingly different to Western sensibilities. For above all else, culture in China is political. This is because the Chinese feel that art and culture cannot and should not be divorced from the political goals of the revolution. The content is just as important as the form, and there is no "art for art's sake."

White-haired Girl

White-haired Girl is a typical example of the new cultural direction. Originally a folktale of Shenxi Province, it was made into a play during the Anti-Japanese War, and is now a ballet. It is also an ingenious combination of old forms with new political ideas, and at the same time a visually and musically beautiful piece, despite what in the describing might seem a sappy melodramatic *Perils of Pauline*. All over China we saw parts of this acted and played, and at Sian we saw a full performance.

The ballet opens with a young village girl tidying up her cottage on the day before the Chinese (lunar) New Year. She spends the early part of the evening celebrating the holiday with village friends, among them a young man who has paid her special attention. After they have left, her father returns home—he is an old man, a widower with just this one daughter. He is also very poor and is only able to afford a gift of a red hair string while the other village girls wear flowers for the holiday. Nevertheless, father and daughter are very close and express their love for each other. A Chinese flute plays a fast, light tune of birds trilling and singing.

After this beautiful scene come violence and disaster. The local landlord and his men arrive to collect the year's debts. The father angrily says he doesn't have any money to pay and tells them to go away. But the landlord has seen the girl. An idea comes to his head, he rolls his eyes around, chuckles an evil laugh, and tells his men to grab the girl. The father tries to defend his daughter, and struggles until he is knocked to the floor. The girl kneels down to look at her father; she screams with horror—her father has been beaten to death. In this moment of grief, she is taken away by the landlord's men.

The following scene has a dark and gloomy setting. In the landlord's home, beneath a scroll which says "The Home of Benevolence," the girl is brought before the landlord's mother. She is still angry and unwilling to serve the landlord and quarrels with the mother. Because of this rebelliousness she is beaten, but with the help of an old servant the girl finally escapes. The landlord's men chase after, trying to recapture her. Tired, cold, frustrated, they give up pursuit when they see one of her shoes lying beside a river. They assume that she has drowned.

The girl flees deep into the mountains, where she gathers wild fruits and vegetables and learns to survive in the wilderness. From time to time, forced by hunger, she goes to a local temple to collect the food left on the altar by worshipers. Due to the lack of salt in this diet, her hair turns white, and her red jacket and pants become tattered and faded. To show the lapse of time and how she has changed physically by living in the mountains, she dances behind a rock to stage left, a different dancer at once appears from the other side of the rock, dances across the stage to disappear behind a tree at stage right, and a third dancer appears a moment later from the other side of the tree. In this way, the dancer changes three or four times, each time the hair becomes whiter, and the clothes fade from red to pink to white and get more tattered.

By this time, the revolution has begun to spread in China. The landlord and his son want to collect their wealth and flee the village. They do it stealthily, without letting the rest of their family and the villagers know about it. The two men, hair uncombed, a jewel box under their arms, run to the local temple, looking back and forth to make sure nobody is pursuing them. The girl is in the temple searching for food. When she hears footsteps, she quickly jumps onto the altar and hides behind the curtains that normally shelter the statue of the goddess of mercy. But when she sees her old enemies, she jumps from behind the altar. The two men fall to their knees with fear, thinking this white-haired creature is the goddess or a ghost. In great anger, she picks up fruit from the altar to throw at them. Chasing after them in the temple, she comes close to the landlord at one point. A clear and loud slap on his face can be heard, and the audience applauds. Just then, the villagers enter the temple, and the girl abandons her enemies and runs away. The villagers catch the two men but do not notice the girl.

Back in the mountains, the People's Liberation Army soldiers appear. In comes the girl's lover, who is now a PLA soldier. He returned to the village, trying to find her, but to his great disappointment she has disappeared. He comes to the mountains to search and suddenly he sees a white-haired girl among the rocks. In fright, the girl tries to run away, but after a brief chase they recognize each other. After this dramatic rediscovery, the girl returns to her village and friends. The landlords are executed, their lands and grain are divided up among the people, and the girl begins a new life.

Such suffering and the breaking up of a family were very common themes for folktales and fiction, dating back to ancient times. In this ballet, it has been rewritten from a revolutionary point of view. The girl's sufferings and her father's death are caused by the landlord's doings, and the people who finally save her are other villagers and the PLA. Class struggle is clearly the main theme of the story.

However, even with newly cast villains and heroes and heroines, the plot of the ancient tale still forms the main part of the ballet. Old and new are also mixed in dancing techniques. There are standard Chinese gestures like holding up one's forearm in front of the face and drying the tears with the sleeve, and revolutionary gestures such as thrusting the chest out angrily with one fist clenched in front. The music is also a new creation for Chinese and Western instruments. The Western violin, cello, and piano are the most widely used instruments, in combination with the Chinese flute, trumpet, cymbals, drum, butterfly harp, and string instruments.

The costumes in this ballet are all Chinese, with both men and women wearing jackets and pants. The main dancer wears silk jackets and pants which are cut very wide; these are especially beautiful when the dancer takes very short and fast steps on tiptoe; the clothes ripple like moving water.

A Western audience would also notice that the main figures in *White-haired Girl* are average peasants and not officials or rich people. In a country trying to eradicate the gross inequalities between city and country, rich and poor, this is only logical. The Chinese are making heroes of average workers and peasants, and are being blunt and direct about their feelings toward all other classes of people. This may help to explain the popularity of the new culture among the Chinese masses—for this sort of portrayal of "real life" is one with which practically all Chinese have had personal and direct experience.

Red Detachment of Women has a theme directly out of China's recent history—but displays a heavy influence of older drama styles. Acrobatic somersaults, swordplay, drums and trumpets flaring . . . all this is straight from the old Peking and Cantonese operas we had seen many times in Hong Kong. There also are some changes in ballet traditions of the West. During a struggle between the heroine and one of the landlord's henchmen (the plot tells the story of the liberation of part of Hainan Island), they are both holding onto a lance. While he crouches, she rises on one toe and turns. This is a familiar ballet movement, with the man supporting the woman, but here instead of the man being merely passive and supportive, he is actively struggling with her. At another point, after she has spoiled her fellow guerrillas' scheme to capture the landlord by beginning the fight too soon, the heroine goes back to the guerrilla camp and is taught better discipline. In this scene she dances alone; but now her emotions are strongly political as well as personal, and the audience can identify with a situation many of them have known.

The content of art can also be propaganda. It can teach lessons, morals, and political maxims. The Chinese are quite aware of this and are not ashamed of putting art to such uses at times. After all, they point out, all art is propaganda for something; the only mistake is to believe that all propaganda is art. They claim that art which expresses the world view of the working classes is art as much as that which expresses the world view of other classes of people. They go on to say that art cannot be separated from certain social classes no matter how hard you try. They are putting the "proletarian" content of art and culture together with old and new forms to create a mass movement which is now encompassing virtually all of the people in China.

Keeping the Old Culture

Yet if the new culture movement has such a radically new basis then the question arises, what is being done with the old art—or to the old art? This question is especially important in light of charges in the West that the Chinese have destroyed their old art, or that they are renouncing their ancient cultural heritage.

Basically, the Chinese have retained and continue to develop the techniques and forms of their traditional heritage. Opera, embroidery, and watercolor painting continue to play important cultural roles, and the Chinese are extremely proud of the great artistic works of the past. For example, visitors to the library at Peking University can see displayed editions of the classics dating back as far as the T'ang dynasty (600–900 A.D.). There are also Ming and Ch'ing dynasty paintings and rare scrolls and documents of every sort. The famous Imperial Palace in Peking, with its Forbidden City, has been undergoing renovation, and has just been reopened to the public. It has thousands of visitors every day, and if you ask them what they think of all this "decadence," they answer, "It's beautiful."

The ancient city of Soochow, besides being famous for its embroidery, is also justly well known for its scenery. Many parks built during the Sung and Ming periods are still meticulously well maintained and open to the public, even though they are remnants of the past. There are museums all over China which display the old works of art, and currently there is an exhibition in Peking showing ten thousand works of ancient art, dating back to 2000 B.C., excavated in sites found since the Cultural Revolution began.

What is happening, however, is that it is being interpreted in light of the political and social changes which have followed the revolution. When you visit the parks of Soochow or the famous Ming tombs outside of Peking, or even the Imperial Palace, they tell you that these great artistic achievements were built with the sweat and toil of the common people, and now the common people finally have the right to enjoy them. At the Ming tombs there are displays showing the contrast between the way the Ming emperors and the common people lived; there are also exhibits describing how the oppressive conditions and the way in which the people were bled by taxes led them to rise up in rebellion. These appear alongside the incredibly lavish and ornate crowns, jewels, and gold of the Ming court. In one of the Soochow parks there is a sign in a pavilion describing how the aristocrats used to come there for their (decadent) aesthetic pleasure to listen to the sound of raindrops falling on the lotus leaves, and asking present-day visitors to reflect on their own goals in life.

Thus, in many ways the Chinese are doing much more than simply preserving their ancient heritage. They are also using it as an educational experience, to illuminate the present as well as the past. To be sure, there are a few things which are considered to be absolutely decadent; for example, in the Summer Palace in Peking we noticed that one panel of a painting had been defaced—it depicted peasants kneeling before a court official. In the United States these works would be said to have "no redeeming social value." These will probably be allowed to disappear, but they are few in number.

Culture After the Cultural Revolution

What have the results of this new cultural movement been? First, the Cultural Revolution itself is a movement to change people's thinking, to get them working together for the goals of the revolution and the development of socialism in China. Cultural productions which express these goals and values are one of the most effective vehicles for carrying out the revolution. Consequently, great efforts are made to get these productions out to the countryside—efforts which are still going on today—with the result that culture and art have virtually exploded onto the rural scene, even in the most remote areas. Culture is coming to everyone now.

Secondly, belief in self-reliance and the determination of the people to improve their own lives through their own efforts has, in cultural areas, released a tremendous potential of creativity and artistic expression. The poetry and drawings on the walls of factories and schools are no accident. This movement is still just beginning, and the future may well see hundreds of millions of potential artists and cultural performers.

Thirdly, the spread of cultural life throughout the countryside will have an important effect on many practical economic, social, and political programs. For example, one of China's main goals is to achieve an even development of industry throughout the country—not just in the cities. Attempts to keep people from moving into the cities, to extol the virtues of living in the country, and to exhort young urban intellectuals and middle-school graduates to go to the countryside will be difficult unless living "out there" can be made as attractive as living in the cities. Cities have always been centers of culture in every society, but if the whole country can be made a cultural center this incentive to move to the cities will be removed. Along with raising the standard of living in the countryside and with the coming of adequate educational opportunities and medical care, the spread of art and culture is helping to reverse the trend.

Perhaps the most important result, however, is the enrichment of people's lives which the art and culture of China now has achieved.

10. WOMEN

Traveling through China we saw old women with feet painfully crippled from foot-binding, younger women working in the fields and operating machinery in factories, and middle-school girls shooting rifles in a militia drill. These contrasts convinced us that the changes in the lives of women since Liberation may be one of the greatest miracles of the Chinese revolution.

The position of women in old China is summed up well in two Chinese proverbs, one for men and one for women: "A wife married is like a pony bought; I'll ride her and whip her as I like," and "When you marry a chicken, stick with the chicken; when you marry a dog, stick with the dog." A young Chinese girl might have been sold during a famine, as were the mother and sister of one peasant we spoke with. She might have been betrothed as a small child, and sent to be essentially a servant in the household of her future husband, as was a retired Shanghai woman we visited. There she would probably be mistreated by her mother-in-law. In fact, the only women who had much power in old China were those who became mothers-in-law in their husbands' households. Ironically, this power was often used to abuse other women. Later in her life, if a woman was widowed, it was socially unacceptable for her to remarry. The anguish of women in this situation of forced marriage is illustrated in Chinese literature by many stories of women throwing themselves down wells or hanging themselves from their marriage bed with their wedding clothes.

Foot-binding ensured the economic and physical dependence of women. When still very young, girls had their feet tightly wrapped and bent until the arch was broken and the toes turned under. The result was a foot half the normal size, and a partly crippled woman. This custom first began in the upper classes, and was a symbol of riches since only a wealthy man could afford such economically useless women. Unfortunately, foot-binding gradually spread through all levels of Chinese society. The tiny, broken feet came to be considered erotic, and thus sexual attractiveness was tied to physical helplessness and economic uselessness. Foot-binding persisted into the twentieth century, and women at Tachai told us that some women's feet were bound until only shortly before Tachai was liberated.

In the early decades of the twentieth century, ideas about women's welfare and equality began to spread. Yet only the upper-class women benefited from legal changes, for the rest of society was still poor, illiterate, and uninformed. Even if a peasant girl discovered that she could no longer be legally forced into marriage, she would have no way to enforce her wishes. In the cities, growing industrialization merely added bad factory conditions to an already burdened existence. We were told of child labor in textile mills where female children were paid not even as much as male children. Older women worked sixteen hours a day in brutal, unsanitary surroundings.

In spring 1950 the new regime of liberated China promulgated the new marriage law. In one blow they made husband and wife equal in the marriage relationship, outlawed dowries and forced marriages, forbade maltreatment of children and infanticide, permitted divorce for women, and gave women property rights. All over the country, from the cities to the countryside, there were women's study groups discussing the new law. In this way, everyone was informed of her rights. Often women backed up by their government and other women struggled against their husbands and old parents or relatives who refused to accept the new law.

The Marriage Law has been so successful that people who were raised in pre-Liberation China find women's lives in the present almost unrecognizable. For example, an old man at Tachai who had witnessed the whole transformation of women in his village told us how much women have changed there, and concluded that women are completely equal now. He was unaware of the inequalities which remain, because all the most glaring and cruel inequalities of the old days are gone.

A Simple Appearance

Chinese women today have a beauty and radiance that comes from good health, confidence, and pride. The clothes they wear are comfortable and practical for their daily work and for riding bicycles, just like the clothes of the men. Women usually wear long pants of a darkish color so they will not soil easily, and simple blouses in white or pastel colors. Men and women alike wear clothes which can be worn without dry cleaning or ironing; once in our hotel when we requested an iron to iron some clothes for meeting with various embassy officials in Peking, our guides laughed at us for wasting time and energy on something so trivial, and said that they never bothered to iron anything. We never did get an iron.

Clothes and hairstyles for women are very plain, except for the occasional flowered blouse or skirt and hair ribbons. Women wear their hair in one of two styles which are practical for work; it is either cut short or worn long in two heavy braids. They never curl their hair or do anything artificial to it, and no one wears any makeup, except when giving cultural performances.

It is impossible to tell whether a woman is married unless you ask her. She may keep her own family's surname for work, and nobody ever calls her "Miss" or "Mrs."; instead they address her as "Comrade," or use other informal titles that do not indicate sex. She usually wears no wedding ring. Even if she works in the same place as her husband, they avoid public display of affection for each other in accordance with Chinese tradition, and each attends to his or her work independently of the other. Therefore, people around them might not know for some time that they are married.

Women at Work

Much of the pride and confidence shown by these women comes from their new, useful role in building China. The Chinese press constantly deplores women who "stay at home all day long and gossip and think of nothing but their families and household chores." The national policy is that all women should work at productive labor for pay outside the home just as men do, and that they should receive equal pay for equal work. This plan has succeeded surprisingly well, considering how backward China's women were only twenty-two short years ago. Women drive heavy trucks and bulldozers, wield picks on road gangs, and fly planes in the air force. Half of the nation's doctors are women, and women comprise more than half the work force in the textile industry. Most nursery and elementary-school teachers are also women.

At each people's commune we visited in the countryside, all the women are full-time workers, except the old women with bound feet whose working ability is very limited. At the Huadong Commune near Canton, 52 percent of the commune laborers are women. All the women are out in the fields working, just like their husbands. In many of the factories we observed, women were working alongside men on the same precision machinery, with no apparent segregation of jobs according to sex. At the Nanking Film Projector Factory, we could detect no discrimination according to type of job—both men and women were doing each type of highly skilled task.

In education, we saw no segregation between male and female students; girls and boys learn side by side at all levels. Each female and male student practices factory and agricultural work on an equal basis. There is no sense that certain types of industrial shop work are for men, and there are certainly no "homemaking" classes into which women are herded. In the militia, too, the number of women is high, though not quite half. We observed some Nanking militia exercises where women and girls were out practicing shooting alongside men and boys. We were told at the Huadong Commune that 43 percent of militia members are women.

Jobs for Men, Jobs for Women

As we traveled around China visiting many production units, we observed that there are some jobs which tend to be done by women, and some which are mostly for men.

In the educational system, for example, the pattern is similar to that found in the United States. The raising of young children, now in nurseries and kindergartens in China rather than only at home, is strictly woman's work. In the large nursery at Textile Mill of Northwest China no. 1 there are forty-four women teachers and one man who cooks meals for the children. We never saw a male teacher in any of the nurseries and kindergartens we visited.

Going up the educational ladder, from nurseries to primary schools to middle schools to universities, the percentage of female teachers gets smaller until male teachers are in the majority at the university level. At the primary school we visited in Nanking, there are thirty-nine women and seven men teachers. The men teach specialized courses, such as factory skills, physical education, and music. At Peking University, there were 646 women and 1,487 men on the faculty. In other words, in the educational system, the most prestigious and highly paid jobs are still heavily male.

In factory work and medical work, we found much more equality between men and women than is found in similar institutions in the United States. At the hospitals we visited, the number of female doctors was less, but not very much less, than the number of male doctors. However, the nursing staff was still entirely female. We visited an embroidery factory and a textile factory, where we were told that before Liberation all such textile work had been done by women. Now there are many men working there too. The Soochow Embroidery Factory is 20 percent men and the Textile Mill of Northwest China no. 1 is 40 percent men. In both factories, we walked around and watched everybody at work, noticing that for all highly mechanized tasks the men and women work together side by side doing the same thing. But wherever a job has not been mechanized, the task is done by women. At the textile mill the only tedious task still done by hand is the final inspection of every foot of cloth produced and the hand repair of all flaws in the cloth, and the workers who do this are all women. At the embroidery factory, some pictures are still totally hand-sewn, with each picture requiring nearly two months of careful work. Only women do this job.

We also visited some factories which in our own country would have all male employees—machine-tool factories, farm machinery plants, heavy-machinery factories, and a rolling-stock plant. In China such factories have mostly male employees, but the occasional woman can be seen painting the finished machines or driving a crane which moves heavy machinery around. The February 7 Rolling Stock Plant, for example, has 9,000 workers and staff. Of these, only 1,700 are women. This includes the women employed to care for children in the nurseries, kindergartens, and primary schools. So, although women are not barred from these jobs as they are in our country, either by company or union restrictions, some jobs are still generally considered to be men's work.

Finally, there are those jobs which are reserved mostly for men. The part of the working world least open to women is the People's Liberation Army. Members of the PLA are highly respected in China today, and they do much more than just prepare for the possibility of invasion. They hold important positions in all sorts of production units and governing bodies. To bar women from any significant role in the army effectively bars them from complete equality in leadership roles in China. We talked with only three women members of the PLA. One heads the PLA medical team at the deaf-mute school we visited in Canton. Another is a young PLA woman of twenty-two who is a student of English at Peking University. (There were other PLA women in the freshman class at Peking University whom we didn't get a chance to talk to.) The third is a member of the leadership at Tsinghua University. They told us that women members of the PLA do mostly logistics, medical, and office work.

When we asked why these differences between male and female employment continue, we were usually told that women are by nature better suited to some tasks, such as gentle care of the sick, patient rearing of children, and meticulous sewing or inspection tasks where perfection is required. Neither the men nor the women seemed to question the assumption that there are these sorts of inherent differences between men and women.

Wage Differentials

Although we met many women all over China whose pay is equal to or greater than that of the men around them, there are some male-female income inequalities built into the job and pay structures. For example, nurses get less pay, on the average, than doctors, and the nurses are all women. Kindergarten teachers get less pay than university teachers, and kindergarten teachers are all women while university teachers are mostly men.

On the people's communes, where the great majority of China's people live and work, pay is in work points which are added up and paid in cash at the end of the year. Each person gets a specified number of work points a day, depending on his or her strength, skill, and training, years of previous work, and political attitudes. For eight hours of work, the pay varies between four and ten work points. The pay for a man tends to be one or two points higher than for a woman. At the Hongqiao Commune, for example, the highest for a woman is eight-and-one-half work points a day, while the highest for a man is ten. Because men still have more years of work experience and more training than women who were not allowed to work outside the home before Liberation, this pay differential will remain at least until the workers are all women and men who began working after Liberation. Even then, the criterion of "strength" may mean that average pay for women on communes will never become equal to that of men unless agriculture is mechanized to the point that physical strength is no longer a factor in productive agriculture labor. Also, there is the built-in inequality that women on the commune who have a baby do not get paid during their almost two months' leave from work, in contrast to women factory workers who do get maternity pay.

Educational Opportunities

Continuing inequalities can be found not only in jobs and pay scales for women, but also in education. The educational system of China treats female students and male students equally in the classroom, but in some places there are more boys than girls in the school system. At the Huadong Commune they said that 45 percent of the students in the commune schools are girls, but 52 percent of the commune's population is female. It is not clear what the reason is for this disparity, but it may be that some commune girls drop out of middle school sooner than the boys. We happened upon a practical school class being given in a commune electric power plant, and the class was almost all male.

It appeared to us that higher education in China is still biased in favor of men. At Peking University, we were told that the student body is 30 percent women and 70 percent men. In recruiting their first year's class after the Cultural Revolution, the university's admissions committee made extra efforts to enroll children of workers, peasants, and soldiers, but not women. When we asked people there why there were only about 30 percent women, they said it was because almost all the students from the army were men, and they saw no inequities in that.

Leadership Roles

Men dominate leadership roles in the People's Republic of China. In almost every organization we saw in China, the leadership is disproportionately male. With one or two exceptions, this means that every commune, every school, every factory, every hospital, every local government branch which we visited had many more men than women in its revolutionary committee and Communist party committee. One of many examples is the May 7 Cadre School we visited outside Peking. The students there are all adults who work in various bureaucratic and teaching positions in Peking. They are some of China's most educated and sophisticated people, and we thought they would be aware of the desirability of having women represented in leadership in proportion to their numbers in the wider organization. The school has 40 percent women cadres, 60 percent men cadres. Yet the revolutionary committee has only five women and eighteen men; the Communist party committee has only one woman out of nine members.

We were fortunate to be able to meet with local leaders

in each city or town we visited. What are called "responsible members" of the city government would meet us at the train or plane as we came into town. Usually the delegation greeting us was three-fourths male, and had a few women as translators or members of the local leadership. The extreme example was Soochow, where all six responsible persons who met us at the train were men.

We found that even in factories where the workers are mostly female, the leadership is heavily male. For example, at the Soochow Embroidery Factory, where 80 percent of the workers are women, the revolutionary committee has seven women, twelve men, and the elected head of the committee is a man, as usual. In the primary school we visited in Nanking, the leading committee is proportionately representative with six women and one man in a school whose teachers are almost all women, but even there the head of the revolutionary committee is its one male member.

Of course in some places the problem of lack of women's representation in government and other leadership roles is recognized and combated with quotas for women, such as the 20 to 30 percent lower limits for women in Shanghai's district committees. The Eastern Peking May 7 Cadre School, which has such poor representation for women on its leading committees, has a quota of 30 percent reserved for women in its lower-level leadership groups. Apparently the Chinese are starting by training women for leadership in these least crucial levels of government. There are only 15 women out of 170 members of the Central Committee of the Communist party. But Yang Fujen, herself one of these fifteen women, is very hopeful about progress in this area. She pointed out to us that since the Cultural Revolution there has been a dramatic rise in the number of women delegates to national conferences.

Out in the countryside where the great majority of the people are, things move more slowly and ploddingly when it comes to something so wrenching as women's equality. Women's role in leadership varies greatly from commune to commune. The relatively advanced ones we visited have about one-third women, two-thirds men in their leadership groups. There are women leaders, yes, but their job for the most part is to lead other women, to confine themselves to women's affairs and women's problems on the commune.

The existence of those women's organizations and women "responsible for women's affairs" is an indication that the Chinese recognize the relative backwardness of the countryside. They see no need for this kind of separation along sexual lines in the city. We met several of these women leaders of other women at Tachai, the brigades near Tachai, the Huadong Commune and Liulin near Yenan. They described their leadership roles to us. Their job is to organize women into the work force, to raise the political level of the women, to assist any woman who is sick, to provide birth-control information, and to help with personal problems. At Liulin the women leaders mentioned that one of their accomplishments had been to see that each woman had a machine of her own to grind grain and also had access to a sewing machine. This mechanization of housework was obviously a big step in the liberation of the woman who formerly ground grain and made her family's clothes by hand.

Why is it that men still dominate leadership in China? One answer can be found by observing the women who have made it into leadership positions. They are almost always young enough to have entirely remolded their lives after 1949. Older women had already been so limited and deprived by the oppression they lived under that they could not shake it off completely. We met two women who are members of the Central Committee of the Communist party, and they are both in their thirties or forties. A housewives' factory we saw is a clear case of older women following and young women leading. The factory is full of older women, but its leader is a woman only twenty-nine years old.

Another reason why women are underrepresented in revolutionary committees and Communist party committees is that these committees are not completely democratically chosen. They are made up only partly of representatives elected by the workers in a factory or the people of a city. The elected members often include some women. But the problem is that these committees also include members of the People's Liberation Army assigned to help lead, and cadres from the local Communist party. These members are usually all men, perhaps including one woman cadre occasionally. The inequities of these committees merely reflect the inequities in other leadership organizations, namely, the Communist party and the People's Liberation Army.

When we had our daylong visit to Peking University, we sat around a big table being briefed on the campus scene, and we asked our usual questions about women's equality, which our guides and some men in our group no doubt got very tired of hearing. The questions were, "How many men are on your revolutionary committee and party committee, and how many women?" The people speaking to us, many of them members of these leadership committees, looked at us blankly and said that they had never noticed. Since women and men are completely equal in China now, who would think to ask that question, they said. We persisted, since women were clearly not equally represented in the largely male group of people telling us about Peking University. So somebody went off to look it up, and came back a little sheepishly with the information that the revolutionary committee has five women and thirty-four men, and the party committee has five women and forty-two men. Three of the five women on each committee are the same, so really only seven women in all get to participate in top leadership at Peking University.

A Housewives' Factory

Although many Chinese women had long been active outside their homes, some women have only recently begun to work. At the February 7 Rolling Stock Plant we saw a curious phenomenon called a "housewives' factory." Apparently in some urban areas of China, large numbers of women were still devoting all their time to household tasks and child raising. But probably even in a planned economy it is hard to fit everyone into a job, and since wives have not traditionally been part of the regular work force, many were unaffected by the socialist economic policies of assuring everyone work. But during the Cultural Revolution a great effort was made to organize everyone to contribute to the socialist construction of new China. Women who had never felt any duty beyond that to their husbands and family spontaneously wanted to or were encouraged to do more. More housewives' factories were started during the Cultural Revolution so that these women could work.

The rolling-stock plant where we saw the housewives' factory is more than just a large factory. It is a whole industrial settlement which includes housing for the workers, schools, and recreational facilities. It is virtually a city in itself and is located several miles from Peking in a suburban agricultural area. It is difficult for people who live here to get into Peking to work, although some do.

The housewives' factory was located on the grounds of the rolling-stock compound, but separate from the main shops. The separation is more than physical, as was immediately apparent when we entered. The buildings are small, the few machines fairly primitive, and the products, mostly recycled wastes, are definitely of subsidiary importance. Initially, women working in the factory received no payment for their labor. Now they receive only thirty yuan a month, lower than the lowest worker's salary in the main plant.

The people who showed us around the factory were very proud of this recent development, stressing over and over again the spirit of self-reliance of the women who had started this shop with nothing and had built it up without asking for aid from the state. They use nothing but waste materials in their production. From old pieces of wood they make small crates for carrying vegetables. Using scrap metal, they make hinges and lanterns for the locomotives. The Chinese need materials so much that they are not willing to let anything go to waste. We even saw a circle of women, most of them elderly, sitting picking little slivers of steel out of oily rags that had been used to wipe the parts of the locomotives in the main plant. They then washed these rags by hand and hung them up to dry so they could be used again and again. We saw that their hands were covered with cuts from the slivers, and one of us asked a woman if it was not painful to do this kind of work. Her answer provides a key to understanding all of this. She said, "When you're working for the revolution, it doesn't hurt."

Human resources, too, are not wasted in China. In other societies, you would see old women sitting in a circle and talking with their friends in the same way, but they would probably be economically dependent upon their children or on the state. The women we saw were proud to be independent and to be able to do something useful, no matter how small, that was contributing to the revolution. In the shop we saw a few men working and asked why they were there. We were told that they were retired workers who were employed in the housewives' shop to teach the women their skills. But it also gave these old men the opportunity to continue to be of use to society after their retirement. We also saw a young handicapped boy, a deaf-mute, working there.

However, it is a little harder to understand why able-bodied young women would be working there with old people and the handicapped. We were told that this was not a training place to prepare women for work in the main factory. In addition, the housewives' factory would never become a "state factory" (a higher-ranking production unit), because its purpose and justification was teaching self-reliance and making use of waste material from the main state-owned factory. This attitude suggests that housewives' factories are not thought to be important, and left us skeptical about this phenomenon. Of course, we have no way of judging these housewives' factories from one visit, but at least the one we saw seems to be perpetuating a second-class or auxiliary status for women. Although they are brought into the working force, they are kept doing menial tasks for low pay. And significantly, even after they have begun to work, they are still referred to as housewives or family members, not as workers.

In spite of *our* reservations, the women there were enthusiastic about their contributions, and about having built up their factory from nothing. There were even more women who would like to work in this factory than there are available jobs.

A Conversation in Shanghai

During our short stay in Shanghai, the seven American women in our group met with eight very liberated Shanghai women. Among them was Yang Fujen, a young woman who is a member of the governing revolutionary committee for the city of Shanghai, and also a member of the Central Committee of the Communist party. The other women included a member of a Shanghai district revolutionary committee, a Communist party secretary for a northern Shanghai district, a woman bus driver, and a member of a university faculty in Shanghai. They all stressed the positive side of the women's equality picture in China, and were themselves examples of the new Chinese woman.

At this meeting they told us that women are for the most part equal to men all over China. In their view, whatever inequalities are left are not major ones, and will be overcome gradually by education, persuasion, and practice. In Shanghai it seems that the days of the "feudal remnants" are numbered. For example, the woman bus driver proudly told us that before Liberation Chinese women were never allowed to drive anything; now there are two hundred women bus and trolley drivers in Shanghai alone. She said that women drivers had proved just as capable as the men drivers. This checked with our observations, for we had seen women driving buses in the city.

The three women who were members of the revolutionary committees at the district and city levels told us of the progress that women have made in acquiring leadership positions in Shanghai. They said that before the Cultural Revolution progress was slow; in the ten districts of Shanghai the vast majority of responsible posts were held by men. Chairman Mao then instructed the city's leadership committees to include a reasonable percentage of women. We were told that now about 20 percent of the leadership in Shanghai at all levels is composed of women. At the district level, three of the ten district Communist party secretaries are women, and on the standing committees of the district Communist party committees, one-third of the members are women. On revolutionary committees below the district level, they said, 30 percent of the members are women. We visited a workers' housing settlement in Shanghai, Chaoyang, which houses 68,000 people. A veteran woman cadre told us that out of twenty-one members of the settlement revolutionary committee, fifteen are women and only six are men. Chaoyang's revolutionary committee was the only unit we visited with a woman as top leader.

We ended our discussion feeling very impressed with these Shanghai women; they are dedicated and happy people. Because their liberation is basically complete and their environment very supportive, they show no resentment toward the male comrades around them. The leading women of Shanghai are a model of what liberated women can be like: relaxed, confident, productive, and a pleasure to be with.

Marriage

The obvious freedom and independence we sensed in the women we spoke with in Shanghai implied other changes in Chinese society, changes in marriage, in number of children, and in child care. We were told that now young people choose their marriage partners themselves on the basis of level of political awareness and compatibility in working together, but not on the basis of physical beauty. There are many chances for people in their teens and twenties to meet members of the opposite sex. This can happen at work or in youth groups, during cultural activities, at university, or just because of the widespread cooperation in Chinese society among large numbers of people on various projects. Of course, as in all modern Chinese societies, whether China, Taiwan, or Hong Kong, most husbands and wives remain emotionally and geographically close to both sets of parents. So while a woman chooses her husband and a man chooses his wife, each of them is likely to listen very carefully to the opinions of his or her parents for guidance in choosing a mate.

The Chinese government discourages early marriages. In pre-Liberation China, child marriages were common, and teen-age girls often had babies. The members of the Huadong Commune told us that the average marriage age for women used to be eighteen, but is now about twenty-three. In the cities the usual marriage age is higher than in the countryside. Late marriage allows each woman to get all the education she can, and to become a productive worker independent of whomever she marries. If she does not have husband and children at too young an age, she is less likely to be dominated in thought and action by her husband and her husband's parents, as in the past. This can be a real problem, because in the countryside a newly married woman often still moves into the home of her new husband's parents.

We were told by some women at the Tachai Production Brigade that criticism about their liberated activities came not from their husbands, but from their more old-fashioned parents, who live in the same house with them and frequently exhort their daughters or daughters-in-law to keep the old virtues and avoid being aggressive and outspoken like men. In the Hongqiao Commune outside Shanghai, some of us visited a household where an old couple lived with their four sons and the wives and children of their sons. If a woman lives in such a traditional environment as this, it is important that she has time to establish an independent identity before she marries. From what we could see on this trip to China, divorce is infrequent because it is discouraged and because couples who do not get along very well can tolerate each other better in China than in the United States. We were told that when a couple goes to court for a divorce, the first thing the court does is to attempt to reconcile the couple and help them work out their differences and reestablish their relationship on a new basis. Only after continued failures at patching up their problems will a divorce be granted.

But incompatibilities can be tolerated in a marriage because the marriage is only one part of life for the woman as well as for the man. A woman in China need not feel that the whole basis of her life is collapsing just because her husband is hard to get along with. After all, she has her own work separate from his and she takes part in various afterwork activities alone. As in traditional

China, she is very close to other women. This is a part of Chinese culture in Taiwan as well as in China; women openly show their affection and friendship by spending a lot of time together, helping each other, holding hands, and putting their arms around each other without embarrassment. Men in Chinese culture are close, too, and express their friendship with one another very openly. So the marriage relationship is not so crucial to either partner that imperfection leads to divorce. Each of them has many other relationships which matter, and each of them is involved in work and other activities outside the home.

Household Labor

The old patriarchal division of labor which relegated all the household tasks to women has not been very much modified in the People's Republic of China. Everywhere we went we asked whether men share in the duties of the home. Occasionally we were assured that men pitch in and do a little something around the house. The women in one household at the Hongqiao Commune proudly told us that all the men in the home know how to cook and do cook sometimes. But almost everywhere when we asked who washes the clothes by hand, who takes care of the children after they come home from school, who buys the food, who cooks the meals, who cleans the house, who does the sewing, the answer was, "The wife, of course."

One of the complaints of American women who work full-time, just like their husbands, is that it is exhausting to come home from a day of work and then start in on the household chores while the husband reads the newspaper or watches TV. The women of China do the same thing, without supermarkets, prepared foods, washing machines, dishwashers, and other time-savers. We asked ourselves how it was possible for China's women to do so much in one day. In the countryside the answer is that they just do it because it has to be done, no matter how exhausted a woman may be. They use lunchtime break and the evening. During the day, young girls work with their mothers and grandmothers to get the clothes washed, or the food prepared, or the baby cared for. Women cooperate with each other, neighbor women as well as women in the same family.

We encountered one striking example of women accepting a subordinate household role traditionally reserved for them. In rural Tachai, we were invited to several different homes for dinner. In each home, the women of the household cooked a lavish meal, then stayed in the kitchen or sat with the guests but did not eat. Meanwhile, the men of each family sat with the guests and ate with us. In each case we asked why the women were not eating, and they replied that it is the custom for women to serve the guests and men of the house, but not to eat themselves until the guests are gone. We pointed out that we felt this custom to be inconsistent with women's equality, and urged the women to eat with us, which they finally did. Most surprising of all, one of the women going along with this old custom was a young woman who is a leader of other women in the commune.

In the cities, the picture has changed. We were told of young couples who cooperate on their one day off per week, sharing the watching of the children and the household chores. It is common practice for people who work in factories or go to schools and universities to eat meals in the canteen. This saves time and costs no more than eating at home. A woman worker at the Soochow Grain Store no. 57 told us how she manages. She and her husband have three very young children, all in nursery or kindergarten during workdays. The whole family eats at the available canteens all the time; she never cooks at home. She and her husband usually do not have the same day off, so on her husband's day off he cares for the children and does necessary housework, and she does the same on her day off.

The people who work in city food markets have sometimes tried to lighten the burden of food shopping and cooking for their customers. We visited a market in a Shanghai housing settlement, and they told us that the market is now open twenty-four hours a day for the convenience of factory workers. Then they proudly showed us a prepared-foods table full of plates of washed, peeled, and chopped vegetables and meats, ready to be cooked and eaten—rather more appetizing looking in their fresh state than our frozen TV dinners.

A few conveniences lighten the burden for city women, but in the countryside the only modern convenience to help women is sewing machines, which are now widely available, and of course the nurseries, kindergartens, and schools which care for China's children while their mothers work outside the home.

Family Separation

During our trip, we began to wonder if the government callously separates husbands, wives, and children for long periods of time without much regard for their feelings. We kept meeting men and women who had not seen their partners for weeks or months because of the requirements of their jobs. We found an extreme example of separation between husbands and wives at the May 7 cadre schools, where each government bureaucrat is required to go occasionally to do manual labor. Male and female members of the bureaucracy sometimes spend six months, a year, or even up to two-and-one-half years far away from their families while reeducating themselves, and see their families only once or twice a year. All four of the guides and interpreters who traveled with us in China had spent one to two years recently at a May 7 cadre school, a great distance from their homes in Peking.

In other cases one member of the couple may be tied down in one place by a job, or by children, while the other goes to the army, to a border area to help with construction, or to the countryside to work temporarily in the fields. This is all very well if everybody is happy with the arrangement, and we questioned many people directly in personal conversations in Chinese about their feelings. The answer was usually something like this: "Oh, I don't mind. My job is exciting, so I want to do it even if it means separation from my husband (or wife). Besides, he (or she) has a good job too, and doesn't want to leave it. We go where we are needed, and don't feel any hardship." Work comes first for both women and men, so if it is necessary for a woman to leave her family or a man to leave his family for work purposes, either one will go ahead and do it.

Those of us who have lived in Taiwan or Hong Kong, where the culture has a lot of elements of old China, have known many couples who separated for months or years just for reasons of convenience or income. People do not seem to mind it there either. This easy attitude toward husband-wife separation may come not from socialism but from traditional Chinese culture. When we asked the women leaders in Shanghai why the government separates families, they responded that it is not intentional, but everybody's work is needed in new China. They said that whenever a couple requests a job change in order to be together geographically, the government changes their jobs as soon as possible, but there may be a lag of a few months while people's positions are shifted.

In one sense, this occasional separation illustrates the independence of Chinese women. In a Hongqiao Commune household, the wife of the eldest son had recently left the commune to go work somewhere far from the Shanghai area. She had left behind her husband, her husband's family, and three grown children, ages fourteen to eighteen. She plans to return only twice a year for a few weeks each time to visit her family. The whole family thought this was a perfectly normal thing to do, and they were proud of her work. They said the daughter-in-law had been very excited about her job, and was happy to go wherever she was needed to do the work. The youngest daughter-in-law of the same household commutes every day into the city of Shanghai to work in a factory and carries her newborn baby with her to the factory nursery, while her husband works in the fields of the commune.

Chinese women separated from their families need not fear for their safety. A great boon to the progress of equality between men and women in China is the fact that a woman can go alone anywhere in China and need not fear rape, theft, murder, or attack of any kind. Therefore, she can carry out her independent role fully without having to depend on a male escort for protection.

Family Planning

Chinese women have been freed from the tyranny of recurring childbirth by the easy availability of family-planning techniques. Couples are told that a small number of children will promote the health of mother and child, and give both parents the time and energy to be productive in their work and study. They learn about family planning from their neighbors, in study groups, local clinics, or their place of employment.

The government at all levels encourages couples to practice family planning. We heard everywhere that women can have abortion on demand, in the city or in the countryside, and that the operation is done safely at no cost in a hospital or clinic. Vasectomies are also available to men. Birth-control devices are available at all the places we visited in China. China produces its own version of the Pill, which looks like a flat piece of paper perforated into twenty-four small sections about one-fourth the size of a postage stamp. We were told that pills are very popular, but it is unclear whether they have managed to produce enough pills to supply all of China's women. Meanwhile, many other types of birth control are used. At the Huadong Commune, a doctor said that 80 percent of the women there use some means of birth control. Approximately half of them use the Pill and half an intrauterine device, with only occasional sterilization practiced. In Shanghai right now they are testing a once-a-month pill and various kinds of injections for birth control. At the textile mill in Shenxi Province, we were told that pills and condoms are the most popular devices.

As we traveled, we asked the people how many children there were per couple in each place. At the Chaoyang neighborhood housing settlement in Shanghai, the women said that the average is two to three children per couple. Most couples agree that three children are too many, they told us, but the problem is that most women want one daughter and most men want one son, so if the couple's first two children are of the same sex, they frequently try for a third. After the third they give up if they still have children all of the same sex. The biggest cities seem to have the most successful family-planning programs, and as you go out into the countryside, the number of children per couple becomes higher. At the textile mill near Sian we were told that the average number of children is almost three per couple. At Soochow Grain Store no. 57 a woman worker said that the female employees have three to four children each on the average. At all the people's communes in the countryside, they said three to four children per couple. These averages are deceptively high because all the older couples who have five or more children are averaged in with younger couples who may have only one or two children during their lives.

Each woman in China gets a leave of fifty to fifty-six days from work for childbirth and recuperation. If she works in a factory job or other salaried position she gets full pay during that time, but if she lives in the countryside she receives no work points and therefore no pay during her fifty-day maternity leave. We were assured at every commune that if she needs money during that time, however, she will get it without question from the brigade welfare fund. Babies are normally delivered by a midwife in the mother's home, but for complicated cases a mother is sent to the local hospital. If a woman has a difficult pregnancy, she can stay off work for an unlimited length of time. We met one woman who had taken ten months off work for pregnancy difficulties, and then returned to work with no loss of position. Since she had worked on her job for more than five years, she received 90 percent of her regular salary during the entire ten months she was on leave. We were told that women never lose any seniority or lose their jobs in China because of bearing a child.

Child Care

There are facilities to care for children from the day the mother's maternity leave ends—approximately six weeks—up to the age he enters school. The infants from six weeks to eighteen months are cared for in "feeding stations." This rather cold, clinical-sounding translation refers to a place that allows a mother to be close to her young child all day long, since the feeding station is located in the place where she works. She is given time off during the day to breast-feed her baby. If she is not breast-feeding, she may just hold or play with the baby. As the child grows, the mother need not be close by, and often the child is transferred to the nursery at the father's place of work, or to a nursery in the neighborhood where the family lives. In addition to these choices, families who have a grandmother living with them, usually leave their children in her care. People are not forced to take their children to child-care centers. They may make the arrangements they wish.

The child-care facilities for children are divided into three levels. The feeding stations are for the youngest, the nurseries for children from eighteen months to three-and-one-half years, and kindergartens for ages three and one-half to seven. The parent usually pays ten to eleven yuan a month for child care. This money is for food, and is about what it would cost for the child to eat at home. The children get three hot meals a day, and four if they stay longer. If a child is sick, there is a full-time nurse on hand, and the child is treated in a special isolation room. Of course, if the illness is serious, a doctor is called or the child is transferred to a hospital. Naturally, in China all this health care is free. Overnight facilities are also available at child-care centers. A small percentage of couples in the cities leave their children at the kindergarten night and day during the workweek, visiting them occasionally but only taking them home on the parents' day off. Children often stay overnight if one member of the couple works a night shift at a factory or if the parents have a meeting and no one to watch the children at home. We visited several such dormitories. They were crowded, but each child had a painted wooden bed with sheets and a colorful quilt—all provided free.

Traditional Americans would be quick to criticize China's women for neglecting their duty and shunting their children off to day-care centers, but the fact is that the many child-care facilities we saw were happy places for children. Perhaps the most pleasant one was at the Shanghai workers' housing settlement some of us visited. When we arrived we were greeted by a group of three-year-olds clapping to greet us in the Chinese custom and then running up to lead us by the hand into their room. The beautiful grounds of the nursery and kindergarten had lawns with sturdy wooden climbing toys and swings. The paths on the grounds were shaded by trellises with vines growing on them. We entered the room and were seated in miniature chairs by children who then ran off to prepare for the performance they were to give us. We were amazed by their poise and self-confidence.

The Chinese have a different orientation toward child care from that of most Americans. The people in our group were disturbed to see that the rooms where children were cared for looked very dull, spartan, and bare. We saw practically no toys, games, or books. The walls were either whitewashed or gray cement, with no pictures but the ever-present one of Mao Tse-tung. Just looking at this, one could easily jump to the conclusion that the Chinese have just done the minimum necessary—provide a place to dump children—so that women's labor can be utilized. However, this is definitely not the way the Chinese see it. They do not see these facilities as in any way inadequate or inferior. Rather, their whole emphasis is not on things for the children to do or play with, but on people-related activities. That is, their games will not revolve around equipment, but will be tag or hide-and-seek types. Instead of painting, a rather solitary activity, they spend a lot of time singing, dancing, and performing skits. We saw even the youngest toddlers doing the same dances that we saw middle-school students and even adult workers do. Their political education starts here too. The children learn quotations from Chairman Mao, and their songs and skits all reflect the belief that art should serve the people.

The children are getting the kind of care parents want for their children. Homes that we visited where there were children did not have great quantities of toys or other things for the children. Nor did other kinds of rooms— school rooms, meeting rooms, or auditoriums—have the bright colors and decorations we are used to. The austerity of the rooms is partly a result of the frugality of the Chinese, who believe that other things are more important at least for the present. As for the children themselves, they were brightly clad, happy-looking, extremely clean and healthy. It was summer, and many of them had heat rash, but all were wearing the white calamine lotion the Chinese use to treat it. We saw no examples of untreated illnesses.

The children certainly received plenty of love and attention. The ratio of staff to children was high in the child-care facilities we saw. In the nursery at Tachai it was practically one-to-one—many of the older women with their painfully bound feet found this was something they could do. When we walked in, they were sitting on a kang playing with and cuddling the children. As the children got older, there were fewer adults per child, about one to ten, but no lack of affection or individual attention. The children also get the valuable experience of developing relationships with one another.

There is a myth that the family in China is being broken up, that children are taken away from their parents, both as a means of breaking the strong familial ties of traditional China and to further utilize or eliminate all family responsibility. According to this myth, then, adults can devote all their time to their work and their children will relate to and love only the Communist party, Chairman Mao, or some other abstraction. We specifically asked about this and were told emphatically that this is definitely not true. The family is considered a positive thing.

Often older parents live in the same house with their married sons or daughters and their families, and the members of three generations then pool their incomes to give the family greater buying power. We visited many family homes where the family had purchased furniture, several bicycles, and radios by combining their resources in this way. If housing units are too small to allow older parents to live with their married children, then they often live just around the corner. For instance, in Shanghai we visited some workers' housing, and an old woman invited us into her apartment, and later took us to visit her son and daughter-in-law who live very close by.

The people who take care of children in the nurseries and kindergartens are not parent substitutes. And it was obvious wherever we went in China that parents, grandparents, and children have close relationships and enjoy doing things and going places together. Far from weakening the family, the employment of women and the childcare facilities that permit this have really strengthened it.

The Road Toward Liberation

The achievements of women's equality since Liberation have been not only on the practical side of life, but also on the spiritual side. It is exhilarating for women to live in the environment of the People's Republic of China even if they have not yet managed to become equal to men in every way. The writings of Mao Tse-tung stress that China needs the productive labor and ingenuity of the female half of the population as well as that of the male half, and that women can do whatever men can. The whole value system of new China supports and encourages women in their struggle for equality. Therefore, once a woman decides that she will be completely equal to all the men around her, the society will support her against whatever obstacles she encounters. For example, we were told about a couple in Shanghai who had marital problems over the issue of women's equality. The husband was a party cadre, and the wife had been just a housewife until the Great Leap Forward in 1958, when she had taken a leap forward herself and gotten a job as a Shanghai bus driver. She then worked her way up into a leadership position in the party too. She gradually spent less and less time in the home, and her husband started complaining bitterly about her neglect of household chores. She took the problem to a study group at her work, and all her coworkers encouraged her and her husband to study Chairman Mao's sayings on the subject together, which they did. The coworkers taught the husband and children of the family to share in the housework, and the result was that the woman continued unhindered in her work and leadership roles.

A husband may just stand aside and let a woman try things on her own, or he may actually help her. At the Huadong Commune, we were told of a forty-year-old woman who was asked by her coworkers to take charge of a warehouse. She was reluctant because she had been raised before Liberation and had never received any education. She was also afraid her husband would object. On the contrary, he encouraged her, and she took the job and did so well at it that she was elected to a leadership position in the commune.

The Chinese woman can thus find support in her environment for seeking new roles and responsibilities. For these women, proudly standing shoulder to shoulder with men, liberation is being able to work and contribute to the building of the new China.

11. CHINA'S FOREIGN POLICY

The *Peking People's Daily* of July 16, 1971, carried a small square box of Chinese characters in the lower right-hand corner of the first page entitled simply "announcement." The "announcement" was brief and restrained, not very different from the morning weather report. Henry Kissinger had been to Peking for talks with Chinese officials, and had arranged for President Nixon to come to Peking for a discussion of "normalization of relations between the two countries" and "an exchange of opinions on problems of concern to both sides." The article was tucked in beneath headline stories on the visit of a government delegation from North Korea.

We were in Peking, having lunch at the Xinqiao Hotel, when we heard the news. After a few seconds of stunned silence, Paul turned and saw one of our interpreters walking past. "Is it true?" he asked. "Have you heard about it?" "Yes, I know," she answered, smiling at our consternation. "It was in the paper today." The hotel dining room was buzzing . . . we began to speculate about the meaning of this news. We all agreed about the most obvious motive Nixon would have for coming to China—a grandstand electioneering trip—but everyone at the table was deeply confused about why the Chinese would invite Nixon. Why were they agreeing to talk to Nixon, whom they consider the archimperialist? What kind of change did this signal in China's foreign policy?

From his bed in the Anti-Imperialist Hospital, *New York Times* correspondent James Reston plaintively sent down a message asking us to find out what the Chinese "man on the street" was thinking of all this. We were curious ourselves, but in Peking that afternoon all was as usual. Everyone seemed to be going about their business very calmly . . . obviously, they did not consider it a tremendous reversal in China's policy, and did not yet expect this event to overturn the present situation. But we were not satisfied with these speculations. We wanted to know why China's leaders had made this decision.

Three days later, on the evening of July 19, we had an opportunity to ask these questions during a four-hour conversation with Premier Chou En-lai. By now there have been pictures of him in many American newspapers and magazines, and his calm, aging face—with the bushy black eyebrows and quick, humorous eyes—is familiar. He greeted us at the door of one of the smaller rooms in the Great Hall of the People, shaking hands with each of us and then following us in. He put us immediately at ease with a few comments about our trip and introduced the others in the room. Two of them we had read about for several years in China's newspapers: Yao Wen-yuan and Chang Ch'un-ch'iao, both members of the Political Bureau of the Central Committee and key figures in Shanghai's Cultural Revolution. We sat in a large semicircle, comfortable in large wicker chairs, with small tables for our notebooks and tape recorders and capped mugs of tea. The premier spoke in Chinese, and we waited while this was translated into English, then replied in English and again waited for the translation to be made. His Chinese was clear and easy for us to understand, but since this apparently is the normal procedure on such occasions, we observed the form. Later, in transcribing the text of the interview from our tapes, we were very glad of this, for it ensured that unclear sections were repeated.

At the beginning of our conversation, Premier Chou assured us that we were invited to take as many photographs as we liked, and also to tape-record the discussion.

The premier's talk centered on Asia, but the comments he made on the Nixon visit reveal the basic Chinese outlook on the likely development of ties with the United States. As such, it is an important document and we include it, in its entirety, as Appendix 1.

The Past

The Chinese believe that they have been the subject of American belligerency and threats for over twenty years. In their eyes, it is America that in the past has slammed the door on the possibility of better relations with China. What has been the Chinese experience in dealing with Americans, and what does it tell about how China will act in the future?

The main fact dominating Chinese-American relations since the Second World War has been the continuous involvement of the United States in Chinese affairs. This involvement began even before the founding of the People's Republic, with several billion dollars of aid and direct military intervention in China's civil war on the side of the Nationalist regime of Chiang Kai-shek.

When General George C. Marshall arrived in China in 1946 with instructions from Truman to settle the conflict between the Communists and the Kuomintang, he presented himself as China's generous best friend; the United States would be accepted as a disinterested mediator; whatever America favored would be in China's best interests.

Such presumptions came naturally. American missionary groups had for almost a hundred years dispensed in China what was "best" in American civilization, and Americans had come to view their bond with China as selfless and uplifting. When the Communists in 1949 won the civil war and turned toward Moscow, the shock and sense of betrayal in America was acute, the scene well set for Senator Joseph McCarthy's quest to find out who had "lost China."

Mao and his comrades had no sympathy for America's injured feelings. For even as Marshall in 1946 was trying to head off war, American war materiel and money were flowing liberally into Nationalist hands. By March 1949, the United States had fed Chiang's armies with *twice* the military aid given to China during the entire war against Japan. And American B-24 bombers were blasting coastal Chinese cities.

So Mao threw his lot in with the Russians. The cold

war, he believed, was carving up the world. "Sitting on the fence will not do," he said in 1949, "nor is there a third road."[1]

What else could Mao have concluded? The United States had not only bet on the losing side in the Chinese civil war, but it had supported in Chiang Kai-shek a regime of unrelieved corruption and one with little popularity. This proved to be an expensive mistake, and left a permanent residue of distrust toward the United States. Yet as late as 1949, it seemed that America might be willing to extend diplomatic recognition to the People's Republic as the legitimate government of China, despite the obvious distaste felt for the new regime. John Foster Dulles suggested that "if the Communist government of China in fact proves its ability to govern China without serious domestic resistance it, too, should be admitted to the United Nations."[2]

Korea

The Korean War dramatically foreclosed any possibility of peaceful Chinese-American relations. Barely a year old, the People's Republic was faced with a fierce war on its Manchurian border, close to important industrial centers. The American forces, which made up most of the "United Nations" or "allied" troops, were led by a general who seemed out of control much of the time and who had ordered air strikes on Chinese cities. The Chinese quickly learned that Truman's public statements had no effect on General MacArthur and that their territory could very well be invaded. In addition to ordering bombing attacks on Chinese border cities, MacArthur in late 1950 was clearly planning for an invasion of Manchuria after North Korea was occupied.

The People's Liberation Army, according to a 1960 RAND study by Allen Whiting, moved into Korea only

---

[1]Mao Tse-tung, "On the People's Democratic Dictatorship," speech, June 30, 1949, in *Selected Works* (Peking: Foreign Languages Press, 1961), vol. IV.

[2]John Foster Dulles, *War or Peace* (New York: Macmillan, 1950).

after repeated and explicit warnings that MacArthur's continued advance toward the Chinese frontier posed a direct threat to the Chinese industrial heartland of Manchuria. Thus, from the Chinese point of view, they entered the war in self-defense, even though it meant risking a total war with the United States, one that they were unprepared for.

Although the Korean War remained a "limited" war, Chinese casualties were very heavy, and they now recognized that America was the principal threat to their security. "For sixteen years we have waited for the U.S. imperialists to come in and attack us," Foreign Minister Chen Yi noted in 1965.[3]

Taiwan

From 1945 to the beginning of the Korean War, the United States, along with most other countries, recognized Taiwan as a Chinese province, an integral part of Chinese territory. President Truman in 1950 stated that "the United States Government has always stood for good faith in international relations. Traditional United States policy toward China, as exemplified in the Open Door policy, called for respect for the territorial integrity of China."[4] Secretary of State Dean Acheson stated the American official position even more strongly at the time: "The Chinese have administered Formosa for four years. Neither the United States nor any other ally ever questioned that authority and that occupation. When Formosa was made a province of China nobody raised any lawyer's doubts about that."[5] This had also been the policy under Roosevelt, and Taiwan was recognized as Chinese territory in both the Cairo Declaration of 1943 and the Potsdam Proclamation of 1945. At the end of the Second World War, Japanese forces surrendered the island to the Chinese army and the island was once again Chinese.

On June 27, 1950, just two days after the opening of

---

[3]Chen Yi, speech, cited in unpublished paper by Jonathan Unger.

[4]*New York Times,* January 6, 1950.

[5]*Ibid.*

hostilities in Korea, Truman ordered the U.S. Seventh Fleet to intervene in the Taiwan Straits. Although obviously a reaction to the Korean situation, Truman's action had the effect of saving the remnants of the Kuomintang government and Nationalist armies from final conquest by the People's Liberation Army. Once more, the American policy was direct intervention in Chinese affairs. This was even harder for the fledgling Communist government in Peking to understand since, six months before, the United States had seemed ready to abandon Chiang after his "final" defeat by the Communists.

The effects of this intervention were not seriously considered at the time, but the State Department earlier in 1950 had recognized what an intervention in Taiwan would mean:

> For the United States Government at this date to seek to establish a non-Chinese administration on Formosa . . . would be almost universally interpreted in mainland China and widely interpreted throughout Asia as an attempt by this Government to separate Formosa from China in violation of its pledges and contrary to its long-standing policy of respecting the territorial integrity of China. The important point from the standpoint of our interests in Asia, including mainland China, is not the technical justifications which we might urge . . . but rather the way such action on our part would be viewed by the people of Asia.[6]

Despite this assessment, the United States did intervene and continues to intervene today, without legal or practical justification for such a policy. The People's Republic has therefore regarded the central issue of American policy on Taiwan to be one of principle—would the U.S. keep up its interference in an internal Chinese matter? Would it insist on supporting Chiang Kai-shek, and would it continue to station troops on Taiwan?

---

[6] State Department report to the House of Representatives in early 1950, quoted in Jerome Alan Cohen, "Recognizing China," *Foreign Affairs,* October 1971.

SEATO

The Korean War shaped Washington's view of China as an "aggressor nation." The U.S. government concluded that China could only be contained through the threat of overwhelming force. The Pentagon accordingly built a military barrier enclosing China's periphery from Japan to Pakistan.

The most important link in this chain was the Southeast Asia Treaty Organization (SEATO), set up in 1954. This closely followed the end of the first Indochina war, in which the U.S. was deeply involved in trying to help the French colonial administration retain control of Vietnam, Laos, and Cambodia. Secret documents published in the *Pentagon Papers* have revealed that the American involvement was not limited to money but also extended to military action. American sabotage teams, led by intelligence officers, were sent into North Vietnam to blow up important transportation and industrial facilities as the conflict drew to a close with the formal French surrender.

From the start, the purpose of SEATO was clearly to encircle China. Yet the immediate justification for the new organization, as reflected in its name, was Southeast Asia. The defeat suffered by the French in Indochina was countered by an American treaty designed to reverse the course of history and bring the region back under Western control. But behind this short-range goal lay the obvious eventual target—China. Why should the struggle of the Indochinese peoples to free themselves from colonial domination have led the United States to see nearby China as a danger?

To American policy makers, and John Foster Dulles in particular, the departure of the French from Indochina was a disaster. It meant that an important region bordering China was no longer a secure pro-Western stronghold. America's control and influence over a strategic part of Asia was threatened. Dulles's answer to this situation was SEATO, which tied a string of Asian countries around China's periphery to American military objectives. The Chinese not surprisingly concluded that SEATO was aimed directly at them. This view of American goals was strengthened in time as the United States established a host of individual treaties with practically every nation on China's borders.

Tibet, India, and Laos

Along the length of its southern border, China has experienced numerous military provocations. These have usually included American involvement, and more often than not Nationalist Chinese participation, too. With a treaty system providing a framework for the American policy of containing China, these actions have often appeared to the Chinese as a deliberate plan. At best, they have fitted neatly with stated American policies.

In Tibet, China was suppressing an uprising led by the rulers of a minority population within China's own boundaries who themselves practiced slavery and serfdom. Tibet is also China's strategic underbelly, and once the Tibetans had risen, Peking felt it had no alternative but to call in the People's Liberation Army. This aspect of the Tibetan revolt is well known in the West. America's role in the 1959 uprising, however, is only vaguely understood. Most accounts have presented the rebellion as a "spontaneous" revolt led by supporters of the Dalai Lama, Tibet's former feudal ruler, and by Khamba tribesmen living in isolated mountainous areas.

A slightly different picture has emerged from disclosures in the *Pentagon Papers*. After the Tibetan revolt began, the Nationalist Chinese government began dropping military supplies to the rebels high in the Himalayas —either in CIA aircraft or with considerable CIA help. This was done through a supposedly private airline, Civil Air Transport, widely recognized as a CIA operation. By 1961, there had been as many as two hundred missions dropping weapons over Tibet, probably using Thailand as a stopover base. Although spokemen for Taiwan's Nationalist regime proudly claimed credit for the drops at the time, few knew of the CIA involvement.

One man involved in these secret missions, from evidence in the *Pentagon Papers,* was Edward Lansdale, by coincidence the man who led the sabotage teams into North Vietnam in 1954. Details of the secret airdrops will almost certainly never be known—how many American planes, how many American pilots, how much taxpayers' money spent secretly. But we do know that Americans were involved and that China's claims then were true. The CIA and Nationalist aid to the Tibetan rebels was also a prelude to the brief war fought on Tibet's southern borders three years later.

The war between China and India has been largely misunderstood by Americans. Ever since the border conflict in 1962, China has been depicted in the West as the expansionist aggressor against helpless India. Yet in fact, throughout the long dispute with India, China was patient and militarily prudent. Indian Prime Minister Nehru, for domestic political purposes, had refused to negotiate the two nations' ill-defined borders, although Peking had been willing to negotiate all of Nehru's claims. These were largely based on highly questionable nineteenth-century British colonial claims. Nehru believed that China would give way entirely without negotiation, and he adopted a "forward" military posture, advancing Indian forces into disputed regions which the Chinese had without protest occupied for years.

Nehru finally precipitated the war by a direct military provocation, the dispatch of 2,500 troops to capture well-fortified Chinese bunkers north of the disputed border line. China easily and quickly defeated India's poorly equipped troops throughout the border areas, then voluntarily withdrew in most sectors north of New Delhi's furthest boundary claims. One expert recently summed up the consensus among China specialists by observing that "the Chinese performance in this dispute, as shown in the Indian record, begins quite early to shine forth as both rational and reasonable, while the Indian performance grows steadily more unreasonable and irrational."[7]

Chinese experience in Laos presents a striking parallel to that in Tibet. Nationalist Chinese aircraft and commandos have been tightly integrated into the huge CIA operation against the Laotian Communists, the Pathet Lao. Only because of newspaper reports and a few sena-

[7] John K. Fairbank, "How Aggressive Is China?" *New York Review of Books,* April 22, 1971.

torial investigations do we now have a picture of the size of the American war in Laos, and much is still to be told. In addition to providing some support for the general American war effort in Southeast Asia, the Nationalist forces in Laos have engaged in military actions not directly linked to that war. At different times Nationalist airplanes have bombed up to and across the Chinese border, and with CIA help have sent raiding parties into China's Yunnan Province.

There is growing confirmation of the role played by the CIA and the Nationalist Chinese in the opium trade in northern Laos. But it is now clear that both have threatened Chinese security in a variety of places on her mountainous southern edge. Indeed, China's basic experience with her neighbors in this region has been one of continuous military provocations. Only Burma, which has remained steadfastly neutral throughout the cold war, enjoys comparatively calm relations with the People's Republic—perhaps because it also refuses to invite the United States to send troops, money, or advisers.

The Third World

Thirty-five years ago, while he and his comrades recuperated in Yenan after the Long March and the dream of Liberation was still far off, Mao Tse-tung told Edgar Snow: "When the Chinese revolution comes to full power, the masses of the many colonial and semi-colonial countries will follow the example of China and will win a similar victory of their own . . ."[8] Today the Chinese are no less convinced that their experience is relevant and valuable for the struggles of other third-world peoples. But the complexities of world diplomacy in a world dominated by hostile powers have always influenced the practical implementation of Chinese diplomatic policies.

The Bandung Conference

For four years, from early 1954 to late 1957, the similarities between intensifying anti-imperialist and inde-

---

[8]Stuart Schram, *The Political Thought of Mao Tse-tung* (New York: Praeger, 1963).

pendence struggles in Africa and Asia and China's own revolutionary experiences created a strong and supportive set of alliances. The first step came in April 1954, in the Chinese-Indian agreement on Tibet. This document outlined five principles which became the basis for China's dealings with all third-world nations during this period. The principles were: mutual respect for territorial integrity and sovereignty; mutual nonaggression; mutual non-interference in each other's internal affairs; equality and mutual benefits; and peaceful coexistence.

These five principles were affirmed a year later at the Bandung Conference of Afro-Asian Peoples, defining a new form of neutralism which was intended to give these nations more freedom of action in the world and more control over their own affairs. The idea for the conference had been raised by Indonesian President Sukarno at an earlier conference in April of that year; the aim would be to forge a political unity of the third world against the pressures of the European-American powers.

The small and "underdeveloped" nations had found that they were unable to determine their own fates and could not sway these world powers. The idea of united action to defend their interests can be traced to 1949, when fourteen Afro-Asian leaders met in New Delhi to discuss the Dutch military actions against the Indonesian independence movement. In 1950 these leaders began to meet in the United Nations on an informal basis. Their problem was relatively straightforward: the definition of "neutralization" which Euro-American and Soviet powers had imposed on Austria and Laos was too restricting. It severely limited the alternatives in policy making open to those nations, and they found themselves isolated and restricted, unable to bargain for what they wanted or needed because involvement with one power meant the enmity of another.

Under these conditions, the third-world leaders had not unreasonably come to the conclusion that their only strength lay in unity—in the formation of a "third bloc." Through Nehru's efforts, China was invited to participate in the Bandung Conference, and together with Nehru and U Nu of Burma, Chou En-lai worked for the affirmation of the five principles at Bandung.

China's Reasons for the New Policy

The five principles and the Bandung Conference represented a clear shift in the Chinese position. In the years since Liberation, the Chinese leaders had been preoccupied with consolidating their position on the mainland, economic recovery from the decades of war and the beginning of the First Five-Year Plan, and fighting a defensive war in Korea. Given these constraints any efforts to actively promote or support revolutionary movements abroad were impossible. Statements of ideological support for other struggles were highly orthodox and rather blunt:

> The course followed by the Chinese people in defeating imperialism and its lackeys and in founding the People's Republic of China is the course that should be followed by the people of the various semi-colonial and colonial countries in their fight for independence and people's democracy.[9]

Liu also said that only a Communist organization, based on the proletariat and a red army, could succeed in making a revolution; the entire statement was vigorously approved by the Soviet Union and reprinted in *Pravda*.

Liu's statement, and *Pravda*'s approval, accurately reflect China's situation between 1949 and 1953. Inexperienced, just beginning to recover from the civil war, and faced by a hostile United States across the Taiwan Straits and in Korea, China was in no position to oppose Soviet leadership.

With the end of the Korean War, however, and the success of its economic recovery, China began to reappraise its role in the world. By 1955 the first signs of a reconsideration of its dependence on the Soviet Union were already there—and China began to see itself allied with the "third bloc" rather than with Russia.

---

[9] Liu Shao-ch'i, quoted in George McT. Kahin, *The Afro-Asian Conference* (Ithaca, N.Y.: Cornell University Press, 1956).

The African Case

After Bandung, the position China took in Africa was conciliatory and realistic. Departing from Liu's position in 1949, it ceased branding Nkrumah and other nationalist, non-Communist African leaders as "lackeys" and "running dogs" of Euro-American imperialism. In large part this policy was based on a new Chinese strategy against the U.S. and Europe in Africa, one designed to prevent the alignment of African states with the major Western powers. In explaining their new support for these nationalist "bourgeois" leaders, the Chinese reminded the world that their revolution had been not only a Communist but also a nationalist struggle against the Japanese, and that—as Lin Piao said—the Chinese Communist party had ". . . made a series of adjustments in . . . policies in order to unite all the anti-Japanese parties and groups, including the Kuomintang."[10]

Under these conditions Chinese diplomacy in Africa was imbued with a spirit of cooperation. The chief criterion of China's support appeared to be the willingness of the African government and nationalist movements to oppose the Western powers. But in a period when many Africans were eager for independence and bitterly resentful of European and U.S. stances, this criterion defined almost all of them as friends.

The Suez crisis of 1956 was the culmination of this third-world defiance of European and American dominance. At that time only four independent states existed on the whole African continent: Egypt, Liberia, Libya, and Ethiopia. Of these, only Nasser in Egypt threatened U.S. and European hegemony because he confronted them with the notion of pan-Arabism, a unified front of all Arab states based on independence from all foreign ties. This front had been outlined at Bandung, in a pact between eight Arab states; the U.S.-European powers indirectly took cognizance of it by forming their own "Baghdad Pact" with selected states in the Middle East.

---

[10]Lin Piao, *Long Live the Victory of the People's War* (Peking: Foreign Language Press, 1966).

Egypt's claim to sovereignty over the Suez Canal, and acceptance of arms from the Soviet Union, brought an open break. The U.S. withdrew from the Aswan Dam project and Egypt found itself, in the attempt to claim its rights, forced into one of the big-power "camps."

By late 1957 China's policies had shifted dramatically. China rejected the Soviet model in foreign policy as it had in economics, and ideological considerations came to the fore as China began to evolve its new style in diplomacy. But these developments were not simply an outgrowth of domestic changes—they were also a reflection of China's experience in its first decade of diplomacy. For the hard line the Chinese now took toward the United States was, to say the least, a logical outcome of events in the 1954–58 period. The United States had not responded seriously to Chinese initiatives, nor had it demonstrated willingness to negotiate issues of substantial worth to both parties. Moreover, the U.S. had sponsored the creation of SEATO, aimed directly at encirclement of China, and the U.S. continued to oppose China's claim to its seat in the United Nations. Finally, by 1961 the U.S. had begun to commit itself to long-term and potentially deeper involvement in Indochina.

The Great Leap Forward campaigns of 1957–62 reestablished the need for self-sufficiency in China. China must be able to go it alone, without Soviet or other foreign help. The general result of this policy was a partially intentional isolation for China from most of the world.

One result was a major split in the Afro-Asian People's Solidarity Organization (AAPSO). Created at the Soviet-initiated World Peace Conference in New Delhi, on the eve of the Bandung Conference, AAPSO had been intended to serve as a vehicle for promoting the Soviet Communist party role in the third world. In the new spirit of independence after Bandung, AAPSO had been ignored. It remained moribund until 1957 when in the wake of Nasser's defiance of Europe and the U.S., the headquarters was permanently based in Cairo and AAPSO took on a new independence, integrity, and momentum. China and Russia held equal membership. Now, at the 1962 Afro-Asian Writers' Conference in Cairo, the

Chinese opposed a Soviet resolution on disarmament and began to attack the Soviets as "outsiders," being neither Asians nor Africans. In February 1963, at a third conference, the Chinese successfully promoted a resolution preventing white delegates from speaking; only those with a mandate from an Asian or African country were allowed the floor. The Sino-Soviet split had come to Africa.

The Question of Revolution

China's third-world policies have been most seriously —even vitriolically—criticized for supporting armed struggle and violent revolution. China has been accused of irrationally endorsing revolution and subversive activities in Africa. Yet evidence shows that—whatever their hopes for ultimate world revolution—the Chinese are more pragmatic than this. They are careful not to explicitly endorse revolutionary groups where their open endorsement would be more detrimental than helpful, or might lead to suppression of that organization by the local government. The Chinese are also well aware of the ways in which they might detract from an organization's nationalist appeal by implying foreign (i.e., Chinese) control, and of the danger that such an implication could serve as grounds for foreign intervention by Western powers. For example, Chinese press reports carry many reports on the revolutionary struggles in Angola, Mozambique, and Guinea Bissau. No particular revolutionary groups are mentioned by name; this is an important point, since some liberation movements in Southern Africa are competing with each other for leadership of the movement as a whole.

Some armed struggles in Africa are not supported by the Chinese at all, explicitly or implicitly. In 1965 in French Somaliland, there was an anticolonial struggle against France in progress. At the Afro-Asian Economic Seminar held in Algiers in February of that year the Chinese delegates endorsed revolutionary struggles in nineteen Afro-Asian areas—but omitted Somaliland, even though the African delegates published a declaration of support for Somaliland's revolutionaries. Why? In January 1964 France had extended diplomatic recognition to

China, and de Gaulle was demanding French independence of U.S. domination. His action converged with the Chinese general international strategy: to build a united front of friends against the main enemy, and to utilize conflicts and contradictions within the enemy camp to isolate the main enemy.

The overriding factor in these cases, apparently, is China's desire not to jeopardize its relations with the governments with which it has formal relations. Nevertheless, the Chinese continue to stress, openly, that true liberation and political independence can be achieved only with the use of armed force. Some governments in Africa (such as the Ivory Coast and Malawi) would very much like to disavow the utility of violence or armed force in attaining liberation. But the fact of the matter is that the present independent states in former French West Africa might not exist were it not for the Algerian people's eight-year war against France or the Mau Mau movement which the British colonialists could not defeat in Kenya. Armed struggle in Algeria and Kenya was the leverage that drove the British and French colonialists to move out of Africa.

All now-independent African nations are committed to the liberation of southern Africa; this has been the case since 1958. The dispute among these states centers on the means to be used in the struggle. It is in regard to this question that China's stress on the utility and rationality of armed force should be seen; for the African states which argue that a "dialogue" should be opened with the racist regimes of southern Africa are those which have the closest ties with the Euro-American imperialists. China is reportedly helping to equip and train revolutionary forces in Tanzania for the fight in southern Africa, and shipping military arms for the same purpose.

In 1964 Chou En-lai toured Africa, and during his trip first proposed the "eight principles on economic and technical assistance." Their main import is to state that assistance programs should not be for the purpose of seeking political control of other governments, suppressing revolutionaries, or exploitation of peoples in the third world. The principles, given below, are China's basic program of economic assistance.

Eight Principles on Economic and Technical Assistance

1. The Chinese government always bases itself on the principle of equality and mutual benefit in providing aid to other countries. It never regards such aid as a kind of unilateral alms but as something mutual. Through such aid the friendly new emerging countries themselves gradually develop their own national economy, free themselves from colonial control, and strengthen the anti-imperialist forces in the world.

2. In providing aid to other countries the Chinese government strictly respects the sovereignty of the recipient countries, and never asks for any privileges or attaches any conditions.

3. The Chinese government provides economic aid in the form of interest-free or low-interest loans and extends the time limit for repayment so as to lighten the burden of the recipient countries as far as possible.

4. In providing aid to other countries, the purpose of the Chinese government is not to make the recipient countries dependent on China but to help them embark on the road to self-reliance step by step.

5. The Chinese government tries its best to help the recipient countries build projects which require less investment while yielding quicker results, so the recipient governments may increase their income and accumulate capital.

6. The Chinese government provides the best-quality equipment and material of its own manufacture at international market prices. If the equipment and material provided by the Chinese government are not up to the agreed specifications and quality, the Chinese government undertakes to replace them.

7. In giving any particular technical assistance, the Chinese government will see to it that the personnel of the recipient country fully master such techniques.

8. The experts dispatched by the Chinese government to help in construction in the recipient countries will have the same standard of living as the experts of the recipient country. The Chinese experts are not allowed to make any special demands or enjoy any special amenities.

Economic Aid: The Tanzanian Case

Tanzania has been independent for ten years. In that time it has sought aid from most of the nations of the world. True to the idea of an independent third-world diplomacy, it has tried to avoid becoming a definite satellite member of any big-power camp.

This has proved in practice to be virtually impossible. Tanzania had projected in 1964 that 78 percent of its development program for the next five-year period would be externally financed. This capital is badly needed, for like most other recently independent nations of the third world, Tanzania does not have enough capital to finance major development projects on its own. But attempts to secure external financing for internally conceived programs have met with political obstacles. Instead of 78 percent, only 34 percent of its programs were externally financed.

Both Great Britain and the U.S.A.—major sources of aid—have responded to Tanzania's attempts to pursue an independent line in international affairs by withdrawing promised aid or curtailing available aid. For example, in 1965 Tanzania broke with Britain over its tolerant policies toward racist Rhodesia; consequently Britain withdrew a loan to Tanzania of $21 million. The U.S.A. has also expressed dissatisfaction with Tanzania's refusal to allow the Peace Corps a free hand in the country, and over Tanzania's friendly relations with China. Of the 34 percent external financing Tanzania's development program received prior to 1969, China's aid was less than 3 percent.

In terms of industrial aid, China has financed, designed, and equipped a $7.7 million "Friendship Textile Mill" in Tanzania. Completed in 1968, the mill will allow Tanzania to concentrate its resources in other sectors of its economy. In the past Tanzania had been a net importer of textiles; now the mill promotes conservation of foreign exchange, and encourages the development of subsidiary industries using domestic raw materials.

In agricultural aid, China has loaned funds for the multipurpose Ruuvu State Farm. When it is completed, the farm—begun in 1964—will cover an area of seven thousand acres and will have cost between $1.1 million and $1.4 million. By irrigating vast areas for the cultivating of rice, cotton, vegetables, cereals, fruit trees, and the raising of dairy and beef cattle the farm will make Tanzania more self-reliant in terms of food supply. A large-scale irrigation control and hydroelectric project will tie in directly to the project.

Finally, there is the Tanzania-Zambia railway, a Chinese-aided project which has received widespread publicity. In 1964 the World Bank withdrew a previously approved loan for this project on the grounds that political rather than economic criteria had led Tanzania to build the railway. (Zambia is dependent on Rhodesia to transport its copper to coastal ports; the railway is an attempt to avoid dealing with—and relying on—this racist state.) In 1965, the Chinese stepped in and offered to build the thousand-mile railway. The total cost of the project, now almost completed, has been estimated at $340–$400 million. Recently the U.S.-aid-financed construction of an asphalt highway in places parallel to the railway has been a source of international amusement —for the U.S. engineers, to their own dismay, are taking far longer and will probably be passed by the Chinese project before the end of 1971.

The dominant trend in Chinese interactions with the third world, then, is one of mutual benefit, even in cases where mutual benefit is defined narrowly as the exclusion of the big powers from Africa. The eight principles are becoming even more important as China's international role grows. China has established diplomatic ties with Chile—the first trip the Chinese ping-pong team made after returning from the world championship in Japan was to Chile—and a trade mission from Peru was recently in Peking; there are also speculations that Argentina will recognize the People's Republic. As the U.S. is increasingly forced to face China's new eminence in the world, more and more Latin American and Middle and Far Eastern governments—previously tied to the U.S.'s restrictive policies—will enter into formal relations with China.

Nuclear Weapons and China's Defense

Chinese ideology advocates "wars of national liberation," and American government spokesmen have been quick to accuse Peking of "subversion," which Washington equates with "aggression." Yet in the making of Chinese foreign policy, questions of Chinese national interest generally outweigh ideological considerations. In line with Mao's military thinking, Peking is prepared to counter a land invasion of China with guerrilla warfare. The People's Liberation Army is almost exclusively defense-oriented. The Chinese navy is negligible and the Chinese air force is backward.

Given China's basic military strategy and planning, why did it commit large resources, at heavy cost to industrial and agricultural development, for the research and manufacturing of nuclear weapons? Is it true, as Richard Nixon once claimed, that China has an "imperial ambition" which will involve it in "foreign adventuring"?

It is now reasonably clear that China built its atomic bomb as a direct reaction to American threats to China's existence.[11] Yet, unlike America's reaction to the Russian technological threat after Sputnik, China's reaction to American nuclear threats was relatively calm. In the Chinese calculation, American behavior had been hostile and belligerent for more than a decade, with the possibility of invasion or a "preemptive" nuclear strike against China's cities often hinted by American officials. In such an atmosphere, there seemed only one option for China: to build its own bomb.

Nuclear threats were first made by America during the Korean War in 1953. MacArthur wanted to "take out" China's industrial plants in Manchuria, but the Chinese could not tell whether he actually spoke for the American government. Eventually he was relieved from his command, and some of his wilder statements about attacking China remained only potential threats. But the Chinese

---

[11] Allen S. Whiting, congressional testimony quoted in *I. F. Stone's Bi-weekly*, September 6, 1971.

were acutely aware that they had escaped war with the United States by a hair.

These potential threats became more concrete when the U.S. gave howitzers capable of carrying nuclear warheads to the Nationalist Chinese forces on the islands of Quemoy and Matsu off the China coast. An air base was also built on Taiwan to handle B-52 bombers, and this was followed by the installation in 1970 of six-hundred-mile nuclear missiles.[12]

Whatever the rhetoric of American policy may have been at the time, the Chinese could see these concrete actions which threatened not just their borders but their very existence. And they had learned to take American threats very seriously during the Korean War. It is certainly hard to imagine a situation in which foreign forces and missiles would be stationed on Hawaii and Long Island, and the United States would not respond. It would be only one of many ironies in Chinese-American relations if the United States forced an unwilling China to develop an atomic bomb to defend itself.

The Soviet Union

It is easy in retrospect to discover the seeds of the present conflict between China and the Soviet Union. The myth of monolithic communism has been dead for well over a decade, and the Sino-Soviet split is a familiar part of our political vocabulary. More surprising, perhaps, is the fact that so few observers—in America—saw it coming.

Territorial Integrity

Just as Japan had demanded China's Shandong Province as spoils for helping defeat Germany in World War I, so Russia demanded and received Dairen and Port Arthur from Japan after World War II. Their value as, respectively, warm-water port and naval base, were evidently well worth angering the Communist Chinese, then fighting a civil war against the Kuomintang. When the Chinese

---

[12]Allen S. Whiting, "What Nixon Must Do to Make Friends in Peking," *New York Review of Books,* October 7, 1971.

won Liberation, they found these territories still occupied by the Soviet Union and that—having driven out the Westerners—they still shared control of the Far Eastern Railroad in Manchuria with Russia through joint-stock companies. In December 1949, Mao went to Moscow to spend almost three months negotiating. At the end of that period, the Sino-Soviet Treaty of Friendship, Alliance, and Mutual Assistance was signed (aimed primarily at mutual defense against Japan); in 1950 Dairen was returned to China, in 1952 the joint-stock companies were liquidated and ownership reverted to China, and in 1955 the Russians withdrew from the Port Arthur base. Khrushchev came to visit in Peking, and good relations appeared to have been restored.

But the Chinese resented what they consider the refusal of the Soviet Union to offer adequate support in two major crises involving their territorial integrity. The first, in 1958, was the Quemoy-Matsu crisis, in which the Russians pointedly did not support Chinese efforts to blockade the islands. The second was the equally serious clash between the Indians and Chinese in 1962. In both of these cases China was quite genuinely threatened, and Soviet unwillingness to aid China left a bitter suspicion in Peking.

To this day China resents the Soviet position on their mutual border. The border, fixed in 18th century treaties between the Manchu (Ch'ing dynasty) and tsarist courts, transferred a large portion of what had formerly been considered Chinese territory to Russia. Despite Lenin's early promises to renounce all tsarist treaties, the Soviets have continued to assert those borders. Compounding the border problems, there are large populations of "national minorities" (Uighurs, Kazakhs, Kirghiz, and other groupings of Mongol and Turkic stock) on both sides of the Sino-Soviet border. Both Russia and China fear attempts by the other to "stir up" these minority groups, some of which number in the millions.

Both of these border problems became acute in the mid-1960s. According to the Chinese, the Russians fomented a rebellion among national minorities in Sinkiang Province in 1962. In 1966 the Soviet Union began a major troop buildup along its border with China and in

1967 minor incidents began to break out along the guarded lines. Two years later a major clash occurred along the Ussuri River to the northeast, between Heilungkiang Province in Manchuria and the Russian territory projecting down to Vladivostok. The focus of the dispute was Damansky, or in Chinese, Chenbao Island. Accounts of the incident are conflicting, but the general consensus among Western observers is that the first incident to break the prolonged tension was probably initiated by the Chinese, with no indication of whether the source was simply local intransigence and foolhardiness, or an actual central directive. In any case, the consensus supports the claim that virtually every incident following this was started by the Russians as "punishment" for the Chinese actions. That October, talks began between the two sides at the vice-ministerial level. The Chinese have continued to insist that Lenin's promises be honored; their position is not to demand territory back, but to seek a precise definition of the boundaries in a document which will acknowledge the inequality of the treaties on which the border had formerly been based.

Economic Aid

Economic relations between the two nations have at times been even rougher than those of a military nature. The brief period of Soviet support—barely a decade in all—ended in bitter recriminations and increasing mutual criticism of domestic policies in both countries.

Soviet assistance took two forms. All materials and financial aid were loans—and not particularly long-term loans. It has been a great point of pride for the Chinese that they were able to repay all of these loans fully, exporting cloth, raw materials, and foodstuffs in order to do so. Today they have no foreign debt. But this type of aid, although it undoubtedly contributed to China's impressive growth, was far less crucial than assistance in the guise of technical expertise. In the fifties, hundreds of Russian engineers, designers, production advisers, and other technically trained persons came to China. With their help the first huge hydroelectric stations and modern heavy industries were constructed and placed in operation.

By the late fifties, however, the Chinese were beginning to feel they had made a mistake. The economic model of development which the Soviets exported, and the Chinese had imported, was dysfunctional. Because the Soviet model was very capital-intensive, where China's greatest resource was its large labor pool, and also because the Soviet Union heavily emphasized development of urban areas and urban-related facilities, where China was still overwhelmingly agricultural, the Russian model simply did not fit. Recognition of this failure led to the Great Leap Forward, in an attempt to reverse the pattern adopted from Russia and to develop a unique Chinese model.

The Great Leap Forward was taken as a serious affront by the Russians. Not only were the Soviet economic models rejected, but the Chinese seemd to be claiming that they had pulled ahead of the Russians on the road to communism. In creating rural communes, the Chinese experimented with the "free-support system," in accord with the Communist idea of "from each according to his abilities, to each according to his needs" (as opposed to the less-advanced socialist stage in which each worker is rewarded according to his productivity). In asserting the unique value of its experience for other underdeveloped nations, China again directly confronted the Soviet model.

The Soviet response in July 1960 was to withdraw all technicians and personnel from China. Only about 150 of the approximately 300 industrial plants and other major projects the Soviets had taken responsibility for were finished—and many of the Russian technicians took the blueprints with them when they went. Coupled with three years of natural disasters (the "three hard years") and bureaucratic mismanagement, the Soviet pullout helped to offset the economic progress of the early years of the Great Leap Forward.

Ideological Disputes

The fierce ideological battles of the early sixties between Peking and Moscow revolved around three questions. First, what attitude should Communist nations take toward non-Communist, but neutralist, governments in the third world? The Russians supported these governments; the Chinese supported more radical liberation movements. Secondly, was there a possibility of coexistence with the United States? The Russians said yes; the Chinese, no. And thirdly, were Russia's changing domestic policies "revisionist," departing from progress toward communism and returning to capitalist forms? In 1964 a major article, "On Khrushchev's Phony Communism" (probably edited personally by Mao), provided a summary of the revisionist tendencies that China perceived in the Soviet Union. From this perspective, the Cultural Revolution can be seen as an attempt to eliminate similar tendencies in China: the adoption of material incentives, increasing bureaucratism, lack of control of bourgeois intellectuals, and increasing inequalities in wages and income. Significantly, Liu Shao-ch'i was commonly called "China's Khrushchev" during the Cultural Revolution.

China's relations with Russia—as with other countries—deteriorated markedly during the Cultural Revolution. But by the late sixties only the last of the three questions outlined above was still a bone of contention. Both China and Russia have a united front position with regard to "national democratic" forces and governments, and China has dramatically demonstrated its willingness to coexist with the United States by inviting Nixon to Peking. But the Chinese still reject Russian domestic policies as a deviation from the path to communism.

Japan

China's relations with Japan, beginning with the Japanese occupation of Taiwan in 1895, have been bitter and intense. For most of a century, Japan has played a partnership role with the Western powers in trying to reduce China to the status of a colony. This culminated, in the Chinese view, in the fourteen-year war with Japan that began in 1931, the first actual fighting of the Second World War. As a result of this war, which cost China millions of casualties, indescribable devastation, and the longest occupation of any allied country, the Chinese feel a deep suspicion toward Japan. It is perhaps comparable in intensity to the Russian feelings toward Germany. After the ever-present American military presence on their borders, the possible revival of a militarized, industrial Japan has perhaps been the main Chinese fear since 1945.

Postwar American policy toward Japan was therefore seen by China as particularly dangerous. After a few years of demilitarizing and democratizing Japan, the American occupation government suddenly reversed course in 1948. The United States set out to rebuild Japanese industrial and military capacities as a keystone of America's new Asian alliances.

This shift in American policy toward Japan brought with it, the Chinese feel, serious consequences for Japanese society. For example, in the attempt to rebuild Japan's war industry, the American forces in many cases installed military officers and businessmen who had been important supporters of the 1930s fascist military regime. Along with this buildup, the American policy was to suppress the labor movement in Japan, which had until then been encouraged as a chief means of making Japan a genuinely democratic country. Japan's economic recovery, an obvious necessity if Japan was to play a vigorous role in the American alliance, was hailed by foreign observers as a miracle; yet it might well have been much less dramatic except for the Korean War. Just as Vietnam provided a business boom in its early stages for large American corporations, the Korean War was largely responsible for bringing the Japanese economy out of its postwar depression.

The most serious consequence of this policy has been the encouragement of militarist and imperialist tendencies in Japan, which have been consistently linked to Japanese investment and involvement elsewhere in Asia. Always aware of past experiences with Japanese imperialism, the Chinese take a very dim view of Japanese expansionism, and they have watched the postwar development and rebuilding of Japan with deep foreboding.

The Present and the Future

What do the Chinese see as the main problems affecting the improvement of Chinese-American relations? Has the Chinese position shifted on important areas of dispute? Will they "soften" their line, for example, on Taiwan? We were constantly thinking of these questions during our interview and wondered just what changes were likely to occur.

The basic impression we got from our conversation with Chou was that the Chinese have certain clear national security and military interests on which they will never budge. This sense of the Chinese policy is so different from most interpretations in the Western press that we have included all of our interview with Chou to give as clear a picture of this as possible. We have let Chou speak for himself, since he is best qualified to do so, but we feel that the main issues in our interview are well worth repeating.

Indochina

Chou's statement of support for the various revolutionary movements in Indochina seemed especially significant to us. His strong reiteration of China's firm support of the seven-point peace proposal of the Provisional Revolutionary Government of South Vietnam, in particular, is contrary to virtually all of the speculation now in American newspapers. But Chou not only made the Chinese position on this question absolutely clear, he made it even stiffer by demanding not just the withdrawal of American troops but of all military installations as well.

Whatever complications may eventually arise from the Nixon visit to Peking, Chou did make this statement: "It might also be said that this demand [to withdraw all U.S. troops from Indochina] is even stronger than the demand to restore relations between the Chinese and American people. . . . And therefore we believe that the question to be solved first should be the question of Indochina . . ."

Before saying this, Chou put the statement in context

by giving us a description of China's experience at the Geneva Conference on Indochina of 1954. He confessed that China had not been wise in assuming that the United States would honor that treaty: "How could it be that a country which would not sign an agreement would agree to truly not disturb the agreement?" As far as the Chinese are concerned, the American forces can be forced to leave Indochina completely only if the United States signs a treaty that absolutely guarantees their departure. This belief led Chou directly to his support of the seven-point peace proposal and implied an answer to the question American newspapers were all asking: Would Nixon get out of Vietnam by going to Peking?

From our talk with Chou En-lai, the answer to that question, though never stated categorically, was clearly that the Vietnam War would be settled *only* at the conference table. This would not rule out moving the conference table from Paris to Geneva or anywhere else. But peace can be made only between the Vietnamese and the United States. On this question, the Chinese agree completely with their Indochinese allies. Chou said that China had learned a lesson in 1954 and would certainly not try to pressure North Vietnam and the National Liberation Front into an early settlement. From our talk with Premier Chou, it seemed clear that Nixon is not going to get any satisfaction on the Vietnam War simply by visiting Peking.

These views were also impressed on us during our visits to the Peking embassies of the three revolutionary governments of Indochina. (See Appendix 2.)

Taiwan

Chou En-lai was equally immovable on the question of Taiwan. He stressed that Taiwan was the chief roadblock, after Vietnam, to better Chinese-American relations. The history of the United States involvement in Taiwan, the intervention and occupation of a Chinese province by a foreign power, has been a part of daily life in China for twenty-one years. Thus there is now very little left to say about the Taiwan problem. The Chinese simply keep reiterating their basic demand that America withdraw its troops from the island and its diplomatic recognition from the Kuomintang government.

Chou listed for us some of the different plans dreamed up to split Taiwan away from China—an "independent" Taiwan, two Chinas, one-China-one-Taiwan—all of them completely unacceptable to the People's Republic. The Taiwan Independence Movement, Chou noted, was influenced and possibly controlled by foreign powers, Japan and the United States. Its leader, we were reminded, had been a student at Harvard and was back at another American university now after having been spirited out of Kuomintang house arrest on Taiwan by unknown agencies.

Chou also mentioned that at Potsdam and Cairo during World War II, Western statesmen recognized that Taiwan was a part of China. Despite this, other officials and lawyers in the West were now trying to claim, by complicated and dubious reasoning, that the status of Taiwan was somehow "unsettled." To the Chinese, the only unsettled thing about Taiwan is the continued presence on the island of American troops. All arguments used to justify, one way or another, the continuation of Taiwan's existence as a separate, distinct country are simply dishonest tricks, he said, to keep China from regaining its territory.

Chou was unequivocal about Taiwan—China would never budge an inch from its position. Naturally this would affect the question of American recognition of the People's Republic. For as long as a country recognized Taiwan as an independent unit, the real China—the People's Republic of China—would not establish diplomatic relations with such countries. So far in dealings with every foreign power, China has not deviated from this basic line. This clearly leaves very little leeway to any American attempt to establish relations, as long as the United States insists on continued support of the Chiang Kai-shek government. Only if the United States cuts these ties, Chou told us, will official relations be considered from the Chinese side. We left our interview with Chou, Yao, and Chang with the feeling that the two issues of Taiwan and Vietnam were the ones which involved Chinese national interests so deeply that they would not and could not compromise.

The Soviet Union and China Today

Premier Chou talked at great length about the dangers of Japan's revived militarism and economic expansion into Southeast Asia. But the Chinese seem to feel that a more immediate danger is posed by the Soviet Union.

Relations between the Soviet Union and China were virtually nonexistent during the Cultural Revolution. In midsummer 1966 the Chinese ambassador was recalled from Moscow (as were the Chinese ambassadors from every other nation except Egypt, where China's representative was Huang Hua, the present ambassador to Canada and the UN). The Russian ambassador left Peking in turn, and the remaining embassy staff were harassed periodically in the next several years. Polemics between the two nations reached new heights of suspicion and outrage.

Only at the end of 1970 had relations been sufficiently restored to allow ambassadors once more to be exchanged. This period of adjustment, through most of 1970 and 1971, has seen accommodation and retrenchment on three general levels.

The first, relations between the two Communist parties of China and the Soviet Union, has shown the least improvement. China continues to be extremely critical of Soviet domestic policies along the line of its attacks in the mid-1960s. The Soviets for their part are equally critical of the Cultural Revolution. The hard feelings evident in this debate are compounded by Chinese charges that the Russians are conspiring with the United States to form a solid front against the peoples of China and the third world, and by recent Chinese diplomatic efforts to jostle that suspected alliance.

Second, border tensions have remained fairly high, but actual confrontations have been more rare since talks began in October 1969. Continued Soviet troop buildups, however, bolster an already massive force. Today missiles abundantly and strategically placed along the border supplement forty-nine Soviet divisions—approximately one million Soviet troops. Many U.S. observers have speculated that the Russians will attempt a preemptive strike (possibly nuclear) against China's nuclear installations before China can develop a retaliatory capability, which means roughly sometime in the next two years. Although this is speculation, there is no question that in a military sense the Chinese consider the Soviet Union their number one enemy.

The third level is that of state-to-state diplomatic relations, and it is here that the situation has most improved since the Cultural Revolution. In 1970, when Chinese and Russian ambassadors returned to their respective posts, trade agreements were signed between the Soviet Union and China. But these agreements were more symbolic of restored relations than a significant binding of the two economies, for that—if the Chinese have their way—will never happen. Still smarting from the pullout of the early sixties and well aware of the manipulative lever foreign aid gives to the "generous" donor, the Chinese are determined to remain independent economically as well as politically.

Future prospects for Sino-Soviet relations are, in each category, basically more of the same. Each claims the mantle of true Marxism-Leninism for itself and rejects the Marxism of the other party as heresy; the intensity of propaganda campaigns in both countries makes the likelihood of reconciliation very remote. China continues to view Russia as an example of what can go wrong with a socialist nation on the road to communism. For China, the threat of Soviet-type ideological revisionism is much more subtle and in the end much more dangerous than the more easily identifiable adversaries of American imperialism or monopoly capitalism. Beneath the streets of Peking we rode the still incomplete Peking subway which is said by the PLA men who run it to have been built largely as a defense shelter. This reveals that the Chinese regard the Soviets as more than just an ideological threat; and are in fact deeply concerned about the possibility of Soviet military attack. We left with a new understanding of how real this possibility is, and how threatened the Chinese feel.

Negotiating with America

China's recent negotiations with the United States, both in the Warsaw diplomatic talks and in more informal exchanges like the Kissinger visits, give another perspective on how much each side will have to change or compromise to achieve better relations. As early as 1964, Chou said that America's "hostile policy toward China" was at issue and noted that "it is for the doer to undo the knot." In this view, America has been more responsible in the past for preventing improved relations, so America has more changing to do now.

Until the successful visit by Henry Kissinger, diplomatic initiatives were regularly proposed, begun, and shot down one by one. Occasionally the United States axed its own moves; "hard-line" military and intelligence officers proved obstructive and undermined presidential feelers; Vietnam contributed to the impasse, as did the Laos and Cambodia invasions.

Yet Nixon apparently was sincere in his statements. On their side, the Chinese declared that they were happy to be dealing directly with the "party of Wall Street." China hoped that the real American ruling class would be more cautious and pragmatic, both in ending the Vietnam War and in making contacts with China. A few problems temporarily blocked this hoped-for pragmatic approach.

Following the 1968 elections, China had agreed to resume the Warsaw talks. The opening session was scheduled for February 20, 1969, but the Chinese never got to the table. In his first weeks in office, Nixon publicly hinted that American policies would not alter till Peking had altogether changed, and he proceeded to pressure Canada to withhold recognition from China. The mainland kept signaling a willingness to talk. In February broadcasts, Peking demanded the U.S. "withdraw your troops of aggression from the Taiwan Straits, from Vietnam, from Asia." China watchers sat up; Peking had omitted specific mention of U.S. withdrawal from Taiwan! Shortly afterward in Holland the CIA, apparently without Washington's foreknowledge, produced international headlines by publicizing the defection of a low-level Communist Chinese diplomat. On February 18, China scuttled the Warsaw talks, citing the incident as a provocation.

In July 1969 the White House was preparing to modify the ban on Chinese goods and to ease restrictions on travel to China. Before this could be announced, Nationalist Chinese forces made a major raid on the mainland and effectively countered the White House gesture. Peking knew American cooperation was required for such an operation. China also was aware that the American commander on Taiwan held veto power over Nationalist offensives under a secret agreement between John Foster Dulles and former Taiwan Foreign Secretary George Yeh. But certain sections of the American military, independent of the White House, had apparently moved to create new tensions in the Taiwan Straits. American diplomacy was again the loser.

During the closing months of 1969, American Ambassador to Poland Walter Stoessel was wooing Peking back to the Warsaw conference table. American reconnaissance flights over the mainland had been halted by President Johnson in March 1968 in his effort to secure peace talks in Paris. Now suddenly and unexpectedly the provocative flights were resumed. And in January 1970, as the Seventh Fleet was pulling back from the Taiwan Straits, another large Nationalist commando raid hit the mainland. The renewed tensions peaked in February, a week before Peking was to resume talks in Warsaw. China reported the downing of a U.S. spy plane over Hainan Island. Chinese radio accused the United States of hypocritically appealing for peace while simultaneously sending spy planes to provoke China. State Department officials crossed their fingers; the Chinese showed up for the talks as scheduled.

Huang Yung-sheng, chief of staff of the People's Liberation Army, in June 1970 offered China's opinion of the Taiwan Straits incidents in a major speech aimed at Washington. Huang argued that by "ceaselessly making intrusions into the territorial waters and airspace of China's mainland and frequently instigating the Chiang Kaishek bandit gang to harass the mainland," America persisted in making itself the enemy of China.

In the more than a year since Huang's message, Nixon

has moved effectively to change America's belligerent stance. Military hard-liners have apparently been restrained (though violations of Chinese waters and airspace do continue); restrictions on travel and trade have fallen one after the other; and the Chinese have finally begun to see concrete evidence of change, especially on the crucial issue of Taiwan.

China has persistently explained that Taiwan's status overshadows all other U.S.-China differences. Chou made this perfectly clear in our interview, taking care to give a detailed discussion of all the significant points to be resolved.

China's terms for detente have been moderate. China has not demanded immediate possession of Taiwan, only that the United States withdraw its forces from the Taiwan Straits and from Taiwan. Peking did not even press hard the issue of U.S. contingents on Taiwan; in the winter and summer of 1969, that demand was quietly dropped from Chinese broadcasts.

Nixon apparently realized that the steps requested by the Chinese were reasonable, for he quietly moved to comply in part. In early 1970 Washington, well aware that Taiwan on its own accord could repel an attack from the mainland, phased out the Seventh Fleet's regular Taiwan Straits patrols. Only some eight to nine thousand American troops, largely logistics personnel, remain on Taiwan. Peking's modest conditions were being met step by step.

By early 1971, the Chinese had hard evidence to believe that Nixon was serious when he said: "We have taken specific steps that did not require agreement but which underline our willingness to have a more normal and constructive relationship." Forty-eight days later, China invited the U.S. ping-pong team to Peking. In July, with election primaries approaching and the unresolved Vietnam War hurting him seriously at the polls, Nixon responded dramatically—and popularly—for direct relations with the People's Republic. This was followed shortly by the invitation to visit Peking. An American president was going to China for the first time.

The Nixon Visit: Ping-Pong Diplomacy

Why is President Nixon going to China? Why is he going now? And what is Nixon hoping to bring back from Peking? Our interview with Chou En-lai and our talks with people all over China suggested to us some very interesting answers to these questions.

Indochina was the almost automatic first response of every Chinese citizen when we asked them why they thought Nixon was coming to China. There seems to be a general feeling that America is finally beginning to admit defeat in Vietnam and is actually, if gradually, withdrawing troops.

The day after the announcement of Kissinger's visit, we went out again to wander around Peking. The Nixon trip was of course still very much on our minds, and at one point, when we had stopped to talk with a middle-aged man in a fruit market, we asked him his opinion of the Nixon visit. He responded at once, as though the answer was so obvious it didn't need to be explained at all. "Have you ever heard of a country called Laos?" he asked us. As far as many Chinese are concerned, the American and South Vietnamese disaster along Route 9 in southern Laos was the crowning blow to an already crumbling war effort.

The second reaction we heard most places was that America was in the grip of a growing and potentially revolutionary crisis. The Chinese have followed very closely the recent economic and political developments in America, and they are very well briefed on the economic recession and the state of dissatisfaction arising from the war. Nixon, in their view, is trying to distract the American public from their real problems by going to China. As Chou colorfully said:

. . . that is like trying to catch ten fleas with ten fingers. When you are trying to catch one flea, another one jumps out. And the result is that all of them escape. And at the most, you can only catch one flea by freeing one of your hands and letting go five fleas instead. That is the predicament that President Nixon is now facing.

This is closely linked in the minds of the Chinese to other American problems such as the astronomical national debt accumulating as a result of the war. Chou demonstrated his excellent knowledge of the American economy by pointing out that the interest on the national debt being paid each year is now greater than any year's national budget before World War II. The Chinese are incredibly astute "America watchers," and Chou—along with other Chinese—places a good deal of stock in President Nixon's statement of July 6, 1971. In it, Nixon expressed great shock and disbelief that America had fallen so rapidly from its top-dog position after 1945 to its current, demoralized condition. It was an unusual admission of candor coming from an American president, and the Chinese think that he was totally serious.

Another explanation, one we didn't hear very often, was the escalating Chinese-Russian tension. If China now feels that the United States is withdrawing partly from Asia and does not want to start another war, the Russians are in a different category. One foreigner, a longtime resident in Peking, told us that in late 1969 the city had been prepared for war. A tank strike was expected from Mongolia, and the government was ready to move to the mountains to begin guerrilla warfare. We cannot say how accurate this description was, but the Chinese definitely have a powerful enemy to the north.

A much more modest reason for Nixon's visit was suggested by Chou En-lai. He pointed out that governments must relate to governments, and that as long as there were no official relations, people-to-people contacts were difficult. The first step, he explained, is to at least make it easier for people to travel between the two countries.

Perhaps the Chinese are being much more realistic than Nixon in not setting high hopes on the coming visit. They have set reasonable goals which they hope to achieve from Nixon's trip, but they know that it can also result in few concrete improvements or even none at all. As Chou said in a recent meeting with other visiting Americans, "From our side, it is all right if the talks succeed, and it is all right if the talks fail."[13] Whatever the im-

---

[13] *New York Times,* October 7, 1971.

mediate outcome of Richard Nixon's visit to Peking, his decision will have a long-range effect hard to estimate now. Would it not be enough, as a short-run result, if Chinese could now come to America and Americans could once again freely go to China?

Postscript

On November 1, 1971, the red flag with the five gold stars of the People's Republic of China took its place in front of the United Nations in New York along with the flags of 130 other UN members. Less than a week before, the *New York Times* on October 26 had clarioned in banner headlines: "U.N. SEATS PEKING AND EX-PELS TAIPEI; NATIONALISTS WALK OUT BE-FORE VOTE; U.S. DEFEATED ON TWO KEY QUESTIONS." A historic watershed had been crossed. After twenty-two years, the legitimate rights of the People's Republic in the UN had been restored.

On November 15, Chiao Kuan-hua, vice-minister of foreign affairs of the People's Republic and head of the Chinese delegation to the UN, arrived at Kennedy airport and publicly expressed wishes of friendship for the people of New York City and of the whole United States.

We had been in China for the fiftieth anniversary of the Chinese Communist party, the one hundred ninety-fifth anniversary of the United States and . . . for Kissinger I. Our book was being written at the time of the historic UN vote. History seemed to be moving fast, very fast indeed. We were reminded of Premier Chou's comment in his conversation with us: "Five years is not a short time."

APPENDIX I

INTERVIEW WITH PREMIER CHOU EN-LAI BY THE COMMITTEE OF CONCERNED ASIAN SCHOLARS FRIENDSHIP DELEGATION TO CHINA

This text is a transcript of tape recordings made by members of the CCAS Friendship Delegation to China during their four-hour interview with Premier Chou En-lai on July 19, 1971, in the Great Hall of the People, Peking. It is as full and complete as possible given the condition of our tapes, which had inaudible words and sentences. Some sections or words were difficult to distinguish: our reconstruction of them was part memory, part guesswork, part translation of the Chinese when this was audible and the English translation was not.

As for the statements made by Chou En-lai, they are clearly not an official, formal statement of the position of the Chinese government. The interview took place in a relaxed atmosphere with a free exchange of views. As Premier Chou En-lai himself points out, there is lots of room for error and misquotation in an interview of this nature. "Maybe I will say something wrong, or the interpreter might interpret wrong." Therefore, as Premier Chou En-lai expressly stated in the interview: "If you are going to show your recordings when you get back to the United States, you must make a statement at the beginning and say there are bound to be some wrong statements in this recording." CCAS urges that any reference to this transcript contain mention of these qualifications.

It was clear to us from our extraordinarily warm and friendly reception in China at all levels that the Chinese government and people are very interested in starting what Premier Chou En-lai called "a free exchange of views" with the American people. Rather than simply publishing our own views and interpretations of this interview, we wanted to let Premier Chou En-lai speak for himself directly to the people of the United States. This is not a "classified document."

The following transcript is issued by Pacific News Service (San Francisco) on behalf of the Committee of Concerned Asian Scholars.

(Premier Chou En-lai introduces Yao Wen-yuan and Chang Ch'un-ch'iao.)

CHOU: Both of them have been elected members of the Political Bureau of the Central Committee during the Ninth Congress.

Comrade Chang Ch'un-ch'iao is a deputy leader of the Cultural Revolution group under the Central Committee of the Communist party of China. Comrade Yao Wen-yuan is also a member of the group. You asked me about the January revolution of Shanghai and they are both members of the January revolution of 1967. Because half of their time is spent working in the Central Committee, when you were in Shanghai they were not there, and were not able to have discussions with you. We heard that you would like to meet Comrade Chang Ch'ing, and she asked me to give you her apology on her behalf because she is not feeling well these few days and she will not be able to come here tonight. She also sends her regards to you.

If any of you want to take photographs, it's all right. We welcome you. It's a rare opportunity for us to be able to meet so many young American friends. We hear that you are a young generation of scholars. You have all spent some time in Hong Kong, I believe. Did you all go there at the same time?

KAY JOHNSON: There are great differences in the time we have spent in Hong Kong. There are some people who have been there for ten years, and some people only for six months. The majority have lived in Hong Kong for about eight months.

CHOU: I think there is also a friend of Chinese origin among you.

DOROTHY KEHL: I'm Cantonese from Xinhui, Guangdong, but I grew up in Hong Kong.

CHOU: When did you go to Hong Kong?

DOROTHY: When I was five.

CHOU: Have you ever gone back to your native area?

DOROTHY: Yes, I went back to my grandmother's hometown, Taishan, for a while.

CHOU: Taishan people play very good volleyball. We

have heard you have said that you think that the present youth movement in the United States is similar to the May 4 movement in China, at the present stage. I was also a participant in the May 4 movement and meeting you it seems that I have gone back fifty-four years—fifty-two years. But I don't think it's exactly the same. Perhaps you also have a bit of the Red Guard movement of China in your movement now. So you have something of both eras. Is that so?

KAY: I think that's very good analysis.

CHOU: I heard that you're the liaison officer. And during the May 4 movement in China we also liked to pick young women to be our leaders. There were a lot of instances like that. For instance, my wife, Comrade Deng Yingqiao, has done that work. At that time she was only fifteen. You see at that time, we had a majority of middle-school students in the movement and the college students were only a minority, and now you are all college graduates.

Therefore you have entered the Red Guard period. We will have to ask these two comrades to tell you something about the Red Guard movement. The Red Guards called themselves members of the "service committee," or members of the "general service committee." It is also a Red Guard trend of thought that they don't like to be called "minister" or "section head" or "director." They like to think that's all bureaucratic and therefore we must do away with the bureaucratic structure and call ourselves "service personnel" of the people. And I think that you also have the same idea. We also see that now some of the men wear their hair long and also grow beards to express their dissatisfaction with the present state of affairs. There are two men here with large beards. There are not many with long hair. What is your name?

PAUL PICKOWICZ: Pickowicz.

CHOU: During the May 4 movement there was a situation which was opposite to your present situation. That is, there were girls who shaved their heads. During the May 4 movement there was also a girl who took part in the movement who was from the Hui nationality. Her name was Guo Dongzhen. She sacrificed her life during the civil war period of 1927–37 and she at that time shaved her head clean—during the May 4 movement—to express dissatisfaction. During the Red Guard movement there was a different trend. At that time they liked to wear coarse clothes, army uniforms, and armbands, and also clothes that were patched that had as many patches as possible. I heard that you were asking why people weren't wearing the colorful cloth produced in the textile mills. It is because it is the custom today to live simply and therefore people like to wear simple clothes, and also as a symbol of discipline. In order to provide a symbol of learning from the People's Liberation Army, people like to wear army uniforms. And the style of simplicity is also in opposition to bourgeois degradation. There is a lady here, Comrade Xie Qingyi. Ask her to sit in the front because there happens to be an empty seat. And she works in one of the offices of the Central Committee. She is also a staff member working under the Central Committee. She has been working there for nineteen years now. Her name is Xie Qingyi. Perhaps you know her. She is quite young. Have you met her?

KAY: No.

PAUL P.: We haven't met her.

CHOU: She also likes to learn from the PLA and she likes to wear an army uniform very much, so finally she was issued one. Now she has been welcomed to join the PLA. At the very beginning she was in the army, and then she became a civilian, and now she is welcomed back in the army again. You haven't met her. If some of the women would like to learn about the equality in political life between men and women in China, you can have some talks with her. She took part in the Great Proletarian Cultural Revolution and she also made a contribution. She went to a factory to support the left and in the factory she participated in the work to bring about the great alliance. It is a well-known printing shop. Perhaps some of your friends might know it. It is the Xinhua Printing Press. And then she went to Tsinghua University to persuade the students to cease their fighting. Have you heard about that? Have you been to Tsinghua University?

GROUP: No, we have been to Peking University.

CHOU: Thus you know Professor Chou P'ei-yuan and Professor Chou Yi-liang. Both of them have the same surname as I do. And also Comrade Chi Qun, also from Tsinghua University, and also from the PLA. Perhaps you are not so familiar with the army—the PLA.

GROUP: No.

CHOU: Have you visited it?

GROUP: No, we still haven't.

CHOU: Then you can visit it; you still have two days. What

about going to see one (*an army unit*) before you leave? I will ask these two comrades to accompany you—one man and one woman.

GROUP: Good.

CHOU: We fully agree with your opinion that you should go among the masses. There is not much to talk about with us (*laughter*)—just the same old issues. And once you read the newspapers you will see that what Mr. Chou En-lai says has all been printed in the newspapers (*laughter*) and to listen to it is nauseating. (*Laughter*.) Isn't that so? And I support that idea of yours. For instance, you have all been taken to either factories or people's communes or schools and other people have already been to them. And when you go back you will say, "All the news about those places has already been printed in the Hong Kong newspapers—what interest is there in our reporting about the same things?" I believe it was a lady among you who expressed such feelings.

COMRADE XI: Mrs. Woodard. (*Laughter*.)

CHOU: I believe it and I thank you. And I was happy when I read that statement. That's the right way to do things —criticize us. It is also criticism for our travel bureau, and above them there is the Foreign Ministry. So your criticism hit the right spot. (*Laughter*.) So we welcome very much this spiritual help from you. It is "rectifying wrong ideas." That is Chairman Mao's wording. It is not brainwashing, it is rectifying erroneous ideas. I haven't thought of a way to wash one's brain yet. In a certain way I would also like to have my brain washed because I also have old ideas in my mind. I have already passed seventy-three, how can it be said that I have no old ideas in my head, because I came over from the old society?

The Old Society

For instance in the old society, I wore a braid, a pigtail. But, of course, you can't see it on me now, nor can you find the old photographs. And also now in China in all the cities and in the great and overwhelming majority of the countryside you can't see that phenomenon anymore. But I cannot dare tell you there is not *one*. For instance, the old custom of the people of Tibet was to wear their hair in braids. But of course the serfs in Tibet have already been liberated, and the old serf system, the aristocratic system, has been overthrown. The laboring people have come to power. But I can't say that there is not a single pigtail left as a manifestation of the old customs, because none of the three of us has been there to inspect on that fact as yet. So if you come on your next trip, or if other friends come to visit China and visit Tibet, and you find some person who is still wearing a pigtail, they can take a photograph of that and publish it to show that what I have said has not been entirely wrong. And another factor or phenomenon, that is there are a number of women whose feet were bound before. This is also a thing left over from the old society, the old system. For instance, my mother had her feet bound. Of course she passed away. So there are no people in Chinese society who have bound feet now? There still are. This seems a very new experience for foreign friends, for instance, our friends from the United States. For instance, if you want to take photographs of this, Chairman Mao has said you can take photographs of this. But naturally because that's a phenomenon which the old society should be held responsible for. We are not responsible for that phenomenon. We were the ones who overthrew the old society, the old system. Of course now after Liberation we have been persuading people not to bind their feet, but what about the old people, their feet have already been bound, and you cannot cut off their feet, nor can they be restored to the original shape, because the bones were broken. There is no way to restore it. And if you did not bind the feet after they have been deformed to such a shape then the women would not be able to walk. And we cannot attempt to hide them all at home. If we attempted to do so, that would be a reactionary way of doing things. For instance, my mother had bound feet. But if it were not for her, how would I have come to be? And my mother herself cannot be responsible for having her feet bound either; she was also sacrificed by the old society. So when foreign friends take pictures of such things, for instance bound feet, you must investigate to see from what position, from what point of view they conceive of doing so. For instance, if they say that this is something left over from the old system, from the old society, that this is a phenomenon, an old, bad phenomenon left over from the old society, even though the Chinese people have now won liberation and stood up, and they show the picture of bound feet, as a comparison of the old and new society, that is very good. The new society always grows up upon the basis of the old society. If there were not the old, where would the new come from? They are opposites, they are in opposition to each other. It's a dialectical matter. If this is a philosophical question, I will have to ask these two comrades (*Yao Wen-yuan and Chang Ch'un-ch'iao*). (*Laughter.*) Who are there among you who would like to talk about philosophy? Later on you can have your say. But I haven't finished yet. (*Laughter.*) The question arose from the taking of photographs. If you take photographs of this sort as comparison between the old and new society, that's one thing; for instance, when you went to Canton I believe you saw a people's commune. The women there do not have bound feet. Their feet are very large and they go barefoot into the rice fields. They are very healthy and strong, isn't that so? And if you take two photographs, one of each phenomenon, wouldn't that be a comparison between the old and the new society? (*To Dorothy Kehl.*) You're from Xinhui, you know that the women go barefoot and their feet are very large, and they carry things on their shoulders. That can serve as evidence. So Chairman Mao does not agree to not allowing people to take photographs. Since you're allowed to go to a place, why shouldn't people be allowed to take photographs of what they see? Therefore if any of you want to take photographs today you are welcome to do it. Please do so.

And if any of you have taken any tape recorders with you, you can also record the talk here if you want. Since we are meeting you, of course we will speak freely. Maybe I will say something wrong here, or perhaps these other two comrades might say something wrong, or the interpreter might interpret wrong. It doesn't matter. It's a free exchange of views. People should be allowed to say wrong things, isn't that so? Otherwise what is the need for exchange? If everyone had the same view, what would be the purpose of an exchange of views? And how would we be able to act about these ideas? So if you are going to show your recordings when you get back to the United States, you must make a statement at the beginning and say there are bound to be some wrong statements in this recording. The Chinese premier also made some erroneous remarks. And the chairman or the vice-chairman of the Shanghai revolutionary committee may also make mistakes. What matters is that we stand on the right position; we take the right position and we have the right views, and as for the concrete expression there might be some flaws. Of course we stand on the position of the stand of the proletariat, and you of course are clear about that. As for our views we do our utmost to see that they are in accordance with Marxism-Leninism-Mao Tsetung thought. Perhaps they (*pointing at Chang and Yao*) are better at this aspect than I am. You say that the youth are better than the older generation. We also agree. We say that those who come later become better. I am much older than they are, and I talk so much that there's bound to be a flaw, when you talk a lot. So it's not a very favorable aspect to be a premier at such an advanced age. But of course if I did not see you, you would probably raise the strongest protest. All right, don't let me be the only one to speak. And so the travel bureau should meet and discuss the two matters that I just now mentioned. They should let you see some places that other people haven't yet seen, isn't that right? And first of all we shall ask these two comrades here—Comrade Xie Qingyi and Comrade Chi Qun—to organize you on a visit to see a PLA unit. That's the first matter. As to the second thing: you can take photographs. Of course you will do so from a position of comparison of the old and new society.

At the same time the present phenomena are also in the process of development. There are some progressive aspects and there are also some backward aspects. You can see the two screens here are empty. Do you know why? Because in the past we had red slogans, red background and gold slogans on them, with some quotations from Chairman Mao Tse-tung. And it was very irritating to the eye, and Chairman Mao did not like it. At the beginning of the Cultural Revolution, there was a necessity to do so. There was a necessity to make it possible for Chairman Mao Tse-tung's thought to be grasped by the broad masses of the people. And in this aspect the vice-chairman of the Central Committee of the Communist party of China, Comrade Lin Piao, has made a great contribution. He selected some of the best quotations of Chairman Mao and made them into a book of quotations. At that time Liu Shao-ch'i and Teng Hsiao-p'ing were opposed to the application of the study of Chairman Mao Tsetung's thought. So at that time Comrade Lin Piao was the first to do so and to advocate the study of Chairman Mao Tse-tung's thought, and the book of quotations among the PLA. And as the Great Cultural Revolution rose up, the broad masses, the millions of the students and the other sections of the people rose up to participate in the Cultural Revolution. And in the movement, the overwhelming majority of the masses were able to grasp some of the crucial points of Chairman Mao Tse-tung's thought in order to solve some of the problems at the time. But by now the Cultural Revolution has deepened; it is already five years since we began. We now call it the stage of struggle, criticism, and transformation, and the time has come for us to study in a deeper way Marxism-Leninism-Mao Tse-tung thought. And those who have had some education should very conscientiously study the works of Marx, Lenin, and Chairman Mao Tse-tung. And therefore these formalistic things should be cut down a little. And this matter was also written in an editorial in the *People's Daily (Renmin Ribao)*, the PLA paper (*Jiefangjun Bao*), and *Red Flag (Hongqi)*. Have you seen the editorial that was put out on the anniversary of the founding of the party, that was the first of July? And in the editorial the struggle between the two lines in the party from the beginning up to the present day was very comprehensively dealt with in simple words. And from that editorial it can be seen why Chairman Mao Tse-tung has such a high prestige throughout the whole party, the whole people, and the whole army, and why we have been able to mobilize the broad laboring masses throughout the country, and also been able to unite with all the patriotic forces, to fight against the common enemy. The result was that we were able to overthrow the Chiang Kai-shek regime and to drive out the imperialistic forces, and then we established the new People's Republic of China. Chairman Mao is now leading us in the socialist revolution. I suggest that we now put forward questions to these two (*pointing to Yao and Chang*) on philosophical and literature and art problems, and we can talk at the end about political problems.

(*Group agrees.*)

KAY: I would like to say a word first, if I may. We are all most honored that you have taken the time to meet with us. The aim of our trip to China has been to further the friendship and understanding between the Chinese and American peoples. We feel that this meeting is certainly a significant contribution toward that end. We've been traveling in China for three weeks now. We believe that our main task when we return to the United States is to communicate to the American people the tremendous achievements and progress that have been made by the People's Republic of China and the Chinese people.

CHOU: You must add something to that. You must say that there has been progress made, but there is still a lot to work on. Otherwise the viewpoint would not be complete, would not be an overall view.

KAY: But we believe, in response to that . . .

CHOU: There are also some phenomena which are in the process of moving from the lower to the higher stage. This is the way things develop. And also the standard of some things is being raised in the process of (consolidation?). If you only simply say that there has been progress, people won't believe you.

KAY: We hope to get a complete and accurate picture of China, and pass this on to the American people. We feel that this has not been done in the past, and that the American people do have a distorted picture of the Chinese people. We hope that we can give an accurate picture *(inaudible)* and that we can contribute in a small way to our main aim, which is to further the friendship between the Chinese and American people.

CHOU: Although the contribution which you make may be small at the beginning, its influence will gradually grow. And that's the way all new things develop.

KAY: Before *(we continue)* we would like to say one thing with regard to our Chinese friends with China Travel Service. I feel that we have been treated in a very good way and well taken care of, and it is us that have given them a great deal of trouble, and we hope *(inaudible)*. And they have worked very hard and gone out of their way *(inaudible)*.

CHOU: We cannot do without troubling them at all, because the Red Guards hold even *more* meetings. For instance, we three here met with the Red Guards many times in this Great Hall of the People. And each discussion could be held until dawn. So this cannot be called a trouble. And we should say that you weren't taken good care of because we heard that some of you fell ill.

KAY: A minor problem.

CHOU: Which one of you fell ill?

KAY: All of our problems in China have been very small. It's because we don't do work, and we are lazy, and we sit at our desks and read books, and that's why when we start moving we get sick.

CHOU: You can't be blamed because it is a very difficult job to come to China, see things, and take notes, and read books, and then take them down and write, and record it all.

KIM WOODARD: After we came to China, we saw that the health of the Chinese people was very good, but health was a great problem for us people here, so we have been eager at every chance to participate in some labor, because we feel that this would improve our own health.

CHOU: Did you take part in some work at Tachai? Didn't Comrade Chen Yonggui let you do some work?

PAUL LEVINE: We hoed a row.

JEAN GARAVENTE: They told us we'd spoil the crops. (*Laughter.*)

CHOU: But have you been to the February 7 Rolling Stock Plant in Peking? And did you do some work there?

KAY: We did some work in a commune in Shanghai, and we picked some tomatoes.

CHOU: That's the place that they (*pointing to Chang and Yao*) two took care of, so they took care of you there.

KIM: But we ate more than we picked.

Philosophical Problems

CHOU: That doesn't matter. Wasn't it Mr. Kruze who was going to put forward some philosophical problems to these two comrades here?

YAO: Probably when you contacted some of the masses you probably asked, you had some discussion with them about philosophical problems.

CHOU: And you also probably have read some articles.

ULDIS KRUZE: Yes, this is true. I'm very interested in the movement to study philosophy. I believe it has great significance, not only for China, but also for the American movement. I'm very interested in the way Marxism-Leninism is practically applied. So I've asked numerous questions about how people apply philosophy in their ordinary lives, and have gotten many answers on how Marxism-Leninism has direct application to their situation. Could I ask either Comrade Chang or Comrade Yao how they particularly study philosophy and how they apply it in their daily work?

CHOU: I'm going to follow you and take off my coat.

YAO: I agree with your idea and your question. That is, that the universal truths of Marxism-Leninism must be combined with concrete practice. And there are many among the workers, peasants, and the People's Liberation Army who have studied Marxism-Leninism in a much better way than we have. Because through their practice they have come to truly understand the points and the views of Marxism-Leninism-Mao Tse-tung thought. They've also summed up their own experience that they have accumulated through their own practice and they have been able to relate these two things. In studying philosophy we study some philosophical works of Chairman Mao Tse-tung and also some of the philosophical works of Marx and Lenin. The aim in studying philosophy is to come to know the world and to transform the world. And in transforming the world there are two aspects: that is to transform society, and also to transform one's own ideas. As you just now mentioned "brainwashing," whether you call it "brainwashing" or the transformation of one's world outlook, what we are talking about is about the same, whatever you want to call it. That is, the transformation of one's own ideology.

For instance, Chairman Mao Tse-tung put forward a thesis of continuing the revolution under the dictatorship of the proletariat, and this is in itself also a very important philosophical problem. That is to say that in a socialist society there still exist classes, there still exist class contradictions, and there still exists class struggle. There exists the struggle between the proletariat and the bourgeoisie, and also the struggle between the socialist road and the capitalist road. And personally it has taken me a gradual process to come to understand this question. Throughout the whole process in the beginning of the Cultural Revolution and in the present stage of struggle-criticism-transformation, this process of understanding Chairman Mao's thesis of continuing the revolution under the dictatorship of the proletariat has never ceased. It is such a process, that is to take part in the class struggle, to have some practice and then to go back to study Chairman Mao Tse-tung's works, and then to summarize one's positive and negative experience in this practice, and to transform; and that is one thing; and then to transform one's world outlook and then to come into contact with new problems, and then to solve them through practice again, and then to study Chairman Mao Tse-tung's works again. This is a continuous process of understanding. This is a process of cognition, throughout the whole process of the Cultural Revolution there is the struggle between the two lines, that is the struggle between Chairman Mao Tse-tung's revolutionary line, and the revisionist line advocated by Liu Shao-ch'i, that is, the struggle between Marxism and revisionism.

And there also is the struggle between the correct proletarian views and various erroneous views, various right or "leftist" tendencies. And all this in the final analysis is a question of one's world outlook, a question of philosophy. And if one does not study dialectical materialism and historical materialism in the gradual process, then one would not be able to make distinctions, clear distinctions between true, genuine and fake Marxism, between Marxism and revisionism. And this is what we call "to study with problems in mind." And in my practice in the revolution the problems that I have come up against most are questions like the ones that I have just now stated, that is, ideological ones. And as I just now said that my study in this field has not been as good as the advanced elements of the workers, peasants, and PLA, and I should continue to learn from them. To study philosophy one must study the present situation, history, theory, and make the correct analysis and draw out the correct conclusions, and be able to find the laws guiding the development. And when the American friend, Mr. Edgar Snow, came to visit China, Chairman Mao Tse-tung talked with him, and he especially asked him (*Mr. Snow*) if it was possible to go to a factory or a farm in the United States to investigate and study. He also put it very prudently: he said that this is also philosophy because we stand for dialectical materialism, that is we stand for investigation and study. This view was opposed by Liu Shao-ch'i. So if when you come next time you will be able to tell us something about a factory or a farm or a school, whether it be a university or a high school in the United States, one of the basic units, if you would be able to dissect one of the basic units in the United States we will be very grateful to you and we will be very happy to learn about these units.

CHOU: I would also like to ask something of you. I believe there are two among you who come from Harvard.

SUSAN SHIRK: I come from MIT, not Harvard, MIT.

CHOU: Isn't there one of you who teaches at Harvard?

GROUP: No.

RAY WHITEHEAD: Could I ask another philosophical question?

CHOU: You can.

RAY: I would like to ask on the question of human nature.

I've read some articles on this and I understand that there is a rejection of the theory of human nature as being a revisionist theory, but just now there was a comment about the transformation of people's ideology, and my question is, is it possible for anyone, any human being to have his ideology transformed, and if so, does this indicate some kind of underlying human nature? Just a short simple answer will be all right. (*Laughter.*)

YAO: I can give you a very simple answer in one sentence. I will refer you to read an article written by Chairman Mao Tse-tung, that is, his speech at the Yenan Literature and Art Forum. There is a paragraph. The speech was made in 1942. There is a very long paragraph in the article specially on the question of human nature, and Chairman Mao expounded the theory there in a very detailed way, so it's a very long paragraph, so I will refer it to you and give you an answer in a very short sentence. Because if we are going to discuss in detail here I believe that there will not be enough time today. And of course we still have a lot of opportunities to discuss in more detail more philosophical questions.

RAY: I have read that paragraph but I don't feel that I completely understand it, but I will reread it again on this advice.

Ping-Pong Diplomacy

SUSAN: I have a nonphilosophical question. The ping-pong team came to China and now we are in China and we hear that President Nixon is coming to China. We were very excited about this, especially excited because we are friends of China and we think this is a good thing for China and also because here we are in Peking, hearing the news.

CHOU: Yes, you come at just the right moment. So when you go back, you can tell your American friends the news. Because Chairman Mao has already told Mr. Edgar Snow that in inviting friends to China, we should invite friends of all spheres. And there is only one president in the United States now, but there are a lot of young friends like you in the United States, that is in numbers, and also no matter whether in quantity or in quality you are in the majority. (*Laughter.*) And in Chinese society there also are a various kinds of people, of course the majority supports the Communist party and agrees with socialism.

SUSAN: Well, I think we are here at a good time and I think it's a good time to ask a question of Premier Chou.

CHOU: Is that the end of your question?

SUSAN: My question is, how did it happen? What is there that has changed the relationship between the Chinese and American people after twenty-two years of separation? And how does Premier Chou see the situation now, what does he think might happen in the future, and what are the biggest problems we still have in developing the friendship between the Chinese and American people?

CHOU: The foremost thing, Miss Susan Shirk, is that the Chinese and American people wish to exchange visits with each other and this strong desire has broken through the barriers. And during the Pacific War there had been a lot of opportunities for the Chinese and American people to contact each other. And taking myself as an example, I know a lot of old friends from your country of an older generation. And I've heard that your committee has two aims. Isn't there one point in your aims, that is that you believe that the older generation of Asian scholars has gotten mixed up with the government? Or they have become silent.

GROUP: That's right.

CHOU: First, I agree with your aims, with your idea. But secondly, I must say some words of sympathy for them. That is that they happened to be oppressed in the fifties, during the McCarthy period, and this was a great harm for them. So I recall what I said, that is what I said at the Bandung Conference in 1955. I said that the peoples of China and the United States *wish* to have contact with each other, friendly contact. It cannot be said that there was *no* response to my words. There were some, I believe a few progressive correspondents wished to come to China, but the Secretary of State at that time, John Foster Dulles, denied them that right. I believe that this issue could be found in the files of the State Department, and I don't think that they should be classified documents. (*Laughter.*) And in this way we were separated. But now we have passed through the sixties and entered the seventies. And it's your generation, your era, and you have broken through the barriers. And so with one sentence of Chairman Mao's we invited the United States table-tennis team that wanted to come to visit China. And so they came! And the barriers were broken through. And so for this we must thank the new forces of your era. Isn't that so? And these new and friendly contacts are bound to continue. Because we received a very quick answer, and there was no way to stop the visit. And so now you also have come, and of course when you go back you will introduce new, even more American friends to us. Also some black friends. Of course if you would be able to introduce some minorities of the United States to us, we would be very thankful.

Let them all come to China to have a look. Of course, we will also return the visits, because your table-tennis team has also invited us to go to the United States, and our table-tennis team is also prepared to return the visit. Do you agree that the interpreter who works in the Foreign Ministry should go on the visit with the table-tennis team? (*Laughter and applause.*) Secondly, your CCAS, the Committee of Concerned Asian Scholars (*said in English*) has also invited us, and since you are so kind, I think that our young Chinese friends should also return the visit. There are a lot of young friends in Shanghai; they should take the lead.

YAO: Because you have already been in Shanghai.

CHOU: Of course, there are a lot of people who would like to go. Of course I believe that you will also will welcome not only men, but also women. (*Laughter.*)

YAO: And complete equality in numbers. I believe that the main thing should be the content.

CHOU: It also would be a good thing to make it equal in numbers. But even though we are a socialist country, a country of the dictatorship of the proletariat, yet, still, male chauvinism comes up now and then. Of course subconsciously.

CHANG: Today, seated here among the Chinese comrades, the number of men and women are not equal yet.

CHOU: See, he's criticizing me. Yet I have tried my utmost to pay attention to the fact. I have paid relative attention to it. When I invited the comrades from Tsinghua University, I invited one man and one woman. The second question . . . Let's not just talk about the first aspect of this question. That is how the barriers have been broken. But the development of the contact between people, in itself alone, is not enough because in the world of today, the state structures of various countries still exist. That is, different states still exist in the world today, and if there is no normalization or no restoration of the relations between the two states then it would be impossible for the contact between the two peoples to develop completely unhindered. And the governments of the two countries will bear the main responsibilities for the normalization of relations between the two countries and the restoration of these relations. If Susan Shirk was the president of the United States, then the matter would be easy to solve. But the problem isn't so simple. Isn't that so? Our philosophical friend understands. (*Laughter.*) That is, it still takes a process of continuing cognition, that is, there still needs to be a process of practice and understanding. A process of the combination, the integration of the universal truth of Marxism-Leninism with the concrete practice of the United States. There still must be such a process before things can develop. It will take process and time. Isn't that so? And your committee also says so. And I believe that it was also Miss Susan Shirk who said that though the revolutionary movement in United States is developing, it cannot be said that it would be able to transform the entire system at the present time. For instance, the opinions in your family differ, don't they? So you can see it will take time to transform society. In recent years, Chairman Mao himself has paid attention to the American situation and he has also asked us all to note the fact that it can be said that the United States is now on the eve of a great storm. But the question of how this storm will be developed exactly is your task, not ours. We can only tell you about something of our hopes. But now, at the present date, in contacting your government to normalize relations we must contact those who are in authority in your country. But in your country, your system is that you have a president, and your president said that he wishes to move toward friendship and he also has said that he hopes to visit China. And of course, naturally we can invite him, in order to seek the normalization of relations between the two countries, and also to discuss questions concerning both sides. And this can promote the solution of the normalization and improvement of the relations between the two countries. But what are the obstructions to the improvement of the relations between China and the United States? What would you say?

On Taiwan

KAY: I wouldn't dare say. (*Laughter.*)

EVERYBODY: Taiwan . . .

PAUL L.: Taiwan certainly will be liberated.

RHEA WHITEHEAD: Indochina . . .

CHOU: You have all mentioned the right problems. It

shows that you have all studied those things. And you, of course, are quite clear about our position on Taiwan. And I would like to take this opportunity to reaffirm our stand: *the first point,* that is, if state relations are to be established with China, then it must be recognized that the government of the People's Republic of China is the sole legitimate government representing the Chinese people. *Second,* Taiwan is a province of China and it is an inalienable part of China's territory. And after the second World War Taiwan had already been restored to China. And the liberation of Taiwan by the Chinese people is an internal affair of China which brooks no foreign intervention. *Third,* the so-called theory that the status of Taiwan is yet unsettled, which is the theory that is going about, some people in the world are spreading it, is absurd. That is, toward the end of the nineteenth century, that is, in 1894, China was at war with Japan and China was defeated in that war and after China's defeat, Taiwan was taken away by Japan, *but* during the Second World War in the Cairo Declaration and later in the Potsdam Proclamation it was reaffirmed that Taiwan should be returned to China. And then in 1945, when Japan surrendered, the Chinese government at the time had already accepted the return of Taiwan to China . . . in taking Taiwan back.

Fourth point. We oppose any advocation of a two-China policy, a one-China-one-Taiwan policy, or any similar policy. And if such a situation continues in the United Nations, we will not go there.

Fifth point. We are resolutely opposed to the so-called "Taiwan Independence Movement." Because the people in Taiwan are *Chinese.* Taiwan was originally a province of China. And a thousand years ago it had already become a part of China. The dialect spoken in Taiwan is the same dialect spoken in the area around Amoy in Fujian Province. Of course there are minority nationalities like the Kaoshan nationality in Taiwan, the minority that lives on the high hills. There is the same case on the mainland. There are also various national minorities on the mainland and we pursue a policy of national equality. Besides, the "Taiwan Independence Movement" is *not* a native movement in itself. It is a special movement which has behind it the special manipulation from foreign forces. One of their leaders is P'eng Ming-min who was originally a student at Harvard, who then went back to Taiwan to become a professor, and now is also back in the United States. There are also some elements of them in Japan. They are supported by the Japanese government.

The sixth point. The United States should withdraw *all* of their present military strength and military installations from Taiwan and the Taiwan Straits. And the defense treaty which was concluded between the United States and Chiang Kai-shek in 1954 about the so-called "defense of Taiwan and Penghu" is illegal, and null and void, and the Chinese people do not recognize that treaty. This is our stand. And we stick to our stand. And our stand has not changed from the beginning of the ambassadorial talks between China and the United States that began on the first of August, 1955, first in Geneva, and later on in Warsaw. They began after the Bandung Conference. And our stand has not changed from that time up to the preset time. And it will not change.

On Indochina

The question also mentioned very correctly that we are also concerned with the Indochina issue.

This question also concerns China and the United States. You have also said that one of your aims is opposition to the aggressive policies of the United States in Indochina and Asia. Isn't that so?

GROUP: Yes.

CHOU: And the aggressive policies of the United States, first the aggression in Vietnam which was later expanded to the whole of Indochina.

China has not gone to Vietnam or Indochina to commit aggression. We are assisting the people there to fight against aggression. Isn't that so? I think we should go back to the beginning. The question began in 1954. At that time during the Geneva Conference we reached an agreement. You friends who are studying various Asian issues probably have already read those documents.

And on this issue at that time we Chinese, and at the time also our Vietnamese friends, lacked experience in international subjects. At that time the representative of the United States was allowed to not sign the documents and to only make a statement that they would not disturb the agreement. But the reality was not so.

How could it be that a country which would not sign an agreement would agree to truly not disturb the agreement? Don't you say that we were lacking in experience in such matters to allow this? You can criticize me for this. I myself, as one of the delegates on the Chinese side at that meeting, at that conference, accept your criticism.

After that time, France, because of its defeat at Dienbienphu, did not wish to continue the war. It was willing to stop the war. But the U.S., which had begun to assist France— the Truman government of the U.S. which had begun to assist France in its aggression in Indochina—did not wish to end the war.

The British representative at that time was Mr. Eden, and he agreed to stop the war, but he wished to draw a line of demarcation and in this way to carve up, to divide the area and also to divide the world by drawing lines of demarcation. This idea of Mr. Eden's was suited to the needs of the brinkmanship policy of John Foster Dulles.

And although there was a clause in the Geneva Agreement that one day after the conclusion of the Geneva Agreement the representatives of the two sides of Vietnam, North and South Vietnam, should meet to form an election committee and that a referendum should be held under international supervision—although there was such a clause in the agreements, it was actually a false clause because they were not prepared to act upon it. Therefore, immediately following the Geneva Agreement, the Manila Conference was held at which SEATO was formed and a line of demarcation was drawn. Of course, SEATO has now broken up by itself, it's now gone bankrupt. But after the Geneva Agreement the election was not held and the U.S. assisted Ngo Dinh Diem to overthrow Bao Dai. The U.S. got control of South Vietnam that way. And all those who participated in the Geneva Conference are prepared to say, will admit, that if an election had been held in Vietnam as stipulated by the Geneva Agreement it would be without question that President Ho Chi Minh would have been elected in any case in Vietnam because through the war of resistance against French aggression he had won great esteem, not only among the Vietnamese people but also among the people of the whole of Indochina. But that was not able to come about and the facts were the United States committed aggression, first in Vietnam, which was then expanded to the whole of Indochina.

Now this question lies before us, before the people of the United States, the people of Indochina and us, and the only way to solve this problem is that we show our complete support for the seven-point proposition put forth by Mme.

Nguyen Thi Binh on the first of July on behalf of the Provisional Revolutionary Government of the South Vietnam Republic and the Vietnamese people, and the Chinese government and the Chinese people completely support this proposition. And the Chinese government and the Chinese people also fully support the stand of the declaration of the four sides and three countries of Indochina which was issued at their summit conference in April last year.

I believe our friends have already met our Vietnamese friends and Samdech Norodom Sihanouk and I believe that on this issue we have the same stand. And we know that the broad masses of the people of the United States are also opposed to the aggressive war in Vietnam which has now expanded into the whole of Indochina. We believe it is also in accord with your aim, the aim of CCAS, to oppose the aggressive policies of the United States in Indochina and the rest of Asia.

We are a neighbor of the Indochinese countries. We assisted them, supported them, in their war of resistance against France. And in the same spirit support them in their war of resistance against U.S. aggression for national salvation.

This is known to the world. No matter whether in the U.S. itself or abroad, we believe the greatest cry is for the U.S. to withdraw its troops from Vietnam and the whole of Indochina. And the troops of other countries which have followed the United States into Indochina should also be withdrawn. I believe that our stand on this is also clear. And we also believe that at the present day among the American people this issue is the most outstanding.

Isn't that so?

Not only for the United States to withdraw its troops from Vietnam but also from the whole of Indochina, not only troops but all military forces and all military installations.

It might also be said that this demand is even stronger than the demand to restore relations between the Chinese and American people. Because the people of the United States do not wish to sacrifice the lives of their people in a dirty war. Isn't that so?

And therefore we believe that the question to be solved first should be the question of Indochina, and by doing so we would be satisfying not only the interests of the Indochinese people but also of the people of the U.S.

But also, we should also mention that Indochina is the

Indochina of the Indochinese people and we should respect the stand of the peoples of the three Indochinese countries. And at the summit conference they've already said that the war of aggression waged by the United States has linked them up in a common fight and after they achieve victory in the war, in the war against American aggression, the peoples of the three countries shall solve their own problems in accordance with the borders that they have already recognized between themselves.

And the Chinese people should respect and support the revolutionary stand of the people and revolutionary governments of the three countries, that is, the governments of the Democratic Republic of Vietnam, the Provisional Revolutionary Government of the Republic of South Vietnam, the Government of National Union under the leadership front of National Union of Cambodia, and the patriotic front, the Pathet Lao. They are all victims of aggression and we should respect their stand.

On Korea

And besides these two issues I think that there should be two other issues that are worth your attention.

I believe you have seen the friends at the embassy of the People's Democratic Republic of Korea. Perhaps you know less of this issue, as it was a long time ago, because there was a cease-fire in 1953. I should like to bring to your attention the fact that in Korea up to the present day there is only a cease-fire, only an armistice agreement was passed. After that there was a meeting held in Geneva, the same Geneva Conference, in 1954.

The first stage of that conference was devoted to Korea. I can try to describe the meeting to you. It was completely without results. On the final day of that stage, as there was no result whatsoever with regard to the Korean question, we put forward the question, what was the use of our coming. We said that at least we should adjourn, we should at least set a date for another meeting. At that time the foreign ministers of certain countries were persuaded, for instance Mr. Spaak of Belgium. He had worked with the United Nations. The chairman of the meeting at that time was Mr. Eden. At that time he wavered a bit and he tended to agree with this view. And at that time there was an authoritative representative who was seated at the conference and who waved his hand in opposition and the result was that it was not passed. Your probably know who he was: the deputy of Mr. John Foster Dulles, Mr. Smith. Of course, it might not have been his own personal opinion but he did so on instructions. He didn't say anything, he couldn't find any words. He just waved his hand.

And as a result of this, the meeting was called off with no result whatsoever. And so now at the thirty-eighth parallel in Korea, there is a military armistice commission that meets every week. One side is the American representative and the representative of the South Korean puppets, and on the northern side there is a representative of the People's Army of the Democratic Republic of Korea and also a representative of China. They meet once about every two or three weeks. There's only a cease-fire, there's no other treaty whatsoever. According to international law the state of war has not yet ended and I believe that there must be people among you who study international law. It is the same case between China and Japan. The state of war has not been called off yet. We still have not concluded a peace treaty. And there are still American troops in South Korea. The Democratic Republic of Korea and we have both demanded that the United States should withdraw its troops from South Korea. Probably our friends at the Korean embassy have also talked about this. Because the Chinese people's volunteers withdrew from Korea in 1958. The American troops in South Korea are there under the banner of the United Nations, yet a lot of countries of the United Nations have either withdrawn their troops or have not taken part in this for a long time. For instance the French parliamentary delegation which met with me yesterday said that they did not believe that they should have anything to do with the Korean situation and that that was a policy that was set in General de Gaulle's time. And in relation with that there is also the question of Japan. You are a Committee of Concerned Asian Scholars so you are probably also very familiar with the Japanese question. And you can also travel to Japan. Have you seen their movies advocating militarism? We should have Comrade Yao Wenyuan tell you about them.

On Japan

YAO: Under the present regime of Sato, the Japanese government personally looked into this matter and put forward a number of films which were on the topic of Japanese militarism. And they laid special emphasis on making propaganda about the Japanese navy because in the Japanese aggression against other countries they relied upon the navy in the past. So a lot of these militarist films centered on the navy. Because during the wars of aggression the air force took off from their carriers.

And in fact we saw these films even before a number of our progressive Japanese friends. So after we had seen these films we showed these films to our Japanese friends and they also felt like us that these films really showed what was happening. One film is called *Great Sea Battle in the Sea of Japan* and another film was called *Yamamoto 56*. And another was called *Our Navy*. Another film was called *The Warlords*. Another film was called *War and Man,* but we haven't completed the translation of that film yet. It specialized on the war af aggression against China. The whole film hasn't been completed yet. In the films *Yamamoto 56* and *Our Navy* they emphasize the Japanese war in the Pacific. They describe the sneak attack on Pearl Harbor. And the common aim of all these films is to distort history. And in actual point of fact it was the Japanese militarists who launched aggression against China, against Korea, and the Asian peoples; who launched the war of aggression in the Pacific. But they turn all these facts upside down and make out as if this war of aggression launched by the Japanese militarists was forced upon them because Japan, they said, lacked resources and they made out as if what they called Manchuria of China was one of their lifelines, and south Asia too was a lifeline, and that they were compelled to launch this war of aggression. And this precisely conforms to the propaganda now spread by the Japanese militarists; that is, that expansionism and aggression are reasonable. The Japanese militarists are now saying that the Malacca Strait is their lifeline. This place is a lifeline; that place is a lifeline. So on and so forth. And the majority of these films have a deceptive side to them. That is because for those who did not experience the Second World War, they have not gone through the savagery and reaction of Japanese militarism in the past and so they thought that these militarists portrayed in these films were all perceived from the position of loyalty and patriotism to the motherland; because there was no way out at home, it was reasonable for them to seek a way out abroad. But once we've analyzed and criticized these films, then these films become very good teachers by negative example not only to the Chinese people but to the Korean people, the Japanese people, and all sorts of peoples of other Asian countries to be vigilant against the revival of Japanese militarism. Our Korean comrades were rather early in taking note of this and they felt very strongly about the dangers of the revival of Japanese militarism. When our premier visited Korea, in the joint communiqué issued by the two sides, this point was particularly emphasized. This has given rise to the attention of the people of the various Asian countries. The revival of Japanese militarism is being fostered single-handedly by U.S. imperialism. President Nixon also admitted this point in his public statements saying that they are fostering their former enemies. But now Nixon is also saying that Japan is his competitor. And so these films, too, reflect these very complicated positions. On the one hand, in order to toady to U.S. imperialism these films help to brag about U.S. imperialism. On the other hand, they portray the sneak attack on Pearl Harbor. These films serving as teachers by negative example can help us see the present aims of Japanese militarism. Perhaps you can select some of these films and see them.

(*Chang Ch'un-ch'iao and Chou En-lai interrupt to suggest that it would be best to see Yamamoto 56, Our Navy, and The Warlords—which, of course, portrays Tojo.*)

FRANK KEHL: Perhaps Comrade Yao would also be interested to having an opportunity to see the film *Tora! Tora! Tora!* which shows from the cooperative American and Japanese side the same kinds of distortions of history. The topic is the sneak attack on Pearl Harbor. But precisely this contradiction is what is dealt with.

CHOU: We haven't yet got a copy of that film, have you seen this film?

FRANK: Yes, I have. Perhaps the patriotic comrades in Hong Kong have made an analysis and perhaps they might have ways of getting it. Its special interest is that it was a cooperative film made by both American and Japanese producers and it showed the attack on Pearl Harbor from both sides, but both sides with a distortion of history to suit the present.

PAUL P.: There was an analysis in the *Hong Kong Ta Kung Pao*.

PAUL L.: Another small point is that a Japanese admiral, a war criminal visited America, I believe, or also in Japan spoke at the same time that the movie came out and there began a lot of big publicity in Japan and at the same time, I believe that it was about the same time last year, a secret treaty was signed between Japan and South Korea, a defense treaty. I was wondering if this has given rise to the tension that Comrade Yao Wen-yuan has just mentioned, a certain amount of rise in tension between South Korea and other countries concerned.

CHOU: Yes, it is a fact that Japanese militarism is being revived because the Japanese economy is developing in a lopsided way. They lack resources, they must import their natural resources and for markets too they depend on foreign countries. And after the war they were not burdened by paying reparations and also for quite some time they spent very little on armaments. How was the Japanese economy developed? There is one characteristic of the development of their economy, that is, they made a fortune on wars fought by others, that is, the war of aggression against Korea and the war of aggression against Vietnam. After the conclusion of the Second World War, less than a year after the end of the Second World War the Chinese civil war broke out. The Pacific War concluded in August 1945, but in July 1946 the Chinese civil war broke out in full force. You are all aware of the fact that in 1945, in order to maintain peace after the world war, Chairman Mao personally went to Chungking to have negotiations with Chiang Kai-shek. I have heard that you have already read the article on the Chungking negotiations written by Chairman Mao; that proves that you are indeed making a study of Chairman Mao's works. Although there were these negotiations, and although we did reach an agreement with Chiang Kai-shek, those agreements were all scraps of paper. They did not count at all. All his troops remained in the rear in the war against Japanese aggression and did not take part in the actual fighting against Japanese aggression. It only turned out to be passive resistance while our People's Liberation Army fought against the Japanese around their cities and on their main arteries of communications. And at this point we would like to express our thanks to the American correspondents of the older generation who wrote a lot of articles reporting these battles. And after the conclusion of the Pacific War the American air force shifted Chiang Kai-shek's troops from the rear areas to the places which were occupied by Japan to accept the surrender of the Japanese authorities, and did not allow the

People's Liberation Army led by the Chinese Communist party to accept the Japanese surrender in those places. So after the surrender of the Japanese warlords all the Japanese weapons were handed over to Chiang Kai-shek. In particular, Chiang Kai-shek received a great amount of military equipment from the United States, especially in the area of lend-lease. All the lend-lease equipment in the East was handed over to Chiang Kai-shek. And the Chinese civil war went on from 1946 to 1949 for two-and-a-half years. The People's Liberation Army had a force of one million and Chiang Kai-shek had a force of eight million and that includes those who replenished Chiang Kai-shek's army later on. But the United States government provided all the military, economic, and financial assistance, and military transport also was taken care of by the United States.

American forces also guarded many of the air bases and naval ports. As for the transportation base in the rear, the United States mainly went through Japan. So even back at that time Japan already was making a fortune through this war. And then with the Korean War and the Vietnam War and now this war throughout Indochina. Although Japan does not directly take part in these wars and Japan is a defeated power Japan makes fortunes through these wars. For instance, the United States estimates that within the past ten years, $120 billion were spent on the Indochina War. And I believe that out of this Japan made quite a lot of money from the military repairs and transportation costs and costs for vacationing of the U.S. troops and also some means of communication. In all these fields I think Japan made quite a lot of money. And so twenty-five years after the Second World War, Japan, a defeated power, has now become the number two economic power in the Western countries. President Nixon praises Japan as his biggest partner. That was when you were already in China, probably you were in Nanking, when President Nixon made that statement on the sixth of July, in Kansas City. Have all of you seen this statement by President Nixon? It also describes Japan as competitor. That was when President Nixon was going from Washington to the Western White House, and on his way there he stopped over in Kansas City, and made this statement to the press. And Nixon praised Japan in these terms: that the output of steel in Japan last year already approached 100 million tons. And that is to say, Japan may either this year or next year catch up with the United States in steel output, because last year the U.S. output of steel was 110 million tons.

CHOU: More. More than 110 million tons. Now where did this output of steel in Japan come from? Where did Japan get such resources? Where did Japan get these markets? Now on the American market there are a lot of Japanese cars. And textiles, a lot of Japanese textiles. You are quite clear about that.

PAUL L.: Except for the resources, the resources come from Australia.

CHOU: And not only Australia, also Latin America, India, and the African countries, and also Indonesia. And so this lopsided development of Japan, what will issue from it? She needs to carry out an economic expansion abroad. Otherwise, she cannot maintain her economy. And so, being in a capitalist system, following this economic expansion, there is bound to come with it, military expansion. Isn't that so? And so, precisely because of that, the fourth defense plan is from 1972 to 1976, and they plan to spend more than $16 billion. About the total amount of military expenditures of Japan after the Second World War to 1971, the first three defense plans, was only a bit over $10 billion. And some American senators, after visiting Japan, reported that this fourth Japanese defense plan exceeded the requirements of Japan for self-defense.

And according to the present economic capacity of Japan, she does not require five years to carry out this fourth plan. As we see it, they may be able to fulfill it in only two or two-and-a-half years. And in this way, it's all further proof that the appetite, the ambitions are becoming much greater. And so they are thinking not only of having up-to-date equipment, but also thinking of manufacturing nuclear weapons themselves. Now Japan is already cooperating with the United States and Australia in building a nuclear reactor and nuclear power, and Japan is already able to manufacture guided missiles, ground-to-air and ground-to-ground guided missiles without a nuclear warhead. So the only problem remaining is how to manufacture a nuclear warhead to put on these missiles. So there does exist this danger. But of course, the Japanese people of the present are not the Japanese people of the thirties or the forties, they have awakened to a certain extent. And also, what is more, the peoples of the Pacific and first of all the peoples of the Far East are no longer the peoples of the thirties or the forties; for instance, the people of the Democratic Republic of Korea, the People's Republic of China, and the three Indochinese countries. And even those countries where there are now still stationed American troops, such as the Philippines, Thailand; or Australia, Indonesia, and also Malaysia, Singapore, they still have a fairly good memory of the disaster of the Second World War. I think the American people too remember the Pacific War. And first of all the Japanese people are aware of the fact that if Japanese militarism is revived, it will not be of benefit to Japan, it will be furthermore harmful to themselves. And so being the Committee of Concerned Asian Scholars, you should also pay attention to this question of the revival of Japanese militarism, and its policies of expansion and aggression. That is, I mean the expansion and aggression of a revived Japanese militarism, because you're opposed to the policies of aggression. And so when you oppose a policy of aggression, of course you're not opposed only to the policies of aggression of the U.S. government but also any policy of aggression of any country of the world. And you are in a more convenient position to contact Japan than we. Any of you here speak Japanese?

FRANK: Some of our organization, not those of us here, but in CCAS do know Japanese.

CHOU: Have you been to Japan? That's a place where it's well worth your while to work.

The Military-Industrial Complex in the U.S.

KIM: Because the slaughter continues in Indochina, of course, this organization and many organizations among the young people of America concentrate their efforts on the question of the war in Indochina, and the question of the role of the U.S. military-industrial complex in the war in Indochina. And yet, of course we recognize that this question of the war in Vietnam, the question of the war in Indochina, is not unrelated to questions of conflict in other parts of Asia. And we cannot separate our opposition to a military-industrial complex and its operations in Indochina from our opposition to the operation of that complex in other parts of Asia.

CHOU: The American military-industrial complex now is not limited to the East Coast and to the central part of the U.S. but has also spread to the West Coast and the southern part of the United States, that is, all these monopoly capitalists must get their orders.

KIM: So we've come to China and we have visited China after the break of relations between the people of the U.S. and China that has lasted for over twenty years. The first group that came to the People's Republic of China, the ping-pong team, when they came here, their feelings were so deep with regard to the reunification of the two peoples after such an extended period of time that many of them wept as they came into China, and as they flew from Canton to Shanghai. We also have experienced these feelings, of course, on our own. This is a feeling of great joy. And yet our feelings for the Chinese people cannot be a fraction of the feelings of a person from North Vietnam having a sense of union with the people of South Vietnam, or the feelings of the people of Taiwan concerning unification with the people of the rest of China. And so when we understand this question of intervention and the question of separation of peoples, in a profound way we see that the various areas of Asia are connected. We also know that these feelings are related very strongly to our own feelings in America concerning the development of our own society. And so we have to ask ourselves the question if there is so much happiness in store in restoring these various relationships, why does the world and Asia continue in its condition of separation? And why do the American youth continue in their feelings of general dissatisfaction toward their society and their government? And we think that we have located the reason, which of course is the destructiveness of the military-industrial complex in our own country. And once we have located the source of such large questions we are very stubborn in pursuing the problems. We, here, are only fifteen people—and most of us are skilled in speaking the Chinese language. There are many people who are like us in our organization, and there are also a great number of people in our country who are also quite stubborn. And the number of people who benefit in the United States from the war in Indochina and the separation of Asian countries is really not very large. Unfortunately, they have more than a little money. But we have located the source of the problem and we hope that our friends will understand that Asian problems cannot be separated from one another.

CHOU: You're right, neither can these Asian problems be separated from one another, nor can they be separated from the United States either, nor from the world. You have five thousand in your organization.

GROUP: That's all. More or less.

CHOU: And how many are in the United States?

GROUP: The great majority.

CHOU: Four thousand in the United States?

GROUP: Almost all of them are in the United States, almost all five thousand.

CHOU: Are all of them college graduates?

GROUP: No, the majority are.

CHOU: They are college graduates in the United States.

GROUP: There are some who are studying in college.

CHOU: Then in our country, you would be considered high intellectuals, and you have a heavy responsibility. And it is your responsibility to link the truth, the general truth, with actual practice. And so that must be put into implementation through you. Some of you friends have said that foreign experience cannot be mechanically brought over to your country. That's right. And Chairman Mao tells us that one must rely on one's own efforts. We cannot impose on you, nor can you just mechanically copy from us. You can see the American youth are gradually raising their political consciousness. According to our experience, it is always intellectuals who start out, because it is easier for them to accept revolutionary theory, and revolutionary experience from books. But for the movement to succeed you must go among the workers, because in the United States the working class is the great majority of the people, and the peasantry is quite small. And so to do that, you must go into them deeply. We have only our experience, but we are not at all well acquainted with your situation. So that must depend upon your own efforts.

PAUL L.: Self-reliance.

CHOU: Self-reliance proceeds from independence, and taking the initiative in your own hands. Yes, one must go through some arduous process. When you go back to your homes you may read over our article commemorating the fiftieth anniversary of the founding of the Communist party. That's only a preliminary, a simple summary of our fifty years.

PAUL P.: I would like to say a word about the process which Premier Chou has talked about, because in the United States, in our struggle, there has been a peculiar process of gaining information and gaining knowledge. This is the question of knowledge. And Comrade Yao Wen-yuan was talking about contradictions and the struggle of gaining knowledge and gaining experience. One of the main contradictions of our process of gaining information about the problems that we deal with is that we were only first awakened by the violent struggle in Vietnam and our learning process then began to go backward. That is as we investigated the origins of the conflict in Vietnam we were taken further and further back. We were embarrassed the other evening when we were talking with our Korean friends that we still do not have a clear understanding of the Korean situation, so we keep on going backward in our understanding.

CHOU: The question of Korea was mentioned somewhat in the secret documents recently published, but those mainly dealt with Indochina.

PAUL P.: We think that our knowledge is imperfect in many ways, that is, we still have very imperfect understanding and knowledge of the origins of the original problems and postwar problems in Asia, and how the American imperialist policy was developed. And we also are imperfect in our understanding of the relations of all Asian nations. Our organization has primarily emphasized Southeast Asia, China, and Japan and we have an imperfect knowledge of many other situations, and also we have an imperfect knowledge of the unity of these problems, not only in Asia, but in other countries, in Africa and Latin America, and so in one sense I think our organization should be criticized, because too often we only talk about Asia, and we only talk about the United States, whereas we should begin to work and link up with other groups and talk about Africa and talk about Latin America, because the problems are really the same everywhere.

CHOU: But you have already begun in this direction. You have this organization of four or five thousand, in practically all the industrial cities?

GROUP: Mainly centered in universities.

FRANK: Yeah, and all over the United States.

CHOU: Do you have one in New York? In Washington?

GROUP: Yes.

CHOU: Boston?

GROUP: Yes.

CHOU: Chicago? Detroit?

FRANK: There is no big university in Detroit. But Michigan has one. But there is one in Ann Arbor.

CHOU: And on the West Coast?

FRANK: Yes, there are many.

CHOU: And in the South?

SUSAN: There are relatively fewer.

FRANK: Not so much because in the South, Asian studies is relatively undeveloped in the universities.

CHOU: But the industry in the South has developed greatly since the Second World War, isn't that so?

GROUP: Yes, but the universities they don't look much into Asian matters. They focus more on Latin America.

CHOU: How about the various research centers in universities? Do they mainly do research about Latin America in the southern universities?

FRANK: In the southern universities, yes. But there are some important Latin America study centers on the West Coast, and also in other parts of the United States.

CHOU: Latin America is well worth studying, because that's your backyard. (*Laughter.*) That is to say, that your backyard is not always tranquil.

FRANK: There was a group very similar to us who became aware even earlier, called NACLA, North American Congress on Latin America. And they are an organization very similar to CCAS who study American imperialism in Latin America.

CHOU: Why are they called the congress?

FRANK: They call themselves a congress because they are very wise. Unlike us, they also include newspaper reporters and nonscholars.

CHOU: So if you use the word "scholar," you may limit the scope of your organization.

FRANK: We are very limited, so we are getting broader in our recruits.

CHOU: What is the membership of the North American Congress?

FRANK: I am not sure, probably as large as we are.

CHOU: Many are from universities too?

FRANK: Yes.

CHOU: Where are their centers?

FRANK: One in New York, that's the one I'm familiar with, and also, my friends tell me, the San Francisco Bay area.

CHOU: And if our friends from the congress would like to visit China, then through your introduction, we would welcome them.

JEAN: I think it would be a good idea to invite some Latin American people from the United States, some Chicanos and Puerto Ricans.

CHOU: Yes, I've mentioned that already, about the minority

nationalities in your country. Those are foreigners living in your country?

ANN KRUZE: Well, they are not foreigners, they are people of Mexican or Puerto Rican parentage who are citizens of the United States, and retain cultural identity with Puerto Rico or Latin America, especially Mexico, some language and customs.

FRANK: Especially Mexican Americans have lived in the Southwest of the United States for generations and generations.

ANN: I would like our Chinese friends to know one thing: While we have shortcomings, and that is a serious consideration to us, we are also aware of our strengths, we do exist as a group. We are aware. We are making progress. We are forming alliances. We are starting to do something. We will not be moved away from this aim.

YAO: That's good. You have hope. And you are very courageous. Because although youthful in years, you have made very serious study and carried out very serious thinking about the major problems of the world. And so that shows there's hope for you.

Ten Fleas with Ten Fingers

CHOU: Since you have addressed yourselves to various problems throughout the world. Yes, indeed, your American friends should have a broad perspective and have a broad range of knowledge because as you know the United States has extended itself everywhere in the world. (*Laughter.*) After the Second World War, it stretched its hands out everywhere in the world. As Chairman Mao said, they look into other people's affairs everywhere in the world. And as a result, they were merely putting nooses about their own necks. And there is a saying in China, that that is like trying to catch ten fleas with ten fingers. When you are trying to catch one flea, another one jumps out. And the result is that all of them escape. And at the most, you can only catch one flea by freeing one of your hands and letting go five fleas instead. That is the predicament that President Nixon is now facing. But it would be fairer to say that it is not only of his own making but also something created by the system itself. Because after the Second World War, monopoly capitalism developed to such a tremendous extent. And in some of these things, not only did your president not preconceive it, not even you could preconceive it. As for us, we could even less preconceive of these aspects. So it is well to read that statement of your president on July 6 in which President Nixon said that to have fallen from such a state of grandeur twenty-five years ago to the present state of affairs is something which he couldn't even have dreamed of in those days. And the opposite of that is that people like you are rising up and taking action. But that latter part, referred to by Comrade Yao Wen-yuan, is something which he did not touch upon. Just citing a single figure would be quite surprising which is relevant to every single one of you. The internal debt in the United States now is approaching $400 billion. And the interest being paid this year alone is already $19 billion. And that is the amount of the annual budget prior to the Second World War during the Roosevelt regime, that is, about $20 billion. So how was that conceivable at that time? That is, the American budget from 1940–41 was that figure only. That was $20 billion. But the amount of interest alone to be paid in one year's time from 1971 to 1972 is $19 billion. That is the change over a period of thirty years. A number of you are apparently not even as old as thirty. Who is the youngest? And you too are only twenty-six? And so I see these changes over the past thirty years. Were any of you here born in 1945? That was just at the conclusion of the Second World War. At that time U.S. imperialists appeared to be almighty. The world is changing, undergoing tremendous changes. But the American people, you, should not feel any discouragement. There is great hope for the American people. Because you have contacts with the people throughout the world, and that is a very fine opportunity as was already found out by our good friends. What place is there in the world which you have not gone to since the Second World War? You have gone to all places in the world . . .

CHANG: Even to the moon. (*Laughter.*)

CHOU: You have such a fine opportunity.

(*Some sentences missed in changing the tape.*)

The monopoly capitalists are blaming each other for their failure to fully control them. But you have found this as a historical lesson. And you can draw different and new conclusions thereby. And also apparently after some members of your Peace Corps went to other countries, when they returned to the States they came to the conclusion that it was wrong.

PAUL L.: That's right.

CHOU: And now this Peace Corps, there are fewer now?

FRANK: There are fewer and fewer Peace Corps volunteers, and those that *are* sent are extremely carefully screened so that all progressives don't get in. That policy began to change about two years ago.

PAUL L.: Also, some Danish friends told me that they had organized a peace corps to send to the United States. (*Laughter.*)

CHOU: It would be better a friendship corps than a peace corps. Actually the Peace Corps in itself is a good, nice-sounding name but they have misused the name, so that it now has a bad connotation. Anyway, what one should not do is to act in place of the people of that region. No matter what the population of a country, when that country sends people to another country they should go there for the purpose of serving the people of that country and after their work is done they return to their country. They must not demand any special privilege. When they go to that other country, they should have the same living standard as the local people and if they commit offenses against the law they must be dealt with in accordance with the law of that country. Even if that country is backward, still you must be dealt with in accordance to the law of the country. And I go back to say that the best way is to withdraw of your own accord. If they show that they do not welcome you, then you should speedily return home. And if you die there, do not ask for any special treatment, just have the corpse cremated. And not to set up a plaque in your honor. We are opposed to that. Even now some places do that for our deceased, but we are opposed to it. And when your work of service is done, then speedily return. Even so, it is still not an easy matter to gain the full confidence of the local people. This is a long-term process, isn't that so? You are a powerful country and you have learned such a huge lesson over the past twenty-five years. We are a country just in the process of development. Anyhow, in our editorial we said we are a country of initial prosperity and if we compare with you, in accordance with the population ratio, then we are far behind you. Although we are a socialist country, we must be vigilant against ourselves. Since Chairman Mao constantly teaches us that we must at all times be on the alert against committing the mistake of big-power chauvinism both at home and abroad.

Because in the world there is another country which is learning from you and sending its hand out everywhere and competing with you. Economic competition is bound to bring with it military competition. Economic development combined with military expansion is bound to occupy various places throughout the world. Having carved up the various continental areas and now wanting to carve up the oceans. So the Latin American countries put forward the position that their territorial sea extends out a distance of two hundred nautical miles and that is indeed a great decision on their part—that's quite something. And according to this proposal, the Mediterranean would become the Mediterranean of the Mediterranean countries, and no other country can use the Mediterranean as open seas. Of course, other countries may be allowed to pass through the Mediterrenean. Friendly countries are still accepted. The point is that the Latin American countries put forth such demands because they are compelled to do so by circumstance or compelled to do so to protect their fisheries. As Comrade Yao Wen-yuan said a moment ago, we need teachers by postive example as well as by negative example. Just as if one just had the experience of success without any experience of failure, once one does suffer from a defeat then one will be at a loss. And so if, after you go back to your country, you are harassed, you should not become discouraged. Now you will also encounter such things. In our revolution, many of our comrades sacrificed their lives. And Chairman Mao often says that we are those left over from the revolutionary wars. What should we do then? Continue the revolution. And only so can we stand up to our martyrs, to our people. You have the spirit of pioneers.

George Washington

Almost two hundred years now, isn't that so? Five more years before the two hundredth anniversary, to celebrate your two hundredth anniversary. Chairman Mao often likes to talk about when George Washington rose up to oppose the British colonial rule with only a population of three million. At that time England had probably a population of some tens of millions, twenty million or more—well, let's say maybe around ten times the population of the United States at that time. But you had the pioneering spirit, fearing no difficulties, and the British colonial army was beaten by you everywhere.

And the Americans at that time precisely carried out guerrilla warfare, firing from this corner and that corner. And you started your struggle in 1775. And afterward you elected George Washington to be your commander in chief—you spent your fourth of July in China. (*Laughter.*) This is highly significant. And on your two hundredth anniversary you will come again. At that time you may only see two of us (*i.e., Chang and Yao*). At that time we will congratulate you. Five years is not a short time.

You have, as I have learned, liked to compare your present situation with the May 4 movement in China. Five years after the Chinese May 4 movement great changes had taken place, the great revolution had already begun. And you will recall that the Great Proletarian Cultural Revolution has just now gone into the fifth year. In fact today is precisely the fifth anniversary of Chairman Mao's return to Peking. You probably have seen an article on the sixteenth of July commemorating the fifth anniversary of Chairman Mao swimming the Yangtze River. But our papers forgot to republish the photo of Chairman Mao swimming the Yangtze River. They try to be creative but yet they've forgotten.

Although the time may not be so long, if one puts in effort and struggles hard, great results will take place. For instance, when the Chinese Communist party was founded in 1921 there were only twelve deputies to the First Party Congress, and the total number of Communist party members at that time did not exceed seventy. But only about three years later in 1924, it had changed tremendously. By 1926 our forces were already above fifty thousand. In 1924, Mr. Sun Yat-sen's Kuomintang started cooperation with Comrade Mao Tse-tung's CCP. Such tremendous changes took place within a period of only five years. What is more, your era is totally different from the era of those days. History will not reenact itself, and while we can make the comparison, it will not completely reenact itself. Since we always say that times are advancing, and time will not turn back, so we hope to see you again in five years. (*Laughter and applause.*)

Frank Kehl, I didn't apologize to you about that episode of taking the photos in Nanking. (*See p. 127.*)

So long as you adopt the attitude of comparison of the present and the past you should be able to take all kinds of phenomena in China, some progressive and some backward. Some things may be in the process of development and going to a deeper stage of progress and development.

So Chairman Mao always tells us when our guests come to visit China, we should let them see all our different facets, all the different aspects of our society, so they can make a comparison and see the process of development, and see the trend of our development, and which are the side currents. And in society we are bound to find some adverse currents. And so I am asking for a discussion with the two PLA, and we will have a discussion on how they support the left in Tsinghua University. It's very interesting. We were asked if people were killed, yes, they were. Even so, the PLA would not fight back. And some of the workers who were there were killed, 5 of them, and a number were wounded among them, 751 were wounded among them, workers and also PLA, but not one of them hit back and they were able, by mere persuasion, to turn this into something quite beneficial, and weed out the bad elements. So this was indeed an arduous task during the Great Proletarian Cultural Revolution (*pointing to Chang and Yao*). They were on the spot, so they can say a word about it.

FRANK: I was just going to say that not only is an apology not necessary, but the incident you refer to was actually a very good opportunity to talk with some of the masses involved, and to understand from the great concern that they have for their motherland.

CHOU: Yes, there is that aspect to it. But from our side, in the aspect of our work, we must examine our shortcomings, because if we had given prior notice to the people there, and had properly informed them of the situation, then things would be better. And so in visiting us you promote our work.

FRANK: I take it that the greater result is that we have learned from the people of their love for the motherland which was expressed in this way.

PAUL P.: I would like to make some closing remarks and it's very difficult to make them, because there is so much to say, in closing of interest and there is not much time. First I want to extend to our friends thanks, to Premier Chou, and Comrades Chang and Yao from the Central Committee and to our PLA friends that are here and our friends from Peking University and our friends from the China Travel Service. And we want to thank all of our friends for meeting with us at this time. Premier Chou has said that he has many old friends in the United States. Well we can say now that he also has some new friends in the United States. (*Applause.*) Unhappily, our visit to China is coming to a close. We have visited Canton, Shanghai, Soochow, Nanking, Peking, Tachai, and Sian, Yenan . . .

CHOU: And Taiyuan . . .

GROUP: Oh yes. (*Laughter.*)

PAUL P.: We have visited people's communes, and we have visited many factories. On our part we had a very valuable opportunity and I think a very symbolic one. Since we have come to Peking we have met with foreign friends from Korea, from Vietnam, and from Cambodia. I can say for all of us this is truly a dream come true. We have come as friends of the Chinese people and we have been warmly received everywhere as friends of the Chinese people. We know that we want to unite even closer with the Chineses people.

We believe that this visit to China and this meeting tonight has been a big step in the direction of uniting closer with the Chinese people. We also believe firmly that friendship is a two-way street. And speaking for the whole group I can say that we are very, very pleased to hear Premier Chou say that he believes that our Chinese friends will accept our invitation for Chinese friends to come to the United States. On the question of unity, we also know that it is very important for us that people who are in the antiwar movement in the United States will unite even closer within our own ranks, for we have many problems and many shortcomings. And we want to say that yes we are representatives of the antiwar movement in the United States, and yes we have done some work in the United States, but we firmly believe again that the real heroes of the anti-imperialist struggle in Asia are in fact the Asian people—the Indochinese people, the Korean people and the Chinese people.

CHOU: But if you make efforts, you will become world heroes.

PAUL P.: I say that the Asian people have suffered the most and they have struggled the most. Our stand is with the Chinese people. We support them in their struggles to build socialism in China and in their opposition to U.S. aggression and U.S. interference in Chinese affairs. We demand immediate withdrawal of U.S. military and equipment from Taiwan Province.

CHOU: Thank you.

PAUL P.: And now in closing I would like to present some symbols to our Chinese friends here, similar to what we have presented as gifts everywhere in China, to friends in all parts of China, and in all walks of life. There are two symbols. One is a photograph of our group. The other one is a button. On both of these symbols is written, "Long live the friendship of the Chinese and American peoples." (*Applause.*) And on both of these symbols can be found the peace symbol.

CHOU: That is our final aim.

PAUL P.: I would like to present Premier Chou with a photograph of our group which has been signed by members of the group. And I would like to give him a second photograph to present on our behalf to Chairman Mao.

CHOU: I will surely present him with it. Thank you for your kindness.

PAUL P.: I would also like to present our button to Premier Chou, I would like to give him another one to also present to Chairman Mao, and I would also like to present buttons to our other friends who have met with us here tonight.

CHOU: Thank you. You should note the plaque to the martyrs of the revolution which is in front of Tiananmen Square with a word on people's revolution, on which it is said that Chairman Mao laid great stress on the importance of the people.

(*Photograph and pin presented to Premier Chou.*)

APPENDIX 2:

VISITS WITH THE EMBASSIES OF THE REVOLUTIONARY GOVERNMENTS OF INDOCHINA AND OF THE DEMOCRATIC PEOPLE'S REPUBLIC OF KOREA

Prince Sihanouk

"Please have some pâté. It's from France," urged our host with solicitude lest we pass up such a gourmet delight. We had met our first non-Marxist-Leninist during our stay in China. This man with the boyish smile and concern for his guests' well-being was Prince Norodom Sihanouk, head of state and president of the National United Front of Cambodia (Kampuchea). He was entertaining us in the simple but elegant receiving room of his Peking headquarters-in-exile.

Though it is just a stone's throw from the Xinqiao Hotel where we were staying, we had barely squeezed through the People's Liberation Army-guarded gates of the headquarters in our touring bus. The headquarters is an old, spacious, nineteenth-century building that would not be out of place on an Ivy League campus. We were shown into the high-ceilinged reception room, and immediately greeted by the prince himself. Once we were seated in the overstuffed chairs placed around the room in an oblong pattern, two of the prince's assistants—one of them a woman in a delicately woven sarong —began serving us Cambodian and French hors d'oeuvres.

One of our group, Ray Whitehead, had already met Prince Sihanouk two years before in Phnom Penh. He reminded the prince of their earlier meeting. The prince replied that it was a pleasure to meet Ray a second time and that he hoped that they would meet a third time; that time in Phnom Penh once again. We laughed and applauded, and the diplomatic ice was broken.

We began by affirming our solidarity with the struggling Khmer people, and the prince thanked us with what was obviously sincere gratitude. He then gave us a brief outline of the position of the National United Front he leads.

The prince started by assuring us, "We are not in any way hostile to the United States. We are sincere admirers of the American people and their tradition of democracy, liberty, and justice." But that didn't mean that the United States should go around interfering in the affairs of other countries.

Cambodia had a very precise, a very particular way of life that involved neutrality and independence. Since the coup and the invasion, everything has been destroyed; not only in the tremendous slaughter of my people, but also our territorial integrity, our national unity . . . everything has been destroyed.

His tone was neither that of depair nor of anger, but rather something closer to exasperation.

Nixon should withdraw his protection from Lon Nol, and let Cambodia continue [sic] war without any interference from outside. Someday we will be able to put an end to such a war. It's also the same in Laos and Vietnam. There are two wars that are linked to each other: war made by external forces in Indochina, and civil war. The first step toward peace is the withdrawal of external intervention . . . and the United States is the major external power. If your government withdraws, perhaps the civil war would continue, I don't know; perhaps the regimes being supported by Nixon will disappear. They don't represent the people; they are not supported by the people.

For example, the regime in Phnom Penh gets three hundred million dollars a year—and it's not Nixon's money. I know President Nixon is not a poor man; but he's not that rich. It's the American people's money; it's your money. This money enables Lon Nol to fight against the resistance of the Cambodian people.

So, it is necessary to have a withdrawal of American forces and American interference—and three hundred million dollars a year is an interference. Nixon sends his planes against us . . . his B52s . . . our Cambodian people get bombed while Lon Nol gets money. To my people America means bombing—napalm, helicopters, B-52 airplanes with their bombs. This is the wrong way for America if they wish to be loved by the people of Asia. The people of Asia hate the U.S.A. because they cannot tell the difference between oppression by the Nixon government and the people of the U.S.A. It's the same in South Vietnam: interference and killing innocent people. Mostly innocent people are killed in Cambodia. The B-52s fly very, very high. They can't be seen. They are like the blind man, they make no discrimination. Our fighters know how to escape. It's the civilians who can't escape . . . so, many of them are killed.

We elite can make the distinction between the U.S.A. government and the U.S.A. people. The government is one thing, the people another. To us in the elite, America is not B-52s and napalm, but people like you. The American people are generous people; they want to be friends, not oppressors. We know that every day the American people fight against the wrong policies of your government. *They* would spend money in a way different from the U.S. government. *They* would spend more on health, schools for people; they would not destroy hospitals and schools in the way the U.S. government is doing. This is not progress. The U.S. government spends three hundred million for what? The result is destruction. Cambodia is returned to the nineteenth century. You have seen that China is growing, advancing, making progress. In Indochina we are going backward . . . because there is war. War is not progress. It suppresses happiness, liberty.

So, I repeat, it is necessary for the U.S. to withdraw its troops, and that includes planes; the U.S. planes that bomb Indochina come from Thailand.

The prince was by now on the edge of his seat, speaking with great intensity and animation. His facial expressions and hand gestures were very Gallic. Each time he made a point, he would try to look in the direction of a different member of his audience.

The U.S. government speaks of two sides in the struggle: the so-called free world and *socialisme*. We are not Communist, but we *are* anti-imperialist. We cannot accept the Nixon government, the *néo-colonialisme* of Washington. It is no different from colonialism. Our independence was guaranteed by the Geneva Accords of 1954 . . . guaranteed by China, the USSR, Britain, and France . . . but the U.S., the U.S. did not support them. Dulles did not like neutrality. He wanted us to be for the U.S., because he felt if we are not for the U.S., then we are against the U.S. But we say that neutrality does not mean hostility. We wanted everyone to respect our neutrality—the Communists too. Dulles said that Sihanouk was a Communist because he dealt with Peking. But the friendship treaty with China was not an alliance. Chinese technicians came to Cambodia to build factories; they left Cambodia after they had built them. This does not mean that we are a satellite of China. The Chinese respect my nationalism, my Buddhism, even my royalism. The USSR sticks with Lon Nol, just like Nixon. They say royalty separates Sihanouk from the people, and that Lon Nol is of the people, so they support him. They say the Chinese are bad Communists because they support royalty, but China wants a neutral and independent Cambodia. We fight beside the Vietnamese people because we are too small to win alone. We have written assurances [here he patted his pockets expressively] from the Communists that they will respect our frontiers and territorial integrity. During World War II the U.S. had a Communist ally in the fight against Hitler, which was the USSR. It is not strange for royalist and Communist to be fighting against the same enemy.

Perhaps because he had visited the United States several times and knew what was on the minds of a segment of the American population, he pursued this further:

Communism is not a problem for the U.S. No genuine internationalism exists as far as communism is concerned. Even the Communists become nationalists—not the Hitler-type nationalism—but nationalism meaning patriotism, attachment to the motherland—not *fascisme*. Nationalism is everywhere, even in the Communist countries. That explains the dispute between China and the USSR. Communism meant internationalism in the past. Now it exists differently in all Communist countries. Yugoslavian communism is not the same as communism in China . . .

There is the socialism of the Vietcong and the socialism of North Vietnam. They will not reunite immediately. After the war, South Vietnam will remain independent for many years.

"Communist camp" does not mean anything anymore. There is no one camp. Cambodia will not be a Communist state. We have many Communists in our united front—but even more nationalists and royalists. The united front represents a compromise of four groups: nationalists, Communists, royalists, and Buddhists. We must unite, Communist or not. We will be a progressive government, somewhat *socialiste*, very nationalistic, very Cambodian, and also neutralist. *We will not align.* Neutrality is the sine qua non of our survival. Neutrality is independence for us. We stand firmly on the basis of neutrality. We shall always have Buddhism as the state religion. Even the Communists are Buddhists . . . They read Marx, but they are also Buddhists. Like de Gaulle who wanted a very French France, we want a very Cambodian Cambodia. In that sense I am *Gaulliste*.

Having expressed this part of his credo, the animated prince rested momentarily and reflected. Then he answered an imaginary skeptic in his audience: "But *what* communism, I ask you? The Communist camp doesn't exist anymore." He reflected momentarily again. Then in a lower key and more slowly, he continued:

> One day we shall win. It is not hope. It is a fact. It is *réalisme*. One day the Indochinese people will win. It is in the best interests of the U.S. to join the people because the regimes which the U.S. supports now will be wiped out. It is better to be on the side of the winner. Nixon can't win. The American people know this. Nixon does not want history to record any defeat for the U.S.A. He can't accept defeat because it will be the first in U.S. history. We don't want to defeat the U.S. Victory means victory against neocolonialism, victory against the puppet regimes, peace and freedom for our people. If the U.S. disengages its forces, history will never record it as a defeat. History will say the U.S. let the situation settle itself. The three countries of Indochina are very much destroyed. The U.S. can help us to rebuild. In the future, if the U.S. will help us in national reconstruction, if the U.S. will give us aid in order to reconstruct our countries, we will be grateful. There is no question of face, of victory or defeat. We will walk together for peace—what you friends here from the Concerned Asia Scholars are doing. You represent the will of the U.S. people.
>
> We shall not forget that China supported us during the *Résistance,* hence China will be our first friend. But we also want the friendship of the U.S. We want the U.S.A. and the government in Washington as our good friend. It was the anti-Communist crusade that caused the U.S. to get into a war in Indochina.
>
> North Vietnam is independent of China and has promised to respect our frontiers and our independence. China will do the same. We shall not be a satellite of China. We are separated from China by Laos and Vietnam. We are a small country of no special interest to China. We are more helpful to China as an independent country and less helpful as a satellite. China has to get back Taiwan, not satellize Indochina. When the U.S. stops supporting Taiwan, U.S. relations with Peking will improve. It is the duty of China to achieve the territorial integrity of her own nation, not to satellize Indochina.

The hors d'oeuvres had been consumed, and now the Cambodian woman in the sarong was serving sherbet, padding noiselessly from coffee table to coffee table with an unobtrusiveness approaching invisibility. Prince Sihanouk had stopped talking about politics and was again urging us to eat. But we had questions on our minds about POWs, Angkor, the National United Front's relationship to the NLF and the North Vietnamese, the liberated areas of Cambodia, the prince's opinion of the seven-point peace proposal . . . We wondered if we would have the chance to raise them. While the prince was occupied with the sherbet, we seized the opportunity.

Did Prince Sihanouk have anything to relay to the antiwar movement in the United States, especially regarding prisoners of war?

"We Cambodians have no U.S. prisoners. We have liberated those journalists who had fallen into our hands. I have contacted my *guerrilleros* about Welles Hangin and Sean Flynn and I can assure you very precisely . . ." He repeated the phrase with gravity:

> . . . assure you very precisely that they are not in the custody of my fighters. Right after they were reported missing, I looked into this. As you know, Robert Anson and Kate Webb were released right after they fell into the hands of the Cambodians. But there is no news of Hangin. We Cambodians liberate prisoners without conditions—automatically. It is too difficult for us to keep them. We have no U.S. prisoners, therefore it is not the same as in Vietnam. There are not many Vietnamese fighting in Cambodia and there is no common command between the two forces. We each have our own command. Perhaps they (i.e., the Vietnamese in Cambodia) have some U.S. prisoners.

"What is the relationship of the forces in Cambodia," we asked him, "that is, between your men and the Vietnamese? You said something earlier about having guarantees in your pocket concerning the territorial integrity of Cambodia. There will be people in the United States, especially in the government, who will say that the Communists will not respect Cambodia's borders once the U.S. has withdrawn from Indochina."

The prince was on the edge of his chair again, speaking with lively intensity.

> I have received solemn declarations that Hanoi will respect our frontiers, our territorial integrity, our sovereignty, and the neutrality of Cambodia and they will never interfere in the internal affairs of Cambodia. By the joint declaration of April 25, 1970, at the Indochinese People's Summit Con-

ference, the Pathet Lao, the Vietcong, and Hanoi all will respect the territorial integrity, the frontiers, and the neutrality of Cambodia. I have these guarantees in my pocket [gestures toward pocket again]. They cannot be more precise. And we of Cambodia made certain assurances to them: (1) we shall not be anybody's ally; (2) there will be no military bases in Cambodia. We also have guarantees from China as well. These are the absolute maximum guarantees. We don't need Nixon's protection. Nixon attracts communism to Cambodia like sugar attracts ants. It is U.S. imperialism which attracts communism.

Many people in the West have expressed concern over the ancient capital of Angkor. How are the prince's forces safeguarding the treasures of Angkor Wat?

The prince plunged right into the answer.

There are many stories about the Communists stealing treasures from Angkor Wat and selling them in Hong Kong and Bangkok. These stories are not true.

We can say many things about the Communists. Perhaps they are too disciplined, too rigid in their thinking. [He gives a Gallic What-can-I-do? shrug.] Perhaps we can criticize them for not being democratic enough, perhaps we can say this, but [now with a tone of finality in his voice] we know that they are honest! They do not steal antiques and sell them in Hong Kong. The units stationed at Angkor are mostly Cambodians who are very respectful of Angkor Wat. All Cambodians are my children, even the Communist Cambodians. They are safeguarding Angkor. The Saigon puppet troops are more noted for theft. Everybody knows that. That's why we are protecting Angkor from them. The things stolen so far from Angkor were stolen by the Saigon puppets . . . by men like General Do Cao Tri, recently killed. He collected antiques from Angkor and opened a shop in Saigon to sell them. Since we liberated Angkor, nothing has been lost. There has been no damage. Lon Nol's artillery destroyed some of Angkor . . . they shelled it from Siem Reap.

He caught his breath, recalled something that must have been fresh in his mind, and plunged in again.

"You are Americans. Do you know of this Asia Society in New York?" He didn't wait for an answer.

They wanted me to neutralize Angkor. They wrote me a letter telling me that I should have the safeguarding of

Angkor at heart, and therefore I should order it to be neutralized. They also reminded me that I had been their guest and should be grateful. Once when I visited New York, we talked and they served me some sandwiches. Now today, you all are my guests here. Do I ask you to be grateful, to feel obligated? I do not. I admit that their sandwiches are delicious but I cannot pay with the price of Angkor Wat. It is the capital of Cambodia and I will keep it. I will not give my Angkor to the Asia Society. No, their letter was really not correct; it is an interference. The Asia Society should tell Nixon to stop the bombing, not to neutralize Angkor. The duty of the Asia Society, if it wants to save Angkor and Khmer civilization, is to tell Nixon to stop the war against Cambodia. We will liberate Angkor and will keep it.

The prince paused, then said:

Lon Nol and Sirik Matak, they have members of my family—my mother, an old and sick woman; my children. I cannot neutralize them. We must accept the consequences of war. We must continue the struggle. When I replied to Senator Fulbright's letter about the journalists Hangin and Flynn, I told him I haven't requested any help to free my children or my mother. We must accept the consequences of war. And as to those interested in saving Khmer culture, there are many treasures of recent history housed in Phnom Penh. Why do they not ask to neutralize Phnom Penh as well?

Note: John D. Rockefeller III and Kenneth Young, former U.S. ambassador to Thailand, are chairman of the board and president respectively of the Asia Society. In a *New York Times* article of October 7, 1971, entitled "Reds Let French Expert Work at Angkor," Terrence Smith reports an interview with Richard Melville, "an official of the Asia Society who visited Cambodia last month on a mission sponsored by the John D. Rockefeller III Fund." In the interview, Melville reports a conversation he had with the French archaeologist Philippe-Bernard Groslier, who has long served as director of Conservation d'Angkor, the archaeological institution which maintains the temples. According to Melville, Groslier is allowed across Communist lines alone and on bicycle every Tuesday and Friday to supervise the several hundred Cambodian workers in the temple area who are carrying out maintenance work. The article suggests that this was made possible by intensive negotiations last year involving Phnom Penh, Paris, Hanoi, and the Indian government; and by direct contact between Groslier and "the deputy commander of the North Vietnamese unit that had occupied the area. He apparently gained the commander's confidence and persuaded him that his sole purpose was to protect the monuments."

Further on in the article when the negotiations are described in greater detail, the Lon Nol government is attributed no role whatever. Groslier reports only minor damage was inflicted during the fighting of last year. The article alleges that "thefts of carvings have apparently increased during the occupation, but not to the extent described in the press reports." The article suggests at one point that the occupiers are Vietcong and North Vietnamese; at another point only North Vietnamese. At no point does the article mention Prince Sihanouk or Cambodian forces loyal to him.

The article concludes, "Diplomatic sources said that the Cambodian Government (Lon Nol) was planning to propose the neutralization and internationalization of the Angkor area at the current session of the United Nations General Assembly."

We asked Prince Sihanouk what was the extent of the liberated areas of Cambodia. He replied:

Two-thirds of the country has been liberated and in the other third, my *guerrilleros* can move freely since they have the support of the people. This has been true since the end of 1970. The military situation has not changed much since then. The countryside has been liberated, the towns have not. Four million Cambodians have been liberated, three million are with Lon Nol, mainly in the towns. We stay out of the towns. If we occupy the towns, the U.S. will bomb them. Even the Vietcong, who have been fighting much longer than we have, who are much stronger than we are, even they have not taken the big towns in Vietnam. The countryside is more important to occupy than the cities. Protracted warfare is the answer. Chairman Mao was right. We are ready to fight protracted war indefinitely.

It was approaching time to leave. We asked a final question concerning the prince's opinion of the seven-point peace proposal put forward by Mme. Binh, and how it affected Cambodia. The prince answered, still speaking as energetically as he had several hours earlier.

We support the proposals put forth by Mme. Binh on behalf of the NLF and the PRG. Since the Summit Conference of the Indochinese People, we promised mutual solidarity. We cannot solve the problem of Cambodia without solving the problem of the other two countries. Peace between America and Vietnam will mean peace between America and Cambodia. The problem of U.S. prisoners is not a problem since the seven-point peace proposal. This is covered in the peace proposal. It calls for withdrawal combined with the solution of the prisoner problem. The government of the U.S. should at least accept the seven-point peace proposal as a basis for negotiations. With this peace proposal there is now a new element for progress toward negotiations for peace and friendship.

Kay and Ken gave the prince several tokens of our solidarity, among them a copy of the CCAS book *Cambodia: The Widening War*. The gifts were accompanied by an expression of our solidarity, which concluded, "We will meet again, and at that time it will be in Phnom Penh."

The prince was obviously moved and he said, almost with surprise: "You have touched my heart and my mind . . . You are much better ambassadors than the regular ambassadors of your government."

We all filed out the French doors of the reception room into the bright sunlight of the garden. We suggested a group photograph and the prince was happy to oblige. When he realized that we hadn't brought a professional photographer, but were going to have one of our own people hold the camera, he called out to his assistant to come take the camera and take a picture of the whole group lest one of us be left out. When the photo had been taken, the prince gestured in the direction of his assistant, smiled wryly to us, and said, "When you return home to your country, you can say you had your picture taken by Prince Sisowath Methavi, the younger brother of Prince Sihanouk's enemy, Sirik Matak."

The Provisional Revolutionary Government of South Vietnam

In contrast with the prince, the representatives of the Provisional Revolutionary Government seemed most interested in discussing American opposition to the war. This visit was followed two days later by a visit to the embassy of the Democratic Republic of Vietnam.

We pulled up in front of an undistinguished, modern, two-story building of white brick. There was only a small black and gold plaque at the entranceway identifying it in Vietnamese and English as the embassy of the Provisional Revolutionary Government of the Republic of South Vietnam.

An embassy official, casual in shirt sleeves, greeted us at the door and escorted us into a long, airy room to the rear of the building. On one side a floor-to-ceiling window-wall looked out on a neatly manicured lawn; several of the glass panels stood ajar and we could hear the high-pitched drone of cicadas. We exchanged introductions with the six other Vietnamese who were there to talk with us. They too were simply dressed and seemed eager to begin the discussion. We arranged ourselves around a long table in the center of the room, sipped tea, and chatted in Chinese, our only common language. Only one of them, their official interpreter, spoke English. All were relatively young and had been with the People's Liberation Armed Forces (PLAF) in Vietnam.

We first presented our hosts with a copy of the People's Peace Treaty signed by all of us. The treaty had been first signed more than a year before, between representatives of the American National Student Association and the National Students' Union of South Vietnam. Since then thousands of Americans have signed to pledge their determination to end the war. We were aware that on several important points the July 1 seven-point peace proposal had superseded it. Yet we felt the People's Peace Treaty—publicized in the U.S. partially by CCAS—symbolized appropriately our solidarity with the Vietnamese people. Our hosts accepted it with thanks but made no further comment. We also gave them copies of several *CCAS Bulletins* dealing with the war and a copy of the CCAS book *The Indochina Story*.

Then we began to talk in earnest. These men of the PRG spoke in a quiet, low-keyed manner and rarely used Marxist terminology, yet their questions and comments indicated unambiguously that these were the categories in which they thought. We talked of the course of the war in Indochina and the antiwar movement in the U.S. They seemed especially interested in the roles that CCAS or we as individuals had played. We related instances of CCAS people helping out GI organizers in Asian "R and R" ports, and we described our research and publications about the CIA's role, done during the protests against the U.S. invasion of Cambodia in 1970. When we discussed the antiwar movement in the U.S., inevitably we talked about splits, divisions, disunity, and the Vietnamese understood this very well.

We asked them what Americans could do to help end the war more rapidly. They offered us four suggestions and one question.

Their first point was "Unify, unify, unify." Create a broadly based front of all those who oppose the war.

Second, they asked us to learn from the antiwar veterans and GIs. They have been to South Vietnam. They have seen war crimes, atrocities, corruption in Saigon, and U.S. profiteering. They understand what the war is really about and they oppose it.

As their third and fourth points, they urged us and all Americans to study the *Pentagon Papers:* "They will teach you much about how the American government works and how it tries to defraud the people"; and to study the seven-point peace proposal: "Understand what it is saying and why at this time it represents a just basis for resolving the conflict in Vietnam." They restated and discussed the text of the proposal.

Text of the Seven-Point Peace Proposal

(1)

Regarding the deadline for the total withdrawal of U.S. forces.

The U.S. government must put an end to its war of aggression in Vietnam, stop the policy of "Vietnamization" of the war, withdraw from South Vietnam all troops, military personnel, weapons, and war materials of the United States and of the other foreign countries in the U.S. camp, and dismantle all U.S. bases in South Vietnam, without posing any condition whatsoever.

The U.S. government must set a terminal date for the withdrawal from South Vietnam of the totality of U.S. forces and those of the other foreign countries of the U.S. camp.

If the U.S. government sets a terminal date for the withdrawal from South Vietnam in 1971 of the totality of U.S. forces and those of the other foreign countries in the U.S. camp, the parties will at the same time agree on the modalities:

A. Of the withdrawal in safety from South Vietnam of the totality of U.S. forces and those of the other foreign countries in the U.S. camp.

B. Of the release of the totality of military men of all parties and the civilians captured in the war (including American pilots captured in North Vietnam), so that they may all rapidly return to their homes.

These two operations will begin on the same date and will end on the same date.

A cease-fire will be observed between the South Vietnam People's Liberation Armed Forces and the armed forces of the United States and of the other foreign countries in the United States camp, as soon as the parties reach agreement on the withdrawal from South Vietnam of the totality of United States forces and those of the other foreign countries in the United States camp.

(2)

Regarding the question of power in South Vietnam.

The United States government must really respect the South Vietnam people's right to self-determination, put an end to its interference in the internal affairs of South Vietnam, cease backing the bellicose group headed by Nguyen Van Thieu, at present in office in Saigon, and stop all maneuvers, including tricks on elections, aimed at maintaining the puppet Nguyen Van Thieu.

The political, social, and religious forces in South Vietnam aspiring to peace and national concord will use various means to form in Saigon a new administration favoring peace, independence, neutrality, and democracy.

The Provisional Revolutionary Government of the Republic of South Vietnam will immediately enter into talks with that administration in order to settle the following questions:

A. To form a broad three-segment government of national concord that will assume its functions during the period between the restoration of peace and the holding of general elections and organize general elections in South Vietnam.

A cease-fire will be observed between the South Vietnam People's Liberation Armed Forces and the armed forces of the Saigon administration as soon as the government of national concord is formed.

B. To take concrete measures with the required guarantees so as to prohibit all acts of terror, reprisal, and discrimination against persons having collaborated with one or the other party, to ensure every democratic liberty to the South Vietnamese people, to release all persons jailed for political reasons, to dissolve all concentration camps, and to liquidate all forms of constraint and coercion so as to permit the people to return to their native places in complete freedom and to freely engage in their occupations.

C. To see that the people's conditions of living are stabilized and gradually improved, to create conditions allowing everyone to contribute his talents and efforts to heal the war wounds and rebuild the country.

D. To agree on measures to be taken to ensure the holding of genuinely free, democratic, and fair general elections in South Vietnam.

(3)

Regarding the question of Vietnamese armed forces in South Vietnam.

The Vietnamese parties will together settle the question of Vietnamese armed forces in South Vietnam in a spirit of national concord, equality, and mutual respect, without foreign interference, in accordance with the postwar situation and with a view to making lighter the people's contributions.

(4)

Regarding the peaceful reunification of Vietnam and the relations between the North and South zones.

A. The reunification of Vietnam will be achieved step by step by peaceful means, on the basis of discussions and agreements between the two zones, without constraint and annexation from either party, without foreign interference.

Pending the reunification of the country, the North and the South zones will reestablish normal relations, guarantee free movement, free correspondence, free choice of residence, and maintain economic and cultural relations on the principle of mutual interests and mutual assistance.

All questions concerning the two zones will be settled by qualified representatives of the Vietnamese people in the two zones on the basis of negotiations, without foreign interference.

B. In keeping with the provisions of the 1954 Geneva agreements on Vietnam, in the present temporary partition of the country into two zones, the North and the South zones of Vietnam will refrain from joining any military alliance with foreign countries, from allowing any foreign country to have military bases, troops, and military personnel on their soil, and from recognizing the protection of any country, of any military alliance or bloc.

(5)

Regarding the foreign policy of peace and neutrality of South Vietnam.

South Vietnam will pursue a foreign policy of peace and neutrality, establish relations with all countries regardless of their political and social regime, in accordance with the five principles of peaceful coexistence, maintain economic and cultural relations with all countries, accept the co-operation of foreign countries in the exportation of the resources of South Vietnam, accept from any country economic and technical aid without any political conditions attached, and participate in regional plans of economic co-operation.

On the basis of these principles, after the end of the war, South Vietnam and the United States will establish relations in the political, economic, and cultural fields.

(6)

Regarding the damages caused by the United States to the Vietnamese peoples in the two zones.

The U.S. government must bear full responsibility for the losses and the destructions it has caused to the Vietnamese people in the two zones.

(7)

Regarding the respect and the international guarantee of the accords that will be concluded.

The parties will find agreement on the forms of respect and international guarantee of the accords that will be concluded.

The thin, soft-spoken leader of the Vietnamese side finished. From the far end of the table another man, somewhat younger, began to speak. He said that he had met with many delegations of foreign friends from different parts of the world, antiwar people, often intellectuals. He had always taken the opportunity to ask them one question, but he could frankly say that up to the present time, he had not yet had a response. So today he would ask us. An answer to it, he felt, would not only help to end U.S. aggression in Vietnam but would contribute to a deeper understanding between our two peoples.

The question was: "How is it that a small country can defeat a large one; a weak country defeat a strong one?" Immediately, another Vietnamese at the table made a gentle move to end the discussion—perhaps it was the leader looking at his watch, for we had been talking for two-and-a-half hours. There was a moment of uncertain silence. Then we were shaking hands all round and moving toward the door.

Once back in our bus, we exploded: "What was his meaning? What was he getting at? He means that the Vietnamese are defeating the U.S. because even though they're small, they're really together . . ." "He means that in order to defeat

Nixon, we've got to heal the divisions in the movement; then even if we're small, the administration will really be in trouble . . ." "He means if you stick with a just principle, you'll win in the end . . ." "He means if you have the ability to analyze his question, then . . ."

There was a cross fire of barely restrainable instant analysis. In the midst of it, Paul said, "He might not like to be called this, but I think he was being the wise Zen master: He asked a question that doesn't have *one* instant answer. The kind of question that, the more you let it thump around inside your head, the more good answers you come up with, the more you begin to see the connections among the different answers."

In our interview with Chou En-lai, the premier referred to the American Revolution as the victory of a small guerrilla force against a strong imperialist nation. We remembered the man from the PRG and his question.

The Democratic Republic of Vietnam

Our visit to the PRG embassy was on the evening of July 14. Two days later, on the morning of the sixteenth, the first word came of Kissinger's visit and Nixon's impending trip. That evening we were scheduled to call on the embassy of the Democratic Republic of Vietnam (DRV).

We were greeted at the door of the embassy by a soft-spoken Vietnamese man who apologized for his inability to speak directly with us in English. The embassy interpreter himself was not accustomed to English-speaking visitors and had some difficult translating the formal language of diplomacy and the nuances of the conversation. Fortunately, Frank spoke enough French to step in as our "people's interpreter"; some parts of the conversation went a tortuous route through two interpreters (Vietnamese-French, French-English) and some of it was carried on in Chinese.

As we had in our visits to other embassies, we began with a presentation of three documents—a statement of solidarity and friendship with the Vietnamese people, a copy of the People's Peace Treaty, and a copy of the national CCAS statement of purpose which condemns scholarly complicity with the U.S. war effort in Indochina. We also expressed our deepest respect for their departed leader, Ho Chi Minh. The Vietnamese delegation accepted the documents and our sentiments regarding Ho Chi Minh with warm thanks for our group, and for all Americans "who have stood up in the face of the aggressive policies of the U.S. government in Indochina."

The leading diplomat from the Vietnamese side then launched into a discussion of the current situation in the Indochina War. He expressed solidarity with the Provisional Revolutionary Government of South Vietnam and the delegation of Mme. Nguyen Thi Binh in Paris. Like the representatives of the PRG, he too urged us to take careful note of the seven-point peace proposal. He carefully explained that this proposal is the only avenue to peace acceptable to the people of Vietnam, and provides for the release of U.S. military prisoners held in northern Vietnam. He also suggested that the *Pentagon Papers* are an important source of information on the origins of the Indochina conflict and the duplicity of recent presidential administrations.

Although their manner was restrained and rather formal, there was no sense of bitterness toward us in the presentations of the Vietnamese diplomats. Each sentence carried a tone of firm determination and dignity, each handshake a sense of genuine warmth and understanding. They did not raise the issue of that day's startling news, and we—still confused by it—did not want to make the first move. Sitting there and listening to the soft tones of Vietnamese, English, French, and Chinese, we could not hold back the flood of remembered images—napalmed babies on the evening news, burned villages, wasted fields.

We watched two short movies with our hosts, seeing flashes of the war through Vietnamese eyes. The first was of cultural troupes in the jungles of southern Vietnam, and the second of a women's antiaircraft unit defending the north.

After the films, we had a short closing meeting. Our hosts presented us with gifts of Hanoi publications and an unusual silver cup. We were told that this cup had been fashioned by a Vietnamese craftsman from the metal remains of the thirty-two-hundreth U.S. warplane to be shot down over Vietnam; it weighs about two pounds, stands eight inches high, and is inscribed in Vietnamese with the date and occasion. In presenting the cup to the friendship delegation, the Vietnamese said with a quiet smile, "It was sent aggressively, but we return it to you with friendly solidarity."

The Democratic People's Republic of Korea

Our first meeting with representatives of the DPRK took place at our hotel in Peking. A secretary from the Korean embassy and his interpreter arrived one morning and greeted us, saying that they had read some of our literature and heard about our activities from Chinese friends. They were happy to meet with a group of young Americans for the first time, and expressed interest in promoting better understanding between Koreans and Americans.

The Koreans showed concern over the fact that their side of the conflict in Korea and their positions have never really been made clear in the United States, and that their attempts to reunify their homeland have been repeatedly rebuffed without consideration by the United States government and the government in South Korea. They began to talk about the progress they had made since 1945, under the leadership of their Premier, Kim Il Sung, but time was short and we decided to meet again. They invited us to come to their embassy for dinner and to see a Korean film, and we accepted with a good deal of anticipation.

Some days later we were received in their new embassy, an impressive, air-conditioned, modern building constructed entirely of Korean materials and by Korean workers. As we nibbled on Korean delicacies and toasted each other with the powerful ginseng liquor, the secretary recounted with pride the Korean struggle against the Japanese and then the Americans. "During the Korean War the whole country was reduced to ashes under a hail of American bombs," they said. "But in the eighteen years since then, we have done as much in rebuilding as would ordinarily have taken a hundred years.

"Now, the problem of peacefully and democratically reuniting Korea is the supreme one." They told us about the efforts of their Red Cross to arrange a meeting with the Red Cross in the south for the purpose of reuniting families long separated by the division of the country. (Since then these meetings have begun.) They also summarized their proposals for unification, made in April 1971, which received almost no publicity in the United States. Briefly, their eight-point program for a settling of the Korean conflict by the Korean people themselves is as follows: (1) All foreign troops should withdraw from southern Korea; foreign troops have already withdrawn from the north. (2) The troops of both northern and southern Korea should be reduced to 100,000 men or less. (3) All treaties which have been made with imperialist countries should be abolished. (4) When these steps are accomplished, a general election can be held on a direct, secret-ballot, democratic basis, from which a united government will result. (5) For this election all political and social activities should be allowed to be carried out freely, and all political prisoners should be released by both sides. (6) If the above is not possible, then a confederation should be established in which the political systems could remain as they are, but in which vital services might cross lines. (7) If even this cannot be arranged, at least travel, postal service, and trade can be. (8) For discussing all these questions all political parties should get together to discuss their views— perhaps in Panmunjom or in some neutral country. When we confessed our ignorance (and the general lack of knowledge in America) of these proposals and of Korean developments in general, they volunteered to send us books and periodicals, and we agreed to send them our literature in return.

After dinner we were treated to a spectacular full-length color film, the *Maidens of Diamond Mountain*. The dialogue was in Korean, but the interpreter performed yeoman service for us in keeping up with the complicated plot. This very pleasant evening ended with exchanges of books and pamphlets, and their wish that we take back their regards to the American people, and interestingly, the American working class.

Then, just before we were scheduled to leave Peking, the Koreans invited us back again for a brief visit. The secretary said he wanted to thank us for our concern and expressed the desire that scholars of Asia would continue to visit Asian countries and that some would be coming to Korea. "We now know of your just cause," he said, "that is, opposition to imperialistic aggression and war and support for the freedom of humanity. We wish you success in your future work for this cause and we also sincerely hope that in the future we shall have closer contacts with you."

BIBLIOGRAPHY

Few Americans realize just how *American* their view of China is. Almost no other country in the world has isolated itself from China so completely over the last two decades. As a result, the China that most Americans "know" is almost unrecognizable to Europeans, Asians, or the Chinese themselves.

To compound this situation, most American books and reporting are basically unhelpful. The reporting is heavily biased and usually anti-Chinese, while most of the scholarly books on China are boring or academic.

The books listed here are among the very few to draw an informative or fair picture of China. Many of them are journalistic accounts and almost all of them are about China since the 1930s.

We have tried to exclude books which require extensive knowledge of China or Chinese culture. The books included are mostly written for the general reader and not the scholar. Books marked with an asterisk are available in paperback editions.

History and Politics

Most of the books which describe Imperial China (pre-1911) are highly specialized and, with few exceptions, dull. Except for translations of early Chinese literature and poetry (Arthur Waley has done a large number of excellent translations of early poetry), a good place to begin would be Wolfgang Franke's *China and the West** (New York: Harper & Row, 1967).

For general background history, *The China Reader** provides a wide variety of documents, as well as analytical and interpretive articles. The first volume covers *Imperial China to 1911;* volume 2 is *Republican China, 1911–1949;* and volume 3 is *Communist China, 1949 to the Present.* All are edited by Orville Schell and Franz Schurmann (New York: Vintage, 1967).

On missionaries: James C. Thomson, Jr.'s *While China Faced West* (Cambridge, Mass.: Harvard University Press, 1969). Written by the son of a missionary born in China, this book provides a new look at the supposedly altruistic efforts of American churches and foundations in China. The most notable results he shows were the failure to bring peaceful nonrevolutionary change and the demonstration to the Chinese of continued American interference in their affairs.

A good short history of twentieth-century China is C. P. Fitzgerald's *The Birth of Communist China** (Baltimore, Md.: Penguin Books, 1964).

For the 1911–49 period, the best treatment of the collapse of the Kuomintang and the rise to power of the Communists is Lucien Bianco's *Origins of the Chinese Revolution* (Stanford: Stanford University Press, 1971).

For a personal account of the disintegration of the Kuomintang from 1945 to 1949, read John Melby's *The Mandate of Heaven** (Garden City, N.Y.: Doubleday, 1971). Melby was an American diplomat on the scene in Chungking and Nanking, and records vivid personal impressions of the demise of Chiang's regime.

Edgar Snow's *Red Star over China** (New York: Grove Press, 1961) is one of the few "classics" on modern China. It is an account of the early years of the Chinese Communist movement and is based on the author's visit to the Communist guerrilla base area in northwest China in 1936 and his extensive conversations with Mao and Chou.

A much more detailed but very interesting book on how the Communists established and expanded their "base areas" in the Anti-Japanese War is Mark Selden's *The Yenan Way in Revolutionary China* (Cambridge, Mass.: Harvard University Press, 1971).

Another American reporter, Jack Belden, wrote of the war years in *China Shakes the World** (New York: Monthly Review Press, 1971), which covers the 1949 liberation as well. While the author is openly partisan on the Communist side, this book is exciting and adventure-packed. Belden hiked and traveled through north China at the height of the civil war.

Derk Bodde's *Peking Diary: A Year of Revolution** (New York: Fawcett, 1967) is an eyewitness account by an American scholar of the way the Communists set up their government in China's new capital.

Because few Americans have been allowed to travel in China since 1949, there are few good books available with an American perspective on life in China during the past two decades. The best general picture is Edgar Snow's *The Other Side of the River: Red China Today** (New York: Random House, 1962). The book is based on the distinguished journalist's return to China and his extensive travels there in 1960.

Another highly readable journalist's account is by Felix Greene, *Awakened China, the Country Most Americans Don't Know** (Garden City, N.Y.: Doubleday, 1961).

For a personal panoramic view of twentieth-century China, see Han Suyin's biographical trilogy, *The Crippled Tree, A Mortal Flower,* and *Birdless Summer* (New York: Putnam, 1965, 1968). The books will be available in Bantam paperbacks in fall, 1972.

Rural China

There are five excellent books in English that describe the human meaning of the new society that is being built in rural China.

The first is William Hinton's *Fanshen: A Documentary of Revolution in a Chinese Village** (New York: Monthly Review Press, 1966). Hinton was a United Nations agricultural adviser in China after World War II who became attached as an official observer to a small team of Communist cadres. They helped the people of a small, backward village overthrow the landlords who oppressed them and redistribute the lands of the village on an equitable basis. The book is long, but it gives us the most vivid picture of the human dimension of the revolution and the true nature of the corrupt rural society which was overthrown.

Two books, Jan Myrdal's *Report from a Chinese Village** (New York: Signet, 1963) and Jan Myrdal and Gun Kessle's *China: The Revolution Continued* (New York: Pantheon, 1970), tell the story of a single village in a very backward part of China before and just after the Cultural Revolution. There is an enormous wealth of detail in these two volumes about ordinary people and how their lives were changed by the revolution.

The last two books, Isabel and David Crooks's *Revolution in a Chinese Village: Ten Mile Inn* (London: Routledge and Kegan Paul, 1959) and *The First Years of Yangyi Commune* (London: Routledge and Kegan Paul, 1966), are written by a husband-and-wife team of foreign visitors who were able to trace the changes in a single small village over several years. There is a great deal of fascinating material here, but on the whole these two books seem more propagandistic and somewhat less sensitive to the problems people face as their society is being transformed than are the first three books.

China's Cities

The study of China's cities has just begun, and unfortunately there are still few good descriptions of life in them and how it has changed since 1949. Perhaps the best work so far is Ezra Vogel's study of the city of Canton, *Canton Under Communism, 1949–1968** (Cambridge, Mass.: Harvard University Press, 1969); this book tells the story of modern Chinese cities from the perspective of a single province, and should not be taken as representative of Chinese cities in general.

Despite its forbidding title, Rhoads Murphey's "Traditionalism and Colonialism: Changing Urban Roles in Asia" (*Journal of Asian Studies,* 29, no. 1 [1969]:67–84) is an excellent and very readable article. It shows how the location and function of *all* Asia's major cities were profoundly changed by four hundred years of Western imperialism, and then goes on to see how China's new government has sought to change the situation. The article thus clearly points out how China's experience differs from countries like India, Vietnam, and Indonesia, which are still a part of the Western imperialist system.

For a more detailed picture of China's cities, one can consult the following volumes recently prepared at Stanford: G. William Skinner, ed., *The City in Late Imperial China* (Stanford: Stanford University Press, forthcoming); and John Wilson Lewis, ed., *The City in Communist China* (Stanford: Stanford University Press, 1971). These books are made up of scholarly articles, the quality of which varies from excellent and readable to dull and boring. Read selectively!

Health

Away with All Pests* (New York: Monthly Review Press, 1969) is the vivid firsthand account of an English surgeon, Joshua Horn, who spent fifteen years in China. Horn describes the importance the Chinese give to tailoring medicine to the needs of the people, especially in the rural areas, and to overcoming the tendency to concentrate and overspecialize medicine in the urban areas. Horn also shows the value of combining "the new and the old," giving credit to valuable traditional medical practices such as acupuncture. The strongest and warmest message in the book is that of a medical service continually developing and adapting to the needs of the Chinese people.

Chinese Medicine, by Heinrich Wallnofer and Anna von Rottaucher (New York: Bell Publishing Company), is one of the few books which explain simply and well the basic philosophical and metaphysical principles behind traditional Chinese medicine. In addition, it has a number of herbal recipes and goes into the theory behind acupuncture.

Education and Youth

China's educational system and the role of young people in its future were two key issues of the Cultural Revolution, so most of our best material on these subjects has been interpreted in light of developments during the Cultural Revolution.

A good place to start in looking at China's educational system is John Gardner's article "Educated Youth and Urban-Rural Inequalities, 1958–66" (in *The City in Communist China,* cited above); this shows how China's Communist educational system, originally based on Western models, encouraged students to seek to advance their personal careers rather than to work to strengthen their country. Thus in the years from 1960 to 1966 the educational system worked to undercut the very values on which Mao Tse-tung had hoped to base China's modernization.

Victor Nee's *The Cultural Revolution at Peking University** (New York: Monthly Review Press, 1969) gives a closeup account of the impact of the Cultural Revolution on an elite college. It is a lively and readable description of intellectual youth questioning the purposes of higher education.

Two other works, both autobiographies of Chinese youths who were shaped by the anti-Maoist educational system, give us a clear picture of how the conflict in the educational sphere helped prepare the way for the Cultural Revolution. The first is Tung Chi-p'ing's *The Thought Revolution** (New York: Coward-McCann, 1966), covering the early 1960s. The second is Gordon Bennett and Ronald Montaperto's *Red Guard:*

The Political Biography of Dai Hsiao-ai* (Garden City, N.Y.: Doubleday, 1971), which covers the first years of the Cultural Revolution.

There is an excellent description of how American children are taught to see China as the "enemy" in Richard and Leigh Kagan's "Oh, Say *Can* You See? American Cultural Blinders on China" (in *America's Asia,** Edward Friedman and Mark Selden, eds. [New York: Pantheon, 1971]).

Women and Family Life

There has been very little written on women and family life in China today outside of stories and novels published in China in English-language editions by the Peking Foreign Languages Press. The reader might consult Ai-li S. Chin's article "Family Relations in Modern Chinese Fiction" (in *Family and Kinship in Chinese Society,* Maurice Freedman, ed. [Stanford: Stanford University Press, 1970]). This article was written for specialists, but it does attempt to compare the patterns of family life found in stories published in Communist China and on Taiwan. Thus it gives some rare insights into the radically different developments in the two societies since 1949.

Report from a Chinese Village and *China: The Revolution Continued* (cited above) contain a wealth of detail about family life, telling the stories of individuals and the changes in their lives. For a good contrast with women in old China, read Ida Pruitt's *Daughter of Han** (Stanford: Stanford University Press, 1967); this is the moving story of a poor woman growing up in China before Liberation.

A brief story of the struggle of Chinese women to free themselves after "official" liberation is told in "Gold Flower's Story," which is in *China Shakes the World,* cited above, and was reprinted as a pamphlet by the New England Free Press (791 Tremont St., Boston, Mass. 02118).

Chinese Communist Political Thought: Maoism

The core of China's political thought is Maoism, and the ways the Chinese have chosen to build their new society have been shaped by Maoist principles. The clearest explanation of Mao's thought is Stuart Schram's *The Political Thought of Mao Tse-tung** (New York: Praeger, 1963). A helpful book with this is Schram's biography, *Mao Tse-tung** (Baltimore, Md.: Penguin Books, 1967).

Better still, one can read Mao Tse-tung himself; for example, the *Quotations of Chairman Mao Tse-tung** (Peking: Foreign Languages Press, 1966) is available in a cheap, red-plastic-covered edition. An American paperback edition of the *Quotations* is available with an introduction and notes by Stuart Schram (New York: Bantam Books, 1967). And there is the *Selected Works of Mao,* in four volumes, from the Peking Foreign Language Press.

John Gurley's "Capitalist and Maoist Economic Development" (in *America's Asia,* cited above) approaches Chinese political thought from the perspective of its theory of economic development, making a comparison with the theory of Western capitalism.

For the interested reader, Franz Schurmann's *Ideology and Organization in Communist China** (Berkeley and Los Angeles: University of California Press, 1968) is a long and comprehensive discussion of how the Chinese put ideology—Marxism and "Mao Tse-tung thought"—into practice.

On the PLA, John Gittings' *The Role of the Chinese Army* (New York: Oxford University Press, 1967) is a detailed explanation of the social and political roles played by the PLA in the period 1946–65, and is the best book on the military in China.

The Cultural Revolution

The best place to start in reading about the Cultural Revolution is Jack Gray and Patrick Cavendish's *Chinese Communism in Crisis: Maoism and the Cultural Revolution* (London: Pall Mall Press, 1968). The book was written while the revolution was still in progress, but it gives us the best and also the most sympathetic description of the key issues involved.

Shanghai Journal,* by Neal Hunter (New York: Praeger, 1969), is the story of a young Australian language teacher in Shanghai during the Cultural Revolution. It goes into detail about the class composition of schools before the Cultural Revolution and describes the dynamics of the mass movement in a blow-by-blow account. The book, however, has the drawback of being a single observer's picture and is therefore not a comprehensive history of the period.

Louis Barcata's *China in the Throes of the Cultural Revolution** (New York: Hart Publishing Company, 1968) is an eyewitness account by an Austrian journalist. This book is valuable mainly for its descriptions of events.

Foreign Policy

Most books on China's foreign policy tend to get bogged down in China-watching games or are affected by the cold war and the containment policy. This list should give the reader a broader background for understanding current events.

The best book on U.S.-China relations before World War II was written in 1938: A. Whitney Griswold's *The Far Eastern Policy of the United States** (New Haven, Conn.: Yale University Press, 1938). For a clearer understanding of the American role in China before and during World War II there is Barbara W. Tuchman's *Stilwell and the American Experience in China, 1911–45** (New York: Bantam Books, 1972).

John Gittings has written the best short summary of U.S.-China relations from the "Open Door" up through Liberation in 1949, "The Origins of China's Foreign Policy" (in *Containment and Revolution*,* David Horowitz, ed. [Boston: Beacon Press, 1967]). This excellent article provides a good background for understanding how relations between America and China got off to a bad start.

Since our first real contacts with the People's Republic came in the form of the Korean War, attention is well directed to that conflict. Allen S. Whiting's *China Crosses the Yalu: The Decision to Enter the Korean War** (New York: Macmillan, 1960), written by an ex-State Department official, makes the case that it was *American* aggression that led China into the fighting. Similarly, Edward Friedman's "Problems in Dealing with an Irrational Power: America Declares War on China" (in *America's Asia,* cited above) shows that China's entry was rational and inevitable in the face of the American threat. I. F. Stone's *The Hidden History of the Korean War** (New York: Monthly Review Press, 1970), originally published in 1952, demonstrates that at least one American at the time thought the Chinese weren't to be completely blamed for the war.

Attempts by Nationalist Chinese propagandists in the 1950s to keep the American public misinformed are revealed in Ross Y. Koen's *The China Lobby* (New York: Harper & Row, forthcoming). Apparently as a result of China lobby pressure on the State Department and on the Macmillan Company, this book was suppressed when Koen tried to have it published in 1960. Richard Nixon was an ardent China lobby supporter in his early political career.

China's relations with other Asian nations are thoroughly explained in two works by John Gittings. "The Great Asian Conspiracy" (in *America's Asia,* cited above) destroys the American propaganda claims that China was part of the Soviet foreign policy apparatus. His *Survey of the Sino-Soviet Dispute* (London and New York: Oxford University Press, 1968) attempts to explain the difficult Chinese-Russian conflict. Especially good is Neville Maxwell's book on the Himalayan border war, *India's China War* (New York: Pantheon, 1970). Maxwell presents convincing evidence that it was Indian provocations and Nehru's stubbornness that started that war.

For an answer to how much the Chinese have actually aided national liberation movements abroad, read Peter Van Ness's *Revolution and Chinese Foreign Policy** (Berkeley and Los Angeles: University of California Press, 1971). A good antidote to the standard American view of China, Gregory Clark's *In Fear of China* (London: The Cresset Press, 1968), is a more sober and useful analysis.

For articles on current affairs see the *Bulletin of Concerned Asian Scholars* published four times a year by the Committee of Concerned Asian Scholars (9 Sutter St., San Francisco, Calif. 94104).

GLOSSARY

agricultural communes. Officially established in August 1958, but actually existing since early summer of that year in the form of amalgamated agricultural producers' cooperatives. Usually coinciding with the administrative village or xian, the communes introduced a revolution in style and methods of peasant work based on the following: collectivization of peasant holdings, new organizational forms such as the production brigade, integration of educational, commercial, industrial, and agricultural functions, and greatly increased military preparedness of the peasantry.

Annam. The traditional Chinese name for Vietnam ("Annan," the pacified south). The name now refers to central Vietnam, between Tonkin in the north and Cochin in the south.

Bandung Conference. A conference of Asian and African Communist and neutral nations convened in Bandung, Indonesia, in 1955. The conference sought a united front of these nations against imperialism and for peaceful coexistence. China's participation in third-world affairs on this basis from 1955 to 1958 considerably raised its diplomatic standing among Afro-Asian countries.

Bao Dai. Became the last emperor of Annam (Vietnam) in 1926, abdicating in 1945. Reinstated in 1949 as the French puppet ruler of Vietnam. After appointing Ngo Dinh Diem as premier in 1954, he was succeeded by the latter as America came to replace France as the dominant foreign power in Vietnam.

baojia system. A system of rural control developed in China in imperial times, featuring mutual control and collective responsibility within units of various numbers of village households. The system was reinstituted by the Kuomintang government in 1932 as a means of supressing rural revolt and was also employed by the Japanese during the occupation of north China.

barefoot doctors (also called *peasant doctors*). Peasants trained in basic techniques of medical care formed during and after the Cultural Revolution in order to alleviate China's extreme shortage of medical personnel. After a six-month training program, the barefoot doctors are sent back to their home areas able to handle most routine medical problems. During subsequent agricultural slack seasons they may be given more medical training.

border region. During the occupation and War of Resistance Against Japan (1937–45) the Chinese Communists established control over a number of "liberated areas" essentially free from enemy incursion. These areas were formally constituted as border regions since they generally lay in the wilderness areas on provincial borders best suited to guerrilla-style warfare. The largest border region was the Shenxi-Gansu-Ningxia Border Region, in which was located the wartime Communist capital of Yenan.

Boxer Rebellion. A popular religious and antiforeign movement which began in north China in 1899 and culminated in the murder of many foreigners in the hinterlands and in the siege of the foreign legations in Peking during the summer of 1900. The siege and the movement were broken by a foreign expedition representing seven powers. A final settlement was reached in the form of a protocol signed September 7, 1901, which made further demands on Chinese sovereignty, such as the right to station foreign troops in Peking and the levying of an indemnity of over $300 million U.S.

cadres. The "backbone personnel of the Chinese revolution," those who play a full- or part-time role in political activity. Their role is to put into practice Communist party and government policies. Generally speaking, anyone whose job it is to lead others. This would include schoolteachers.

cadres, revolutionary. Those who were characterized as progressive elements during the Cultural Revolution and not in need of reeducation, retraining, or ideological criticism.

Cairo Declaration. Issued December 1, 1943, after the conference attended by Chiang Kai-shek, F. D. Roosevelt, and Winston Churchill affirmed their purpose "that . . . all the territories Japan has stolen from the Chinese, such as Manchuria, Formosa (Taiwan), and the Pescadores (islands near Taiwan) shall be restored to the Republic of China."

Cambodia, Royal Government of National Union of. Established May 5, 1970, in Peking two days after a congress of the National United Front of Kampuchea (NUFK or, in French, FUNK) held under the leadership of Prince Sihanouk. Prince Sihanouk is simultaneously chief of state of the Royal Government and president of the NUFK. Penn Nouth is the prime minister of the Royal Government, which opposes the illegitimacy of the coup-installed Lon Nol–Sirik Matak regime in Phnom Penh. The NUFK is a broadly based united front of royalists, Buddhists, nationalists, and Communists united to oppose the Lon Nol regime and U.S. and Saigon aggression in Cambodia. It has liberated over two-thirds the area and one-half the population of Cambodia since spring 1970.

catty. Basic unit of Chinese weight measure. Has various values, but generally equals about 1⅓ pounds.

Central Committee. Elected by the National Party Congress, it is the highest body in the Chinese Communist party when it is in session. During the Ninth Party Congress, 170 members were elected to the Central Committee. The Central Committee in turn elects the Political Bureau and approves decisions made by the latter body.

Chang Ch'ing (b. 1913). Has been Mao Tse-tung's wife since 1939. (It was not the first marriage for either.) Before the marriage, she had been a movie actress, using the stage name of Lan P'ing.

There is no indication that Chang Ch'ing had had any important political role until the Cultural Revolution, when she emerged as an important spokeswoman and theoretician on questions of culture and theater. Possibly most responsible for the development of revolutionary ballet in China since the Cultural Revolution. She was also one of five members of the Cultural Revolution Group, which guided the Cultural Revolution in many localities and institutions.

Chang Ch'un-ch'iao. No information is available on Chang's early career. After Liberation, he was involved primarily with propaganda work in the Shanghai region, also became involved with cultural work, not as an artist himself but as one concerned with safeguarding ideological purity in art and literature. By the mid-1950s he was an important figure in the Shanghai political scene. His ardent support of the efforts of Mao, Chang Ch'ing, and Yao Wen-yuan in Shanghai earned him a primary position in directing the Cultural Revolution in Shanghai, and the responsibility of leading the culture and art section of the Cultural Revolution group of the Chinese Communist party's Central Committee. In October 1967 he became the "leading member" of the Shanghai Municipal Revolutionary Committee. His power was augmented by concurrent appointments in positions of military authority in east China such as first political commissar, PLA Nanking Military Region.

Chang Hsueh-liang. The son of Manchurian warlord Chang Tso-lin, he succeeded to his father's rule after the elder Chang was murdered by the Japanese. After acceding to nominal Nationalist control in 1928, he was ousted from the northeast by the Japanese invasion of 1931. By 1936, he had come to head the Kuomintang "bandit suppression headquarters"—an organization whose objective was to suppress the Communists who had recently arrived in northwestern Shanxi Province from the Long March. On December 13, 1936, after Chiang Kai-shek had gone to Sian to convince the reluctant Chang and his troops to fight the Communists, the latter kidnapped Chiang in an effort to convince him not to fight other Chinese, but to resist Japan. The effort was successful, as a united front was formed a few months later, but Chang was taken prisoner by Chiang in reprisal and has remained a prisoner to this day on Taiwan.

Chen Yi. After joining the Chinese Communist party in France in 1923, he gradually rose through the military hierarchy, becoming the commander of the southern branch of the Communist forces in the forties. During the civil war of the late forties, he was in charge of the Communist forces in the area north of the Yangtze River above Nanking, as well as those which liberated Nanking and Shanghai. He became mayor of Shanghai in 1949, a position he held until 1958, when he became foreign minister. He was criticized during the Cultural Revolution.

Chiang Kai-shek. A native of Zhejiang Province, eastern China, Chiang Kai-shek was born in 1887. He headed the Whampoa Military Academy and was a follower of Sun Yat-sen. He attained political and military leadership of the Kuomintang during the Northern Expedition (1925–27) which supposedly united the Republic of China under KMT suzerainty. Chiang Kai-shek was supreme commander of the armed forces of the Republic of China during the Japan War and was elected president in 1943. Since 1949, when his armies were defeated by the Communists, he has lived on the island of Taiwan, where he still holds the title of president.

China Administration for Travel and Tourism (CATT). Parent body for China Travel Service. That segment of the Chinese government responsible for the well-being of foreign tourists in China: travel, accommodations, guide-interpreters, liaison with other segments of the government that the tourist might be interested in contacting. Decision-making body for extending visas to foreign guests.

China Travel Service (Luxingshe). Official travel bureau of the People's Republic of China for visitors coming from overseas or Hong Kong-Macao. China's only recognized travel agency.

Chinese Communist Party (CCP). Has been the leading force in the Chinese revolution and in the construction of socialism. Like other Communist parties, the CCP is an organization of professional revolutionaries based on democratic centralism.

The CCP was founded in 1921 and at first maintained close contact with the international Communist movement (Comintern) and the Nationalist party (KMT) in China. Since 1927, it has been politically, organizationally, and ideologically independent. During the 1930s and 1940s, it developed a revolutionary strategy and mobilized resources for the struggle against the Japanese invaders and the KMT.

After Liberation, the CCP expanded membership from 4.5 million in 1949 to 17 million in 1961. During the Cultural Revolution, Mao expressed fear that some sections of the CCP were losing revolutionary spirit, and might become a new exploiting class. After fierce political struggle, revolutionary committees assumed command and the party was reorganized.

Chou En-lai (b. 1898). One of China's most important revolutionary leaders—in student activities, in building the PLA, and in negotiations with allies and enemies.

Since 1949, he has been premier of the State Council and was generally considered to rank third in the official hierarchy. He was involved in many phases of government activities, especially those dealing with scientists and intellectuals.

More than any other Chinese leader, Chou has been active in foreign affairs. He has been foreign minister and has represented China at important conferences. He has also made goodwill trips abroad, to Asia and Africa in 1963–64. Played a major role in the Cultural Revolution, serving on the committee that made critical judgments about its progress. Continues to be a major figure since the Cultural Revolution, especially in China's new foreign policy. In the fall of 1971 he became the second-ranking person in the government.

comprador. The class of Chinese who served as intermediaries between Western merchants and capitalists in their dealings with the Chinese people. This group is condemned for their cooperation with Western economic imperialism, thereby impeding native Chinese economic development. Comprador mentality, consequently, is the label applied to people who exhibit a slavish dependence upon Western methods, thereby impeding independent Chinese development.

Cultural Revolution (Great Proletarian Cultural Revolution). In Marxist terminology, a revolution in the superstructure. A historically unprecedented political revolution in what was already a socialist China. Begun in 1965 with a piece of heavily political literary criticism written by Yao Wen-yuan against the deputy mayor of Peking, it burst fully on the scene when dazibao went up on the Peking University (Beida) campus criticizing the Beida leadership for revisionism and bourgeois reaction. Mao himself subsequently wrote a dazibao, "Bombard the Headquarters" (i.e., of the Communist party) and the movement spread throughout the country on the energy of the radical middle-school and university Red Guards. At the outset, the supporters of Mao were the underdogs, but the January revolution in Shanghai (January 1967) turned the tide in their favor and against Liu Shao-ch'i, "China's Khrushchev," and his supporters in the party bureaucracy. When Red Guards proved unable to develop the triple alliances upon which the new revolutionary committees were based, workers, Mao thought propaganda teams and the People's Liberation Army moved in "to support the left" in factories and schools around the country. During the Cultural Revolution, the masses were encouraged to take part actively in the "three great struggles": class struggle, the struggle for production, and the struggle for invention. The final stage of the Cultural Revolution is still continuing.

Dalai Lama. Religious and political ruler of Tibet enthroned in 1940 and assuming full power in 1950. He fled to India in 1959 after the abortive Tibetan uprising.

dazibao (big character poster). Medium of expression of political views, especially by those who have no access to the press. Essays or manifestos written on posters and often put up on walls. These were used in early mass movements —May 4, the student anti-Japanese imperialist movement of the 1930s, and most recently in the Cultural Revolution.

Democratic People's Republic of Korea. After the withdrawal of the Japanese forces from Korea, people's committees were set up in both North and South Korea to form some sort of transitional organization. In February 1946, representatives of these committees in the north met at Pyongyang and proclaimed the Democratic People's Republic of Korea, to be headed by Kim Il Sung. In August 1948, elections were held in North Korea and members were elected for a Supreme People's Assembly, a constitution was adopted, and Kim Il Sung was made prime minister of the Democratic Republic of Korea. This democratic republic was subsequently recognized, first by the Soviet Union, as the legal government of all Korea, both north and south of the thirty-eighth parallel.

Democratic Republic of Vietnam (DRV). Formed in 1945 with its capital in Hanoi, the DRV has consistently fought against intervention by France and the U.S. in the affairs of Vietnam. Giving support to the resistance against the U.S. in the south, the DRV supports the seven-point peace proposal of the Provisional Revolutionary Government of South Vietnam.

dictatorship of the proletariat. The intermediate stage predicted by Marx between capitalism and communism (at which point the state would go out of existence), when the proletariat, or urban working class, would seize state organs of power and use them to suppress the bourgeoisie, until the proletariat could consolidate its control over the society and the economy.

Eighth Route Army. New name assumed by the Chinese Workers' and Peasants' Red Army in 1937 to indicate the Chinese Communist party's willingness to cooperate with the Kuomintang in a united front against Japan. Nominally under the control of the Nationalist government, this army operated primarily in north China, combining military defense against Japan with major political and economic reforms. The superior ability of this army in winning and maintaining the support of the local population in 1937–45 proved essential to a Communist victory in the subsequent civil war.

feudal remnants. Since the official Communist party view of China's history is that the nation was feudal for the three thousand years preceding 1842 and semifeudal, semicolonial until Liberation in 1949, any undesirable manifestations of the ways or thinking of the old society in the countryside are labeled feudal remnants, e.g., discrimination against women.

Geneva Conference. On May 8, 1954, nine countries, the United States, France, Britain, the Soviet Union, the People's Republic of China, Cambodia, Laos, North Vietnam, and South Vietnam took up the problem of the first Indochina war. The declaration that resulted included the following stipulations:

1. Laos and Cambodia would not request foreign aid unless for purposes of self-defense.
2. The seventeenth parallel in Vietnam was not to be

"interpreted as constituting a political or territorial boundary."

3. General elections would be held in Vietnam "under the supervision of an international commission composed of representatives of the member states of the International Supervisory Control Commission." The date was set as July 1956.

4. All who signed the declaration should "respect the sovereignty, the independence, the unity, and the territorial integrity" of Cambodia, Laos, and Vietnam, while refraining from any "interference in their internal affairs."

The United States refused to sign the declaration but promised not to disturb the agreements arrived at.

Great Leap Forward. Initiated by Mao in 1958—a plan to utilize China's vast manpower to effect improvement in industry and agriculture without foreign help. Cooperatives were merged into people's communes. All agricultural resources were mobilized, and new techniques such as early planting were employed. Industry was largely decentralized, and small-scale production at the family and village level was encouraged. Natural disasters and serious crop failures in 1959, 1960, and 1961 led to the failure of the Great Leap and a temporary lessening of Mao's direct leadership.

Huang Yung-sheng (b. 1906). Chief of general staff of the People's Liberation Army. A native of Jiangxi, he began his military career in the Red Army in 1931. Participated in the Long March. Rose rapidly through the ranks to position of commander by mid-1940s. After Liberation, he built his career in south China, becoming commander of that military region in 1953. He was in the vanguard of the Cultural Revolution in Canton and became chairman of the Guangdong Provincial Revolutionary Committee in February 1968. He was appointed to his present position as head of the PLA in November 1968.

Kuomintang (KMT). The Nationalist party, founded by Sun Yat-sen in 1912. Since the 1927 purge of left-wing elements, the Kuomintang has been under the control of Chiang Kai-shek and has claimed to represent the whole Chinese people. In 1949 the Kuomintang and its adherents were driven from the Chinese mainland by the Communists and took refuge on the island of Taiwan, where they remain as the "Republic of China."

Lao Patriotic Front (Neo Lao Hak Sat). Formed in January 1956 as the political wing of the Pathet Lao. The front opposes any U.S. intervention in the affairs of Laos and calls for a "peaceful settlement" of the Laotian problem based on the 1962 Geneva Accords on Laos. It supports a foreign policy of peace and neutrality and advocates national unification without foreign interference.

Liberation. The victory of the Chinese Communist party (CCP) over the military forces of the Nationalists (KMT), in a civil war which was fought off and on from 1927. It was carried on with resolute vigor from the time of the surrender of the Japanese forces in China in 1945. The official day celebrated for this Liberation is October 1, 1949, the day of the founding of the People's Republic of China.

Lin Piao (b. 1907). Has been one of China's most important and brilliant military commanders ever since the creation of the PLA in 1927. In 1959 named minister of defense, after the previous holder of that position, P'eng Te-huai, had criticized Mao's strategy of the Great Leap. As minister of defense, Lin Piao stressed that the human factor is more important than weapons, and that politics and ideology are more important than technique. In late 1971 Lin Piao lost his position of power in the government.

Liu Shao-ch'i (b. 1898). One of the important leaders of the Chinese revolution. Specialized in organizing industrial workers during the 1920s and 1930s, and also set up the underground activities in north China in the late 1930s. In the early 1940s, Liu was a leading theoretician on organizational questions of the Chinese Communist party, and by 1945, the second highest leader, after Mao.

After 1949, one of the top leaders of party and state; chairman of the state and president from 1959 to about 1967, during which time he was actively concerned with the development of the economy and the party. At this time he was Mao's heir apparent.

Liu came under sharp attack during the Cultural Revolution, because the policies that he advocated were such as to increase class differences in China. As a result of these attacks, Liu was removed from his leadership position, and his whereabouts are now unknown.

loess. Known in Chinese as huangtu (yellow earth), this is soil and dust blown from the inner Asian deserts into China over the millennia. In many parts of north China it reaches a depth of fifty feet or more; because of its unique composition it is particularly adapted for the digging of cave dwellings. The soil, while fertile, is susceptible to severe erosion.

Manchuria. Known in Chinese as the Northeast (Dongbei), this pivotal area between Russia, Mongolia, and Korea has traditionally been an area where outside pressure has been exerted, from Russian harassment in the nineteenth century, to Japanese invasion in 1931, to saber rattling by General MacArthur in 1950–51, to Russian encroachment in the late 1960s.

Mao Tse-tung (b. 1893). Unquestionably the most important leader of the Chinese revolution. Son of a Hunan peasant. One of the roughly dozen men who founded the Chinese Communist party in 1921, and became the leader of the party in 1935, a role he has continued to hold to the present time.

In the revolutionary struggle, Mao early recognized the potential of the peasantry, especially when combined with a disciplined party-army and a rural base area. As the war with Japan developed, Mao realized that nationalism was an important demand of many patriotic Chinese, and supported a united front against Japanese aggression. The final element of Mao's revolutionary strategy—a self-conscious revolutionary party based on Marxism-Leninism—was added in the early 1940s.

After liberation in 1949, Mao was chairman of both the government of China and the CCP. As before, he continued to play a critical role in sensing broad needs and implementing them. In 1955, he insisted that rural China should become collectivized. In 1965, Mao initiated the Cultural Revolution to prevent a rigid class structure from developing in China.

While Mao has always been revolutionary in his goals, his tactics have been marked by caution and pragmatism.

Marriage Law of 1950. Promulgated in May 1950, it is essentially a bill of rights for women, defining for the first time in law such basic rights as equality of the sexes, and freedom of marriage and divorce, as well as outlawing the remnants of the old society such as bigamy, concubinage, child betrothal, and interference with the remarriage of widows.

mass line. This term designates the type of leadership expected of cadres dating back to the 1930s. They are to inquire among the masses for their ideas and desires, translate these into specific policy proposals, and take those back to the people to be put into practice, and to be improved upon depending upon the experience of the practice. The principle is summed up in the slogan "From the masses, to the masses."

May 4 movement. A demonstration held on May 4, 1919, to protest China's shoddy treatment at the Versailles Peace Conference became the keystone of a broad movement directed against imperialist incursions and certain aspects of Chinese tradition inimical to development. The movement came to focus primarily on such cultural phenomena as promotion of the vernacular language as against the classical, and a new willingness to accept Western ideas.

May 7 cadre schools. Novel institution created out of the struggles of the Cultural Revolution. Named after a Mao directive. Modeled after Kangda, the Anti-Japanese Imperialism University of the Yenan days. Urban cadres, several thousand at a time, go to suburban or rural wasteland areas to build from scratch a farm with accompanying factories, dormitories, and classrooms. Cadres stay there from six months to two years spending half their time in manual work, and half studying the classics of Marxism-Leninism-Mao thought. Purpose is to purify the cadres' world view, and combat tendencies to elitism and bureaucratism. It is planned that all China's cadres will do a six months' "sabbatical" in a May 7 school in future.

mu. The Chinese unit of land measurement, equal to approximately ⅙ acre.

Ngo Dinh Diem. Vietnamese Catholic nationalist who ousted Bao Dai as ruler of South Vietnam in 1955. After an eight-year reign noted for its oppression and lack of flexibility in the face of popular revolt, and during which American dominance of the political process increased, he was deposed and killed in a U.S.-sponsored coup in November 1963.

Nguyen Thi Binh. Foreign minister of the Provisional Revolutionary Government of the Republic of South Vietnam. After serving three years in prison under the French, eventually became member of the National Liberation Front Central Committee. Appointed to present position upon formation of the Provisional Revolutionary Government on June 10, 1969, she succeeded Tran Buu Kiem as leader of its delegation to the Paris talks.

Ninth Party Congress. Convened from April 1 to April 24, 1969, it was the first to be held since the Cultural Revolution. At this time Lin Piao delivered a major policy speech, a new revised constitution was adopted, the Central Committee was elected, and Mao was elected chairman of the Central Committee. The 1,512 delegates were convened under the theme of unity in order to signal a new stability after the disorders of the Cultural Revolution. In contrast to previous party congresses, delegates came overwhelmingly from the ranks of workers, peasants, and soldiers.

offshore islands. The islands of Quemoy and Matsu near the mainland ports of Amoy and Foochow were held on to by the Kuomintang after 1949 and have been a constant source of tension between Taiwan and the People's Republic of China, as has been the nature of America's defense commitment to Taiwan.

Opium War. 1838–42, the first major armed conflict between China and the Western powers, signaling the irreconcilability of traditional Chinese methods of foreign policy and the demands of Western imperialism. In this war, China sought to end the growing British opium trade in Canton, while England hoped to secure and expand its commercial interests on the China coast. The Nanking peace treaty of 1842 was the first of a long series of unequal treaties forced upon China by a superior Western military might as a result of China's loss of the Opium War.

Pathet Lao. Formed in August 1950 from various nationalistic Laotian groups who had fought against the French until independence in 1949. Has continued the struggle for independence and nonintervention by foreign powers as part of the war against the United States in Indochina.

Peking University (Beida). The first modern university in China, founded in 1898. Beida was the center of intellectual life in China from the May 4 movement—it led academic resistance to Japan in the thirties, became militantly anti-Kuomintang in the late forties, and was one of the centers of the Cultural Revolution in the late sixties.

People's Daily (Renmin Ribao). The newspaper published daily in Peking which serves as the official organ of the government of the People's Republic. All official policy announcements appear first in this paper.

People's Liberation Army (PLA). The name given to the Red Army (Eighth Route Army) in 1946, signifying the readiness of the Communists to battle against the Kuomintang until final victory. Lin Piao took command of the PLA in 1959, and it has served as the vanguard in promotion and study of the thought of Mao Tse-tung. Policy making and operational direction of the PLA rest with the military affairs committee of the Communist party's Central Committee. PLA strength in 1970 was estimated at 4,180,000 active duty personnel. Relative to the country's population, one of the smallest armies of any country in the world. PLA includes navy and air force as well. Since the Cultural Revolution, PLA men and women can be found on almost all major revolutionary committees in the civilian sector. This is an institutionalized continuation of its Cultural Revolution role of "supporting the left."

"people's livelihood." The third of the "three people's principles" (sanmin zhuyi) of Sun Yat-sen, the first two being nationalism and democracy. As vaguely outlined by Dr. Sun, the "people's livelihood" entailed "restriction of capital" and "equalization of rights in the land." The "three people's principles" is still used as the official ideology of the Kuomintang.

people's militia. The voluntary self-defense forces existing in most major Chinese production and residential units. The tens of millions of members of both sexes all train only part-time in small weapons handling. The "people in arms" according to the Marxist formula. Also serve as an adjunct to local security forces and as work vanguards during time of natural disaster.

Political Bureau. Elected by the plenary session of the Central Committee of the Chinese Communist party. Within this body, a smaller standing committee is elected, and debate within this small group results in party policy decisions and directions. When major policy changes are to be decided upon, the Political Bureau will convene a plenary session of the Central Committee. When the Central Committee is not in session the Political Bureau exercises all its functions and powers.

Potsdam Conference. On July 17, 1945, Truman, Churchill, and Stalin met at Potsdam, Germany, to confer on postwar policy toward Axis powers and liberated areas. Stalin reiterated his Yalta demands that Dairen port (Manchuria) be Russian although open to international trade. The U.S. concurred with this policy. The "unconditional surrender" policy toward Japan was also developed at this conference. Reaffirmed that Taiwan be returned to China upon Japan's defeat.

production brigades. Work groups actually organized in winter of 1957 and spring of 1958 with the launching of the waterworks program. Although the production brigades did go through several stages, one can say that they radically transformed the organization of peasant labor by enlarging the scope and geographical area in which peasant work and cooperation took place. The brigade is an integral part of the commune organization and usually coincides with the natural village. Currently it is a decision-making body midway between the larger commune and the smaller work team.

Provisional Revolutionary Government of the Republic of South Vietnam (PRG). The government formed jointly on June 10, 1969, by the South Vietnamese National Liberation Front and the Alliance of National, Democratic, and Peace Forces (a coalition of non-Communist, anti-imperialist groups). This government represents a broad front of South Vietnamese anti-American, anti-Thieu forces.

Red Guards. In May 1966, the students of a Peking middle school began to put up "big character posters" (dazibao) protesting certain activities of the teachers and administrators of their school. As this practice spread to other middle schools and universities, the students formed groups and called themselves Red Guards. When Chairman Mao met them in Tiananmen Square and put on a red armband with the name Red Guard on it, this name became official. These students were instrumental in closing down schools all over China and carrying the Cultural Revolution to all parts of China. Many eventually volunteered or were sent down to the countryside to work with and serve the peasants.

Revolution of 1911. Initially, an uprising in the city of Wuchiang (present Wuhan) in central China, on October 10. As similar uprisings broke out throughout the country the Manchu emperor was forced to abdicate and retreat to Manchuria on Februrary 12, 1912. The republic which was subsequently set up marked its national day as October 10 to commemorate this uprising.

revolutionary committees. One of the new organizational forms created during the Cultural Revolution whose purpose was to better represent the "revolutionary masses" against the entrenched party bureaucracy, thus reflecting the main political direction of the Great Proletarian Cultural Revolution. The committees were conceived after the pattern of the Paris Commune, but this was later deemphasized in favor of a "triple alliance" comprised of soldiers, revolutionary masses, and "loyal" cadres. The revolutionary committees currently are the leadership bodies of all social units of Chinese society from communes to provinces.

SEATO. On September 8, 1954, Australia, Britain, France, New Zealand, Pakistan, the Philippines, and Thailand signed a collective defense treaty under the sponsorship of the U.S. The Southeast Asia Treaty Organization was to provide a collective response not only in the event of armed aggression but also in cases of "subversive activities" or "any fact or situation (other than armed attack) which might endanger the peace of the area." The areas to be covered were the "general areas of Southeast Asia" and the "general area of the Southwest Pacific" south of Taiwan. A protocol to the treaty provided for "assistance and protection" of nonsignatories Cambodia, Laos, and South Vietnam.

seven-point peace proposal of the Provisional Revolutionary Government. Presented by Mme. Nguyen Thi Binh, head of the PRG delegation at the Paris peace talks on July 1, 1971. The seven points proposed were:

1. Simultaneous withdrawal of U.S. and other foreign troops from South Vietnam and release of National Liberation Front– and North Vietnamese–held prisoners of war, accompanied by a cease-fire.

2. U.S. withdrawal of support from the Thieu government, and an end to U.S. interference in internal Vietnamese affairs (e.g., elections), a new administration to enforce measures forbidding terrorism or reprisals against persons of either side, and an agreement upon measures for holding genuinely free elections.

3. Vietnamese parties themselves to negotiate settlement regarding the question of armed forces.

4. Reunification of North and South Vietnam to be achieved peacefully, with neither side participating in foreign alliances or allowing foreign bases on its soil.

5. South Vietnam to follow a policy of peace and neutrality, maintaining economic and cultural relations with all countries, including the U.S.

6. U.S. government to bear responsibility for the destruction it has caused to the people of North and South Vietnam.

7. Vietnamese parties to negotiate forms of international guarantee of the settement.

On July 6, 1971, Le Duc Tho announced that the question of military withdrawal and return of prisoners of war could be negotiated independently of political questions.

Shanghai worker rebellion of 1927. On March 20, 1927, the armed workers of Shanghai succeeded in capturing most of the city from warlord forces. This move was in conjunction with the joint Northern Expedition of the Kuomintang and the Chinese Communist party. When Chiang Kai-shek and his forces arrived in the city some days later, he called for the workers to lay down their arms, and on April 12, with the aid of hired thugs, "Greengang," and the tacit agreement of the foreign police, began a systematic slaughter of every identifiable Communist and left-winger. This action precipitated the first KMT-CCP civil war, which was to last until the united front was re-formed in 1937 against the Japanese invasion.

Sihanouk, Prince Norodom. Hereditary monarch of Cambodia, he abdicated in 1955 to become premier. After pursuing a course set on keeping his country out of the struggle in Indochina for fifteen years, he was deposed in March 1970 while out of the country. Soon after, he announced the formation of the Front of National Union of Cambodia (FUNK), headquartered in Peking.

Smith, General Walter Bedell. After serving as Eisenhower's chief of staff in 1945, Smith served as ambassador to the Soviet Union from 1946 to 1949 and later as CIA director from 1950 to 1953. Upon resigning from the army in 1953, he became Undersecretary of State to Dulles and represented the U.S. at the Geneva Conference of 1954.

state factory. A factory owned by the state (ownership of "all the people"), which may be under either central (therefore a central state factory) or regional (therefore a regional state factory) economic coordinative control. It contrasts with the collectively owned factory (ownership by the "collective"), which is usually of smaller scale, often involved in recycling wastes and based within a residence unit such as a commune, university, or (larger) state factory. Salaries in a state factory are determined by the state, those in a collectively owned factory by the workers working in it and their coresidents in the commune, university, etc., of which it is a part.

Taiwan. Island province of China about 150 miles from the mainland. Also called Formosa after the Portuguese colonial designation, Ilha Formosa (Beautiful Island). Originally an area of cultural contact between the Han Chinese and peoples of Malayo-Polynesian origin. Han Chinese began settling there as frontier pioneers in the sixteenth century (Ming dynasty) from the region around Amoy, Fujian Province, gradually pushing the non-Han groups into the high mountains where they remain today as an internal colony. A Dutch colony in the seventeenth century, Taiwan was the refuge of anti-Manchu forces after the collapse of the Ming, led by the loyalist Koxinga. Han Chinese migration continued and Taiwan was officially designated a province by the Ch'ing

(Manchu) dynasty. After the loss of the Sino-Japanese War, China was forced to cede Taiwan to Japan and the island became a Japanese colony in 1895. According to the Cairo and Potsdam agreements, Taiwan was to be returned to China upon Japan's defeat in World War II. Thus in 1945, Taiwan reverted to China with the people of Taiwan greeting the Kuomintang troops as liberators. However, two years later, as a result of the army's corruption, there was a island-wide revolt put down viciously by Chiang Kai-shek's troops. In 1949 with Chiang defeated on the mainland, he and two million bureaucrats and troops loyal to him fled to Taiwan. The People's Liberation Army, massed on the mainland coast, was about to cross over and deliver the coup de grace of the civil war when the Korean War broke out, and the U.S. reentered the Chinese civil war by interposing the Seventh Fleet in the Taiwan Straits and stationing troops on the island. There are currently about nine thousand U.S. troops on Taiwan, though the patrolling of the fleet recently stopped.

Taiwan-U.S. Defense Treaty. Signed December 2, 1954, this treaty stipulates mutual assistance in the event of armed attack against Taiwan and the Pescadores and "such other territories as may be determined by mutual agreement." It also calls for strengthening capacity to resist armed attack and Communist subversion directed "from without."

treaty port. After the Opium War of 1838–42, five cities were designated treaty ports, where the Western powers were allowed to set up trading posts and live under the provisions of the Nanking treaty, which provided immunity from Chinese law. As Western pressure increased, the number of these ports expanded into the scores. At the larger ones, such as Shanghai, Tientsin, and Hankow, the powers were granted territorial concessions, which, in effect, were small colonies totally under the rule of the various Western nations.

two-China policy. A policy recognizing the legitimacy of both the People's Republic of China (Peking) and the Republic of China (Taiwan). This policy has been denounced by both Chinese regimes as imperialistic and unfounded in fact, since both regimes consider China an indivisible national unit. The United States (1971) proposal regarding the admission of the People's Republic to the United Nations followed this line, under the rubric of "one China, two governments," as a device for retaining a seat for the representatives of Chiang Kai-shek's Kuomintang.

united front. A characteristic feature of the Chinese revolution's bourgeois democratic stage, the united front is a method of uniting the Communist party with a wide range of democratic classes or groups. It was used in 1924–27 in uniting with the Kuomintang against the warlords. It was used to unite China's peoples against the Japanese invasion from 1937–45 and finally, it was used as an ideological tool in post-1949 campaigns to transform society and economy. A united front is used to achieve political, military, or social goals unachievable by the party alone or more efficaciously achieved by the interaction of the party and other less progressive but still democratic groups or classes.

warlord. A military official who gathered a personal army and officer corps loyal to him and "ruled" a territory within the Chinese polity. During the 1911–49 period many areas of China were controlled exclusively by such semifeudal warlords. Previous dynasties also saw this phenomenon, which included fealty to the overlord and rewards of land grants (with tenant peasants) to loyal subordinates. Chiang Kai-shek allied himself with many warlords in order to succeed in the Northern Expedition to unite China (1925–27).

wars of national liberation. As summed up by Lin Piao in his 1965 article, "Long Live the Victory of the People's War," this type of war is viewed as the struggle of third-world nations to free themselves from the control of the imperialist powers. The key to victory is the innate advantage possessed by a people fighting for a just cause on their own soil over the material superiority of the imperialists. The concrete manifestation of these theories lies in the experiences of China, Korea, Vietnam, Laos, Cuba, and Algeria in successfully battling against imperialist aggression or occupation.

Yao Wen-yuan. Main author of the article "On the New Historical Play *Hai Jui Dismissed from Office*," which was the opening shot of the first stage of the Cultural Revolution. The article raised political issues that went far beyond the questions of historical accuracy to which the protégés of Liu

Shao-ch'i tried to limit the ensuing debate. Yao, about forty, is one of the younger members of the Central Committee of the Chinese Communist party and the youngest member of the Political Bureau. He was elected to the Central Committee at the Ninth Party Congress in April 1969 as a result of his extremely active participation in the Cultural Revolution, both in Peking and his native Shanghai. One of the Chinese Communist party's foremost ideologists. Has also written *Comments on Tao Chu's Two Books,* an attack on bourgeois idealism in the writings of Tao Chu, Guangdong Province kingpin ousted during the Cultural Revolution.

Yeh, George K. C. Appointed foreign secretary in 1950 in the first Kuomintang cabinet to be formed after the Nationalist government fled to Taiwan in 1949. He held that post until 1958, when he was appointed ambassador to the U.S., a position he occupied until 1962.

Yenan Forum on Literature and Art. A series of talks held in May 1942 in which Mao outlined the Chinese Communist party view that the function of literature and art was to serve the people and stressed the necessity for artists from nonproletarian backgrounds to come to grips with this concept. Always regarded as important, these talks have received even greater emphasis since the Cultural Revolution as the embodiment of the mass line in the arts.

yuan. Basic unit of the renminbi (people's currency). Worth approximately forty cents U.S. The yuan is divided into one hundred fen.

INDEX

ABOUT THE AUTHORS

THE COMMITTEE OF CONCERNED ASIAN SCHOLARS is a broad antiwar group which was formed in 1968 by a representative group of students, historians, political scientists, and sociologists who have devoted their lives to the study of the people and countries of Asia. They are the authors of four other books: *The Indochina Story, Cambodia, The Widening War, Laos: War and Revolutions,* and *America's Asia. CHINA! INSIDE THE PEOPLE'S REPUBLIC* is the result of a group of CCAS scholars' visit to China in the summer of 1971. The group consisted of fifteen young American students and teachers who were trained scholars of China, had been through the best American universities, spoke fluent Chinese, had spent many months in Hong Kong, and who represented the best current American knowledge on China. They were the first group of American scholars admitted into China in twenty-two years.